THE CHINESE COLLECTION

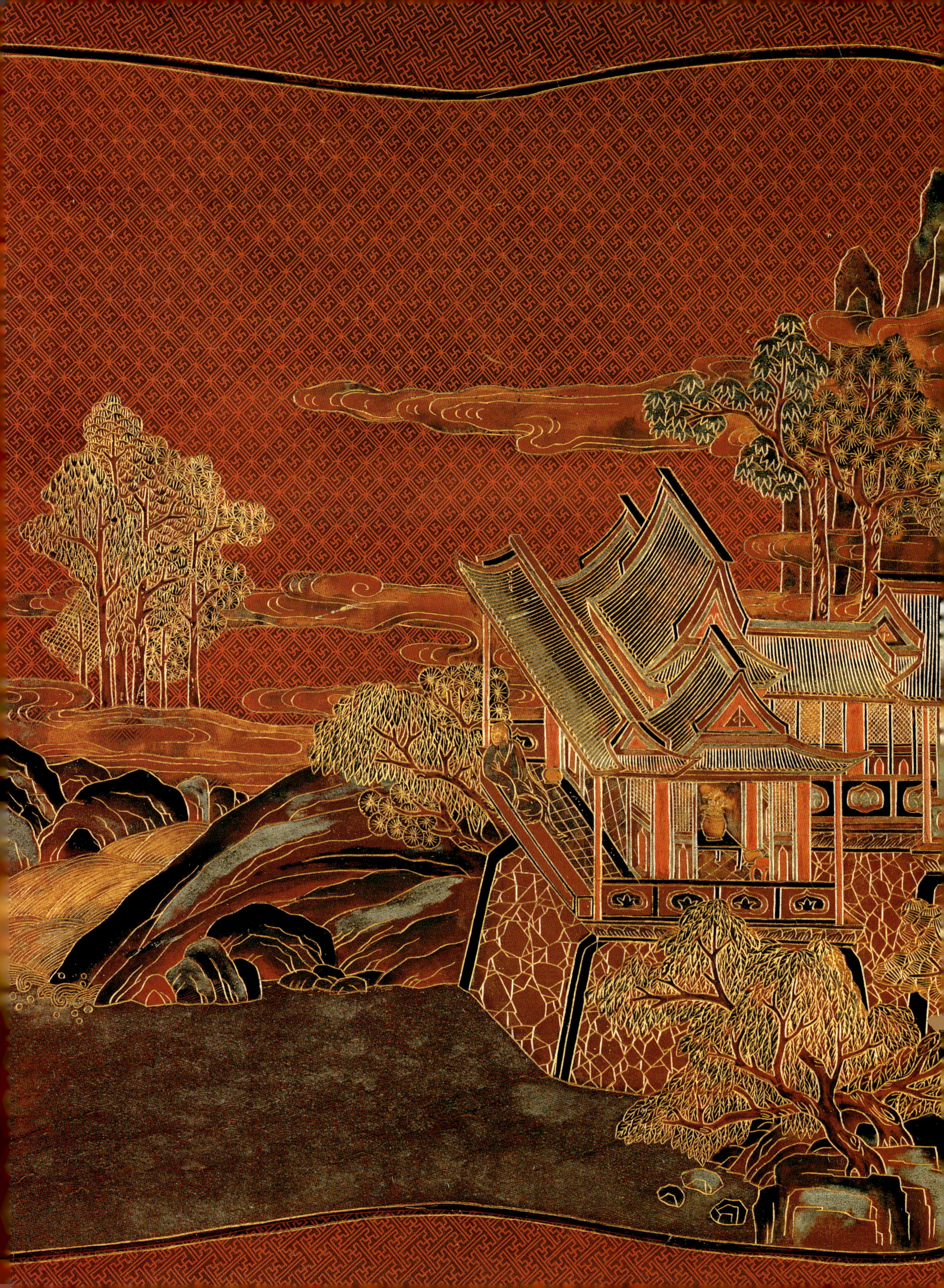

John R. Finlay
with essays by Colin Mackenzie and Jenny F. So

the CHINESE collection

selected works from the NORTON MUSEUM OF ART

The Norton Museum of Art | West Palm Beach, Florida

Dedicated to the memory of Sophie Davis, whose personal enthusiasm for the Chinese collection and boundless energy in support of all the Museum's goals are remembered with gratitude and deep affection.

The Chinese Collection: Selected Works from the Norton Museum of Art is published on the occasion of the opening of four galleries for Chinese art in the new Southwest Wing, March 8, 2003.

The catalogue is sponsored by an anonymous foundation and the E. Rhodes and Leona B. Carpenter Foundation.

Published by the Norton Museum of Art
1451 South Olive Avenue
West Palm Beach, FL 33401
Tel: 561-832-5196, Fax: 561-659-4689
E-mail: museum@norton.org
Web site: www.norton.org

Distributed to the trade by Weatherhill, Inc.,
41 Monroe Turnpike
Trumbull, CT 06611
Tel: 1-800-437-7840, Fax: 1-800-557-5601
E-mail: order@weatherhill.com

Library of Congress Control Number: 2003090229
ISBN 0-8348-0532-4 (trade hardcover)
ISBN 0-943411-40-8 (museum hardcover)
ISBN 0-943411-41-6 (softcover)

Edited by Elizabeth Powers and Ray Furse
Book design and production by Binocular, New York
Principal color photography © Bruce M. White
Chinese character glossary typeset by Birdtrack Press
Index compiled by Robert J. Palmer
Separations, printing, and binding by Mondadori
Map by Anandaroop Roy

This book was typeset in Celeste and Meta and printed on 150 gsm Job Parilux Silk.

Front cover: *Dragon pendant*, jade, 5th century BCE (cat. 43); frontispiece: *Pair of lacquered cabinets with cupboards*, mid- to late 17th century, detail showing palace buildings (cat. 109)

Printed and bound in Verona, Italy

CONTENTS

DIRECTOR'S FOREWORD

The history of the Norton Museum's collection of Chinese art is an illustrious one, founded in large part on a series of devoted collectors who have shepherded it over time to become one of the finest, although purposefully not the largest, collections of Chinese art in any museum. Initially, the Museum's founder, Ralph Norton, in concord with its first director, E. Robert Hunter, made the decision to develop a Chinese collection to parallel the Western culture collections that he had previously donated with his wife, Elizabeth Norton. The impetus behind the decision was a forward-thinking one, "as a worthy means to ... serve to direct attention of visitors to the art of the Far East." Fifty years later museums would espouse this philosophy as an enlightened multiculturalism and a statement that Eurocentrism was to be avoided. For Ralph Norton the root behind this thinking was identical—an opportunity to expose museum visitors to a completely different culture of supreme quality and thereby to widen their perceptions of the world, its cultures and its history. Perhaps this was particularly relevant given the geographic isolation of Florida as a peninsula.

Initially Mr. Norton was attracted by a diverse collection of 18th- and 19th-century jade and hardstone carvings, which had been developed by the prominent dealer Stanley Charles Nott, acquiring it for the collection in 1941. In 1950, the Norton Gallery and School of Art, as the Museum was originally named, hosted a groundbreaking exhibition of ancient Chinese jades organized by the dealer and connoisseur C.T. Loo and his New York business partner Frank Caro, Sr. From this exhibition Mr. Norton and his family acquired the almost forty examples of ancient jade that are the heart of the Chinese collection today. In 1953 the Museum purchased, again from C.T. Loo, the majority of the Shang and Zhou ritual bronzes now in our collection. In his lifetime, Mr. Norton directed the acquisition of early Chinese ceramics and, interestingly, a small group of tomb figures, all with the goal of finding the best, most representative examples of Chinese art. In keeping with the Museum's philosophy of art collecting, which always emphasized quality over quantity, Norton encouraged deaccessioning and exchanges whenever the holdings could be augmented by better examples and discouraged a "study collection," in the belief that all of a museum's works should be of the best quality and interchangeably suitable for exhibition. Jades acquired from Stanley Nott, for example, were exchanged in the 1960s for a range of objects, including early ceramics and tomb figures. Following this lead, collectors in the community, including the Nortons' daughter, the late Beatrice Richards, continued to gift works to the Museum's Chinese holdings.

In the early 1970s the Chinese collection was extensively studied by Horace H.F. Jayne, the former vice-director of the Metropolitan Museum of Art and former director of the University of Pennsylvania Museum of Archaeology and Anthropology, whose expertise was in Chinese art. He met the Nortons through Frances Hunter, the wife of E. Robert Hunter, who provided him with Ralph Norton's original notes on the collection as the basis for his further research. Mr. Jayne produced the first catalogue of the collection, which has been out of print for two decades. His extensive knowledge and trained eye taught us much about the objects, and his catalogue remains a valuable resource to this day.

In the Norton Museum's planning in the mid-1990s, both the need for physical expansion and the care and development of the collections were emphasized. In particular, one trustee, Sophie Davis, described the Chinese collection over the last decades as the "stepchild." Indeed, the Norton had never had a curator designated for Chinese art, and although it amply cared for its Chinese collection, there had been no complete reinstallation in forty-five years. Mrs. Davis, who passed away in 2000, was a "take action" trustee as was her colleague on the Norton's board, John McGraw. He then endowed a major curatorial position for Chinese art in honor of his mother, who particularly enjoyed Chinese art. As a result, John Finlay, the primary author of this new collection catalogue, became the first Elizabeth B. McGraw Curator of Chinese Art. Mrs. Davis had already donated significant monies through the Leonard and Sophie Davis Foundation to begin the funding campaign for a new wing that would include major exhibition space for the Chinese collection. The principal gallery now carries the name "The Leonard and Sophie Davis Gallery." Other donors devoted to Chinese art came forward, happily turning the stepchild into a favored child. Indeed, from the 1950s onward, many donors have contributed to the collection, which currently has approximately 600 objects. Originally scrolls, textiles, lacquerware, and furniture were not collected due to the climatic conditions in Florida, but with the introduction of computerized climate control systems this is no longer a collecting issue. The Museum is now working to add these important types of objects to the collection.

China's opening to the West, further advances in scientific analysis, and much new scholarship in the field have made this new catalogue even more important for the Museum and for those who wish to study or to simply enjoy our Chinese art collection. Many people are to be acknowledged for their contributions, but in particular it is most appropriate to acknowledge Sophie and Leonard Davis, John and Marjorie McGraw, and Beatrice Richards, whose interest in Chinese art at the Norton spanned those many decades until her death in 2001. John Finlay, the Elizabeth B. McGraw Curator of Chinese Art, has devoted his time and energy to this publication and to the study and presentation of the Norton's Chinese art collection. He has called upon his colleagues in the field to join him in this exceptional publication. It is my privilege to thank all those who have assisted this project in reaching fruition.

Christina Orr-Cahall
Director

ACKNOWLEDGMENTS

It was never the intention that this catalogue would rewrite the history of Chinese art, which has been done so ably by other authors and curators working with larger collections. The Norton Museum's Chinese holdings, however, contain groups of objects and individual pieces that are little known in the field, and we wanted first to bring them to the attention of scholars, collectors, and all who might have an interest in Chinese works of art—or art in general. The strengths of the collection, including the extraordinary archaic jades and ritual bronze vessels, provided the inspiration to include three essays at the front of the catalogue. These, which have, perhaps, a more specialized readership, are intended to explore important issues in Chinese art historical scholarship in greater depth than a catalogue entry usually permits.

While the bulk of this project was funded by a foundation that wishes to remain anonymous, the E. Rhodes and Leona B. Carpenter Foundation gave important initial financial support. Generous underwriting makes it possible to include full-page color photographs of all objects discussed in the entries. Individual donors of works of art are acknowledged in the credit lines for all objects in the catalogue, but their generosity extends far beyond the pages of this book.

Colin Mackenzie and Jenny F. So, who have each contributed essays, also shared their knowledge of ritual bronzes and archaic jades during visits to examine the Norton collection. Annette L. Juliano examined our Buddhist sculptures and provided valuable insight in this field. Nicholas Grindley provided an abundance of information on lacquer furniture, and David Priestley made available research on tomb figures and 18th- and 19th-century jades. Other visiting scholars and dealers have had a chance to examine the collection, and we have always profited from their informed observations. They, along with individual donors, have provided substantial information on objects in the collection.

In the production of the catalogue, Tony Wimpfheimer provided practical editorial guidance in the initial stages of the project, and E. Gabriel Perle gave us the benefit of his knowledge of publishing and intellectual property. Elizabeth Powers and Ray Furse agreed to take on the task of editing the catalogue on short notice and against a tight deadline. Bruce M. White provided most of the wonderful photographs of the Museum's Chinese works of art, and C.J. Walker completed the photography of our Chinese paintings. The design is the work of Joseph Cho and Stefanie Lew of Binocular, who also oversaw the production of the book. Kelli Woodham Marin, Karol Lurie, and Lisa Heard of the Museum's Curatorial Department took on many of the thankless tasks that attend any publication project, and we want to recognize, too, the willing and cheerful cooperation of all the Museum's staff. It is conventional in Chinese publications for the author to thank colleagues for all that is worthwhile in a book, to take full responsibility for any errors that make it into print, and to invite corrections from all sources. Having completed the Museum's second catalogue of the Chinese collection, I am beginning to understand the truth contained in these sentiments.

John R. Finlay
The Elizabeth B. McGraw
Curator of Chinese Art

CHRONOLOGY OF CHINA'S HISTORIC DYNASTIES

Xia dynasty (unconfirmed)	ca. 2100–ca. 1600 BCE
Shang dynasty	ca. 1600–ca. 1100 BCE
Zhou dynasty	ca. 1100–256 BCE
Western Zhou	ca. 1100–771 BCE
Eastern Zhou	770–256 BCE
Spring and Autumn period	770–481 BCE
Warring States period	481–221 BCE
Qin dynasty	221–206 BCE
Han dynasty	206 BCE–220 CE
Western (Former) Han	206 BCE–9 CE
Wang Mang interregnum	9–23
Eastern (Later) Han	25–220
Six Dynasties	220–589
Three Kingdoms	220–265
Southern Dynasties	317–589
Northern Dynasties	386–581
Northern Wei dynasty	386–535
Sui dynasty	581–618
Tang dynasty	618–907
Five dynasties	907–960
Liao dynasty	916–1125
Song dynasty	960–1279
Northern Song	960–1127
Southern Song	1127–1279
Jin dynasty	1115–1234
Yuan dynasty	1272–1368
Ming dynasty	1368–1644
Qing dynasty	1644–1911

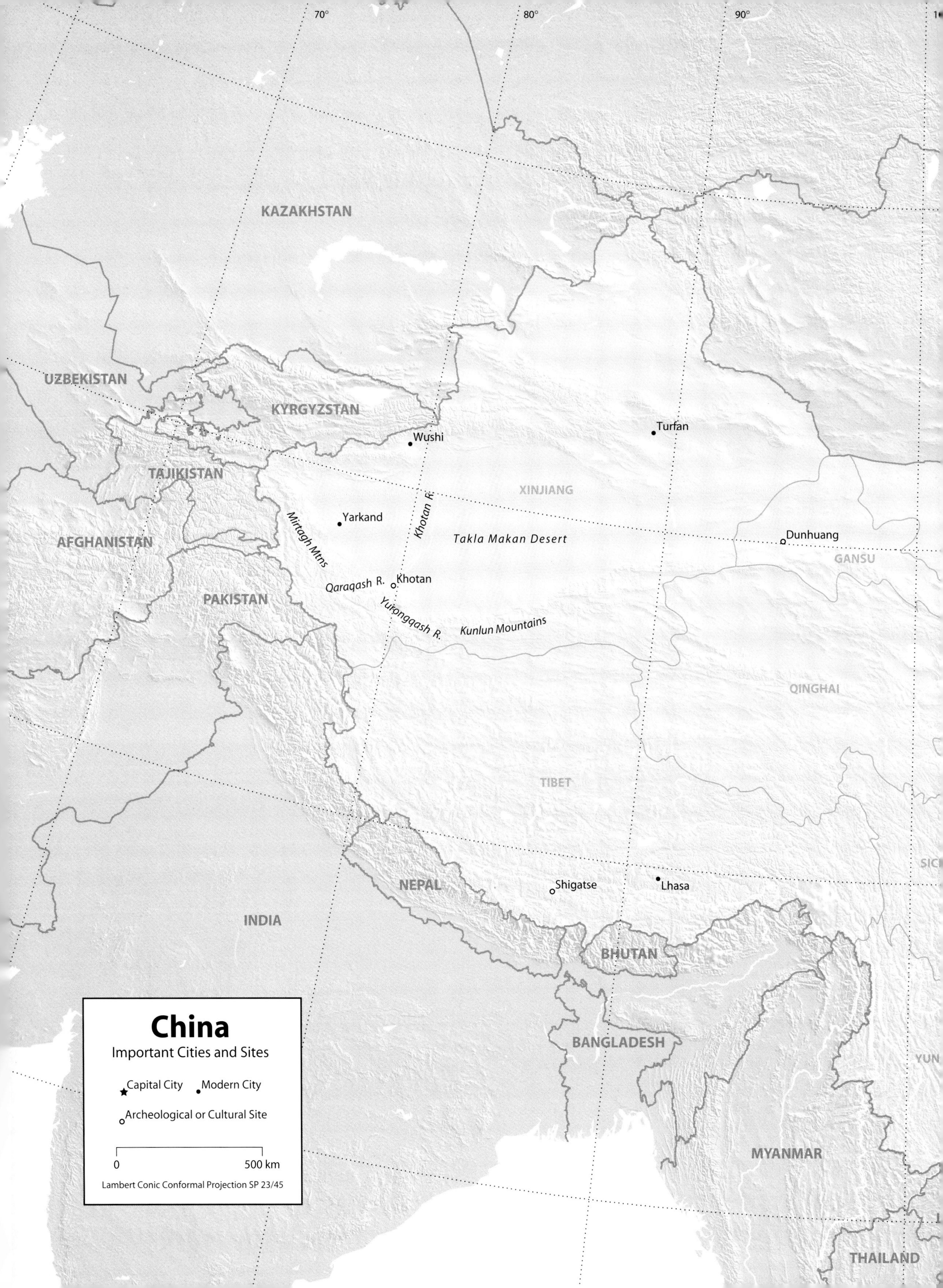
70°
80°
90°
KAZAKHSTAN
UZBEKISTAN
KYRGYZSTAN
TAJIKISTAN
AFGHANISTAN
PAKISTAN
Wushi
Turfan
XINJIANG
Yarkand
Mirtagh Mtns
Khotan R.
Takla Makan Desert
Dunhuang
GANSU
Qaraqash R.
Khotan
Yurongqash R.
Kunlun Mountains
QINGHAI
TIBET
NEPAL
Shigatse
Lhasa
INDIA
BHUTAN
BANGLADESH
MYANMAR
THAILAND
China
Important Cities and Sites
Capital City
Modern City
Archeological or Cultural Site
0
500 km
Lambert Conic Conformal Projection SP 23/45

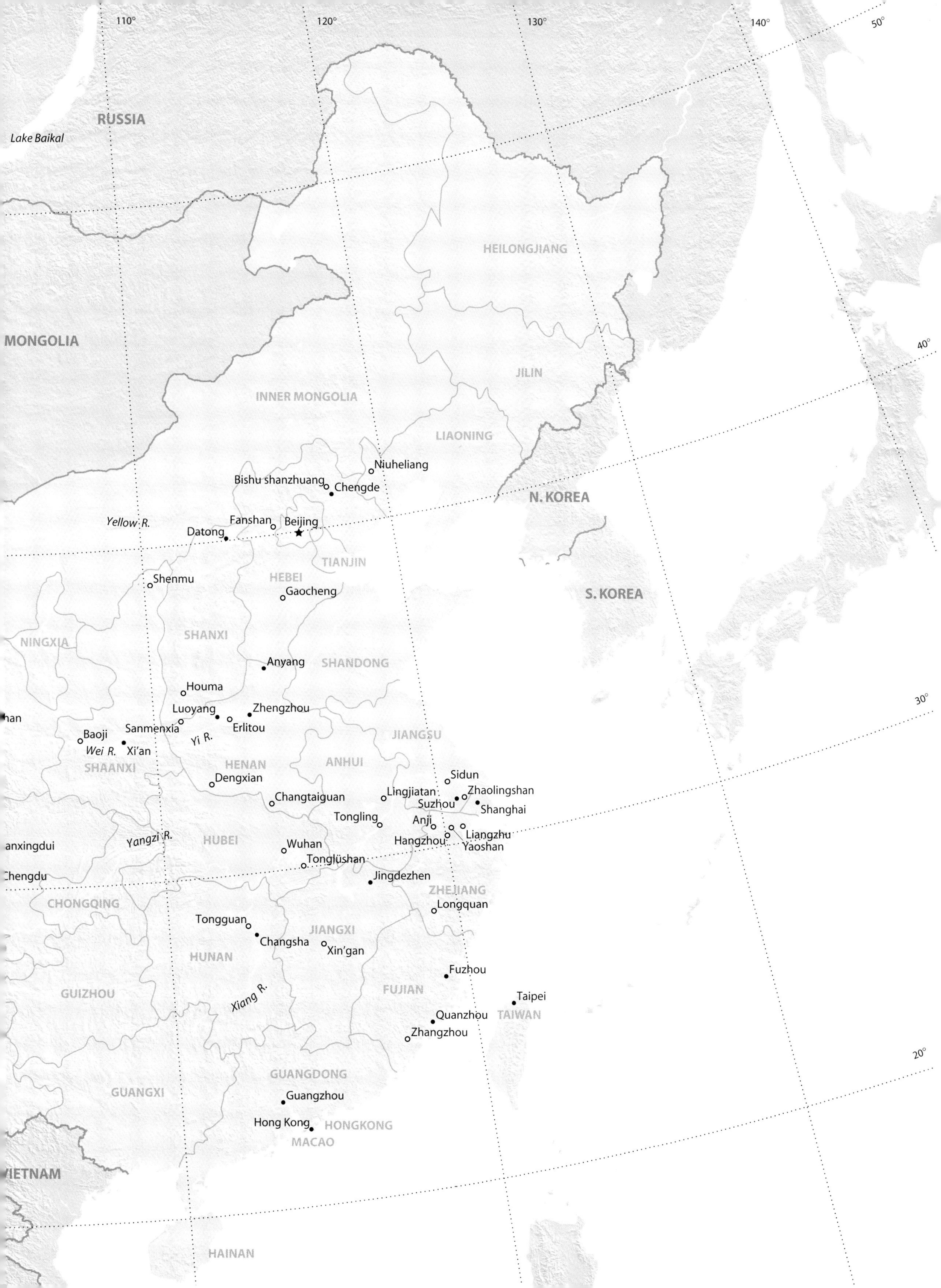

110°
120°
130°
140°
50°
40°
30°
20°
RUSSIA
Lake Baikal
MONGOLIA
HEILONGJIANG
JILIN
INNER MONGOLIA
LIAONING
N. KOREA
S. KOREA
Niuheliang
Bishu shanzhuang
Chengde
Yellow R.
Fanshan
Beijing
Datong
TIANJIN
HEBEI
Shenmu
Gaocheng
NINGXIA
SHANXI
Anyang
SHANDONG
Houma
Luoyang
Zhengzhou
Sanmenxia
Erlitou
Baoji
Wei R.
Xi'an
Yi R.
JIANGSU
SHAANXI
HENAN
ANHUI
Dengxian
Sidun
Changtaiguan
Lingjiatan
Zhaolingshan
Suzhou
Shanghai
Tongling
Anji
Liangzhu
Hangzhou
Yaoshan
Yangzi R.
HUBEI
anxingdui
Wuhan
Tonglüshan
Chengdu
Jingdezhen
ZHEJIANG
CHONGQING
Longquan
Tongguan
Changsha
JIANGXI
Xin'gan
HUNAN
Fuzhou
GUIZHOU
FUJIAN
Xiang R.
Taipei
Quanzhou
TAIWAN
Zhangzhou
GUANGDONG
GUANGXI
Guangzhou
Hong Kong
HONGKONG
MACAO
VIETNAM
HAINAN

ESSAYS

THE NORTON COLLECTION OF ARCHAIC CHINESE JADES—FIFTY YEARS LATER

Jenny F. So

INTRODUCTION

In February 1940, C.T. Loo, a preeminent dealer in Chinese art, organized an exhibition of archaic Chinese jades at the University of Pennsylvania Museum of Archaeology and Anthropology, Philadelphia. Included in the exhibition were over three hundred jades spanning almost two thousand years, dating from the second and first millennia BCE.[1] Many of the jades in that exhibition have since formed the core of such important museum collections as the Freer Gallery of Art and the Arthur M. Sackler Gallery in Washington D.C., the Metropolitan Museum of Art in New York, the Avery Brundage collection in the Asian Art Museum of San Francisco, and the Norton Gallery (as the Norton Museum of Art was then called) in West Palm Beach. The short introduction to the catalogue of the Philadelphia exhibition, written by Horace H.F. Jayne, revealed insights and a critical attitude in regard to traditional scholarship that are still valid today.[2]

In 1950, the Norton Gallery organized an exhibition of Chinese jades from C.T. Loo's gallery through Loo's New York partner, Frank Caro, Sr. In this exhibition many of the jades shown in Philadelphia in 1940 were again on display. It was from this exhibition that the core of the current collection of over forty archaic Chinese jades was selected, thirty-four of which were obtained for the Gallery immediately after the close of the exhibition in March 1950. H.H.F. Jayne, who retired to Florida in the 1950s and moved to Palm Beach where he formed a close relationship with Ralph H. Norton and his wife, became in the following years the de facto curator of the Chinese art collection. In his 1972 catalogue of that collection, Jayne published the group of thirty-four jades.[3] In 1991, six remaining jades from the 1950 purchase were given to the Gallery by members of the Richards family, descendants of the Nortons. Compared to other private collections of archaic jades assembled during the early twentieth century in America — the Grenville L. Winthrop Collection at the Harvard University Art Museums or the Edward and Louise B. Sonnenschein collection in the Art Institute of Chicago, which contained several hundred jades each[4] — Ralph Norton's purchase was by no means comprehensive. About one-third of Mr. Norton's selection consisted of large, plain pieces that fall under the ritual implement category; the remaining two-thirds are smaller, more decorative, ornamental pieces. The motives and incentives behind the selection will probably never emerge, but individual examples have continued to grow in meaning and significance with our knowledge of this material over the last half-century.

Much of what we know about ancient Chinese jades is a direct consequence of the early Chinese custom of burying the dead with their treasured belongings. Although graves had been opened by accident, war, or looting throughout Chinese history, it was the controlled excavations carried out by China's Western-trained archaeologists in the late 1920s that first brought the archaeological context to the attention of Western scholars and collectors alike. A second major wave of discoveries came with the economic development and construction that began after the end of the Cultural Revolution. Excavations since the early 1970s have significantly enhanced our understanding and appreciation of ancient Chinese jades, and the end is nowhere in sight. The Norton collection was formed during the earlier of these two activities. C.T. Loo wrote in his preface to the 1950 exhibition catalogue that the collection on view was "gathered during the last few years," that is, before 1950. But in fact, some of the ancient Chinese jades subsequently acquired by Ralph Norton were already in Western hands by the 1920s and 1930s (cats. 28, 39) or previously shown in C.T. Loo's New York exhibition of 1941–42 (cats. 17, 20, 24, 43),[5] in other words, before collectors, dealers, or scholars had the full benefits of the objects' archaeological contexts. Fifty years later, with much more information from controlled excavations at our disposal, we can look at them again with new insights.

JADE AS VIRTUE'S EMBODIMENT

It has long been recognized that the term "jade" (*yu*), although widely used and accepted, is a mineralogical misnomer.[6] In both Chinese and English, it has become a term loosely applied to a variety of hard and soft stones susceptible to polishing. The most commonly worked stone in ancient China was nephrite, a silicate of calcium and magnesium with a hardness of 6 to 6.5 on the Mohs scale (diamond is 10). Almost all of the archaic jades in the Norton collection are nephrite. Other minerals, such as serpentine, soapstone, agate, rock crystal, turquoise, and even softer stones (cats. 18, 21), have also been used since antiquity.[7] Jadeite, the brilliantly translucent green, gem-quality mineral now commonly associated with the name "jade," was unknown in China until the seventeenth century, when it was first introduced from northern Burma.[8] The richest sources of nephrite, even today, are located in modern China's far western province of Xinjiang in Central Asia. But recent analysis of excavated examples indicates that throughout the Neolithic period and the Bronze Age (ca. 5000–500 BCE), Chinese jade workers depended largely on sources closer to home.[9] Only late in the first millennium BCE do we see a significant increase in the use of top-quality, pale yellowish-white, translucent nephrite typical of Xinjiang sources (see cats. 40, 43, 46).

In its purest state, nephrite is glowing, semitranslucent, and milky white. The wide-ranging hues of gray, green, brown, and yellow commonly seen on nephrite are the results of mineral impurities in the stone. Discoloration can also occur over time—through exposure to varying conditions of weathering, burial, and man-made processes. The ancient burial custom of sprinkling mercuric oxide (cinnabar) over the corpse and burial goods often leaves powdery red accretions on the surface of the stone (cat. 27). Chemical reaction to substances in the earth and decomposing organic matter in the grave can also affect its color. Artificial methods of coloration, enthusiastically practiced by dealers to enhance the appeal of the object, are often encountered on jades handed down for generations.

The hardness of nephrite coupled with its distinctive felted crystalline structure means that it cannot be scratched or cut by ordinary metal tools. It is therefore misleading to say that a piece of nephrite is "carved," because it was never carved in the conventional sense with the sculptor's tool in direct contact with the stone; rather, the tool holds and guides the abrasive. Today, as was the case millennia ago, the jade worker would shape and polish nephrite using an abrasive paste made from crushed harder stones, such as quartz sand (hardness 7 on the Mohs scale), which was applied to tools generally made of soft materials like wood, bone, bamboo, cord, or leather. Technically, the jade worker's tool never comes into contact with the nephrite. Jade working is therefore a quintessential art form of societies before the advent of metal working, as it involves only the action of stone against stone.

Large nephrite boulders, often weathered rough and dull and resembling ordinary rocks on the exterior, have to be cut open to expose the pristine stone inside. Even under modern conditions, with electric saws and hard abrasives like corundum or synthetic Carborundum (hardness 9–10), it still takes several weeks to make a single cut through a one-foot cube of jade. The same task, executed in ancient China with far less sophisticated tools and abrasives, must have been nothing short of formidable. The prestige of worked jade artifacts, in ancient and modern societies alike, must stem not just from the material's natural beauty and endurance, but also from a tacit recognition of the extraordinary effort required to work it. An often-quoted passage from the *Book of Rites* (*Liji*) attributed to Confucius, China's ancient sage-philosopher, describes jade as the epitome of human virtue:

Ancient superior man found the likeness of all excellent qualities in jade. Soft, smooth and glossy, it appeared to them like benevolence; fine, compact and strong, like intelligence; angular, but not sharp and cutting, like righteousness; hanging down (in beads) as if it would fall to the ground, like (the humility of) propriety; when struck, yielding a note, clear and prolonged, yet terminating abruptly, like music; its flaws not concealing its beauty, nor its beauty concealing its flaws, like loyalty; with an internal radiance issuing from it on every side, like good faith; bright as a brilliant rainbow, like heaven; exquisite and mysterious, appearing in the hills and streams, like the earth; standing out conspicuous in the symbols of rank, like virtue; esteemed by all under the sky, like the path of beauty and duty.[10]

Proof of the high regard for jade in ancient China is seen when even broken fragments of nephrite were given new life by reworking them into new forms. The small bird-shaped ornament (cat. 32) in the Norton collection must have been refashioned in antiquity from a fish: the pair of "fins" under the belly does not belong on a bird, and the upturned end of the tail reveals lines and motifs that appear to be abruptly cut short. Likewise, an even older object, the half of a squared cylinder (*cong*, cat. 14), testifies to the continuation of this reverence into more recent times. Its warm ivory-colored surface suggests that, in spite of its incomplete state, the object was nevertheless much loved and handled over a long period of time.

Because of its beauty and durability and the skill and challenge required to work it, nephrite has been one of the most highly regarded materials throughout China's history. Its importance goes back to distant antiquity, to the Neolithic communities of over five thousand years ago, where nephrite consistently appears as the material of choice for leading members of those communities in the northern, southern, and western parts of China. Nephrite artifacts were buried with only a few individuals, suggesting the special status the deceased had enjoyed in their communities. One individual was buried about 3000 BCE at Sidun, Wujin county, in Jiangsu province, with over one hundred jades, of which thirty-three were the squared cylindrical *cong* (fig. 1) similar to the one in the Norton collection (cat. 14). Many of them also show the mysterious facelike images placed at the four corners of the object that are arranged in horizontal segments along its

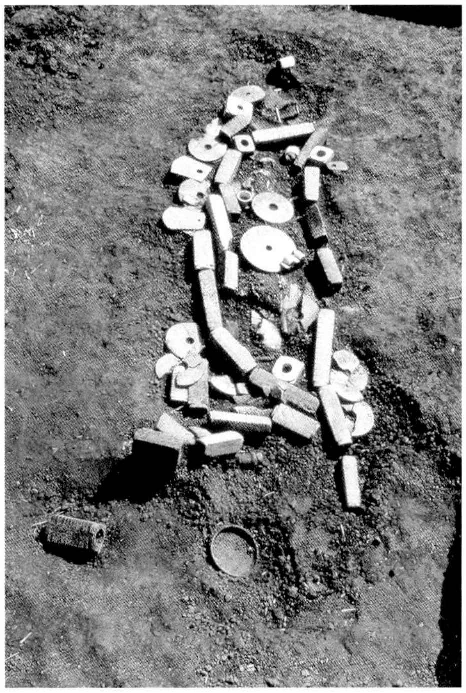

FIGURE 1 Tomb 3 at Sidun, Wujin county, Jiangsu province, showing jade discs and *cong* surrounding the contours of the occupant. Late Neolithic period, ca. 3000–2500 BCE

length. On the Norton *cong*, the upper register is simple, with incised, small, double circular eyes; the lower is more elaborate, with large oval eyes and a wedge-shaped nose-bridge in relief. In the absence of writing from the time, we will probably never know exactly the meaning of these images. Their extensive use in burials and their compelling presence, however, convince us that the *cong* and other jades on which these images appear must have functioned as important symbols in a religious or spiritual world known only to the Neolithic peoples who created and used them.

These *cong* were often found in the same grave with a distinctive three-pronged object, which can be smooth and plain like the one in the Norton collection (cat. 15), or elaborately decorated with similar facelike motifs (fig. 2). Shared imagery might indicate that the *cong* and the three-pronged object also shared the same religious or spiritual meaning or that they functioned under similar ritual circumstances. But while the three-pronged object might have been worn, perhaps with additional components inserted into the three holes at each prong, the *cong* were probably made solely for ritual purposes.

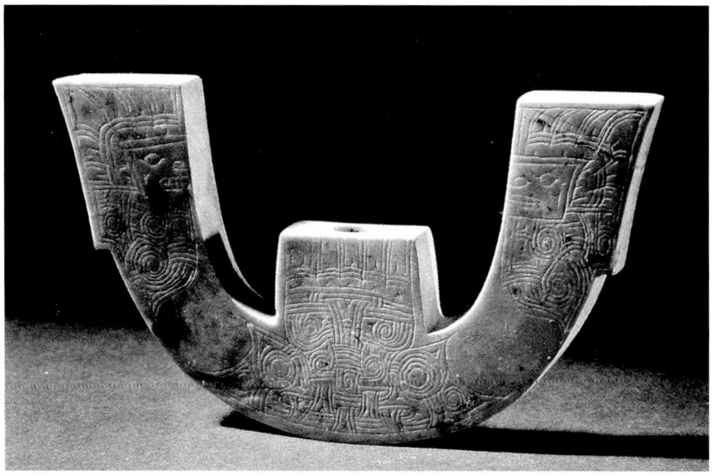

FIGURE 2 Three-pronged ornament with incised mask motifs. Height: 1 7/8 in. (4.8 cm). From Tomb 7 at Yaoshan, Yuhang county, Zhejiang province. Late Neolithic period, ca. 3000–2500 BCE

The flat blade (cat. 18) in the Norton collection represents another late Neolithic and early Bronze Age artifact with strong religious associations. Its shape is distinguished at one end by a curved, fork-shaped tip, and at the other end by an irregular series of serrations above a rectangular butt. The meaning and function of these unusual blades have long baffled scholars, but recent discoveries from two Bronze Age (ca. 1200–1100 BCE) sacrificial pits at Sanxingdui in the southwestern province of Sichuan have supplied the first glimpse of their possible use and meaning.[11] There, a bronze figure is shown kneeling with such a blade clasped forked end up in its hands (fig. 3); and incised motifs on another jade blade from the site show forked blades standing upright next to hill-like mounds and kneeling figures (fig. 4).

Although the blades from Sanxingdui came from a Bronze Age find, less elaborate earlier versions have come from late Neolithic or early Bronze Age contexts (ca. 2000 BCE) in northern Shaanxi province. Thus, although we might conclude that such blades were an important part of ritual worship in natural (perhaps mountainous?) settings in southwestern China during the Bronze Age, we do not have sufficient evidence to say the same of their earlier prototypes from the north. The forked blades that were made and used in large numbers in the southwest are separated by time and space from those found in the northwest. The shape may have survived or been transmitted over these distances, but its original meaning or function may not have come with it. The Norton collection includes two other jades (cats. 16 and 17), both having the same shape as the *cong* (cat. 14), that illustrate how time and space can distort or change an object's appearance or meaning. One of these (cat. 16) closely resembles an example recovered in Gansu province, far away from the southeastern coastal home of the *cong*.[12] In Gansu, not only is the *cong*

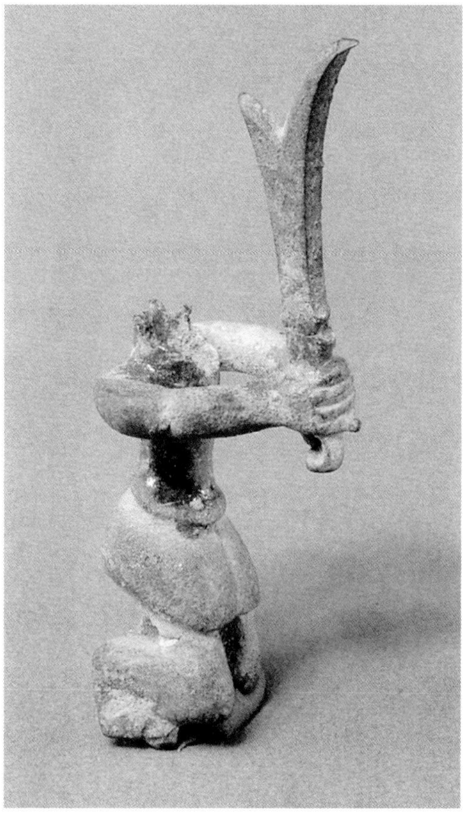

FIGURE 3 Miniature bronze figure holding forked blade. Maximum height: 1 7/8 in. (4.7 cm). From Pit 2 at Sanxingdui, Guanghan county, Sichuan province. 12th century BCE

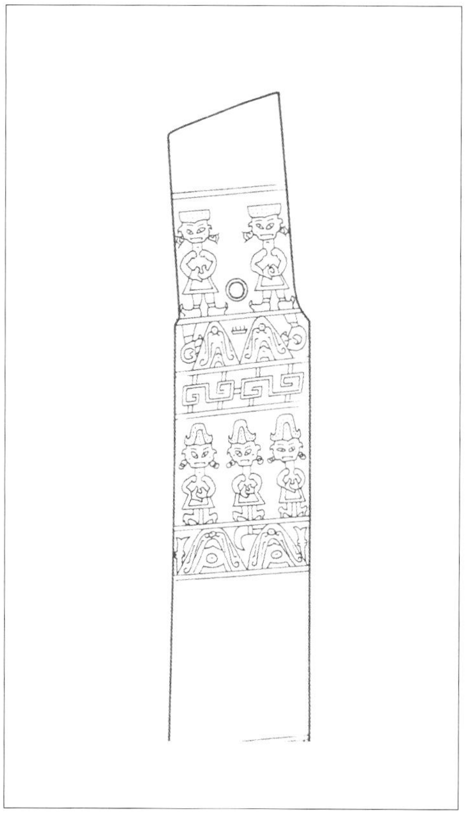

FIGURE 4 Drawing of bottom half of stone blade with incised decoration showing figures and sacrificial mounds (or mountains) flanked by forked blades. Height of complete blade: 21 3/4 in. (54.2 cm). From Pit 2 at Sanxingdui, Guanghan county, Sichuan province. 12th century BCE

shape a rarity, but the mysterious imagery of the southeastern prototypes is also often replaced by simple geometric motifs, such as the ribs on the Norton example. The second object (cat. 17), from the Eastern Zhou, represents the *cong* as it was understood from the sixth to fifth century BCE, over two thousand years after the Neolithic versions were made. The surface is decorated with motifs fashionable at the time, and the holes drilled into three of the four corners suggest an as yet unknown function or attachment. The jade workers who made these two artifacts may have known the ancient shape but not the ancient religious beliefs that inspired them.[13]

JADE AS A SYMBOL OF POWER

The spiritual powers associated with jades also translated into prestige for their owners. In ancient communities, spiritual and worldly power often resided in the same individual, and so it was that jades in ancient China were often not only religious symbols but also markers of extraordinary status. The best representatives are the large ax and halberd (*ge*) blades (cat. 22 and fig. 5), which were modeled after functional weapons made from ordinary stone or metal. Made of nephrite (or fine-grain stone in the case of fig. 5), they would have been too brittle and too valuable to be used and must have functioned only in ceremonial display. The ax blade (cat. 22) was already an important part of elite burials in Neolithic times (fig. 6), with large numbers of similar blades buried with an individual perhaps signifying exceptional prowess. The halberd blade (fig. 5) was modeled after a Bronze Age weapon that only came into being in the late second millennium BCE. When

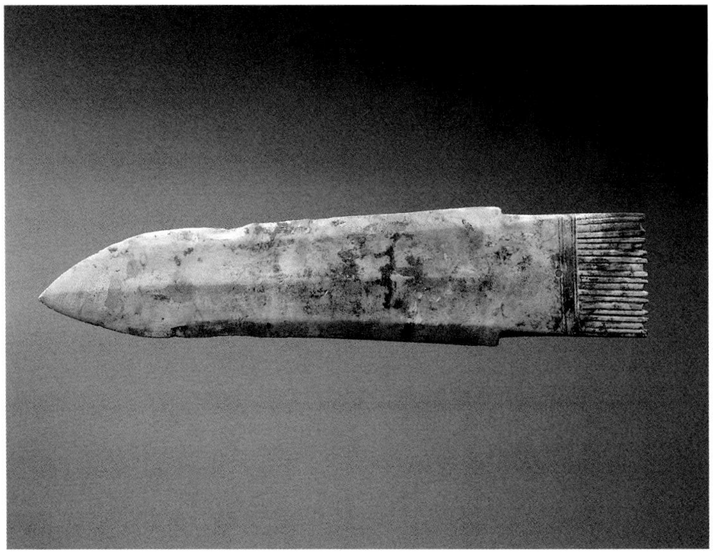

FIGURE 5 Stone halberd blade. 14 1/2 × 3 1/4 × 1/4 in. (36.8 × 8.3 × .6 cm). Late Neolithic period–Shang dynasty, ca. late second millennium BCE. Gift of R.H. Horton, 50.17

such a blade was matched with a turquoise-encrusted bronze butt (cat. 20), the effect must have been grand indeed.

Less obvious than ceremonial weapons as indicators of status, personal ornaments in the form of pendants or other accessories made of jade were also important signs of rank. In Neolithic communities in northeastern China (ca. 3500–2500 BCE), select individuals were buried with large sculptural ornaments worn at the chest, as seen in a tomb excavated in southwestern Liaoning province (fig. 7). One characteristic type shows an animal head at one end of a C-shaped piece. The Norton collection has a much smaller Bronze Age descendant of this type (cat. 27). Its greatly diminished size compared to its Neolithic counterpart would seem to suggest a corresponding change in meaning and significance over time. Again, the outward form and superficial function of the Neolithic ancestor seem to have been preserved, absent the earlier spiritual or political meaning.

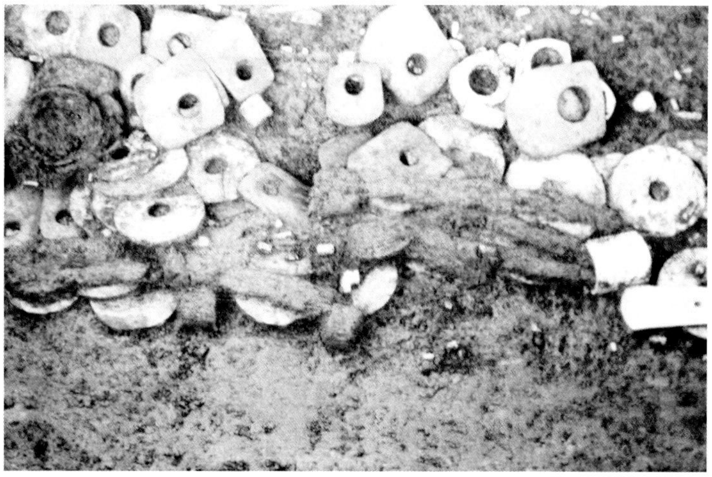

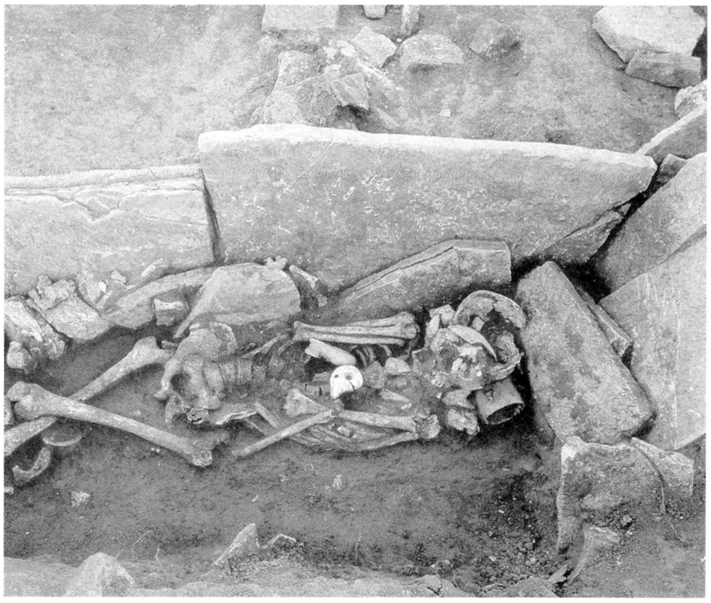

FIGURE 6 Tomb 20 at Fanshan, Yuhang county, Zhejiang province, showing ax blades in situ. Late Neolithic period, ca. 3500–2500 BCE

FIGURE 7 Tomb 4 at Niuheliang (Site 2, Cairn 2), Jianping county, Liaoning province, showing two C-shaped ornaments in situ. Late Neolithic period, ca. 3500–2500 BCE

Excavations of another flourishing Neolithic (ca. 4000–3000 BCE) culture in southeastern China yielded prototypes for two other Bronze Age descendants in the Norton collection (cats. 26, 25). The first (fig. 8), conceived as a flat rather than sculptural pendant, is also C-shaped and terminated by an animal head. It was recovered from excavations at a fourth millennium BCE site at Lingjiatan, Hanshan county, Anhui province, and is currently the earliest known example of its type from the south. The second ornament (fig. 9) is arc-shaped and shows a profile figure with knees bent, arms at the chest, and a human-like head with a fancy headdress.[14] In Neolithic contexts, these ornaments with their distinctive imagery must have indicated both the spiritual and personal powers of those who wore them. Whether their specific meanings were transmitted with their distinctive forms into the Bronze Age remain as yet unclear.

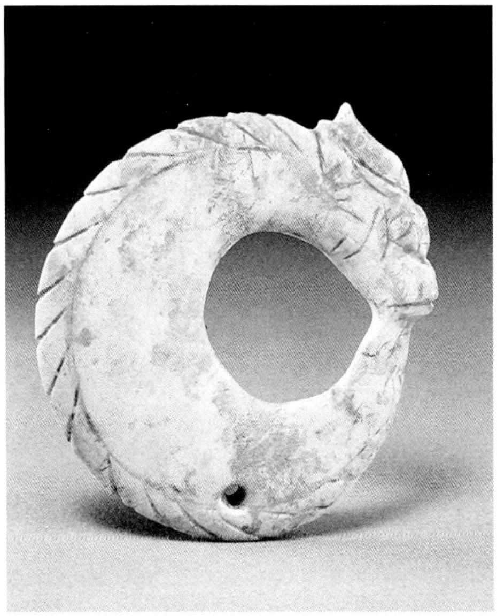

FIGURE 8 C-shaped dragon plaque. Width: 1 ¾ in. (4.4 cm). Lingjiatan, Hanshan county, Anhui province. Late Neolithic period, ca. 3000–2500 BCE

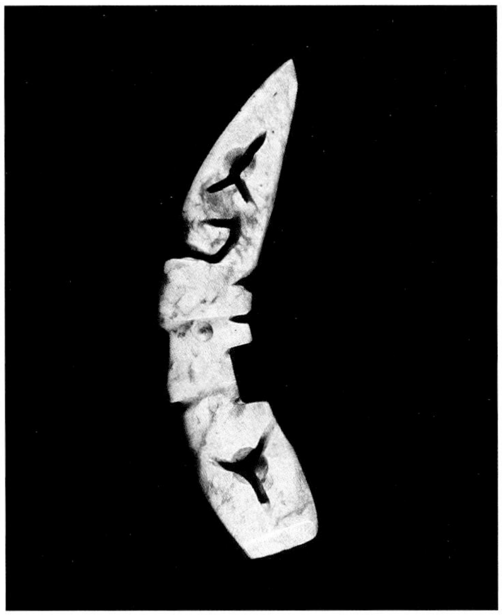

FIGURE 9 *Xi* (knot-opener?) showing a human figure in profile with fancy headdress. Height: 2 ⅜ in. (6 cm). From Tomb 5 at Zhanglingshan, Wu county, Jiangsu province. Late Neolithic period, ca. 3000–2500 BCE

Aside from inheriting ready-made icons from their Neolithic predecessors, Bronze Age jade workers also created their own new symbols of power. A magnificent bird-shaped plaque in the Norton collection is a forceful pronouncement of its owner's status (cat. 24). The large bird stands in proud profile, with hooked beak, tall crenulated crest, back, chest, and tail feathers creating a fiercely aggressive jagged silhouette. A perforated tab at its claw was probably inserted into something that allowed the bird to be prominently displayed. The only bird-shaped plaques comparable in size, complexity, and strength have been recovered from the tomb of Fu Hao (ca. 1200 BCE), royal consort to the Shang king Wu Ding, at Anyang, the Shang capital in northern Henan province.[15] Bird plaques like the Norton's, whether worn as pendants or displayed in some other context, represent one of the most outstanding second millennium BCE additions to this rich repertoire and certainly served as preeminent status symbols for the ruling nobility.

While we still have little information on how the Shang jade ornaments were used or worn, recent archaeological excavations of first millennium BCE tombs have given us glimpses of a practice that has changed the way we look at these ornaments. The opening of several undisturbed royal tombs dating to the tenth and ninth centuries BCE in southwestern Henan province has revealed that a variety of plaques were strung together (probably with silk cord) as components of a grand necklace or chain, or they were sewn onto a fabric funerary face cover (figs. 10, 11).[16] For the first time, we understand that the multitude of individual jade plaques collected, exhibited, and published for over half a century as isolated objects of beauty were actually parts of a grand design. Worn in life and buried with the dead, these impressive assemblages must have been the ultimate emblems of rank and status symbols of their time.

The Norton collection has a number of jades that might have functioned in this capacity as parts of complex ornamental chains (cats. 38, 39, 40, 43). Dating mostly from the fifth century BCE, they display the typical shapes and surface decorations of the Warring States period. How they might have been strung together is suggested by lacquered wooden attendant figures excavated from fourth-century BCE tombs in Henan province

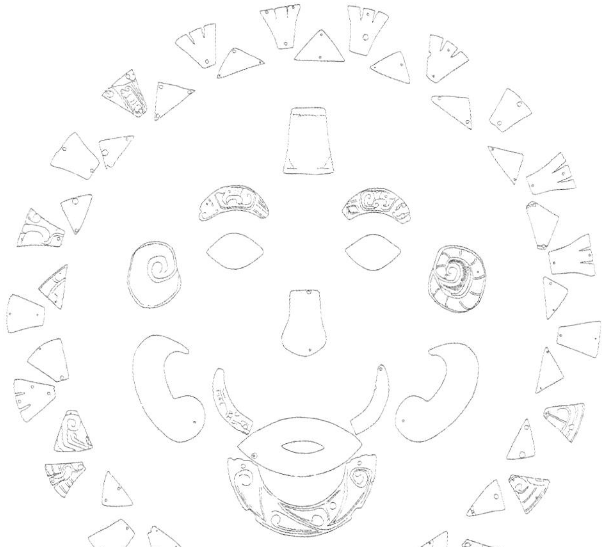

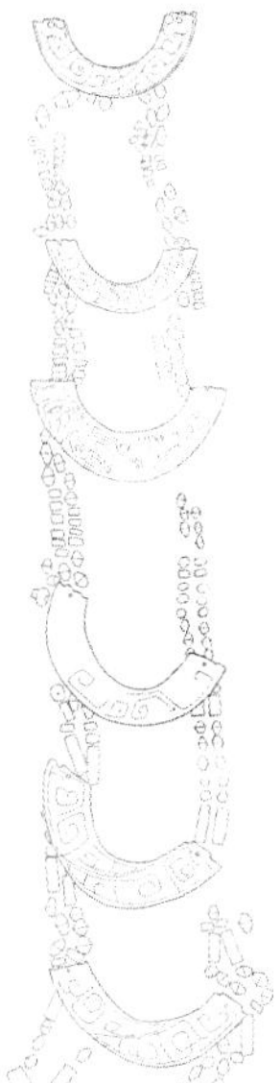

FIGURE 10 (left) Drawing of jades sewn on a face cover, from Tomb 2001 of the Guo state cemetery at Sanmenxia, Sha'an county, Henan province. Late Western Zhou dynasty, 9th–8th century BCE

FIGURE 11 (right) Drawing of jade pendants and beads forming necklace, from Tomb 2001 of the Guo state cemetery at Sanmenxia, Sha'an county, Henan province. Late Western Zhou dynasty, 9th–8th century BCE (fig. 12). These attendant figures are shown wearing fairly simple pendant chains on which a small handful of circular and arc-shaped pieces are strung together with twisted (silk?) cord. A nobleman or prince would merit more elaborate configurations using components of great variety, such as one worn by the rebel King of Nanyue, buried in Guangzhou (Canton) in the late second century BCE (fig. 13).[17] Literary sources of the time suggest that strict sumptuary regulations governed the appearance of complex pendant chains according to rank and status:

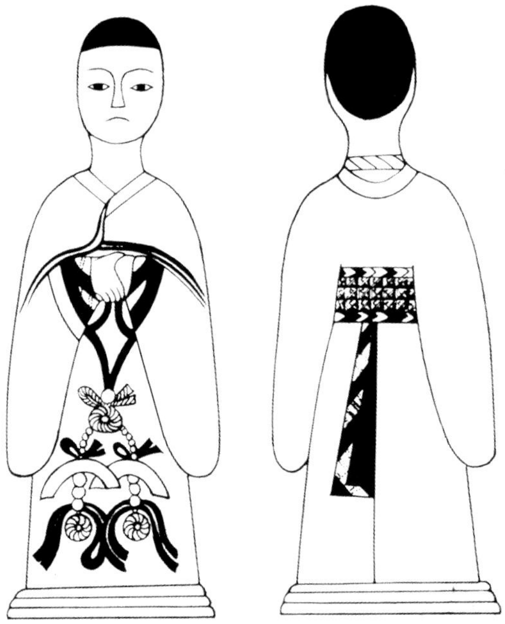

FIGURE 12 Drawing of lacquered wooden figure showing jade pendant suspended from waist, from Tomb 1 at Changtaiguan, Xinyang county, Henan province. Warring States period, 4th century BCE

The Son of Heaven had his pendants composed of beads of white jade, hung on dark-colored strings; a Duke or Marquis, his of jade beads of hill-azure, on vermilion strings; a Great Officer, his of beads of aquamarine, on black string; an Heir-son, his of beads of yü *jade, on variegated strings; an ordinary officer, his beads of jade-like quartz, on orange-colored strings.*[18]

Although this hierarchy is not yet supported by archaeological evidence, the passage from the *Book of Rites* nevertheless illustrates clearly the rankings associated with different jade pendant chains. The "white jade" worn by the Son of Heaven (that is, the ruler) must have been the high-quality material similar to the lustrous nephrite used for the disc- and dragon-shaped pendants in the Norton collection (cats. 40, 43). The refined workmanship that went into the making and polishing of the pearl-like surface of raised commas matches the beauty of the material.

An arc-shaped pendant (cat. 42) measuring over one foot in length and 2 ½ inches in width would almost certainly have been too large to wear. Originally part of a pair (now separated), it is worked and finished on both sides, which excludes its use as an ornamental inset into the surface of another object. It is possible that large pendant assemblages were hung as decorations in palace interiors, as suggested by the scene on the funerary banner of the Marquise of Dai buried at Mawangdui, Changsha, Hunan province (fig. 14). In the lower section of the banner, which shows the ancestral hall, a large arc-shaped pendant hangs over the altar table on which containers of food and wine were laid out for the dead marquise. If modern-day customs may be taken as a guide, oversized items may simply have been presented as tokens or awards in ceremonial situations. A contemporary parallel might be the gigantic checks presented with pomp and ceremony as symbols of a donor's generosity.

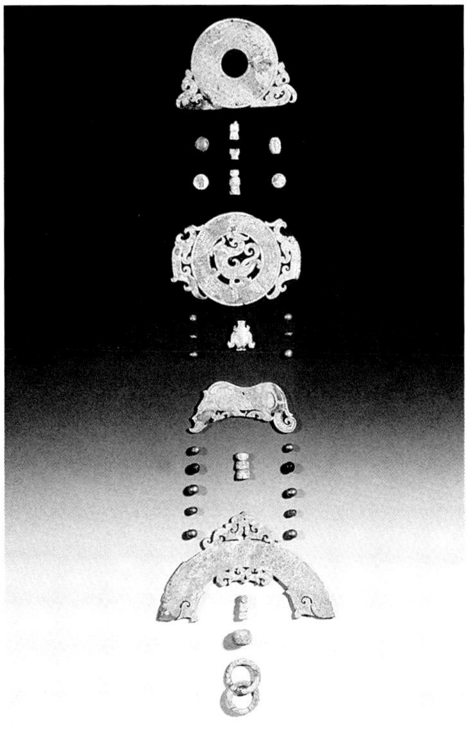

FIGURE 13 Reconstructed configuration of gold beads and jade plaques and beads, from the tomb of the King of Nanyue at Xiangshan, Guangzhou, Guangdong province. Western Han dynasty, late 2nd century BCE

JADE AS A CULTURAL SYMBOL

Aside from serving as powerful status symbols, singly or in complex groupings, some jade shapes or types reflect different cultural heritages. The small, three-dimensional tiger in the Norton collection (50.29) is the jade cousin of numerous similar bronze tigers that have come to be closely associated with parts of southern and southeastern China during the late second millennium BCE. There, tigers are often encountered as small ornamental additions on bronze vessels and, more rarely, as a large free-standing sculpture like the examples excavated from a burial at Xin'gan in Jiangxi province.[19] Similar jade tigers excavated from the tomb of Fu Hao suggest that tiger-shaped amulets were probably collected and treasured as exotica and insignia of distant lands that had succumbed to Shang authority.

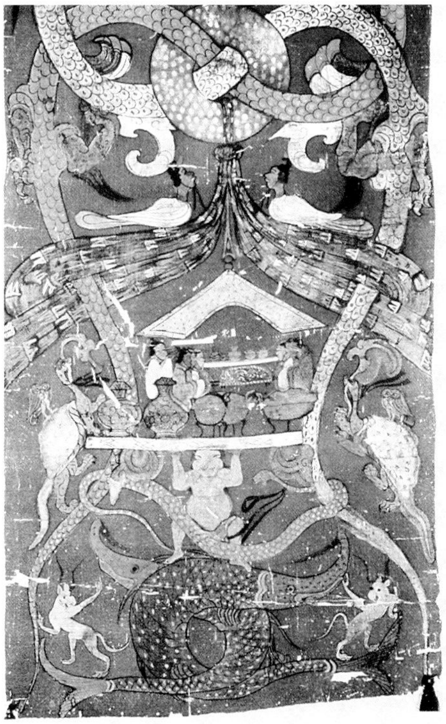

FIGURE 14 Detail of bottom section of painted silk funerary banner showing arc-shaped ornament above ritual altar, from Tomb 1 at Mawangdui, Changsha, Hunan province. Western Han dynasty, early 2nd century BCE

The antlered deer (cat. 37), plump water fowl (cat. 35), and long-eared hare (cat. 36) are all creatures commonly represented in jades excavated from the tombs of Zhou nobility in their homeland in western Shaanxi.[20] Although these are also flat two-dimensional plaques, they are distinguished by a direct and simple realism. The deer, in particular, is a signature Zhou motif. As an animal of the northern and central Asian grasslands, the deer symbolizes the Zhou people's links with the herders of the Eurasian steppes and the cultural heritage that came with them. It appears to have been particularly popular during the tenth century BCE, perhaps a quiet prelude to the influx of new cultural forces that would have far-reaching effects on ritual practices in the following century.[21]

By the late first millennium BCE, other distinctive shapes emerged that also pointed to exotic connections. The elegant, florid openwork pendant (cat. 45) represents a totally transformed, ornamental version of a second millennium BCE accessory, worn by an archer over the thumb of the right hand to help grip the string of a long bow as it is pulled back (fig. 15).[22] The long double-curved bow came to China by way of the nomadic hunters north of the border who acquired it from the Neolithic communities of Transbaikal.[23] Within very few centuries, archery was considered an essential part of a nobleman's upbringing. The contents of an inscription on a bronze food container (*gui*) in the Arthur M. Sackler Gallery, Washington, D.C., records a tenth-century BCE Zhou king's reward to one Jing, an archery trainer, for the success of his students (namely, the sons of nobility and court officials) in a state archery contest.[24] A thousand years later, during the first and second centuries CE, when the long bow had been displaced by the more powerful crossbow in China, the archer's thumb ring had become the symbol of an elite upbringing. In the Norton example, only the circular opening in the middle and the unusual pointed outline of the central element remind us of its utilitarian origin. The focus of attention is the elegant surrounding openwork scrolls.

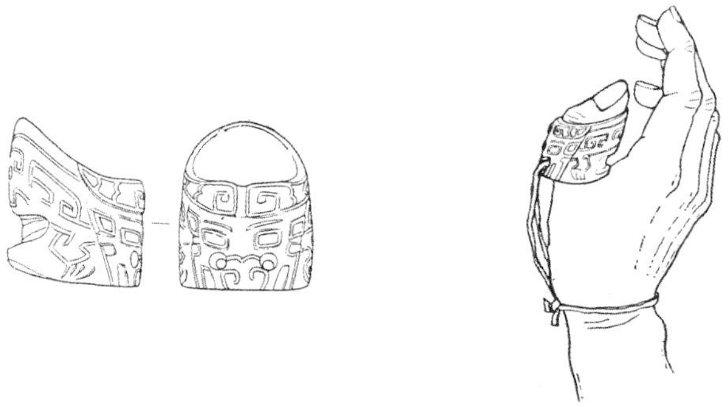

FIGURE 15 Drawing of jade archer's thumb ring (left), from Tomb 5 at Anyang, Henan province, and recreation (right) of how ring might have been worn. Late Shang dynasty, 13th–12th century BCE

The so-called "knot-opener" (*xi*, cat. 44) with its pointed end appears to be closely associated with the ornate archer's thumb ring in post–Bronze Age culture.[25] Jayne suggested a possible nomadic origin for this shape as well, since horseback riding and herding gear required frequent use of knotted leather and rope. However, in a more recent discussion it was argued that it could well have been an equally essential item in Chinese life, for opening fabric belts tied over a lapped robe and the cords of headdresses.[26] Regardless of its ultimate origin, the custom of wearing a handy tool slung from the belt, for easy access to the essential tools of one's trade, marks a mobile way of life.[27]

A sword guard in the Norton Collection (cat. 46) may be taken to mark the end of an era in the history of ancient Chinese jade. Used as an ornamental fitting on a bronze sword, this Western Han guard shows a large and a small feline in playful engagement across its front, a popular motif on fittings of the last centuries BCE. Modeled in high relief with sculptural realism, the larger feline also appears to weave in and out of scrolls incised into the surface. The creature's effortless movement between the physical and implied boundaries of the guard, rendered in a subtle but compelling three-dimensional space, is new to the world of jade designs. Where jades had once served as symbols of spiritual or earthly power that could be paraded on grand occasions or buried with elaborate rituals, or as emblems of human virtue that were worn and displayed with pomp and pride, this small sculpture suggests that from this time on jade will participate in a more concrete human realm. By acknowledging human or worldly space, China's mysterious stone of antiquity has reached out and made itself accessible to everyone. If we are already captivated by jade's ageless and more transcendent mystique, its very human and accessible qualities will also delight us. ✦

NOTES

1 Loo, *Archaic Chinese Jades* (1940).
2 Ibid., pp. 7–11.
3 Jayne, *A Handbook of the Chinese Collections*. Norton, trained as an engineer, arranged the jades himself and secured them to two display panels with minute steel clips of his own devising. Photographs of the panels appear as illustrations in Jayne's catalogue.
4 The catalogue of the jades in the Winthrop Collection contained 630 entries (Loehr, *Ancient Chinese Jades*); the Sonnenschein gift of jades to the Art Institute of Chicago in 1950 totaled 853 (Pearlstein, "Ancient Chinese Jades").
5 Loo, *Exhibition of Chinese Arts* (1941).
6 See Laufer, *Jade*, p. 22.
7 The collection also contains a late Neolithic–Shang stone blade (acc. no. 50.17, ca. late second millennium BCE) that is approximately 14 inches long; see fig. 5.
8 For a succinct description of the different types of materials and their possible sources, see Watt, *Chinese Jades*, pp. 15–16. See Hansford, *Chinese Carved Jades*, ch. 2, for a more detailed description of nephrite sources.
9 Wen and Jing, "Chinese Neolithic Jade."
10 Legge, trans., *The Li Ki*, reprint, vol. 2, p. 464.
11 For the most recent discussion of these blades, see So, "Jade and Stone at Sanxingdui."
12 See Yang Boda, "Gansu Qijia Yu Wenhua Chutan," p. 15.
13 For a discussion of several later "understandings" or "interpretations" of this shape, see So, "Revising Antiquity."
14 See *Zhongguo wenwubao*, August 2, 1992, for the example excavated in 1990–91 from Tomb 77 at Zhaolingshan, Kunshan city, Jiangsu province; see Mou Yongkang and others, *Lianzhu wenhua yuqi*, for the example excavated in 1977 from Zhanglingshan, Wu county, Jiangsu province.
15 *Yinxu yuqi*, nos. 44, 47. For an English description of Fu Hao's tomb, see Bagley, "Shang Archaeology," pp. 194–202.
16 For other examples, see *Wenwu* 1994.1, p. 23, figs. 31–32; p. 24, fig. 33; *Wenwu* 1994.8, inside front cover: 1; p. 9, fig. 12; p. 11, fig. 19; p. 20, fig. 29; p. 27, fig. 7; *Wenwu* 1995.7, p. 10, figs. 10–11; p. 15, fig. 17; p. 16, fig. 18; p. 17, fig. 19:1
17 For a full presentation of the jades from this tomb, see Lam, *Nanyue Wang mu yuqi*.
18 Legge, trans., *The Li Ki*, reprint, vol. 2, p. 19.
19 Although tigers were known in many different parts of China, as can be seen on Bronze Age artifacts, they seem to have been more localized in southern and western China (see Bagley, *Shang Ritual Bronzes*, p. 35). For examples from Xin'gan, see Peng Shifan and others, *Jiangxi Xin'gan chutu qingtong yishu*, nos. 5–11, 35, 38.
20 *Baoji Yu Guo mudi*, pl. 183–184.
21 For the early history and origins of the Zhou, see Shaughnessy, "Western Zhou History," pp. 299–307. For a discussion of the Zhou ritual revolution, see Rawson, "Western Zhou Archaeology," pp. 433–40.
22 For a detailed discussion of the development of this archer's accessory, see Yeung Kin Fong, *Zhongguo guyu yanjiu lunwenji*, pp. 128–38.
23 Watson, *Cultural Frontiers*, pp. 118–20.
24 See Rawson, *Western Zhou Ritual Bronzes*, no. 53.
25 See Rawson and Michaelson, *Chinese Jade*, pp. 286–87; no. 20:5.
26 See Loo, *Archaic Chinese Jades* (1940), pp. 9–10; *Zhongguo wenwubao*, April 11, 2000, p. 4.
27 For tools and implements associated with a nomadic way of life, see So and Bunker, *Traders and Raiders*, ch. 2.

CHINESE BRONZE CASTING AT ANYANG DURING THE LATE SHANG DYNASTY

Colin Mackenzie

INTRODUCTION

On present evidence, bronze casting seems to have arisen in China relatively late in comparison with Bronze Age cultures in western Asia. Although sporadic finds of early bronze and copper artifacts have been reported from northern and northwestern China, arguably the most significant early metal artifact is a bell of lenticular cross section from grave M3296 at Taosi in Xiangfen county, southern Shanxi, composed of 97.8% copper, 1.54% lead.[1] Radiocarbon dating of the skeletal remains in the tomb yielded a calibrated result of 2085 ±130 years BCE. Interestingly, the bell was the only metal object found among the 400 graves at the site, indicating that at this point bronze was still very rare or at least not usually consigned to graves. Surprisingly, in view of the very high proportion of copper, which makes casting difficult, the object was cast in a two-section ceramic mold. Ceramic molds were used during the late Neolithic period to mold the legs of *li* tripods, and it seems likely that the use of a mold to cast the bell represents an adaptation of this technology. Despite the crudity of the object, it is of great significance, since it foreshadows the use of ceramic molds for casting vessels.[2] This method was unique to China, but it offered many advantages over the methods for working metal used elsewhere—notably the capacity to produce very fine decoration that needed little coldworking—yet it also required considerable organizational and technical skills.[3]

Despite its lateness, in scale of production and sophistication of its technology China's Bronze Age stands unrivaled among the civilizations of the ancient world. From about the second quarter of the second millennium BCE, bronze begins to appear frequently in the tombs of the elite, becoming a primary focus of social and economic activity and involving an expenditure of labor and resources on a scale unparalleled elsewhere. In Egypt, for instance, bronze does not appear to have been a material of outstanding prestige. The contrast between two unplundered Egyptian and Chinese tombs, that of Tutankhamen (ca. 1370–1352 BCE) and that of Fu Hao, a consort of Wu Ding, a Shang dynasty ruler of around 1200 BCE, is striking. In the former, gold, rather than bronze, was prominent; the latter yielded 1,625 kilos of bronze, almost all in the form of vessels and weapons.[4]

In most ancient cultures, the nonmilitary use of bronze focused as much on sculpture and ornaments as on vessels. In this respect, the discovery of life-size statues in pits at Sanxingdui in Guanghan county, Sichuan, has revealed the importance of statuary in at least one Chinese Bronze Age culture. In mainstream casting associated with the historical dynasties, however, the primary nonmilitary use was the casting of vessels and musical instruments in the form of bells for ritual and ceremonial use. This emphasis on ritual vessels rather than on sculpture perpetuates the ceramic traditions of the Chinese Neolithic period and is a defining feature of mainstream Chinese bronzework.

The rise of large-scale Chinese bronze production in the second millennium corresponds broadly to the Xia and Shang dynasties recorded in later histories. Certain sites, such as Erlitou in Yanshi county, Henan, have been identified by Chinese archaeologists as Xia dynastic remains. However, none of these sites has yielded any inscriptional evidence that confirms this identification, so the historicity of the Xia remains to be definitively proven. The historicity of the Shang dynasty (ca. 16th century–1050 BCE), on the other hand, is well established. The discovery at the end of the nineteenth century of enormous quantities of inscribed divination turtle plastra and ox scapula, commonly referred to as "oracle bones," at the modern town of Anyang in northern Henan has provided a wealth of information about the Shang state.[5] Inextricably linked to divination were the sacrifices and libations offered to ancestors. A wide range of animals as well as human victims were sacrificed. Libations of alcohol made from millet were also important, as shown by the large variety of wine vessels in the Shang ritual bronze repertoire. The centrality to Shang religion of the ancestor cult fostered lavish expenditure on graves and grave goods, among which bronzes held pride of place.

It should be emphasized, however, that although Shang was probably the most powerful state and, on present evidence, the only one with a developed script, it was only one of a number of independent polities with which it interacted militarily, diplomatically, and economically.[6] The recent spectacular discoveries of bronzes at sites as far afield as Sanxingdui and Dayangzhou in Xin'gan county, Jiangxi, have thrown new light on the bronze casting industries that were patronized by such independent polities. Not surprisingly, these discoveries have shifted interest away from the sites in northern China that had previously held attention. Despite these recent discoveries, it should be emphasized that the sites of the central plains of northern China—Erlitou, Zhengzhou, and Anyang—remain crucial to our understanding of the development of early Chinese bronze casting. The overwhelming majority of unprovenanced Shang period bronzes are associated stylistically with northern sites. The Shang period bronzes in the collection of the Norton Museum of Art fall into this category and thus provide an opportunity to review this mainstream tradition as it is known from Anyang.

THE SITE OF YINXU

The Shang remains at Anyang, which are usually referred to by the historical name Yinxu (Wastes of Yin) by Chinese archaeologists, constitute the largest conurbation of pre-Qin China discovered so far.[7] The overall size of the site has been estimated at thirty square kilometers (see map of Anyang sites, opposite), compared with an area of twelve square kilometers at Sanxingdui and twenty-five square kilometers at Zhengzhou.[8] The area in which the remains are found stretches from Guojiawancun in the east, to the west as far as Beixinzhuang. To the north of the Huan River at Xibeigang lies the cemetery of large-scale, possibly royal, tombs. To the south, Shang remains are found as far as Sanjiazhuang, and to the southwest as far as Qijiazhuang. The core area of the city was a complex of tamped earth platforms for buildings and altars that probably served as the palace and ritual center. Unlike Zhengzhou, Sanxingdui, and other Shang cities, but like Erlitou, the city lacks a defensive wall. Instead, a moat surrounds the palace complex on two sides (the other two sides were no doubt protected by the Huan River).[9] Nevertheless, it should be noted that the area enclosed by the moat is considerably smaller than that within the wall at Zhengzhou.

Although Yinxu has been accepted by most scholars as the site of the last Shang capital, the date of its founding is still unclear. According to the *Shiji* (Historical Records), 273 years separated its founding by Pan Geng from the overthrow of Shang by Zhou. This latter event is considered by most scholars to have taken place around 1050–1040 BCE, so, if the *Shiji* is to be believed, the move to Yinxu would have taken place around 1320 BCE. However, as a number of scholars have argued, the archaeological evidence does not support such an early date.[10] The building of the capital, to judge from the palatial foundations, the moat, and the earliest of the monumental tombs at Xibeigang north of the Huan River, is dated by excavations to the end of Period I or the early part of Period II, equivalent to the reign of Wu Ding, about 1200 BCE.[11] The early phase of Period I, on the other hand, is represented only by a number of mid-scale tombs and modest habitation sites that in no way resemble a capital. The lack of oracle bones that can be associated with any ruler earlier than Wu Ding further raises questions about the status of the pre–Wu Ding habitation at Anyang.[12] The recent discovery of traces of an earlier walled Shang city to the north of the Huan River raises further questions about the date of the establishment and, indeed, the role of Yinxu. A preliminary analysis of the finds at this site suggested to archaeologists a pre–Pan Geng date for the city, at least in its founding. Whether this site will reveal bronzes and oracle bones that immediately precede those of Yinxu must await further excavation.[13]

The dramatic increase in activity at Yinxu during Wu Ding's reign was not limited to the core area of the city. Sites dated by archaeologists to this reign include Sipanmo, Gaolouzhuang, Hougang, Guojiawancun, and Miaopu Beidi, all to the south of the Huan River, and Dasikongcun and Wuguancun to the north of the river, covering an area of about twelve square kilometers. During the early phase of Period II (late 13th century–first half of 12th century BCE), the distribution further widened to include the foundry and small tombs at Limintun in the west, Liujiazhuang in the south, and Qijiazhuang in the southwest.[14] During Period III (second half of 12th century–early 11th century BCE) and Period IV (ca. second quarter of 11th century BCE), the distribution of sites continued to widen, eventually covering an area more than double that at the beginning of Wu Ding's reign. Although there exist no accurate estimates of the population of the Shang city, this expansion seems to imply a dramatic increase in population.[15] However, it may be that royal control in parts of the city weakened in the later periods, since it seems that some sites constructed during Period II for use by the elite were subsequently taken over by the common populace. For instance, the ridge on which Fu Hao's tomb is located became a common habitation site by Period III.[16]

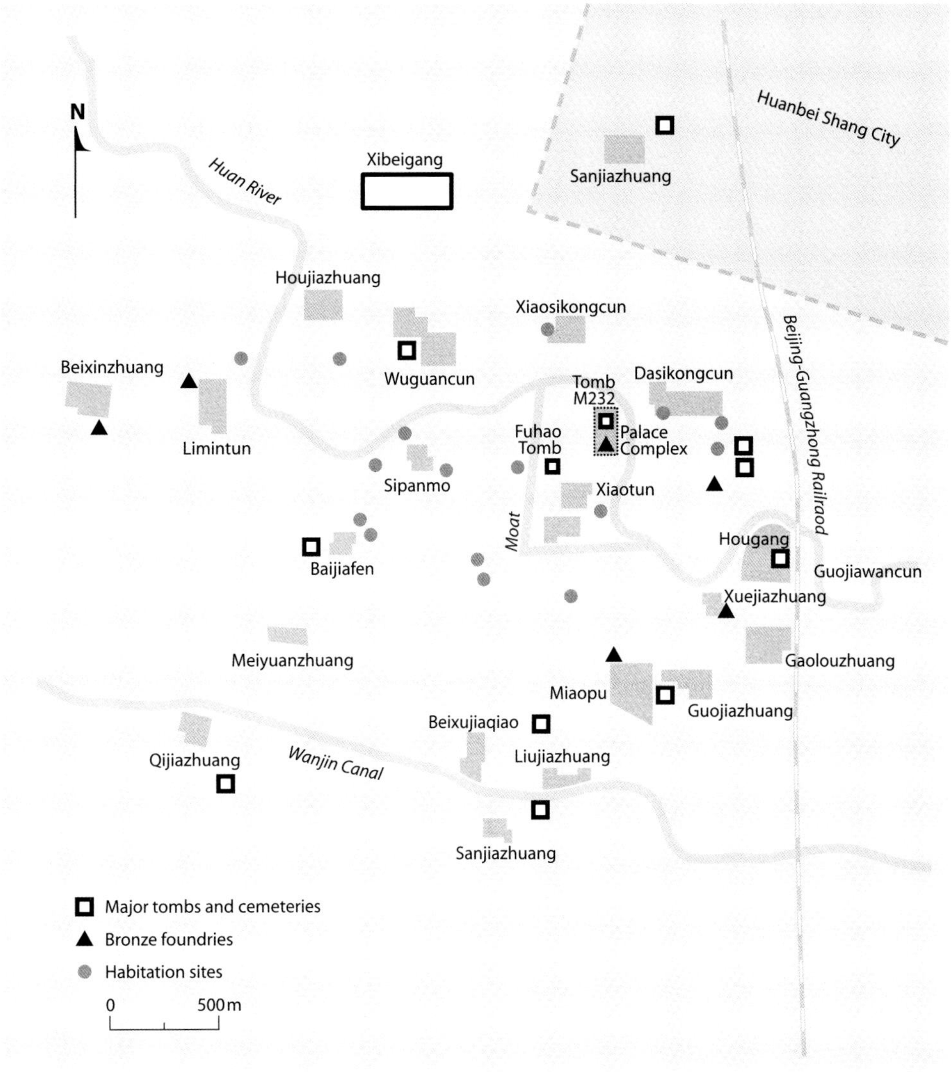

MAP OF ANYANG SITES (YINXU)

THE BRONZE CASTING WORKSHOPS

At least four foundries have been discovered at widely dispersed sites at Anyang. Remains of a foundry were found in the 1930s in the northern part of the palace complex at Xiaotun, but the other foundries were located well outside the defensive moat that defines the palace area.[17] The foundries seem to have specialized to a degree. At Limintun, two kilometers west of Xiaotun, the molds discovered indicate that the main production was weapons and tools. At Miaopu, the largest Anyang foundry, one kilometer south of Xiaotun, the production was almost exclusively of bronze vessels.[18] The site covers an area of more than ten thousand square meters and was in production from Period II until Period IV. The western sector yielded few remains that directly related to bronze casting, but included houses, presumbably those of foundry workers, and some tombs that yielded molds for casting bronzes. The presence of molds in the tombs implies that the bronze casters believed that they, like their rulers, would perform the same profession and retain the same social status in the afterlife as they had during their lifetime.

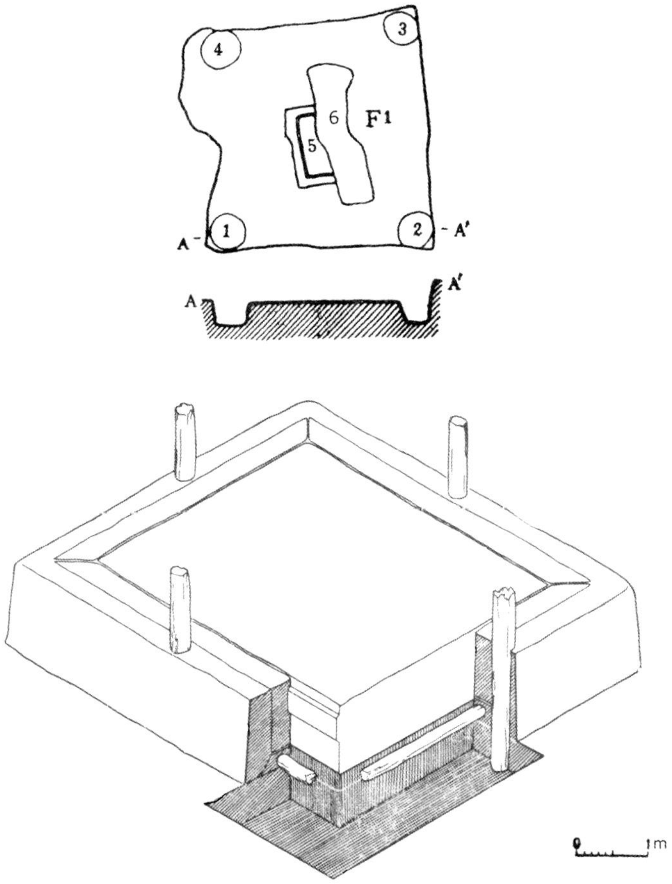

FIGURE 1 Plan of a foundry at Miaopu. Top: 1–4: post holes; 5: remains of ceramic mold; 6: later burial; bottom: reconstruction of ceramic mold and core for casting a large rectangular *ding*

In the eastern sector of this foundry, large numbers of casting paraphernalia were found, including fragments of furnaces, some up to a meter in diameter, and crucibles made of sand-tempered clay up to thirty-four centimeters in diameter. Most important were the twenty thousand mold, model, and core fragments, among which were identifiable square and round *ding, gui, fang yi, you, zhi, jia, jiao, jue, gu, he,* and *zun* (see glossary).[19] Tools included stone polishers, bronzes knives, and awls and bone awls.[20] A cast copper-tin alloy ingot (97.21% copper, 2.71% tin) confirms the assumption that metal was brought to Anyang in the form of ingots probably cast at the site of the mines, rather than as ore.[21]

The remains at Miaopu reveal the highly specialized nature of the foundry process and hint at a division of labor. Among the twenty houses in the eastern sector at least three different types of workshops have been identified on the basis of their contents. A twin-roomed house (PNVF6), which yielded ceramic molds as well as the plant ash that may have been added to the clay molds, was probably a mold workshop. Another house (F17) has been identified as a kiln for firing molds, since it included a furnace with a chimney and many fired and unfired ceramic molds. A third house (F16) was probably a foundry, since many broken molds, some with traces of bronze slag adhering to them, were found both inside the house and surrounding it. Of particular interest is a square semisubterranean structure (PNV IV F1) 3.3 by 3.5 meters with a hard-fired floor (fig. 1).[22] The roof had been supported on pillars, but there do not seem to have been walls. In the middle were the remains of a large rectangular mold and core for casting a large rectangular *ding*. Wooden poles had been inserted in the mold section to give it greater strength. The intact side of the mold measured overall 117 centimeters on the exterior, and the interior face of the mold corresponding to the wall of the vessel is about 20 centimeters shorter. The *ding* cast from this mold must therefore have been about a meter long, considerably larger than the two Si Mu Xin *fang ding* (64 centimeters long) from Fu Hao's tomb and approaching the size of the Si Mu Wu *fang ding* (length 110 centimeters), the largest bronze vessel in existence. Since *ding* of such monumental size would have been restricted to the highest echelons of the elite, the discovery of this mold testifies to the importance of the Miaopu foundry, which no doubt produced bronzes for the royal family.

THE EVIDENCE AT ANYANG FOR THE PERIODIZATION OF CHINESE BRONZES

The stylistic evolution of early Chinese bronzes was first charted by Max Loehr in 1953.[23] His scheme of Five Styles posited the gradual elaboration of decoration, its increase in area over the surface of the vessel, and the eventual emergence of motifs set off against a background of fine lines. The validity of Loehr's sequence as a relative chronology has since been confirmed by archaeological discoveries, but it was only the discovery in 1976 of Yinxu tomb M5 that offered a firm chronological benchmark on which to hang the stylistic development of Anyang bronzes. Now generally accepted as being the tomb of Fu Hao, a consort of the Shang ruler Wu Ding who is thought to have ruled around 1200 BCE, this tomb also undermined assumptions about the absolute chronology of Loehr's Five Styles.[24] In particular, it provided indisputable evidence that the most advanced of Loehr's styles, Style V, in which the motif is executed in relief against a dense background of spirals, had matured by this date, significantly earlier than had previously been thought. By pushing back the emergence of Style V, the discovery of Fu Hao's tomb raised questions not only about how decorative style developed post–Fu Hao, but also about the stages immediately preceding Fu Hao. These two questions—the immediate antecedents of the Fu Hao style, and the subsequent development—are discussed further below.

THE EARLIEST BRONZES AT YINXU

The earliest evidence of Shang activity at Yinxu is represented by tombs M232, M333, and M388, all at Xiaotun, and by tombs at Sanjiazhuang some 3.5 kilometers north of Anyang.[25] Although the former are located in the area of the palatial complex at Xiaotun, none is related stratigraphically to the foundations. Measuring 3.4 by 2.3 meters, tomb M232 is considerably smaller than Fu Hao's tomb, and it yielded a set of ten bronze vessels, including two types of *gu, jue, jia, pou,* a short-necked *lei, pan,* and *ding* (fig. 2).[26] Some of these vessels are typical of the Erligang phase at Zhengzhou (16th–early 14th century BCE): the *ding* with tapering pointed legs and Loehr's Style II decoration (narrow bands of decoration executed in raised ribbons), a *lei* with a late version of Style II, and an undecorated *gu* beaker lacking the bulge at the belly of later *gu*.[27] The Norton *gu* (cat. 3) exemplifies this early shape, but its relatively advanced Style III decoration indicates that it is a post-Erligang casting. The *pou,* on the other hand, a vessel type that is virtually unknown during the Erligang period, becomes common in the immediate post-Zhengzhou phase known from such sites as Gaocheng Taixi in Hebei (ca. 14th–early 13th century BCE).[28] The *pou*'s scheme of densely packed fine lines from which the mask and dragons are beginning to emerge represents an advanced stage of Style III and is also indicative of a post-Erligang

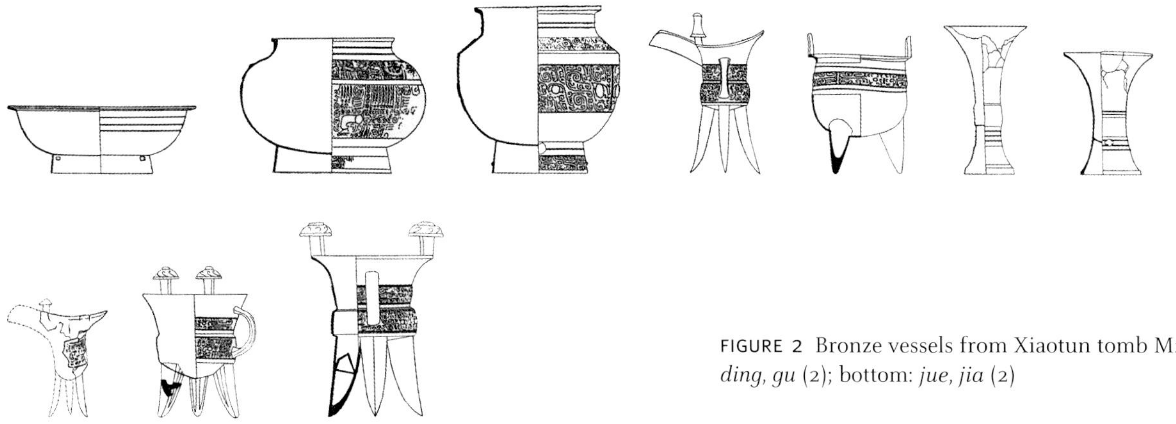

FIGURE 2 Bronze vessels from Xiaotun tomb M232. Top: *pan, pou, lei, jue, ding, gu* (2); bottom: *jue, jia* (2)

date. The *jue* also shows advances compared with earlier versions. Whereas the majority of *jue* from the Erligang period possessed flat bases, *jue* from all three of these tombs included both flat-based and round-bottomed versions, the latter becoming the majority in subsequent bronzes from Yinxu.[29]

A slightly later phase is represented by tomb M331 at Xiaotun and by tomb 59WGM1 at Wuguancun. Although the majority of the bronzes from the former tomb (fig. 3) are still in Style III, advanced features occur on several. For instance, the *ding* with pointed legs survives, but a new type with cylindrical legs has appeared. Style IV decoration (defined by fine spiral decoration forming a background for the motifs) occurs on a *zun*, and Style V (motifs in relief) on a square *you*. The tomb at Wuguancun shows a further development (fig. 4). Both *ding* now have column legs, and, although Style III still survives on the two *gu*, Style IV decoration is well established, occurring on a *ding* decorated with cicadas as well as on a *pou* and a *jia*. The *jia* is a new variant of the type, distinguished from pre-existing versions by a shorter neck and more bulbous

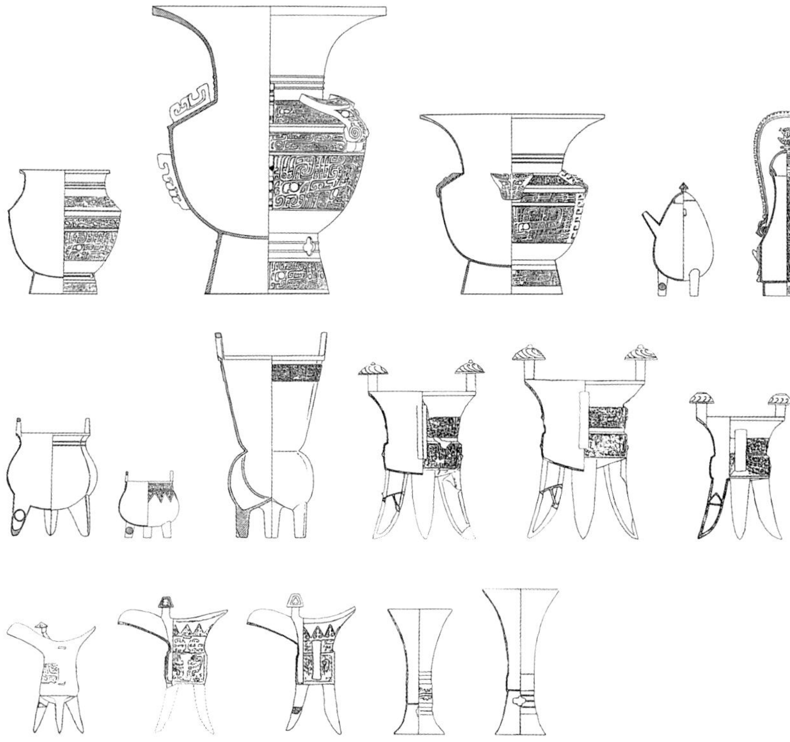

FIGURE 3 Bronze vessels from Xiaotun tomb M331. Top: *lei*, *zun* (2), *he*, *you*; center: *ding* (2), *yan*, *jia* (3); bottom: *jue* (3), *gu* (2)

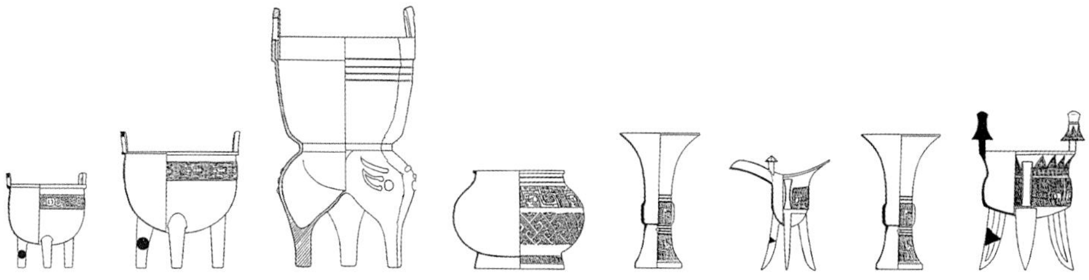

FIGURE 4 Bronze vessels from Wuguancun tomb 59WGM1: *ding* (2), *yan*, *pou*, *gu*, *jue*, *jia*

belly forming a smooth S-profile. This new version is particularly associated with late Style III and Style IV, and the Norton *jia* (cat. 9) represents a slightly later version of this type.

The absolute dating assigned by Chinese archaeologists to these tombs, however, presents problems. The bronzes from tomb M232 are similar to those at the site of Gaocheng Taixi and must therefore at least overlap with them. It is significant that the Chinese excavators recognize that M232 precedes Dasikongcun I and Miaopu I, which represent the habitation sites corresponding to Period I at Anyang. M331 and 59WGM1 are clearly post-Gaocheng and have been assigned by some Chinese writers to the late phase of Period I, that is to say, the early part of Wu Ding's reign. This latter dating seems significantly too late, since there is a stylistic lacuna between the bronzes from these tombs and those from Fu Hao's tomb.[30] Whereas the majority of the bronzes from tombs M331 and 59WGM1 are still decorated in Style III, Styles IV and V predominate in Fu Hao's tomb, with hardly any bronzes in Style III. Because of the large number of bronzes it yielded, if Fu Hao's tomb followed directly on the preceding group, one would expect to see some Style III bronzes, especially among the more common vessels, such as *gu* and *jue*. In fact, there is a telling contrast between the *gu* and *jue* from tomb 59WGM1, both decorated in Style III, and those from Fu Hao's tomb, which are in Style IV and have acquired flanges running up the sides of the foot and the belly (fig. 5). The same stylistic gulf exists between the *jia* from M331 and the Si X Mu *jia* from Fu Hao's tomb, with the former decorated in late Style III and the latter in fully developed Style V. Similar gulfs separate the *pou* from 59WGM1 (decorated in Style IV and

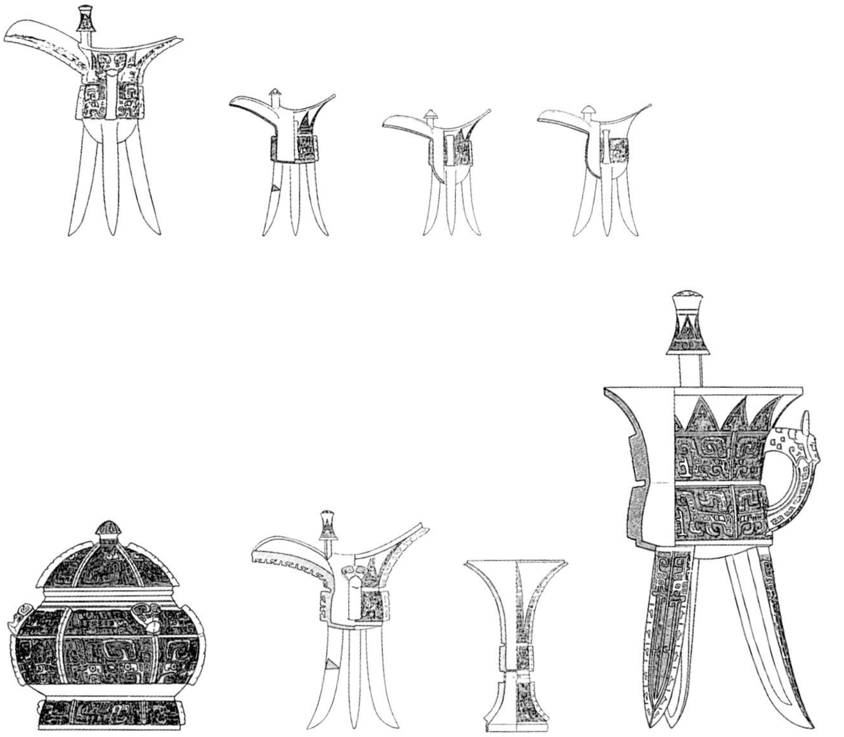

FIGURE 5 Bronze vessels from the tomb of Fu Hao (Yinxu tomb 5). Top: *jue* (4); bottom: *pou, jue, gu, jia*

lacking flanges) from the one from Fu Hao's tomb (Style V and embellished with flanges). The maturity seen in the Style V designs is particularly startling. Moreover, whereas a high proportion of Fu Hao's bronzes are inscribed, none of those for the preceding group bears inscriptions. Pre–Wu Ding inscriptions are extremely rare; indeed, the unidentified character on the interior wall of the foot of the Norton *gu* (fig. 6, and see cat. 3) is one of the few that can be confidently ascribed to a pre–Wu Ding date.[31]

It is possible, of course, that Fu Hao, as a consort of the Shang king, was able to commission more advanced bronzes than those that were available to less important members of the Shang hierarchy. This, however, does not seem a very convincing line of argument. Style V may have been marginally more difficult to execute than decoration that was flush with the surface of the vessel, but the real investment in time and labor came from the fineness of the lineament that composed the design and the proportion of the surface area of the vessel that was covered in decoration. If Fu Hao's tomb dates to about 1200 BCE, M331 and 59WGM1 would seem to be at least another half-century earlier. The stylistic lacuna between the two strengthens the argument that these earlier tombs pre-date the establishment of the capital at Anyang.[32]

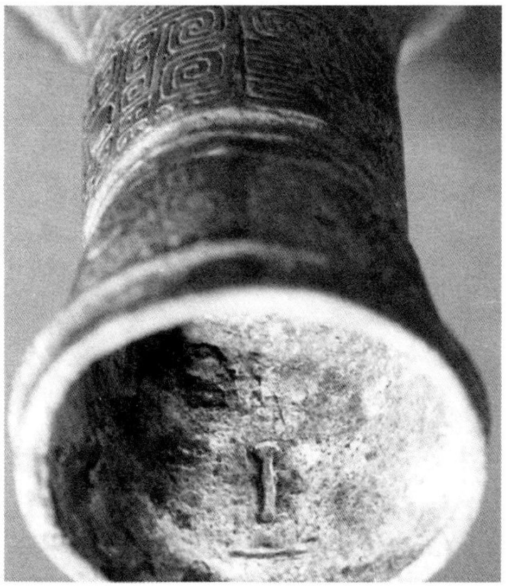

FIGURE 6 Detail of inscription on interior foot of Norton *gu* (cat. 3)

The Fu Hao bronzes are our most complete evidence of the bronze repertoire at its most elaborate during the reign of Wu Ding. New vessel types that appear for the first time in the archaeological record at Anyang include the *zhi*, the *fang yi*, the *hu*, and the *lei* with rounded shoulder and straight neck. Versions of the *you* had occurred intermittently in pre-Anyang contexts, but, from Fu Hao onward, the *you* becomes more popular. Because of the high status of its occupant, the tomb included vessels that were apparently unavailable to lower-ranking members of the royal hierarchy, either because of sumptuary restrictions or lack of resources or because they were not part of the core repertory of ritual vessels. Large rectangular *ding*, such as the Si Mu Xin pair, are represented in only a few other tombs at Anyang, although smaller versions were introduced around the time of Fu Hao and continued to be popular into early Western Zhou. Other vessels from Fu Hao's tomb, such as the *he*, seem to have been deliberately archaistic throwbacks to Erlitou and early Erligang-period bronzes. Square versions of *jia* and *zun* (*fang jia*, *fang zun*) seem also to have been favored at the highest levels, although, as we shall see, concentrations of them occur later in certain tombs or are associated by inscriptions.

Guang pourers seem to have a similarly restricted clientele. Although unprovenanced examples, some of which may have come from the large tombs at Xibeigang plundered during the 1920s and 1930s, exist in collections, the form is extremely rare in mid-sized and smaller tombs at Anyang. The origin of this type is enigmatic. The *guang* does not appear at Erligang or at the transitional sites; the earliest *guang* known is one in the British Museum decorated in Style III.[33] Its asymmetrical juglike form does not seem to have been a ceramic borrowing and it is possible that it instead represents a conversion into bronze of a gourd vessel. The asymmetrical form provoked the bronze casters to abandon the compartmentalized approach to the surface that was the norm for bronze vessels. Initially, they seemed happy to ignore the mold divisions and, indeed, the divisions between lid and body as far as decoration was concerned. On the British Museum *guang*, for instance, a serpent runs from the lid onto the body, a feature perpetuated on a number of *guang*, including the one in the Norton Museum (cat. 1). The Norton piece relates closely to a *guang* from Fu Hao's tomb and another in the Grenville L. Winthrop Collection in the Arthur M. Sackler Museum at Harvard University.[34] Both of these have large tiger faces at the front of the lid and bird and dragon decoration in relief, elements of which run across the divisions between lid, body, and foot, a feature they share with the Norton *guang*. Compared with the Fu Hao and the Sackler *guang*, however, the introduction of vertical flanges and a plain horizontal band make the surface of the Norton *guang* more compartmentalized. This does not necessarily indicate that the Norton piece is later, since another *guang* in Style IV from Fu Hao's tomb (fig. 7) shows an even stricter surface compartmentalization. It seems, therefore, that compartmentalized and uni-decor approaches to the surface represent parallel styles. At any rate, the Norton *guang* is unlikely to be much later than Fu Hao's tomb. One other possible source of influence on these elaborate *guang* should be mentioned—stone funerary sculptures placed in the royal tombs at Xibeigang. These hint at a sculptural tradition practiced mainly in perishable materials that has not survived but that may

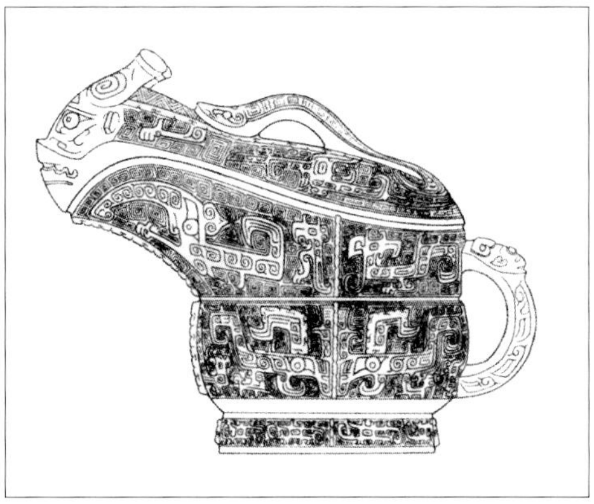

FIGURE 7 Bronze *guang* in Style IV from tomb of Fu Hao

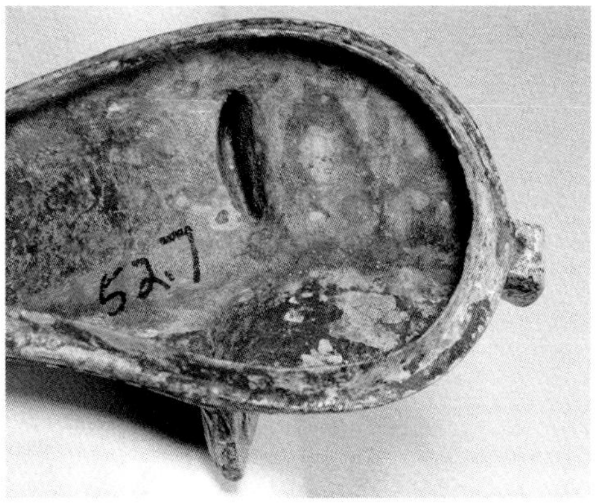

FIGURE 8 Underside of lid of Norton *guang* (cat. 1), showing the joint between the ears and lid

have exerted an influence on some of the more unusual vessel types around the period of Fu Hao.[35]

Guang are often particularly finely decorated, with bold sculptural elements in addition to the elaborate surface decoration. On the Norton *guang*, the small bearlike figure suspended from the base of the handle must have been pre-cast and inserted into the mold before the vessel was cast. The upright ears half-way down the lid, on the other hand, seem to have been cast integrally, since the smooth transition from the underside of the lid to the hollow interior of the ears would have been impossible to achieve if the ears had been pre-cast or cast on (fig. 8). Although there have been a number of attempts to cast replicas of Shang bronzes using piece molds, recent experiments have highlighted the complexity and labor involved in the casting process. The replication of an owl *you* in the Shanghai Museum required twenty-five steps and a total of 110 days.[36] Although the bronze casters of ancient China were undoubtedly more practiced than their modern counterparts, a complex, elaborately decorated vessel such as the Norton *guang* would nevertheless represent a considerable investment of man-hours.

Hu were another vessel type that seem to have had a restricted production. Again, it is not certain whether this restriction stems from sumptuary regulations or whether the *hu* was simply not considered a core ritual vessel in bronze. Ceramic flasks with lug handles occur as early as the Erlitou period, and by the Anyang period they had assumed an oval cross section that became characteristic of the bronze *hu*.[37] The earliest bronze *hu* are two examples from the Dayangzhou tomb in Xin'gan county, Jiangxi, one decorated in Style V and the other in an early version of Style IV.[38] Although a number of unprovenanced *hu* in collections may have come from the large tombs at Xibeigang (two were found in Xibeigang tomb HPKM 1005 and two in Fu Hao's tomb),[39] bronze *hu* are only rarely found in medium- or small-size tombs in Anyang. The closest parallel to the Norton *hu* (cat. 2) is an example from Xiaotun tomb M238 (fig. 9). The reason for the decline in popularity of this type after Period II is not clear. As mentioned below, it may have been replaced by a new type of wide-bodied *you* that became a regular component of ritual vessel sets from Period III onward.[40]

In contrast with these exotic vessels, the core repertoire is represented by smaller tombs such as tomb M539 at Dasikongcun (fig. 10), which is contemporary with Fu Hao. These show new additions to the typical sets of *gu*, *jue*, *jia*, *yan*, and *ding* seen in pre–Fu Hao tombs. In addition to these vessels, a new form of owl *you* has appeared. Unlike the *guang*, which retained its asymmetrical form into the Western Zhou period, the new type of owl *you* has a more symmetrical form compared with the Fu Hao version. The owl *you*, like the *guang*, however, remained a relatively rare vessel, while the deep bowl shape known as *gui* and the lidded goblet *zhi* became regular members of the vessel sets. The *gui*

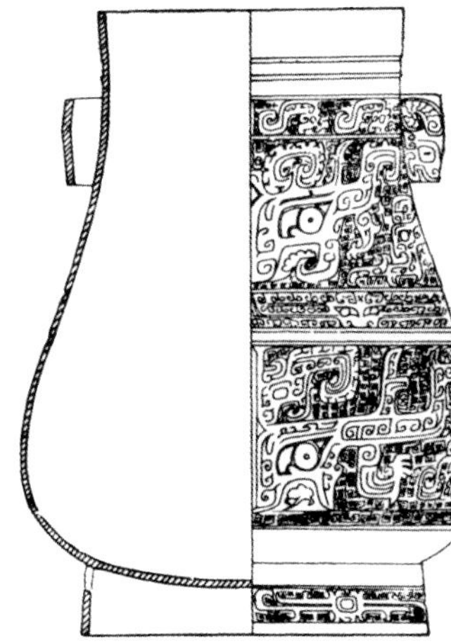

FIGURE 9 Bronze *hu* from Xioatun tomb M238

had appeared as early as the Erligang period, but it is still rare before the Anyang period. By the time of Wu Ding, however, jade as well as bronze examples in Fu Hao's tomb indicate that it had become an important form.[41]

Tomb M539 also yielded a *jia* very similar to the Norton *jia* (cat. 9). Like the Norton piece, it is rare in being provided with a bronze lid. Possibly lids in perishable materials were routinely supplied for *jia* and other open vessels, but have not survived. On early *jia*, the belly tended to form a distinct angle with the flat base. One line of development, represented by monumental *jia* in both round and square cross sections from Fu Hao's tomb, retained the flat base and tall flaring necks of these earlier *jia*. In the evolution represented by the *jia* from tomb M539 and the Norton *jia*, on the other hand, the base gradually became more rounded, the belly more bulbous, and the neck shorter. Whereas the tall-necked version was frequently decorated in relief, the S-shaped version was usually decorated in Style IV. The reason for this stylistic dichotomy is not clear; possibly it was a purely aesthetic decision to match relief decoration to a more architectonic form and the flush decor to the more rounded profile.

POST–FU HAO BRONZES

The Fu Hao bronzes mark the culmination of a consistent stylistic trend that saw the elaboration of decoration from a simple pattern restricted to limited areas of the vessel surface to vessels in which much of the surface is animated with decor, from diffuse scrolls to clear motif-background distinction, and from individual vessels to coherent vessel sets. In terms of decoration, a limit was reached. The post–Fu Hao bronzes do not reveal the emergence of any definable single style that could be characterized in the same way as Loehr's previous Five Styles. Whereas each of Loehr's styles represents a conceptual advance over the previous (even if, in practice, there was overlapping), the subsequent history of bronze ornament during the last 150 years of Shang rule instead represents refinements, reworkings, and manipulations of existing schemes rather than a fundamental stylistic shift. As Bagley has argued, in the post–Fu Hao period it is not possible to talk in terms of a single line of development but rather of a number of parallel trends.[42] Indeed, it was the gradual shift in vessel repertoire, rather than any dramatic change in decor, that is the most significant development of post–Fu Hao bronzes at Anyang.

FIGURE 10 Bronze vessels from Dasikongcun tomb M539. Top: *ding, yan, gui, pan,* owl *you, jia, gu* (2); bottom: *jue* (2), *zhi, qi, dou* (ladle)

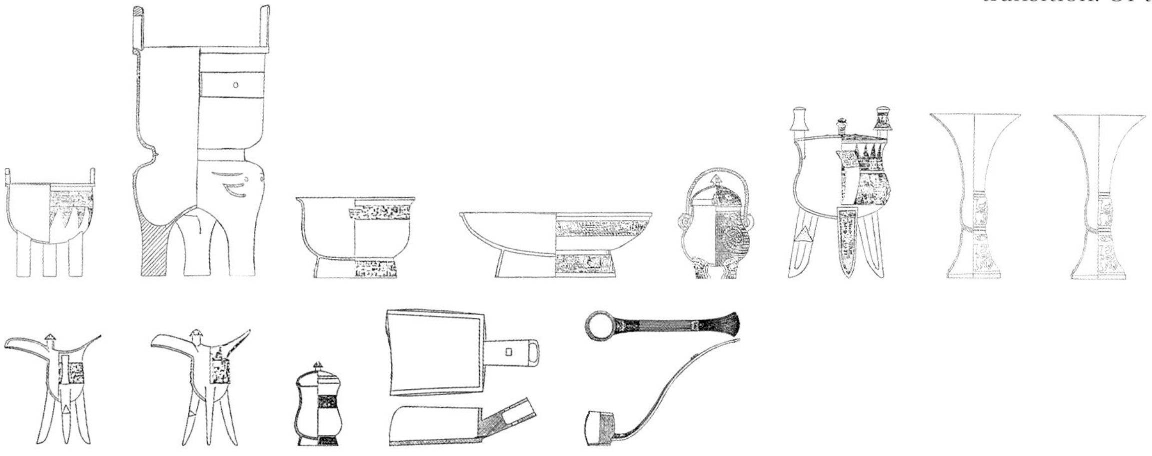

PERIOD III

Although we lack later tombs of comparable richness to that of Fu Hao, discoveries of smaller tombs provide enough evidence to trace a broad outline of subsequent developments. That the typical Fu Hao decor survived into the following period is shown by the Norton *ding* (cat. 5). A similar *ding* occurs in the Period II tomb M539 at Dasikongcun, but the addition of a narrow band at the neck filled with long-tailed dragons indicates that the Norton *ding* may date as late as Period III, when this motif first becomes popular.[43]

Tombs from Period III show the ritual bronze vessel repertoire in transition. Of these, tombs M269 at Qiajiazhuang and M160 at Guojiazhuang are the most important. It may be significant that both are located a considerable distance from Xiaotun, reflecting the expansion of the Shang capital during this phase. The first, a small- to medium-size tomb measuring 3.4 by 1.9 meters at the base of the pit, yielded seventy-three objects, including fifty-eight bronzes of which twenty were ritual vessels and three were bells (fig. 11). Many of the bronzes are inscribed with the character "Yuan," probably the name of the owner.[44] The vessel repertoire has much in common with that of the preceding period—round *ding* with columnar feet, *fang ding*, *ding* with feet in the shape of dragons, *gu*, *jue*, *fang yi*, *lei*, *zun*, and the *zhi*, but the *pou* has now disappeared and new types have appeared. Among these are a wide-bodied *you* with a handle aligned along the long axis and a *gu*-shaped *zun*, both possibly based on ceramic prototypes.[45] Although the traditional, trumpet-mouthed *zun* still survives, it was virtually to disappear by the end of Period III. The *gui* with handles had appeared earlier, but it now becomes more a more impressive vessel. Not only have the handles been enlarged, but the foot is taller and heavier, endowing the vessel with greater presence.

More important is tomb M160 at Guojiazhuang. Measuring 4.5 by 2.9 meters, it is the largest undisturbed burial discovered at Anyang after Fu Hao's tomb.[46] Compared with the latter, however, which measured 22.4 square meters, it is still modest at 13 square meters. Interred in the tomb were four accompanying humans and three dogs. Altogether 353 items were recovered, including sixteen ceramics, on the basis of which the excavators date the tomb to fairly late within Period III, that is to say around 1100 BCE. The majority of the finds were bronzes, primarily weapons, including three *yue*, two large knives, and nine heaps of arrowheads (comprising a total of 906 heads). The weapons were distributed around the coffin (largely decayed), as if in a protective formation. Most seem to have been *mingqi* (burial substitutes), judging from the high proportion of lead and the lack of tin, which would have made them useless in actual combat. The use of high-lead *mingqi* weapons foreshadows the use of lead for *mingqi* vessels at the end of

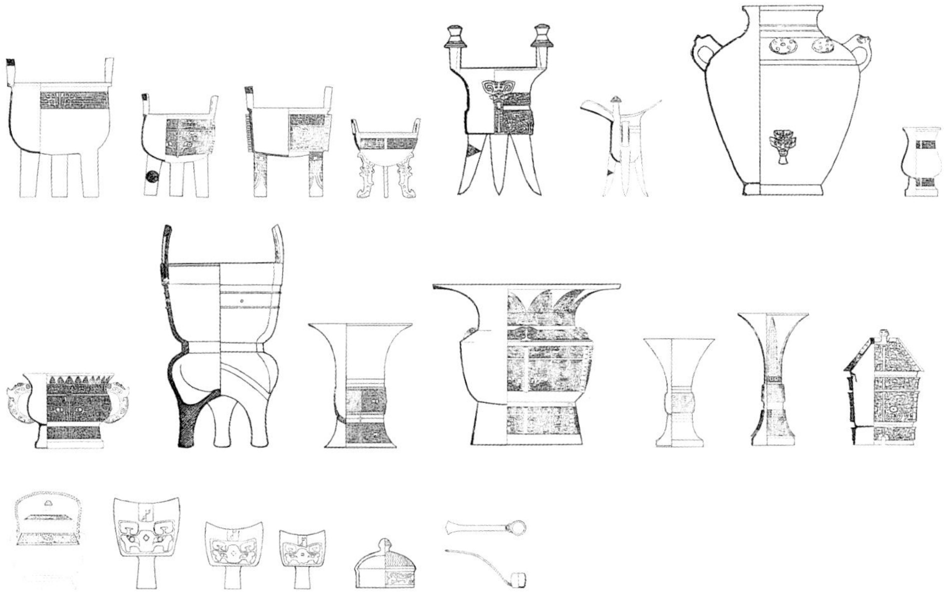

FIGURE 11 Bronze vessels from Qiajiazhuang tomb M269. Top: *ding* (4), *jia*, *jue*, *lei*, *zhi*; center: *gui*, *yan*, *gu*-shaped *zun*, *zun*, *gu* (2), *fang yi*; bottom: *you*, *nao* bells (3), cover for an unidentified vessel, *dou* (ladle)

the Shang period, when tin may have been in short supply.[47] The forty-one ritual vessels and three bells in this tomb (fig. 12) contained conventional proportions of copper and tin, and thirty-three of these were inscribed with the name Zhi, most likely the owner of the bronzes and the occupant of the tomb. Although Zhi was clearly not of the same rank as Fu Hao—the forty-four ritual bronzes pale in comparison with Fu Hao's 210—he or she must have been a personage of considerable status.

A comparison between Zhi's vessels and those of Fu Hao reveals both absences and new additions. Some of the types prominent in Fu Hao's tomb, for instance, the *guang*, *fang yi*, *pou*, and *hu*, are absent. Unlike Fu Hao's tomb, in which the largest vessel is a *fang ding*, the largest vessel in tomb M160 is a round *ding* with bowed legs, a type that was to become common in Western Zhou. Smaller *fang ding*, however, are present and continue to be popular into Western Zhou. The *ding* with lobed body is represented by an example decorated with a *taotie* mask close enough to that on the Norton *ding* (cat. 6) to suggest that the two vessels are roughly contemporary. Apart from the large round *ding*, the most impressive vessels from this

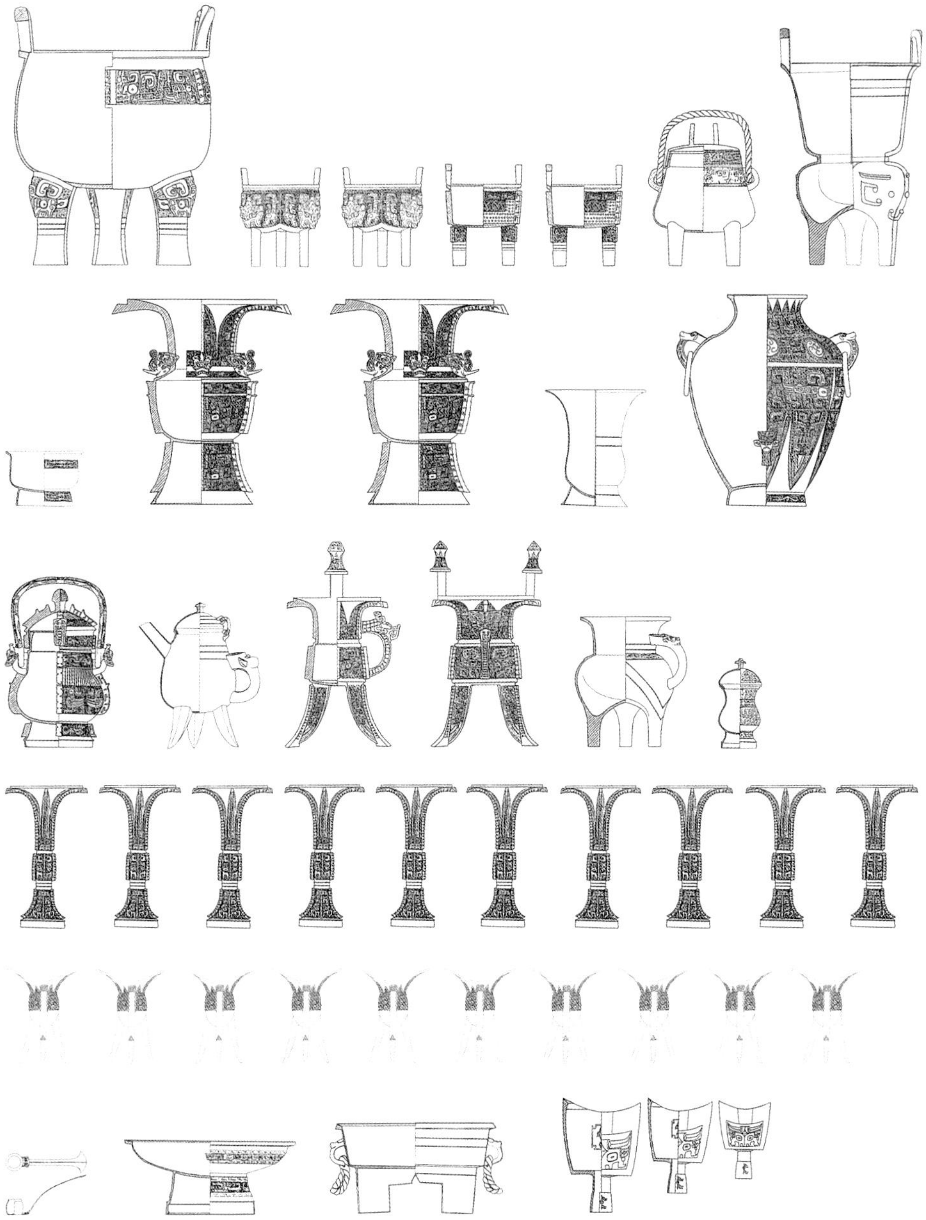

FIGURE 12 Bronze vessels from Guojiazhuang tomb M160. Top: *ding* (5), *you-fang ding*, *yan*; second row: *gui*, *zun* (2), *gu*-shaped *zun*, *lei*; third row: *you*, *he*, *jia* (2), *li-jia*, *zhi*; fourth row: *gu* (10); fifth row: *jiao* (10); bottom: *dou* (ladle); *pan*, square basin (*lu*?), *nao* bells (3)

tomb are, as in the case of the Fu Hao bronzes, of square cross section. Indeed bronzes cast in square section comprise an even higher proportion of the total than at Fu Hao, 41 percent in the case of M160. Some of these, such as a pair of *fang zun*, bear a close resemblance to the *fang zun* from Fu Hao's tomb, but have slightly squatter proportions and more elaborate animal heads on the shoulder. The *fang jia* also bear a close resemblance to the Fu Hao *fang jia*, but their squatter proportions rob them of the architectonic poise of that pair. Most unusual are a set of ten *fang gu* with flanges running from the foot to the rim, paired with a set of ten *jiao*, a symmetrical variant of the more usual *jue*.[48]

The *fang gu* and *jiao* exemplify a new trend, casting sets of vessels of uniform size, shape, and decoration. Whereas the *gu* and *jue* in Fu Hao's tomb include a number of different sizes and decorative schemes, the *fang gu* and *jiao* from tomb M160 differ in size only by four and two millimeters, respectively, and the decoration of each vessel closely matches the others in the set. Indeed, the pair of *fang jia* differs in size only by one millimeter and likewise bears matching decorative schemes. In view of this interest in replicating designs, it is surprising that the bronze casters did not reutilize the models to create sets of molds. But close examination of the matched vessels has revealed that in no case is the decoration identical, implying that a new model and a new set of molds were created for each vessel.[49]

Whereas the *fang zun*, *fang jia*, *fang gu*, and *jiao* are all decorated in relatively similar styles, other vessels from tomb M160 exhibit striking contrasts of style. For instance, a new version of the *you*, distinguished by a flattened body with swing handle across the shorter section and pronged flanges, is decorated with large-scale birds rather than a *taotie* mask. The rendering of the birds in smooth relief against a fine *leiwen* (squared spiral) ground seems to reflect a heightened sensitivity to textural contrasts between motif and background. Subsequent versions of this type of *you* were to become increasingly dominated by heavy flanges and appendages in late Shang and early Western Zhou.[50] Other vessels in this tomb possess svelte profiles and understated decoration; a pair of *lei*, for instance, are decorated in a Style IV that would not look out of place in Fu Hao's tomb. A *zhi*, decorated in a smooth rounded relief, is remarkable for the complete absence of *leiwen*. Two other vessels, both based on ceramic prototypes, an S-shaped *zun* and a *jia* with a lobed body reminicent of the *li*, are almost completely undecorated. Both these forms were soon to displace their traditional counterparts.[51] Since all these vessels bear Zhi's name, there can be no doubt that they are coeval; indeed, it is likely that they were all cast in the same foundry. No doubt, the relative importance of a particular vessel type in the staging of a ritual was a factor in determining how elaborate the decoration it received. Nevertheless, the stylistic contrast between such vessels as the *zhi* and *jia* in tomb M160 seems to reflect a deliberate and conscious decision to include vessels of contrasting styles within a full ritual set. We do not know whether this is a reflection of their different uses, or whether aesthetic choices or financial constraints played a role. The elimination of the *leiwen* on the *zhi* would certainly have reduced the man-hours needed to produce the model.

PERIOD IV

The shift in vessel repertoire that was underway in Period III gathered further momentum in Period IV. The wide-bodied *zun* had by then been largely replaced by the narrow type, while the older type of *jia* had completely vanished. *Gu* and *jue* remained the most common basic ritual vessel set, but they are frequently accompanied by *ding* and *gui*.[52] This addition foreshadows the shift in emphasis from wine to food vessels that was to continue during the early Western Zhou. Despite the existence of some finely cast unprovenanced vessels that can be attributed to this period on account of their inscriptions or stylistic features, the picture that emerges from the contents of the small- and mid-sized tombs at Anyang is one of decline. Apart from one large *ding* from a sacrificial pit, the other excavated bronzes from Period IV are mostly uninspired and often undecorated. Burial substitutes, either in lead or ceramic, occur frequently, indicating either that fewer bronze vessels were cast or that, instead of being consigned to burial, they were stored in ancestral temples over generations.[53] The occasional occurrence of earlier bronzes in later Anyang-period tombs implies that bronzes were sometimes kept for a number of generations. This would have allowed the revival of older styles, a trait that gains ground in Period III to IV. The lack of motif-background distinction on vessels such as the Geng Shi Ma *gui* from Xiaotun tomb 82M1 (fig. 13) clearly evokes Loehr's Style III.[54] The most significant innovation occurring in Period IV, however, is the appearance of longer inscriptions, sometimes recording gifts from the Shang king to the caster of the bronze. The use of bronzes as vehicles for commemorative inscriptions was one of the most important legacies of late Shang bronze casting to that of Western Zhou.[55]

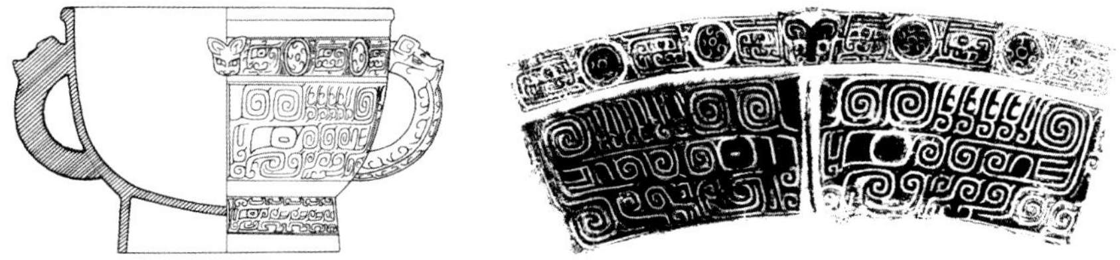

FIGURE 13 Drawing of Geng Shi Ma *gui* from Xiaotun tomb 82M1

BRONZE CASTING AT THE END OF SHANG

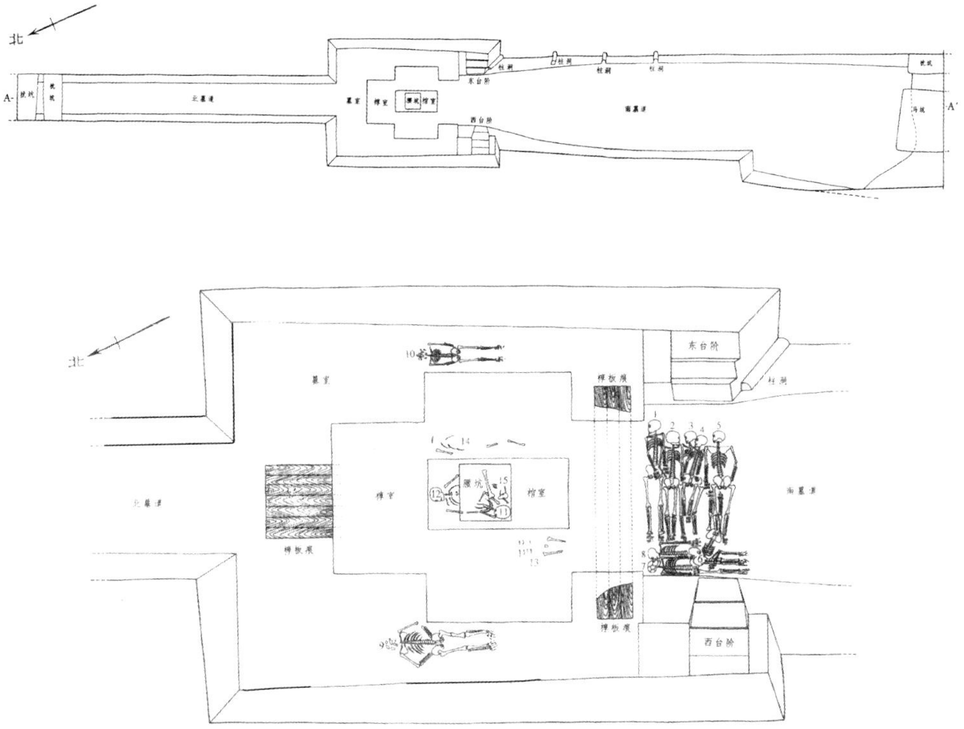

FIGURE 14 Plan and detail of tomb of Chang Zi Kou at Taiqinggong, Luyi county, southeastern Henan

The recently reported discovery of another bronze foundry at Yinxu may change our picture of late Anyang bronze casting.[56] Until it is published, however, the best archaeological evidence for bronze casting at the end of Shang comes from sites outside the Anyang area, and it is in these that we can see the transition from Shang to Western Zhou repertoires taking place. This seems to have been an uneven process, one that varied from location to location. The recent discovery of a tomb at Taiqinggong in Luyi county exemplifies the survival of Shang traditions into Zhou in southeastern Henan. In terms of shape, with its two long ramps and waste pit, and the large number (14) of sacrificial victims buried with the occupant, the tomb clearly perpetuates Shang traditions (fig. 14).[57] The repertoire of bronzes is transitional (fig. 15). Wine vessels still predominate, and many of the bronzes retain Shang shapes and decoration, particularly the *fang zun* and *fang lei* (both direct descendants of the *fang zun* and *fang lei* in Guojiazhuang tomb M160), the large number of *gu* and *jue*, and the *nao* bells, and the relatively high proportion of square vessels. However, other vessels, such as two four-handled *gui* with a tall foot, indicate clearly that this is an early Western Zhou–period burial. Many of the bronzes are inscribed with the name of the occupant of the tomb, Chang Zi Kou (Baronet Kou of Chang). The state of Chang is mentioned in oracle inscriptions as a supplier of turtles to the Shang court and seems to have had fairly close relations with the Shang. Based on the evidence of

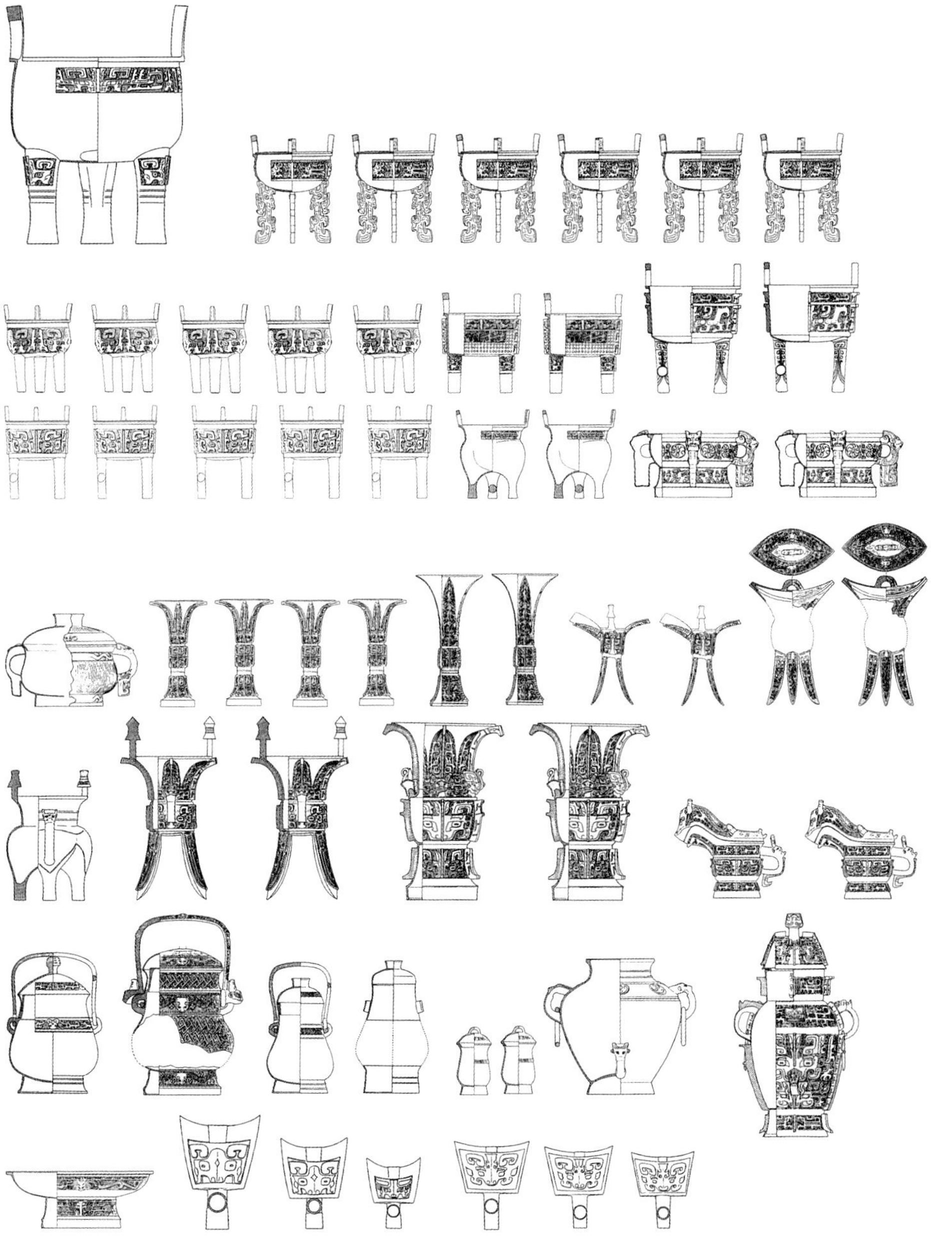

FIGURE 15 Bronze vessels from tomb of Chang Zi Kou at Taiqinggong, Luyi county, southeastern Henan. Top: round *ding* (7); second row: round *ding* (5), *fang ding* (4); third row: *fang ding* (5), *li* (2), four-handled *gui* (2); fourth row: *gui*, *fang gu* (4), *gu* (2), *fang jue* (2), *jiao* (2); fifth row: *jia*, *fang jia* (2), *fang zun* (2), *guang* (2); sixth row: *you* (3), *hu*, *zhi* (2), *lei*, *fang lei*; bottom: *pan*, *nao* bells (6)

his skeleton, Kou is estimated to have been around sixty years old when he died. Since the bronzes indicate that tomb is unlikely to have been later than three decades after the overthrow of Shang, Kou would have lived about half his life while the the Shang dynasty was still in existence. Not surprisingly, he retained many Shang traditions even after the dynasty was overthrown. The presence of the Zhou-style four-handled *gui* in his tomb suggests, however, that he was aware of the new bronze forms fashionable among the Zhou. Indeed, Kou's possession of the *gui* may well signify that he, like many Shang vassals, had switched political allegiance to the Zhou while continuing to adhere in other aspects to Shang tradition. ✦

NOTES

1 "Shanxi Xiangfen Taosi yizhi shouci faxian tongqi," *Kaogu* 1984.12, pp. 1069–71, and Zhu Fenghan, *Gudai Zhongguo qingtongqi*, p. 8, table 1:2, and p. 12. For a review of the origins of metallurgy in China, see Bagley, *Shang Ritual Bronzes*, pp. 15–16, and Bagley, "Shang Archaeology." For a skeptical view of the metal finds from Neolithic sites, see An Zhimin, "Zhongguo zaoqi tongqi de jige wenti," *Kaogu xuebao* 1981.3, pp. 269–84, and An Zhimin, "Shi lun Zhongguo zaoqi tongqi," *Kaogu* 1992.12, pp. 1110–19. Zhu Fenghan, *Gudai Zhongguo qingtongqi*, pp. 13–14, and Hua Jueming, *Zhongguo gudai jinshu jishu*, p. 15, argue that two finds of copper-zinc (i.e., brass) alloys in sites from the Yangshao and Longshan periods (5th–3rd millennium BCE) should not be dismissed as intrusive and may be evidence of familiarity with metals during the Neolithic period.

2 The earliest evidence of a cast bronze vessel in China is a fragment from pit H617 at the site of Wangchenggang, Dengfeng county, western Henan. A piece of charcoal from the pit yielded a radiocarbon date of 3850 ±165 years, i.e., around 1800 BCE. See "Dengfeng Wangchenggang yizhi de faxian," *Wenwu* 1983.3, pp. 8–20, pl. I:1, and Li Xiandeng, "Wangchenggang yizhi chutu de tongqi canpian ji qita," *Wenwu* 1984.11, pp. 73–75.

3 The most complete description of Shang foundry methods is to be found in Bagley, *Shang Ritual Bronzes*, pp. 37–45. See also Bagley, "Shang Archaeology," p. 141. However, the archaeological record has so far yielded little information regarding the organizational structure and economic investment necessary for large-scale bronze production to flourish. Recent attempts to reproduce Chinese bronzes using traditional methods have given some indication of the complexity of the process and the number of man-hours needed to produce a vessel. See the discussion of Fu Hao bronzes below and note 36.

4 Lu Liancheng, *Qingtong wenhua de baoku*, p. 56. For a lucid statement on the unique importance of bronze in China compared with other ancient civilizations, see Bagley, "Shang Archaeology," p. 137.

5 See Keightley, *Sources of Shang History*.

6 Bagley, "Shang Archaeology," provides a persuasive argument in favor of a multipolity model of early Bronze Age China.

7 For a description of the site, see *Yinxu de faxian yu yanjiu*, pp. 40–42. The name Yinxu was applied to the area at least as early as the Han period, since it is mentioned in the Biography of Xiangyu chapter of the *Shiji* by Sima Qian (ca. 145–ca. 85 BCE) (Lu Liancheng, *Qingtong wenhua de baoku*, p. 23). It is not certain, however, whether the Shang referred to themselves as "Yin," since it does not occur in the divination bone inscriptions or in Zhou bronzes (see Keightley, *Sources of Shang History*, p. xiv, note 8).

8 For a description of the Sanxingdui site, see Xu, "Bronze at Sanxingdui," p. 27; for a description of the site at Zhengzhou, see *Zhengzhou Shang cheng*, vol. 1, p. 7.

9 The moat ranges from 7 to 21 meters in width and is around 1,750 meters long. Forming an L-shape to the west and south of the palace complex, it probably linked two stretches of the Huan River and would undoubtedly have formed an effective defense against an attack on the palace and temple complex. See *Yinxu de faxian yu yanjiu*, p. 44, and *Yinxu fajue baogao*, pp. 94–96.

10 For instance, Bagley, "Shang Archaeology," p. 181. Keightley, moreover (*Sources of Shang History*, pp. xiii–xiv, note 6), casts doubt on the reliability of the *Shiji* tradition.

11 The four-period division of the Yinxu site adopted here follows the chronology proposed by Chinese archaeologists on the basis of ceramic typology and oracle bone inscriptions. These periods have been broadly correlated with the reigns of Shang kings recorded in the *Shiji*. The absolute dates attributed to these periods in this essay should be regarded as approximate. For a discussion of the periodization of Yinxu and the expansion of the activity at the site, see *Yinxu de faxian yu yanjiu*, pp. 25–26, 41–42.

12 Keightley, *Sources of Shang History*, pp. 97–98, note 24. See also *Yinxu de faxian yu yanjiu*, pp. 172–73, in which the authors cite an oracle bone fragment from Xiaotun tomb M331 as evidence of pre–Wu Ding divination activity. However, since none of the other pre–Wu Ding tombs have yielded oracle bones, it is possible that its presence in the tomb was intrusive.

13 The archaeologists who carried out the survey cautiously suggest that this city may be Xiang, the capital founded by Pan Geng's predecessor, the twelfth Shang king, He Tang Jia. See Tan Jigen, Jing Zhichun, and George Rapp, "The Largest Walled Shang City Located in Anyang, China," *Antiquity*, vol. 74, no. 285 (September 2000), pp. 479–80. I am grateful to Professer Jing Zhichun for bringing this article to my attention. See also "Huanhe liuyuqu kaogu yanjiu chubu baogao," *Kaogu* 1998.10, pp. 13–22. On the question of Pan Geng's move, see also Yang Xizhang and others, "Pan Geng qian Yin didian lice," *Zhongyuan wenwu* 2000.1, pp. 15–19.

14 *Yinxu de faxian yu yanjiu*, p. 44.

15 Estimates of the population of Shang cities have been based on the ratio of dwellings to total area. The population of Yinxu has been estimated as 230,000 during Period IV and 140,000 in the preceding periods, compared with 100,000 for Zhengzhou and 95,000 for Erlitou. Even if, as seems likely, these are overestimates, they still represent major population concentrations. See Song Zhenhao, "Xia Shang renkou chutan," *Lishi yanjiu* 1991.4, pp. 92–106.

16 *Yinxu de faxian yu yanjiu*, Beijing 1994, pp. 43–44.

17 In addition to a foundry to the west of Limintun and the one at Miaopu, discussed below, a foundry was also discovered near Xuejiazhuang, to the south of Xiaotun. See *Yinxu de faxian yu yanjiu*, pp. 45 and 83. For the Xuejiazhuang excavation, see Zhou Dao and Liu Dongya, "1957 nian qiu Anyang Gaolouzhuang Yin dai yizhi fajue," *Kaogu* 1963.4, pp. 213–16, 220, pl. 7.

18 The following description is based on the report in *Yinxu de faxian yu yanjiu*, pp. 45, 83–91, and *Yinxu fajue baogao*, pp. 11–60.

19 *Yinxu fajue baogao*, pp. 34, 53.

20 Ibid., pp. 55–57.

21 Recent studies of the lead isotope ratios of some of the Fu Hao bronzes have indicated that Yunnan was the source of the lead component of the alloy (see Xu, "Bronze at Sanxingdui," p. 70). The sources of copper were probably the middle and lower reaches of the Yangzi, where a number of copper mines have been found, of which those at Tongling, Ruichang county, Anhui, and Tonglüshan, Daye county, Hubei, are the most important. See Hua Jueming, *Zhongguo gudai jinshu jishu*, pp. 48–49; Liu Shizhong and Lu Benshan, "Jiangxi Tongling tongkuang yizhi de fajue yu yanjiu," *Kaogu xuebao* 1998.4, pp. 465–96, pls. 1–8; and *Tonglüshan gu kuangye yizhi.*

22 *Yinxu fajue baogao*, pp. 20, 47–48; *Yinxu de faxian yu yanjiu*, pp. 263–64.

23 Loehr, "The Bronze Styles of the Anyang Period," pp. 42–53.

24 For a discussion of the date of Fu Hao's tomb, see Bagley, *Shang Ritual Bronzes*, p. 54, note 100.

25 For M232, see Shi Zhangru, *Xiaotun*, vol. 1: *Yizhi de faxian yu fajue*: fasc. 3, Yinxu tombs part 3: *Nanzu muzang fu beizu mu buyi.* M333 and M388 are coeval with M232. Their excavation is reported in the same series volume, fasc. 3, Yinxu tombs part 5: *Bing qu muzang shang* (unavailable to this author), cited by Zhu Fenghan, *Gudai Zhongguo qingtongqi*, p. 626, note 62. Individual bronzes from these tombs are published in the series *Gu qiwu yanjiu zhuankan*, Li Ji and Wan Jiabao, editors, no. 3: *Yinxu chutu qingtong jia xing qi zhi yanjiu*; no. 4: *Yinxu chutu qingtong ding xing qi zhi yanjiu*; and no. 5: *Yinxu chutu wushisan jian qingtongqi zhi yanjiu.* Small-scale tombs at Sanjiazhuang, some 3.5 kilometers north of Anyang, have yielded bronzes coeval with M338 and M331. See "Anyang Yinxu Sanjiazhuang dong de faxian," *Kaogu* 1983:2, pp. 126–32, pl. V.

26 The importance of studying bronze vessels as components of a ritual set has been central to Chinese bronze studies since *Shang Zhou tongqi qun zonghe yanjiu* (written by Guo Baojun in 1965, but not published until 1981). Jessica Rawson was the first Western scholar to grasp the importance of this methodology as a tool for charting vessel changes. See Rawson, *Chinese Bronzes*, p. 11, and *Western Zhou Ritual Bronzes*, passim.

27 For instance, the *ding* from M232 is indistinguishable from two from Baijiazhuang tombs M2-3, which are among the latest tombs at Zhengzhou. Since they are located close to the wall, it has been argued that they postdate the abandonment of the city. Yet they cannot be much later than that event and certainly precede the tombs at Gaocheng Taixi. See Zhu Fenghan, *Gudai Zhongguo qingtongqi*, pp. 609–10.
28 An example from Gaocheng Taixi tomb M112 is reproduced in *Gaocheng Taixi*, color pl. III, p. 131, fig. 78:1.
29 Round-bottomed *jue* occur among the later tombs at Gaocheng Taixi. See *Gaocheng Taixi*, p. 130, fig. 77:2–6, and pls. 83:2, 84, and 85:1–2.
30 Tomb M18, located in the vicinity of Fu Hao's tomb, yielded bronzes that at first glance seem slightly less advanced. The paucity of decoration in Style V and the presence of a *jia* in Style III might suggest that M18 is somewhat earlier than Fu Hao's tomb, but the *jia* seems out of character with the rest of the bronzes and was probably an heirloom. Moreover, the presence of inscriptions on many of the bronzes suggests that they cannot be more than a couple of decades earlier than Fu Hao. See "Anyang Xiaotun cun bei de liang zuo Yin dai mu," *Kaogu Xuebao* 1981.4, pp. 491–517, pls. 9–18.
31 Although a small number of unprovenanced bronzes bearing inscriptions have been cited by various authorities as being of Erligang date, no excavated Erligang-period bronzes bear convincing inscriptions. Nor do any appear on bronzes from transitional sites such as Gaocheng Taixi (although a minority of the signs incised on the ceramics from this site can be related to later bronze graphs). Of the motifs on excavated bronzes proposed by Cao Shuqin, none relate convincingly to late Shang script, although a few may be insignia. See Cao Shuqin, "Shang dai zhongqi you mingwen chutan," *Kaogu* 1988.3, pp. 246–57, 218. See also Li Xueqin, "Lun Mei Ao shoucang de jijian Shang Zhou wenwu," *Wenwu* 1979.12, pp. 72–76.
32 The fact that none of the large, possibly royal, tombs at Xibeigang north of the Huan River can be shown to significantly pre-date Fu Hao supports this argument. For a discussion of the dating of these tombs, see *Yinxu de faxian yu yanjiu*, pp. 109–12.
33 Rawson, *Chinese Bronzes*, pp. 62–64, no. 6.
34 For the Sackler *guang*, see Seiichi Mizuno, *Bronzes and Jades of Ancient China*, pl. 54.
35 Stone sculptures were found in a number of the Xibeigang tombs. Tomb HPKM 1001 yielded a crouching beast with a head that resembles those on some *guang* and an owl that relates closely to *you* in the form of owls. See Liang Siyong and Gao Quxun, *Houjiazhuang*, part 2, pls. lxxi–lxxiv.
36 Tan Derui, "Zhongguo qingtong shidai tao fan zhuzao jishu yanjiu," pp. 236–38. The number of man-hours required to cast monumental *fang ding* would have been a multiple of that needed for the smaller vessels. The pair of Si Mu Xin *fang ding* from Fu Hao's tomb suggest that the time required would, nevertheless, have been months rather than years. If Si Mu Xin, as the Fu Hao excavation report argues, is Fu Hao's posthumous name, then the Si Mu Xin bronzes must have been cast during the interval between the consort's death and her burial. See *Yinxu Fu Hao mu*, p. 96. See also note 3 above.
37 See *Yanshi Erlitou*, p. 228, fig. 143:1–4.
38 See *Xin'gan Shang dai da mu*, color pl. 16:1–2.
39 See *Yinxu de faxian yu yanjiu*, pp. 284–85, figs. 153:3 and 154:1–2; and *Yinxu Fu Hao mu*, pl. 28:1–2.
40 See discussion below of Period III finds and note 45.
41 For jade *gui*, see *Yinxu Fu Hao mu*, color pl. 14:1,2.
42 Bagley, *Shang Ritual Bronzes*, pp. 28–29 and no. 49, pp. 293–307.
43 Long-tailed dragons appear on a number of bronzes from Period III, for instance, Miaopu M172. *Yinxu qingtongqi*, color pl. 67.

44 "Yinxu Qijiazhuang dong 269 hao mu," *Kaogu xuebao* 1991.3, pp. 325–52, pls. 7–16.

45 It is not certain what prototype lay behind the new type of *you*. It shares the ovoid cross section with *hu*. *Hu* possess tubular lugs that were, no doubt, originally furnished with rope handles. The substitution of a bronze version of the rope handle would in effect convert a *hu* into a wide-bodied *you*. The handles on certain *you* betray a clear generic relation to rope handles. A plain bucket-shaped vessel with a handle in the form of a rope, found in Period II tomb M26 at Guojiazhuang, is illustrated in *Kaogu* 1998.10, p. 40, fig. 9 and pl. IV:2.

46 *Anyang Yinxu Guojiazhuang Shang dai muzang*, pp. 70–126.

47 Only one of the fourteen weapons tested contained significant amounts of tin, whereas the vessels ranged from 10 percent to 17 percent (Ji Lianqi, "Henan Anyang Guojiazhuang 160 hao mu chutu tongqi de chengfen fenxi yanjiu," *Kaogu* 1997.2, pp. 80–84, 92, chart 1). Little research has been done on the sources of tin during the Shang period. A number of lead *mingqi* are known from Period IV at Anyang, perhaps indicating a scarcity of both copper and tin at this time.

48 The only bronzes showing a comparable emphasis on square sections are a group linked by their inscriptions, which include the name "Ya Chou," and which were probably cast at the beginning of Western Zhou. Yin Zhiyi, "Shandong Yidu Sufutun mudi he 'Ya Chou' tongqi," *Kaogu xuebao* 1977.2, pp. 23–34, pls. 1–2.

49 Liu Yiman, "Yinxu Guojiazhuang 160 hao mu de faxian ji zhuyao shouhuo," *Kaogu* 1998.9, pp. 64–72, esp. p. 72.

50 The *you* is paralleled by the Ge *you* from Ningxiang in Hunan (*Zhongguo gu qingtongqi xuan*, no. 21). For a discussion of the subsequent evolution of this type, see Loehr, *Ritual Vessels*, pp. 96–100, nos. 40–41.

51 The ceramic prototypes for the new type of *zun* appear about the same time in Period III. See *Yinxu fajue baogao*, p. 159, fig. 119:2–6. Although bronze *jia* with a lobed body had occurred earlier, these do not seem to have been the direct inspiration for the new form of lobed *jia*. Not only were the earlier versions extremely rare, but they differed from the new type in possessing the legs in conventional triangular section. It is possible that the new bronze type was inspired by ceramic versions (for an example of the ceramic version, see *Yinxu fajue baogao*, p. 160, fig. 120).

52 Yang Xizhang and Yang Baocheng, "Yin dai qingtong liqi de fenqi yu zuhe," in *Yinxu qingtongqi*, p. 88, chart 5.

53 *Mingqi* (burial substitutes) in lead and ceramic appear during Period III, though it is unclear whether this practice indicates that bronzes were being preserved in temples rather than buried, or whether it simply reflects a decline in the scale of bronze casting. See ibid., pp. 87–89, charts 7 and 8, where it is stated that ceramic copies of bronzes begin to appear in tombs in Period III.

54 *Yinxu qingtongqi*, figs. 86:1, 87:5.

55 Bagley, *Shang Ritual Bronzes*, pp. 521–36, no. 103.

56 I am grateful to Lothar von Falkenhausen for bringing this discovery to my attention.

57 For the full excavation report, see *Luyi Taiqinggong Chang Zi Kou mu*. Other articles on the tomb include the following: Han Weilong and Zhang Zhiqing, "Luyi Taiqinggong Chang Zi Kou mu chutu qingtongqi," *Zhongyuan wenwu* 2000.1, pp. 4–7; Henan Sheng wenwu kaogu yanjiusuo and the Zhoukou diqi wenhuaju, "Henan Luyi xian Taiqinggong Xi Zhou mu de fajue," *Kaogu* 2000.9, pp. 9–23, pls. 1–3; and Han Weilong and Zhang Zhiqing, "Chang Zi Kou mu de shidai tezheng ji mu zhu," *Kaogu* 2000.9, pp. 24–29.

QIANLONG IMPERIAL JADES IN THE NORTON MUSEUM OF ART

John R. Finlay

INTRODUCTION

The Qing imperial uses of objects made of jade go far beyond the traditional Chinese production of finely carved objects for display in imperial temples, halls, and palaces. Jade objects produced for the imperial court in eighteenth-century China embody policies and practices that would legitimize the rule of the Manchu Qing dynasty (1644–1911). Like the earlier Mongol Yuan and Jurchen Jin dynasties, the Manchu Qing was a conquest dynasty that had invaded China and established itself as rulers over the native Han Chinese population. The Manchu conquest of territories in Central Asia that were the sources of nephrite—true jade—in extraordinary quantities provided an unparalleled opportunity for the imperial institutions to produce and use objects of jade. The Qianlong emperor's (r. 1736–95) equally unprecedented emphasis on written texts provides a crucial contemporary context for these objects. The texts in question include the emperor's own voluminous writings (some only nominally authored by him), records of the emperor's day-to-day activities, and archival documents generated by the various imperial government bureaus. Because of the contemporary publication of imperial writings and the preservation of bureaucratic documents, we have invaluable sources for the study of Qing imperial material culture. With the purchase in 1941 of just over 100 jades from the dealer Stanley Charles Nott, the Norton Museum of Art acquired four important Qianlong imperial jades. These are the *Bowl with seven Buddhas,* dated 1777 (cat. 94), two *Individual chimestones* from a set dated 1761 (cats. 91, 92), and a large *Vase in the form of a hu* (cat. 93), dated in accordance with the year 1778. Nott mistakenly believed that all were products of the Ming dynasty,[1] but, as the following discussion of these objects reveals, each is an important document of the Qing Qianlong imperial court. Each jade has at least one long, dated inscription on it, and each of these was recorded in the great compendia of the Qianlong emperor's official writings. An examination of the written record provides the background for an understanding of the various roles these objects played in the Qing court and of the way they embodied some of the crucial concerns of imperial rule.

BOWL WITH SEVEN BUDDHAS, DATED 1777

Tibetan Buddhism was the private religion of the Manchu Qing imperial clan.[2] From before the conquest of China, Manchu imperial patronage was extended specifically to the Yellow (or Gelugpa) sect of Tibetan Buddhism. Although two lineages of lamas (spiritual leaders regarded as incarnations of deities), one based in Outer Mongolia, the other in Inner Mongolia and China proper, were the most immediately influential in the Qing court, formal visits by two heads of the Yellow sect—the Dalai Lama, in 1652, and the Panchen Lama, in 1780—were important state occasions in the Qing.[3] The *Bowl with seven Buddhas* was carved in direct response to the Panchen Lama's presentation of a Tibetan scroll of seven Buddhas to the Qianlong emperor. Its size and the use of jade reflect the value placed on the scroll and the emperor's devotion to Tibetan Buddhism.

On the outside of the bowl, seven brief texts alternate with seven identical high-relief images of seated Buddhas. (These are Shakyamuni, the historical Buddha, and the six Buddhas that preceded him in past ages.) Engraved into the surface, the characters are filled with gold to make them stand out against the dark green jade (see fig. 1 for a detail of one of the texts and one Buddha image). A much longer text is engraved on the gently rounded bottom of the bowl using the same gold-filled technique. Comprising twenty-five long columns of small characters, it is the Qianlong imperial "Stele Record of the Stupa of the Seven Buddhas." Like Qing imperial texts of every kind, the "Record" was carefully transcribed and preserved in the corpus of imperial writings, in this case in the Second Collection of Qianlong texts, compiled in 1786.[4] The "Record"

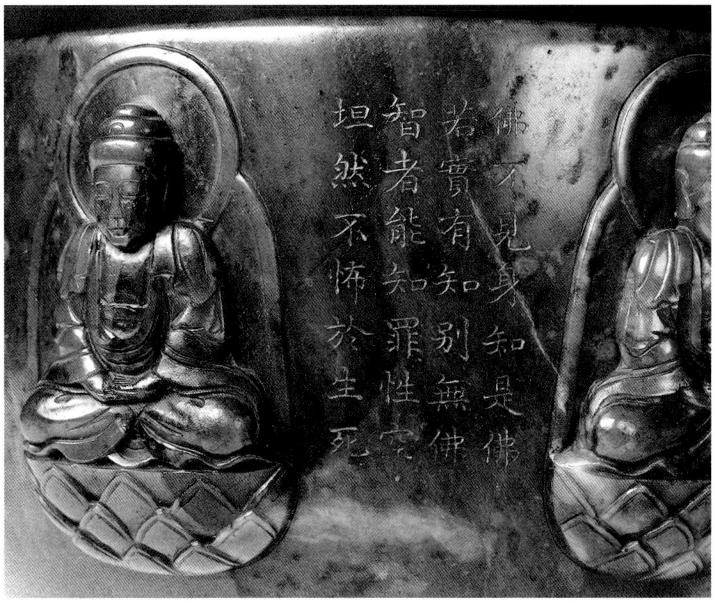

FIGURE 1 Detail of Buddha image and section of text from *Bowl with seven Buddhas*. Norton Museum of Art, Gift of R.H. Norton, 42.66 (cat. 94)

carved on the Norton bowl is identical to the published versions, with the minor exception of characters written in slightly different forms. It is signed as *yubi*, or "imperial calligraphy," a phrase indicating that it is a replica of the Qianlong emperor's own hand. Engraved versions of two of the Qianlong emperor's seals, *bide* and *langrun*, which usually appear together,[5] and the cyclical date equivalent to 1777 are part of the signature line.

The "Stele Record of the Stupa of the Seven Buddhas" must have been considered an important text, since at least two other versions still exist, both carved on the pages of jade books. On the one in the Chester Beatty Library, Dublin,[6] the text and other decorations are engraved and filled with gold on four thin sheets of gray-green jade that make up the "pages" of the book. The jade pages have silk frames of imperial yellow, and the book has carved wooden covers. The signature at the end of the text reads "Respectfully written by Dong Gao." Dong Gao (1740–1818), the son of the painter Dong Bangda (1699–1764), was a Hanlin Academician who held other high government offices. In addition to being a painter and calligrapher, he served in the Wuying Dian, the hall that housed the imperial printing presses.[7] A second jade book, in the Metropolitan Museum of Art, New York, preserves a version of the "Record" by a different hand.[8] Here the pages are sheets of jade set in paper and cloth mounts and bound in accordion style with carved wood covers. The original calligraphy, carefully copied, engraved, and filled with gold on the jade, was written in gold ink on black paper, and the pages are mounted in the album facing the inscribed jades. The calligrapher, whose signature appears at the end, was Liang Guozhi (1723–1787), who served in several high positions, notably as the emperor's personal secretary in the Imperial Study after 1774.[9] Liang's signature appears on other Qianlong-era jade books, and his calligraphy appears to have been favored by the emperor.[10]

The text of the "Stele Record of the Stupa of the Seven Buddhas" begins with a description of how the *Sayings of the Seven Buddhas*[11] came to China:

The Sayings of the Seven Buddhas *were first placed in the canon by the Buddhists of the Chan sect. Their import is to be found scattered in Sanskrit writings, although they were never compiled [in Sanskrit] in a single sutra. Recently the tribute received from the Panchen Lama E'erdeni*[12] *included a Tibetan scroll of the seven Buddhas.... No ordinary Buddhist priests appear to know how the* Sayings *came to be composed, but on consulting the Zhangjia Guoshi we learn that the origins of the doctrine can be traced, point by point, in various Tibetan and Chinese sutras.*[13]

"Zhangjia" is part of the Chinese transcription of the Mongol term Jangjya Hutuktu, one lineage of lamas of the Gelugpa sect. "Guoshi" is an unofficial reference to some of the most important court officials and aides to the emperor.[14] The third Jangjya Hutuktu, Rolpay Dorje, was a classmate of the prince who would become the Qianlong emperor and his close advisor after he ascended the throne. Rolpay Dorje served as Grand Lama of Beijing and was intimately involved in the production of Tibetan-style art and architecture for the emperor.[15] He identified the names of each of the seven Buddhas, the names of their parents, sons and attendants, and the places where the Buddhas supposedly lived. This information concerning the lineage of the Buddhas, which makes up the bulk of the "Record,"[16] is followed by an explanation of the doctrine that the seven Buddhas are in reality manifestations of the one Buddha. In view of this doctrine and the importance of the scroll with the images of the seven Buddhas, so the imperial "Record" continues, "this text has been engraved on pure white stone and a stupa of the seven Buddhas has been built and dedicated."[17] The stele currently stands near the Beihai in the Western Park (the imperial gardens, lakes, and buildings just west of the Forbidden City), north of the Five Dragon Pavilion.[18] The stupa has not been identified and possibly no longer exists. It was not necessarily a freestanding building but more likely a small shrine in the form of a stupa, perhaps a gilt-bronze container for the scroll.[19]

Images of seven Buddhas appear relatively early in a Chinese cultural context. A miniature stone stupa from Gansu province, which bears the images of seven Buddhas with Maitreya, the Buddha of the Future, is dated by inscription to 428 CE. One of a group of fourteen such votive carvings, it combines an Indian stupa form with Chinese deities, eight trigrams from the *Book of Changes*, high-relief images of the seven Buddhas and Maitreya in small niches, and a passage from a Chinese translation of the *Ekottaragama sutra*.[20] Such miniature stupas are found only in Turfan and Gansu, on China's northwestern frontier, and are almost all dated to the brief Northern Liang dynasty (398–439). A gilt-bronze image of seven Buddhas in the Nezu Museum, Tokyo, from the Sui dynasty (589–618), takes the form of seven lotus flowers branching from one single stem, each lotus supporting a seated Buddha. This imagery perhaps implies the same doctrinal identification of all seven as manifestations of the one Buddha that is cited in the Qianlong emperor's stele inscription.[21] The Bishop collection, now in the Metropolitan Museum of Art, includes an eighteenth-century white jade bowl with nine images of Amitabha seated on lotus pedestals (fig. 2). Taking the form of a Buddhist monk's alms bowl, it is carved in Tibetan style with identical images of

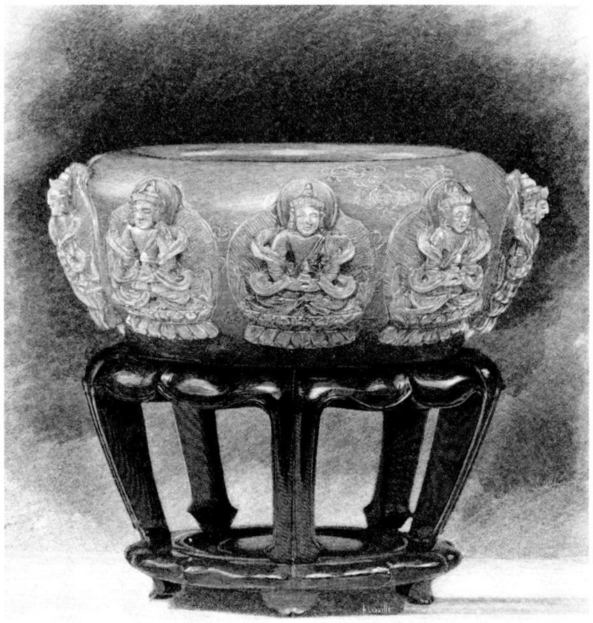

FIGURE 2 White jade bowl carved with images of nine Buddhas, 18th century. The Metropolitan Museum of Art, 02.18.622a,b

seated Buddhas each holding miniature Tibetan stupas.[22] On the bottom of the bowl is the Qianlong reign mark *Qianlong nian zhi*, "made in the Qianlong reign." Also from the eighteenth century, a carved lacquer alms bowl in the National Palace Museum, Taipei, has the *Sayings* carved between images of seven Buddhas (fig. 3).[23] Clouds surround identical images of Buddhas seated on lotus pedestals, and the names of the Buddhas appear above the images. Rolpay Dorje's research in the Tibetan and Chinese sutras presumably brought these texts to light, and each short text seems to be associated with a specific Buddha.

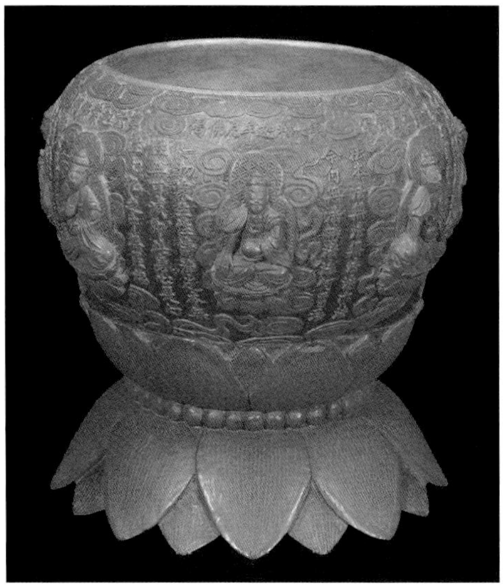

FIGURE 3 Red and black lacquer bowl carved with images of seven Buddhas, 18th century. Taipei, National Palace Museum, T6731/*chung-ch'i* 89/*chung* 4882

In 1779, the sixth Panchen Lama, E'erdeni, who had sent the seven Buddhas scroll in tribute, expressed his desire to be present at the celebrations of the Qianlong emperor's seventieth birthday in 1780.[24] The request was of great religious and political significance, and the only real precedent was the visit of the fifth Dalai Lama during the reign of the Shunzhi emperor in 1652. At that time the emperor had the Xi Huangsi, the Western Yellow Temple, constructed just north of the Inner City wall to welcome the Dalai Lama.[25] Similarly elaborate plans were made for the Panchen Lama's visit to the Qianlong emperor, which entailed a grueling journey of several months from Tashilhunpo, the lama's seat at Shigatse, southwestern Tibet, to the Bishu Shanzhuang, the Qing imperial summer villa at Rehe (Jehol), north of the Great Wall near Chengde. For the lama's reception, the Qianlong emperor ordered the construction of the Xumifushou Temple at Rehe. This was begun in 1779 and was completed by the time of the lama's arrival in 1780. Xumifushou is the Chinese transcription of Tashilhunpo, and the temple was in some ways a recreation of the Panchen Lama's monastery and temple in Tibet. Here he stayed during his visit to Rehe and preached with the emperor in attendance.[26] The Panchen Lama went on to Beijing with the Qianlong emperor's entourage and was received by the emperor at various times in the Yuanming Yuan, in the imperial villa at Xiangshan, and at the Western Yellow Temple, where he resided during his stay in the capital. Unfortunately, while in Beijing the Panchen Lama contracted smallpox and died suddenly. The horrified Qianlong emperor ordered the construction of a golden stupa to contain the lama's embalmed body on its journey back to Tibet, and he also had built a white marble Tibetan-style stupa at the Western Yellow Temple to hold the relics that the lama had brought with him for presentation to the emperor.[27]

Two jade *teqing*, or individual chimestones, in the Norton can be traced back to the chance discovery of a group of eleven bronze bells in Linjiang prefecture, Jiangxi province, in 1759. Identified by their inscription as dating to the Zhou dynasty,[28] they were specifically *bozhong*, bells that were played individually (in contrast to a carillon of bells or *bianzhong*) as part of ancient ritual music.[29] The Zhou bells were brought to Beijing and installed in a hall in the Western Park, the Yungu Tang—the Hall of Echoing Antiquity—which was renamed for the bells.[30] Inspired by what must have been regarded as an auspicious omen, the Qianlong emperor ordered sets of bronze *bozhong* cast in the style of the Zhou examples. He also ordered at least four corresponding sets of jade *teqing* or "individual chimestones" (fig. 4) since, "having replicated the bells, the *qing* should not be omitted."[31] (As will be discussed below, *teqing* are played individually, in contrast to *bianqing*, which are played in sets.) The emperor's motivations went beyond his delight at this reappearance of ancient musical instruments. Music was an essential part of imperial ritual and ceremony, and the proper performance of music on instruments sanctioned by the authority of ancient tradition helped establish the legitimacy of the Manchu Qing dynasty.[32]

From before the official proclamation of the Qing dynasty in 1635, Manchu rulers had used court and ritual music based—at least in part—on Chinese models. In 1616 Nurhaci (Ch. Nu'erhachi) declared himself khan of the Later Jin dynasty, the forerunner to the Qing, and established music for the use of his new dynasty in the court at Shenyang, the Manchu capital north of the Great Wall. Contemporary records do not detail the instruments played or the specific musical forms.[33] Court records from 1636 describe ritual music played with drums and other instruments, but no chimestones or bronze bells. When the Manchu Qing established their rule in Beijing in 1644, the new dynasty almost

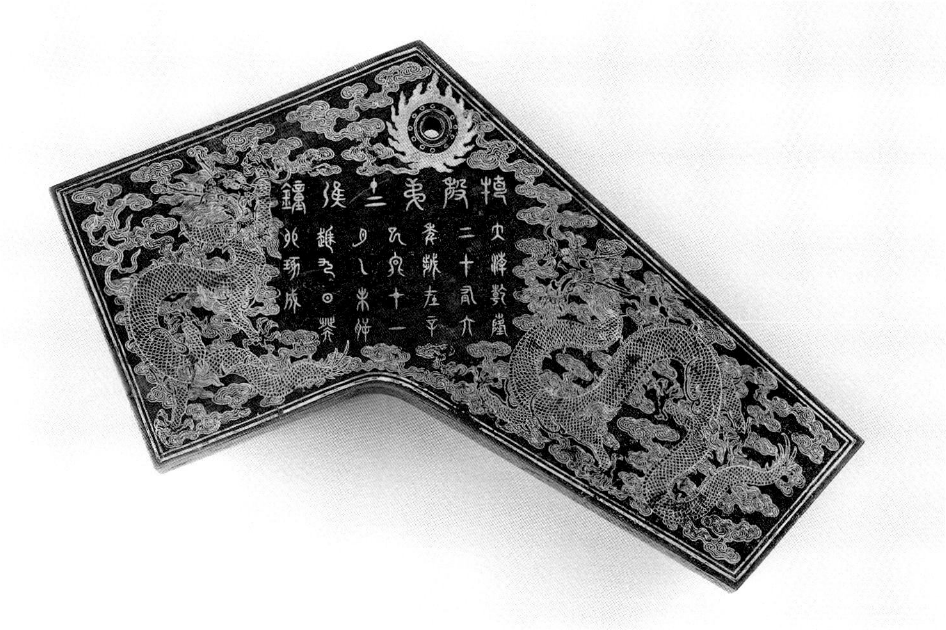

FIGURE 4 Individual chimestone number twelve, front, with date corresponding to the twenty-sixth year of the Qianlong reign (1761), eleventh month, fifth day. Norton Museum of Art, Gift of R.H. Norton, 42.20 (cat. 91)

immediately adopted music for ritual use, court assemblies, and banqueting that was closely based on Ming dynasty precedents.[34] For example, the first Sacrifice to Heaven, the ritual that signaled the legitimate succession of the new dynasty, was accompanied by Ming ritual music played by musicians from the former dynasty.[35] Qing court ritual music effectively followed Ming precedents until 1713, when the Kangxi emperor (r. 1662–1721) ordered the compilation of the *Lülü zhengyi* (True essentials of music). Under the editorship of He Guozong (d. 1766), a mathematician and high court official, the text was printed in 1723 with a preface by the Yongzheng emperor (r. 1722–35).[36] The entry on *qing* chimestones describes both sets of sixteen stones, or *bianqing*, and the twelve individual chimestones categorized as *teqing*.[37] Both arrangements of chimestones—ensembles of smaller stones and large-scale individual stones—have long and complex histories, which are supported by textual records, the discovery of ancient instruments, and recreations of ancient forms.[38] The Norton chimestones are specifically *teqing*, individual chimestones.

The Qianlong emperor recognized that the *Lülü zhengyi* did not account for much of court musical practice, and in 1741, the sixth year of his reign, he ordered officials under the supervision of Zhang Zhao (1691–1745) and the imperial Prince Yinlu (1695–1767) to compile a voluminous sequel and revision of the earlier text, entitled the *Lülü zhengyi houbian*.[39] The emperor set out to establish all details for court music, including the scores, instruments and instrumental ensembles, ritual movements, paraphernalia, and even the costumes of court musicians. A comprehensive Music Bureau was established the following year, 1742, with a staff of approximately 1,030 officials and court musicians. The *Lülü zhengyi houbian* listed five broad categories of court music (sacrificial music, music for court assemblies, banquet music, welcoming music, and processional music).[40] The ritual music for which individual chimestones were created was the *Zhonghe shaoyue*, which was performed during sacrifices at the most important imperial altars and the emperor's ascent to the throne. It derived from the *Shao* music of the mythical emperor Shun, music supposedly heard by Confucius.[41]

The Confucian Classics, which record the use of chimestones in ritual music, provided ample precedent for the restoration of earlier traditions by the Qianlong court. For instance, the *Book of Rites*[42] listed the ritual musical instruments of the ancient state of Lu (in modern Shandong province): "They had the drum of Xia supported on four legs; that of Yin supported on a single pillar; the drums of Zhou, pendant from a stand; the peal of bells of Sui; the differently toned *qing* (sonorous stones) of Shu; and the organ of Nüwa, with its tongues."[43] This text is cited in the *Huangchao liqi tushi* (Illustrated regulations for ritual paraphernalia of the present [Qing] dynasty), which describes the individual chimestones commissioned by the Qianlong emperor in 1759 and completed in 1761.[44]

Illustrated here (fig. 5) is the first and largest stone, after a 1759 Qing imperial woodblock edition of the *Huangchao liqi tushi*. The large single column of characters to the right of the illustration reads "Individual chimestone number one, *huangzhong* [tone], for the *Zhonghe shaoyue* for court assemblies." The description of the stone on the following page begins:

Respectfully following the Liji, *"Positions in the Mingtang" chapter, concerning the individual chimestones of Shu, and Chen Yang's* Book of Music,[45] *for sets there are various small* [*stones*], *and if separate then they are individual large* [*stones*]. *If they are the separate chimestones of Shu, then those are* teqing [*individual chimestones*] *with special suspension frames with crossbars.*[46]

In the illustration can be seen the massive rack with a stout crossbar that was necessary to hold the heavy pieces of jade.[47] The text continues, detailing what we see in the illustration: the top of the rack decorated with heads of *feng* phoenixes, the uprights inserted in the backs of wild ducks, and a cord for suspending the jade chimestone from the crossbar. Extant examples in the Forbidden City and the Shenyang Palace Museum show how closely illustrations in the *Huangchao liqi tushi* resemble the objects actually produced for the court.[48]

The measurements of individual stones recorded in the *Huangchao liqi*

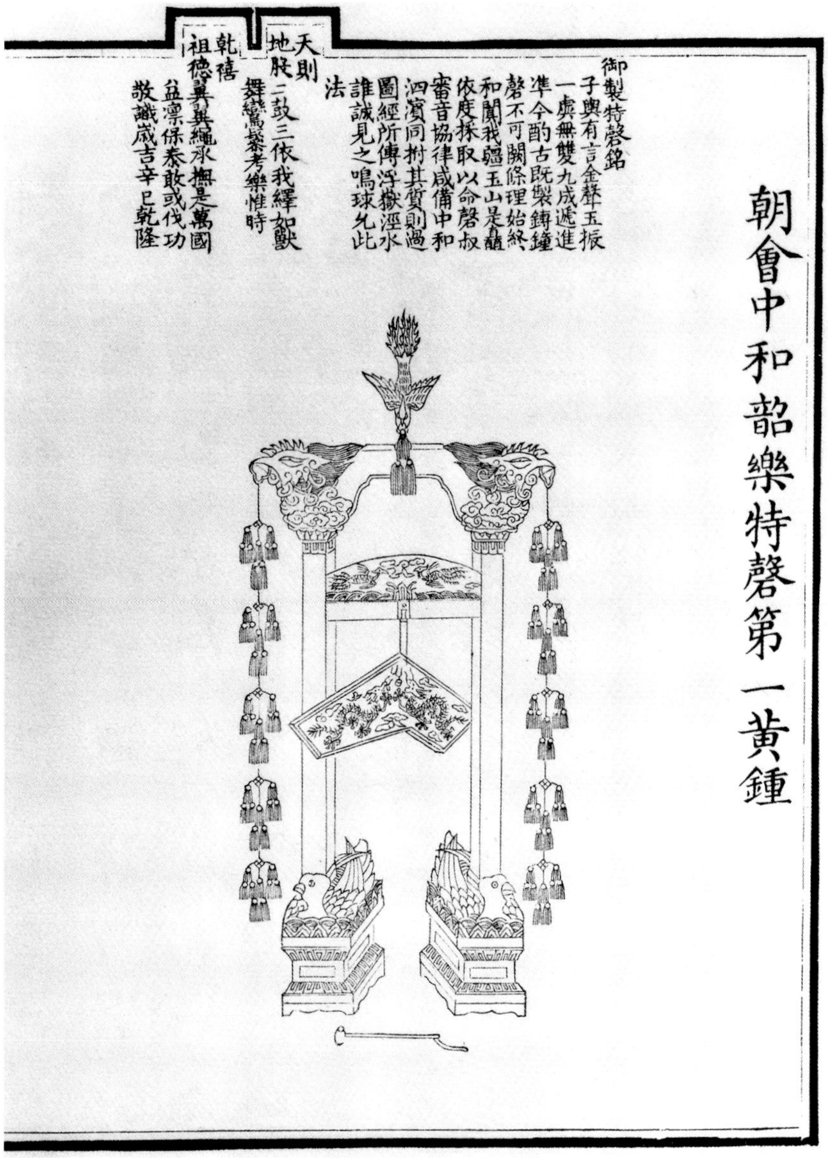

FIGURE 5 Woodblock illustration from 1759 edition of *Huangchao liqi tushi, juan* 8, showing individual chimestone number one

tushi (and the *Lülü zhengyi houbian*) show an even more careful concern with detail. The measurements are given for all twelve individual chimestones in Chinese feet and inches, with each stone described by the length and width of its two ends. One is dubbed the *gutiao*, literally "thigh end," and is the shorter, broader part of the stone. The other is also called the *gutiao* (but the *gu* is written with a different character) and is the "drum end" or "striking end" of the stone. This is the part that would be struck with a wooden mallet (depicted at the bottom of the illustration in fig. 5) to produce the clear, ringing tone.[49] The measurements are extraordinarily precise, almost always specifying length, width, and thickness to one-hundredths of a Chinese inch. The extreme detail of the measurements—down to one one-thousandth of an inch in some instances—must be related to the tuning of the chimestones, with the exact measurement producing the correctly tuned musical note.

The *Huangchao liqi tushi* is in large part descriptive, giving in its pages the precise details of a panoply of court paraphernalia, including chimestones. The "Inscription for Individual Chimestones," which appears above the illustration just described, was also inscribed in seal script characters filled with gold on each of the individual stones in the sets of twelve *teqing* commissioned by the emperor.[50] (In fig. 5, the characters that extend beyond the upper border of the illustration have deceased emperors as their grammatical subject; the "elevated" characters are a sign of respect.) The inscription takes the form of a poem in archaistic four-character couplets that begins with a well-known phrase from Mencius: "Metal sounds and jade responds."[51] That is, bronze bells are struck at the beginning of the musical line in ritual music, and the jade chimestones with the corresponding pitch are struck at end of the line in the performance of the *Zhonghe shaoyue*.[52]

One of the couplets of the imperial inscription notes that the jade for the chimestones comes from Khotan, on the Chinese frontier in Central Asia. (The role of Khotan jade is discussed in detail below, in reference to the *Vase in the form of a hu*.) Further, according to the emperor's poem, the sound of the musical jades resonates throughout the empire, and the ritual music evokes in the participants in imperial ceremonies the proper solemn spirit. The emperor says of his own feelings, "Beating time to the music, we ponder [ritual], / Heaven's blessings, and our ancestors' virtue." In the published text of the "Inscription for Individual Chimestones," a note was inserted following the lines "Khotan is our frontier, / The Jade Mountains rising high." The compilers explained that from the jade discovered on one particular mountain "craftsmen are ordered to choose it according to the measure of [a stone for] the *huangzhong* pitch [the first and largest individual chimestone] to serve for use on imperial altars, in shrines, and audience halls."[53] Most likely this refers to the imperial commission of 1759, which had resulted in the manufacture of more that 160 jade *qing*,[54] most of those being individual chimestones, including the two Norton examples.

Two complete sets of twelve chimestones from 1761 still exist in China—these are in the Forbidden City and in the Shenyang Palace Museum, the preconquest Qing imperial palace north of the Great Wall.[55] At least five stones dated 1761 are currently in Chinese museum or gallery collections in Beijing or Hubei province.[56] Six individual chimestones from at least one 1761 set (and possibly others), including the two in the Norton, are documented in the collections of American museums or accounted for in auction sales.[57] Because four individual chimestones numbered four and eleven exist, we can be certain that there were once at least four additional complete sets.[58] The sources of individual chimestones dispersed from their original locations cannot be determined with certainty, but there are intriguing, and occasionally confusing, leads. In 1967 the New York dealer Frank Caro informed Horace H.F. Jayne, author of the 1972 Norton catalogue, that one stone from a 1761 set was in the Gurie Gallery in Montreal.[59] According to a letter from Alex Gurie, son of the then recently deceased owner of the gallery, "[the] Spinach Jade Resonant Stone was bought by my father in Peking in 1931 and the Chinese dealer at that time informed him that it was stolen from the Summer Palace during the Boxer Rebellion by a French officer who was with the Allied Expeditionary Forces."[60] Gurie's letter contained a photograph that clearly shows a number four stone dated 1761.[61]

The Chinese dealer's story—or Gurie's recollection—seems at first glance to conflate the widespread looting in the wake of the Boxer Rebellion of 1900 with the 1860 looting of the Yuanming Yuan, one of several imperial villas outside Beijing loosely referred to as the "Summer Palace." Although Jayne's reply prudently noted, "one takes such stories with several grains of salt,"[62] he wrote in 1972 that the chimestones may have been taken from the Confucius Temple during the Boxer Rebellion.[63] James Hevia, however, has described auctions of Boxer Rebellion loot that "continued well into the winter of 1900–1901 and included a much larger pool of buyers than in 1860. There were members of the diplomatic corps, foreign residents in Beijing and from other treaty ports, members of the eight allied armies, and eventually curio shop owners from Shanghai and Hong Kong, some of whom were reported to have commissions from European auction houses and art dealers."[64]

The text for stone number one in the *Huangchao liqi tushi* lists three imperial altars where individual chimestones were used in court ritual, and two of these are part of the Altar of Heaven, a huge enclave just inside the southern wall of the Outer City of Beijing.[65] The relatively exposed position of this imperial ritual complex during the Boxer Rebellion made it, too, a possible candidate for looting. The Chinese dealer's story, however, receives support from an unsuspected source. James Legge's translation of the *Shoo King* (*Shujing*) contains the following note: "I have seen a *king* [a *qing* chimestone], brought in 1861 from the 'Summer palace,' that had been made for the emp. K'een-lung [Qianlong] of jade stone fully an inch thick, and like a ship-builder's *knee*, the form in which the instrument is commonly represented. When suspended and struck with a piece of metal, it emitted a rich ringing sound."[66] Published imperial texts and inscriptions on chimestones provide a wealth of detail, but individual stones are not identified in their inscriptions with specific palace buildings or imperial temples, leaving us unsure of the sources of so many jade chimestones removed from their original locations. Their numbers, however, hint at the scale of production of such ritual instruments for the Qianlong court.

VASE IN THE FORM OF A HU, DATED 1778

The front of the very large and heavy *Vase in the form of a hu* is engraved with a long text, the "Huiyu xing" or "Essay on Muslim Jade." It begins by telling a familiar story of the Central Asian sources of jade:

Since the Muslim lands have already returned to [Chinese] dominion, Muslim jade is thus appropriate for the payment of taxes. They dredge it [from the rivers] in spring and autumn. Now, as in the rivers, there is also production from the mountains, but it is considered inferior. What they take from rivers annually makes up the regular choice [for tribute]; but what [comes from] the various mountains is rarely superior. Because of its weight and size it is difficult to transport.[67]

The largely Muslim territories of East Turkestan, comprising modern Xinjiang and the nearby regions along modern China's far western borders with India, Pakistan, Tajikistan, Kyrgyzstan, and Kazakhstan, came under Qing control in the military campaigns of 1755–59. The campaigns were considered a great success for the Qianlong emperor. Jade from the nephrite deposits of Central Asia began to appear in centers of Chinese culture by the late first millennium BCE, and historical texts from the reign of the Western Han emperor Wudi (r. 140–87 BCE) onward had recorded this region as the source of jade.[68]

The rivers to which the "Huiyu xing" refers are specifically the Yurongqash (the White Jade) River and Qaraqash (the Black Jade) River, which rush down from the Kunlun Mountains, flowing on either side of the city of Khotan and merging as the Khotan River that runs into the Takla Makan Desert (see fig. 6). A contemporary account describes the method of dredging jade from the swift rivers:

[Jade boulders] are gathered in this way: one official supervises from the far bank, while a battalion official watches from the near side of the river. A gang of twenty or thirty experienced Muslims are sent to span the river shoulder to shoulder and walk over the stones barefoot. The Muslim knows when he treads on jade. He bows down and lifts it onto the bank. On the shore a guard bangs a gong, and at each crash of the gong the official makes a red mark [in a register]. When the Muslims emerge from the water, the stones are collected in accordance with the [number of] red dots.[69]

A jade rock in the National Palace Museum, Taipei, carved in the form of a mountain landscape, illustrates this technique for recovering what was supposedly the finest quality jade (fig. 7).[70] Many jades retain the original shape of the natural rock—or are cut to suggest such a shape—and depict mountain landscapes (see cats. 96, 97).

The jade mined from the mountains, mentioned in this text as inferior because it did not partake of the "essence" (*qi*) of water,[71] came from Mi'ertaishan, the Mirtagh Mountains, approximately 190 miles west of Khotan. Mining jade in the mountains was at least as arduous as gathering stones from rivers. Muslim workers were conscripted to climb high on the mountainsides and dislodge jade boulders with hammers and chisels. In the commentary to the published text of the "Huiyu xing" is a long note that elaborates on jade from Mi'ertaishan.[72] Despite the slightly inferior quality of the mountain jade, which is not as "glossy and moist" as the riverine variety, it has one advantage: the blocks can be very large, and special government agents in the past had been sent to supervise the collection of boulders big enough to make sets of chimestones.[73] In addition, some of the difficulties of transporting large jade blocks can be overcome by moving them

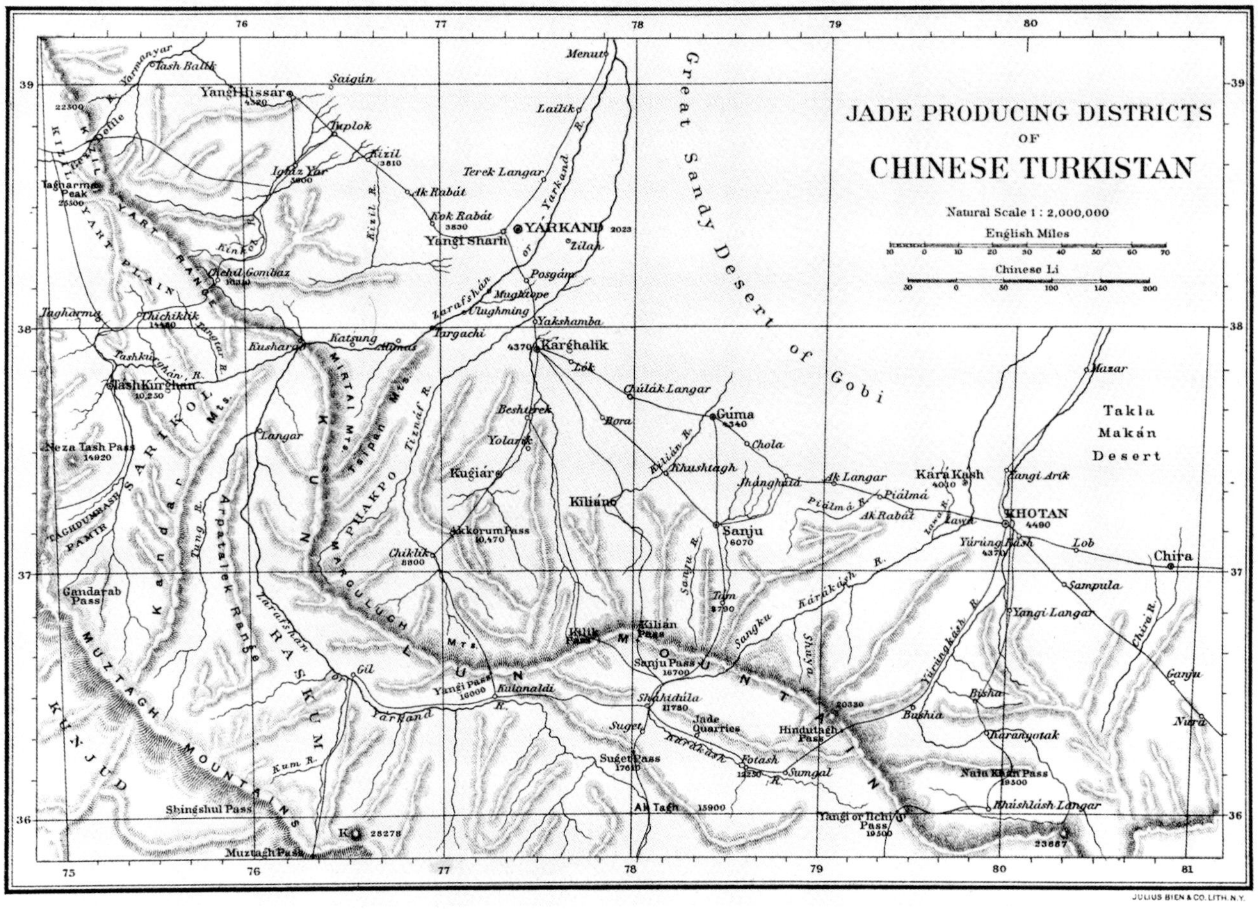

FIGURE 6 Map, ca. 1906, showing jade-mining region of Central Asia

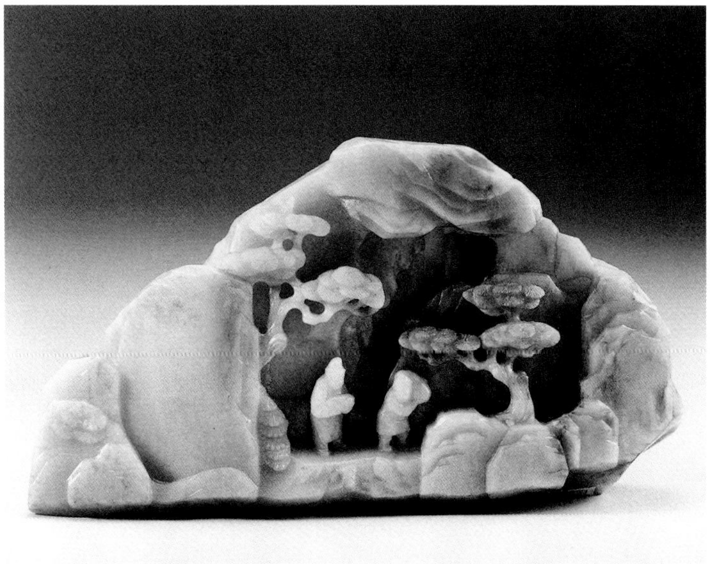

FIGURE 7 Miniature mountain of carved jade showing Muslims gathering jade, 18th century. Taipei, National Palace Museum

on sledges over the ice to the capital where "masters carved this [or 'a'] great jade urn." This note may possibly refer to the Norton jade *hu*.[74]

The engraved text of the "Huiyu xing" continues, stating that the Muslims were under orders to present the jade to the Detached Grand Minister,[75] the title of Qing officials sent to Xinjiang to govern certain cities and the regions immediately around them, and it alludes to corrupt practices in diverting this mountain jade from the imperial court, its legal destination. Again, it is only in the commentary to the "Essay" that one learns the circumstances of official corruption and the names of the most important conspirators. While officials might bestow rewards on Muslims or Chinese involved in collecting jade for the court—relatively small amounts of jade legally released for private sale—in the case referred to here in the "Huiyu xing" and the commentary, local merchants in collusion with corrupt officials had launched a scheme to divert extraordinary amounts of jade into private hands. The text engraved on the *hu* asks, rhetorically, how officials, knowing that the Muslim peoples coveted profit, and though aware of this scheme, did nothing to counter it. Clearly in the Qianlong emperor's voice, it asks, "And how, if they did seek secret commerce, could it be so? Among the officials, how could the Grand Minister do such a thing?... Various others set straight the laws, and he suffered severe punishment."

Another note in the commentary to the published text of the "Essay" identifies the official in question as the Detached Grand Minister at Yarkand,[76] Gao Pu. Yarkand lies west of Khotan and, like Mi'ertaishan, fell under Gao Pu's jurisdiction:

Now Gao Pu in his role as Detached Grand Minister unexpectedly colluded in secret with the profiteers to misappropriate and sell [jade]. First he asked them to mine Mi'ertaishan, and then he put to work over 3,000 of the Muslim people to go to the mountain and extract it, where they obtained large and small jades beyond number. He secretly sent his family members to transport it to the heartland,[77] *and then with the profiteer Zhang Luan in Suzhou had it made into objects and sold privately. He already sold [the equivalent of] 200,000 taels of silver, and from Shaanxi and Gansu he continued to transport a further 4,000 and more catties of raw jade. The large and small pieces of jade that he had accumulated and hidden in Yarkand were calculated at several hundred pieces.*[78]

Gao Pu (d. 1778) was the grandson of Gao Bin (1683–1775) and the member of a family of Chinese origin attached as *baoyi* or bondservants to the Manchu Bordered Yellow Banner.[79] In 1735 one of Gao Bin's daughters, Gao Pu's aunt, was taken as a concubine by the Qianlong emperor and in keeping with this honor the family was officially released from their hereditary bondservant status.[80] Gao Bin's son Gao Heng (d. 1768), who was Gao Pu's father, served in various high government posts, although his admission to the imperial bureaucracy came through the *yin* privilege, which provided exemptions from the official examination system.[81] His most important office was that of Lianghuai Salt Censor, to which he was appointed in 1757. Although the Qianlong emperor had previously praised Gao Heng for his seeming diligence in rooting out corruption in various government offices, in 1768 it was revealed that the minister had concealed the extraordinary sum of more than 10,900,000 taels[82] of silver from the Lianghuai Salt Administration. He was executed for his embezzlement, and the family was punished by a return to bondservant status.[83]

Despite Gao Heng's infraction, in 1776 Gao Pu was ordered to Yarkand as Detached Grand Minister, and he arrived at his post in Central Asia in 1777. Almost immediately he became familiar with Zhang Luan (d. 1778) and other Muslim and Chinese merchants engaged in the long-distance trade between Central Asia and the major cities of China. In just one episode of their collusion to smuggle jade diverted from the Imperial Household Department, Gao Pu, Zhang Luan, and others agreed to transport approximately 2,800 catties (roughly 1,400 kilos) of jade to Suzhou in Jiangsu province, the city where Zhang had his business base and also the leading center of jade carving outside of the imperial workshops in Beijing. Arriving in Suzhou, Zhang discovered on reexamining the shipment that the jade weighed almost 3,200 catties, and he conspired to conceal this unexpected bonus from Gao Pu and share the extra profit with his collaborators.[84] Complex arrangements were necessary to return the profits to Gao Pu in Yarkand or deliver silver and other valuables to his house in Beijing. Although almost all private trade in jade was illegal, jade was one of the few products of Central Asia for which there was a ready market in China, and the many merchants and officials involved in—and corrupted by—this trade gained further profits by sending such marketable products as Chinese silks and tea back to Xinjiang.[85]

The extent of Gao Pu's corruption came to light largely as the result of political appointments in the region.[86] The Detached Grand Minister governed with the assistance of a local Muslim official, whose loyalty to the Qing dynasty was an important factor in his appointment. On the death of the *ak'im beg*, the local governor of Yarkand, Gao Pu requested the appointment of the man's son as his successor, but the emperor refused, appointing one Setiba'erdi[87] instead.

The emperor rightly feared the creation of hereditary posts where an official's loyalty was compromised between local allegiances and the distant imperial court. In 1778 the imperial agent in Wushi (the city of Ush), the Manchu Chuoketuo, finished his term and was replaced by Yonggui, an elderly official from the Board of Rites and Board of Civil Appointments. Setiba'erdi learned of Gao Pu's exploitation of the Muslim population. As the commentary to the "Huiyu xing" records, among other offenses Gao Pu had conscripted 3,000 Muslims to work without pay. The emperor's fears of revolt are expressed in the "Huiyu xing" itself, where he worries that the Grand Minister's actions might have caused an uprising like "the revolt in Wushi." There the exploitation of the local population led to a bloody uprising in 1765 that decimated the population of the city.[88]

Setiba'erdi gathered evidence of Gao Pu's illegal dealings in jade, but sent them only to Yonggui in Wushi. As he was legally required to do, Yonggui went to Yarkand to inquire into the matter and determine the truth of the allegations, and sent the information to the emperor. Gao Pu was removed from his post, pending the outcome of the investigation. Under Yonggui's interrogation, Gao Pu refused to speak or defend his actions. The Qianlong emperor declared that Gao Pu's crimes were even worse than those of his father and ordered his execution in Yarkand.[89] Preston Torbert comments, "We do not know under what particular statute Gao Pu was put to death, but merchants who later illicitly dealt in jade from Xinjiang received the severest punishment prescribed for theft—strangulation."[90] As a posthumous humiliation, his body was forbidden the customary return to his home for burial.[91]

CONCLUSION

The above discussion of three imperial jade objects in the Norton Museum of Art suggests that jade as a material was intimately bound to the Tibetan Buddhist faith, Confucian rituals, and the economic underpinnings of the Qing imperial court. The last of these, the jade *hu* with the inscription detailing the case of Gao Pu, has an additional inscription on the bottom reading *Qianlong fanggu* or "imitating antiquity in the Qianlong [reign]." Corruption was not the only result of the trade in jade. The arrival of large amounts of Central Asian jade in the workshops of Jiangnan, especially the city of Suzhou, also coincided with the emergence of a "new taste" for elaborately carved jades. This new taste was strongly criticized by the emperor, who deplored the vulgar expansion of the jade market and the new designs that brought a better price than more tasteful ones. He urged an aesthetic conservatism, and the inscription *Qianlong fanggu* on archaistic vessels is one indication of the emperor's aesthetic preferences.[92] In a perceptive exhibition and catalogue, Chang Lituan explored the persistence of the Qianlong emperor's aesthetic choices through the approximately 800 poems and essays he authored on the subject of jade or inscriptions he wrote for specific jade objects.[93] These document the emperor's evolving taste, which focused on the connoisseurship of ancient jade artifacts, the production of archaistic vessels and objects in jade, and the preference for carvings in a so-called "painterly style," which is exemplified by jade mountain landscapes (see fig. 7 above). The formal severity of the Norton *hu* fits securely within the self-declared Qianlong aesthetic. The vessel is almost insistently archaistic in its form, the walls are remarkably thick, the supports for the ring handles are simply—almost crudely—carved, and the surface includes small areas of the original, weathered skin of the block from which it was carved. Bearing the text that it does, it is a declaration of the emperor's victory in, at least, this outrageous instance of the unstoppable smuggling that was filling the jade market with designs and objects of unacceptable "new taste." The emperor, too, was the economic victor, since just the amount of fines levied in the case totaled over 270,000 taels of silver, which were paid into the Secret Accounts Bureau, the imperial treasury administered by the Imperial Household Department.[94]

The revival and recreation of ancient rites under the Qing dynasty produced lavish versions of ancient objects. Chimestones, which had formerly most often been cut from various hardstones other than jade,[95] were now manufactured from the enormous quantities of Xinjiang jade available to the court. The Qing imperial monopoly on Central Asian jade production was intended to guarantee the supply—and the income—from jade production for the imperial court, but the parallel production of large numbers of ritual and decorative jades in the court workshops and jades for the private market were supported by the unmatched output of jade mines in the mid- to late eighteenth century. The use of huge slabs of jade for individual chimestones for court ritual and celebration, in the context of the Qianlong reign, could not be seen as an outrageous extravagance.

The *Bowl with seven Buddhas* embodies the devotion to Tibetan Buddhism of the Manchu Qing imperial clan, translated into a Chinese medium that implied additional qualities of virtue—and value. The surface treatment of the bowl is telling. In contrast to the elaborate openwork and detailed carvings of the so-called "new style," which concealed the substance of the stone (and its flaws) under decorative elaboration, the bowl has the smooth but not glassy surface of the best eighteenth-century imperial jades. This treatment allows the nature of the stone to show clearly and gives a tactile sense of the material from which it is carved. Surely such refinement must reflect the emperor's knowledge of the many ancient jade objects in the imperial collection[96] and his desire to recreate their ancient qualities. ✦

NOTES

1 Nott, *Chinese Jades*, specimen no. 67, *An Alms Bowl or Shui-cheng*; specimen nos. 21, 22, *Te-ch'ing or Stone Chimes*; and specimen no. 78, *A Massive Ming Temple Vase*.

2 The relationship was a complex one, involving varying degrees of support and control over Tibetan, Mongol, and Chinese Buddhist institutions in pursuit of sometimes competing religious and political goals. See Farquhar, "Emperor as Bodhisattva."

3 Bartholomew, "*Thangkas*," pp. 170–71.

4 *Yuzhi wen erji* (Second collection of imperial writings), *juan* 30, Stele Inscriptions. For the text of the "Record" (*Qi Fo ta beiji*), see the *Siku quanshu*, reprint, vol. 1301, pp. 464–65.

5 See Shanghai Museum, *Zhongguo shuhuajia*, vol. 1, p. 242, nos. 1, 2; see also Contag and Wang, *Seals of Chinese Painters*, p. 588, no. 154.

6 See Watson, *Chinese Jade Books*, no. 4.

7 Hummel, *Eminent Chinese*, vol. 2, pp. 791–92.

8 Leidy and others, *Chinese Decorative Arts*, pp. 28–29 (MMA acc. no. 02.18.527).

9 Hummel, *Eminent Chinese*, vol. 1, p. 501.

10 Leidy and others, *Chinese Decorative Arts*, pp. 28–29.

11 Although Watson (*Chinese Jade Books*, no. 4) renders the word as "sutra," the Chinese *ji* (also pronounced *jie*) can mean a Buddhist hymn as well. In this context, "sayings" is probably more accurate, since the texts in question, which appear between the seven Buddha images, are short. They may, however, have been chanted or sung. The "Record," however, specifically uses the standard term *jing* to refer to sutras.

12 E'erdeni is the Chinese transcription of the name of the sixth Panchen Lama.

13 Translation after Watson, *Chinese Jade Books*, no. 4, with modifications.

14 In the Yuan dynasty the *guoshi* was the official in charge of the Commission for Buddhist and Tibetan Affairs which supervised Buddhist clergy in China and Tibet. See Hucker, *A Dictionary of Official Titles*, nos. 2654 and 3530.

15 On Zhangjia Hutuktu, see Bartholomew, "*Thangkas*," pp. 170–73. I am grateful to Dr. Bartholomew, e-mail message of October 8, 2002, for providing the identification of Rolpay Dorje and the reference to the alms bowl in the National Palace Museum, Taipei, which is discussed below.

16 In addition to Watson's rendering of the beginning and end of the "Record," a complete translation appears in Bishop, *Investigations and Studies*, vol. 2, no. 527 (pp. 173–74). Another complete but inaccurate translation appears in Nott, *Chinese Jades*, pp. 350–52, along with unreliable renderings of the texts between the Buddha images.

17 Watson, *Chinese Jade Books*, no. 4.

18 Tsai, *Monarchy and Its Buddhist Way*, cat. 85, giving the location of the stele. On the Five Dragon Pavilion, see the *Rixia jiuwen kao*, *juan* 28, reprint, vol. 2, p. 396.

19 I am grateful to Professor Susan Naquin, Princeton University, who discussed this possibility in a personal communication, October 2002. In the Chinese title *Qi Fo ta beiji* (see n. 4 above), the word *ta* can refer to a Tibetan stupa as well as a Chinese pagoda, and a number of small-scale stupa-shaped shrines remain in the Palace Museum, Beijing. See Palace Museum, *Qinggong Zangchuan*, cat. 119. See also Tsai, *Monarchy and Its Buddhist Way*, cats. 29, 30.

20 Juliano and Lerner, *Monks and Merchants*, cat. 48. The *Ekottaragama sutra* (Sutra of gradual sayings) was first translated into Chinese in the 4th century.

21 Matsubara, *Chinese Buddhist Sculpture*, vol. 2, no. 218(a).

22 Bishop, *Investigations and Studies*, vol. 2, no. 622, white jade, 2.72 × 5.62 inches; four-character seal script inscription (*Qianlong nian zhi*) on the bottom; (MMA acc. no. 02.18.622a,b).

23 Tsai, *Monarchy and Its Buddhist Way*, cat. 85.

24 On the sixth Panchen Lama's journey to China, see Naquin, *Peking*, pp. 473–74; see also Bartholomew, "*Thangkas*."

25 Naquin, *Peking*, p. 342.

26 See Bartholomew, "*Thangkas*," pp. 173–76.

27 See Wang Jiapeng, "Liushi Banchan de yifeng zoushu," which includes illustrations of the Chinese text of the memorial listing the Panchen Lama's gifts to the emperor. My thanks to Susan Naquin for bringing this article to my attention.

28 Modern publications describing the bells do not include the text of the inscription and date, and the author has not been able to locate an 18th-century citation of the find.
29 See Lang Xiuhua, "*Biyu teqing*," p. 250, for a brief note on the discovery.
30 *Rixia jiuwen kao*, *juan* 22, reprint, vol. 2, pp. 298–300, which identifies the bells as having been unearthed in Linjiang prefecture, Jiangxi.
31 Bartholomew and Clark, "Walters," p. 135, n. 28, citing Lang, "*Biyu teqing*." The present discussion of *qing* chimestones is indebted to Bartholomew and Clark's comprehensive survey.
32 See Evelyn Rawski's excellent summary of the role of Qing court music, "The Creation of an Emperor in Eighteenth-Century China," in Yung and others, eds., *Harmony and Counterpoint*, pp. 150–74. The present discussion here of Qing ritual music is indebted to Rawski's study.
33 See Wan Yi, "Qingdai gongting yinyue," pp. 8–9, for a summary of early Qing court ritual music. See also Rawski, "The Creation of an Emperor," p. 164.
34 Wan Yi, "Qingdai gongting yinyue," p. 8, citing the *Qingchao wenxian tongkao* (Qing [history of institutions and] critical examination of documents).
35 Rawski, "The Creation of an Emperor," p. 164.
36 On the compilation of the *Lülü zhengyi*, see Hummel, *Eminent Chinese*, vol. 1, pp. 285–86, the biography of He Guozong (Ho Kuo-tsung). The text, in 5 *juan*, was part of the *Lüli yuanyuan*, a compendium on the calendar, mathematics, and music.
37 *Lülü zhengyi, xiabian*, *juan* 2. See the *Siku quanshu*, reprint, vol. 215, pp. 175–79.
38 See So, *Music in the Age of Confucius*, esp. pp. 101–13.
39 The 120-*juan houbian* was printed in 1746, and 8 supplemental *juan* were added in 1789. See Hummel, *Eminent Chinese*, vol. 1, p. 24, the biography of Zhang Zhao (Chang Chao); and vol. 2, pp. 925–26, the biography of Yinlu.
40 Rawski, "The Creation of an Emperor," p. 165.
41 This and other classifications of court music are described in the *Da Qing huidian shili* (Statutes of the Qing dynasty), cited in Wan Yi, "Qingdai gongting yinyue," without a specific chapter or page reference. See also the *Qinding Da Qing huidian tu* (Imperially sanctioned illustrated statutes of the Great Qing), *juan* 36, cited in *Zhongguo yinyue wenwu daxi, Beijing juan*, cat. 10. Earlier dynasties used ritual music called *zhonghe* music, but the term *Zhonghe shaoyue* first appears in records of music in the Ming Hongwu reign (1368–98). See Rawski, "The Creation of an Emperor," pp. 165–66. It designates the musical scores played, the texts or lyrics sung at various rituals and ceremonies, and the ensemble of instruments and musicians who performed it.
42 For the *Book of Rites*, considered by tradition to have been edited by Confucius, see Nienhauser, *The Indiana Companion*, p. 313.
43 Legge, trans., *The Li Ki*, vol. XVII, p. 37 (book 12, paragraph 25; the transcription of Chinese names has been changed to *pinyin*). On the reliability of book 12, the "Mingtang wei," see vol. XVIII, pp. 28–30. For the Chinese text and extensive commentary, see the *Liji zhushu*, *juan* 31, pp. 22b–23a, in the *Siku quanshu*, reprint, vol. 116, p. 12.
44 *Huangchao liqi tushi*, *juan* 8; see the *Siku quanshu*, reprint, vol. 656, pp. 454–62. On this Qing imperial text, see Margaret Medley, *The "Illustrated Regulations for Ceremonial Paraphernalia of the Ch'ing Dynasty,"* cited in Dickinson and Wrigglesworth, *Imperial Wardrobe*, p. 29. Medley notes that the section on music quotes an imperial edict from 1760; presumably the 1759 date is that of the Qianlong emperor's preface.
45 The Song dynasty *Yueshu* (Book of music), in 200 *juan*, compiled by Chen Yang (act. late 11th century), contains earlier writings on music in its first half; in the second half it sets forth the meanings of music, musical instruments, and scores, thereby constituting a broad-ranging, illustrated discussion of music. See the *Siku quanshu*, reprint, vol. 211, pp. 23–949.
46 *Huangchao liqi tushi*, *juan* 8, p. 31b, *Siku quanshu*, reprint, vol. 656, p. 454. Unless otherwise noted, all translations are my own.
47 Although the *teqing* were suspended individually, there were four racks presumably scaled to the sizes of the stones. Stones 1–3 hung on one rack, 4–6 on another, and 7–9 and 10–12 on their own racks. See *Lülü zhengyi houbian*, *juan* 62, pp. 22a–30a; see the *Siku quanshu*, reprint, vol. 217, pp. 12–16.
48 See, for example, Wan Yi and others, *Qingdai gongting shenghuo*, no. 42.
49 A *qing* could be struck with two levels of force. See Legge, trans., *The Shoo King*, p. 87, the text of book IV, chapter ii, paragraph 9: "K'wei said, 'When the sounding-stone is tapped or strongly struck....'"
50 The *Teqing ming* (Inscription for individual chimestones) appears in the *Yuzhi wen chuji*, *juan* 27, containing *ming* or "inscriptions," pp.12a b. See the *Yuzhi wen chuji*, reprint, vol. 10, p. 542.

51 See Legge, trans., *The Works of Mencius*, p. 372, book V, paragraph 6, rendering the sentence: "A complete concert is when the *large* bell proclaims the *commencement of the music*, and the ringing stone proclaims its close" (italics in the original translation).
52 Wan Yi and others, *Qingdai gongting shenghuo*, nos. 41 (bells), 42 (chimestones).
53 The note was inserted in an 18th-century imperial publication of the *Teqing ming*; see note 50, above.
54 Bartholomew and Clark, "Walters," p. 136, n. 29, citing Lang, "*Biyu teqing*."
55 *Zhongguo yinyue wenwu daxi, Beijing juan*, cat. 10; *Imperial Tombs of China*, p. 154.
56 *Zhongguo yinyue wenwu daxi, Beijing juan*, cat. 11, a stone in the National History Museum; and *Zhongguo yinyue wenwu daxi, Hubei juan*, cat. 7.
57 Bartholomew and Clark, "Walters," pp. 136–37, n. 35 (the Norton chimestones), and Table 1.
58 Two of the number four stones are part of the complete sets in the Forbidden City and the Shenyang Palace Museum; there is an isolated number four stone in the Hubei Provincial Museum; the fourth was sold at Sotheby's Hong Kong, November 24–25, 1981, lot 413. For this last, see Bartholomew and Clark, "Walters," n. 37. There is a slight chance that the Hubei stone is the one sold at Sotheby's—and possibly the same number four stone discussed below. Four other *teqing*—all numbered eleven—are parts of the Forbidden City and Shenyang Palace Museum sets or in the Asian Art Museum (San Francisco) and the Wuhan Cultural Products Store, confirming a minimum of four different sets, all dated 1761.
59 Norton Museum of Art Registrar's files, letter dated April 7, 1967. Caro had a long-standing relationship with the Norton, and it was through him that the 1950 C.T. Loo exhibition of Chinese archaic jades came to the Museum. See Jenny F. So's essay in this catalogue on R.H. Norton's jade purchases, which form the bulk of the Museum's holdings. C.T. Loo was also the source, in 1953, of most of the Museum's bronzes.
60 Norton Museum of Art Registrar's files, undated letter, probably late 1960s.
61 This may possibly be the number four stone offered at Sotheby's Hong Kong in 1981. See previous note.
62 Norton Museum of Art Registrar's files, letter dated June 29, 1967.
63 *The Chinese Collections*, cats. 226, 227. Jayne was possibly thinking of the reference to chimestones and matching individual bells in the Confucius Temple, described by Kaufman, *Musical References*, p. 82. (See Bartholomew and Clark, "Walters," p. 134 and n. 19.) Unfortunately, few of Jayne's research notes are preserved in the Museum's files.
64 Hevia, "Looting Beijing," in Liu, *Tokens of Exchange*, p. 199 and n. 34, citing *The Celestial Empire*, November 19, 1900, p. 617. The newspaper, published in Shanghai, ceased publication with the September 28, 1929, issue.
65 The *Huangchao liqi tushi* identifies these altars as the Altar of Heaven (Tian Tan), the Hall for Prayers for Good Harvest (Qinian Tang, part of the Altar of Heaven), and the Altar of the Heavenly Spirit (Tianshen Tan, unidentified); see note 44 above. See also Naquin, *Peking*, map 11.1, Qing Peking. The Altar of Heaven is unlabeled at the bottom, right of center. (The Confucius Temple is just inside the north wall of the Inner City.)
66 Legge, trans., *The Shoo King*, p. 87, note to chapter ii (see note 49, above; spelling, quotation marks, and italics as in the original).
67 The "Huiyu xing" appears in the *Yuzhi shi siji, juan* 55, pp. 7a–9a, reprint, vol. 7, pp. 151–52.
68 See, for example, the *Gujin tushu jicheng, fangyu huibian, bianyidian, juan* 55, *Hedian bu huikao* (Synthesis of books and illustrations of ancient and modern times, geography of the world, borders and frontiers, chapter 55, investigation of Khotan), reprint, vol. 213, pp. 36–42. See also Jenny F. So's essay in this volume, pp. 17–18.
69 Millward, *Beyond the Pass*, p. 181 and n. 59, citing Qishiyi (Chunyuan), *Xiyu wenjian lu* (Record of things seen heard and seen in the Western regions), 1777, *juan* 2:29b–30b. The discussion of jade production in Central Asia and the case of Gao Pu is indebted to James Millward's *Beyond the Pass* and Preston Torbert's *The Ch'ing Imperial Household Department*.
70 The subject is not unique. See Millward, *Beyond the Pass*, fig. 6, p. 181, for another carving of Muslims gathering jade.
71 The distinction among jades appears in the "Huiyu xing" and elsewhere.
72 The commentaries are inserted in the text of the "Huiyu xing" in the *Yuzhi shi siji, juan* 55, pp. 7a–9a. See note 67 above.
73 See the discussion p. 65 above, and notes 50, 53.
74 The text of the "Huiyu xing" reads "*shi zhuocheng da yu weng*." *Weng*, urn or jar, is not the usual title for such jades, which are usually called *hu*. Neither singular or plural is specified, nor a specific "urn." See note 72 above.

75 The suffix *Da Chen*, Grand Minister, is added to the titles of imperial princes and other senior officials serving the Neiwufu or Imperial Household Department. See Hucker, *A Dictionary of Official Titles*, no. 5888. Here the title is modified by *ju bi* or "resident in another place," that is, deputed to the region. See the following note.

76 The title is *zhucha Ye'erjiang dachen*. Ye'erjiang is Yarkand, and *zhucha* indicates an official "detached at" or assigned to a specific place. See Hucker, *A Dictionary of Official Titles*, no. 1358.

77 *Neidi*, that is, China proper as opposed to the Central Asian frontier of Xinjiang.

78 4,000 catties is approximately 2,000 kilos or about 4,400 pounds.

79 Gao Pu's biography appears in the entry on Gao Bin (Kao Pin) in Hummel, *Eminent Chinese*, vol. 1, pp. 412–13. See also Torbert, "The Case of Kao P'u [Gao Pu]," in *The Ch'ing Imperial Household Department*, pp. 136–71. And see Millward, *Beyond the Pass*, especially pp. 185–91.

80 *Baoyi* or "bondservant" is the Chinese transliteration of a Manchu word meaning enslaved prisoner of war or simply slave. Manchu and Chinese bondservant families served the emperor or imperial princes, first in menial tasks but often in important and sensitive posts in the government. Administered by the Imperial Household Department, their attachment through personal, hereditary bondage to the emperor ostensibly made such officials more loyal than other officials to the Manchu Qing dynasty. See Hucker, *A Dictionary of Official Titles*, no. 4482. See also Spence, *Ts'ao Yin and the K'ang-hsi Emperor*, esp. pp. 2–18. Spence comments (pp. 17–18): "The bondservants worked for the emperor only; just because they were his servants, he protected them and appointed them to lucrative office, so that at some indeterminate point servility became prestige."

81 Legally freed from *baoyi* status, his appointment to official position had to come through other channels. On the *yin* privilege, see Hucker, *A Dictionary of Official Titles*, no. 7971.

82 It is extremely difficult to give even a rough equivalent for the monetary value of a tael, or Chinese ounce, of silver, but the amount in question is huge.

83 Torbert, *The Ch'ing Imperial Household*, pp. 136–39. Torbert's research is based in large part on the *Da Qing lichao shilu* (*Ta-Ch'ing li-ch'ao shih-lu*) or "Veritable Records of the Qing Dynasty," which provide exhaustive accounts of the activities of the emperor and the government. On these texts, see Wilkinson, *Chinese History*, ch. 50.4. On the return to *baoyi* status, see Torbert, *The Ch'ing Imperial Household*, p. 139, n. 39, citing the *Shiliao xunkan* (*Shih-liao hsün-k'an*, Journal of historical materials), published in Beijing, 1930–31.

84 Torbert, *The Ch'ing Imperial Household*, pp. 149–50, 153.

85 Millward, *Beyond the Pass*, pp. 184–85, 190–91. The author notes that jade was one of the few regional products with intrinsic value.

86 On the administrative changes in Ush and Yarkand, see Torbert, *The Ch'ing Imperial Household*, pp. 156–59.

87 Setiba'erdi is the transliteration of his name in Chinese characters.

88 On the revolt in Ush, see Millward, *Beyond the Pass*, pp. 124–25.

89 For Gao Pu's arrest and execution, see Torbert, *The Ch'ing Imperial Household*, pp. 158–63.

90 Ibid., p. 163, n. 69.

91 Watson, *Chinese Jade Books*, p. 14, n. 2, citing Sugimura Yūzō, *Kenryū Kōtei* (The Emperor Ch'ien Lung) (Tokyo: Nigensha, 1961), pp. 207–8.

92 Millward, *Beyond the Pass*, pp. 186–87 and n. 74, citing Yang Boda, "Jade: Emperor Ch'ien Lung's Collection in the Palace Museum, Peking," *Arts of Asia* (March–April 1992), pp. 84, 86.

93 Chang Li-tuan, *Gongting zhi ya*, National Palace Museum, 1977.

94 Torbert, *The Ch'ing Imperial Household*, pp. 190–91.

95 See the *Lülü zhengyi houbian*, *juan* 62, p. 51a, where *bianqing*, the sets of sixteen chimestones, may be made of jade or *lingbi* stone, which is also famous for its musical resonance. See the *Siku quanshu*, reprint, vol. 217, p. 26

96 Evidence of the Qianlong emperor's close attention to ancient jades is his many poems and other writings on the subject—published in the collections of imperial poems and writings, written on the elaborate boxes or decorative stands for jades, and in many cases engraved on the jades themselves. For just two of many examples of ancient jades with Qianlong inscriptions, see Fong and Watt, *Possessing the Past*, pls. 5, 36. Chang Li-tuan, National Palace Museum, Taipei, kindly provided the author with an exhaustive list (unpublished) of Qianlong poems, writings, and inscriptions on ancient and contemporary objects that includes texts from almost every year of his sixty-year reign.

CATALOGUE

1 RITUAL WINE-POURING VESSEL *(GUANG)*

Shang dynasty, Anyang period, ca. 12th–11th century BCE
Bronze, 7 1/4 × 8 × 4 13/16 in. (18.4 × 20.3 × 12.2 cm)
Gift of R.H. Norton, 52.7

Identifiable animals, fantastic beasts, and zoomorphic forms animate the entire surface of this *guang*, a wine-pouring vessel. The grinning face and bottle-shaped horns at the front of the lid belong to a dragonlike creature whose body drapes downward onto the vessel below, its forelegs appearing just under the spout and hind legs with talons reaching down to the vessel's foot. The face of a tiger, peering out over the handle with ears pricked up, forms the back end of the lid. Both main motifs share the lid with two boldly striped, crouching tigers (not visible in this photograph) and small, snakelike dragons. The various compartments of the vessel's sides are filled as well with dragons of various sizes, most reduced to heads with characteristic bottle-shaped horns and schematic bodies, while miniature elephants with raised trunks appear on the foot, just behind the small, arched openings on each side of the *guang*. And from the base of the handle—itself an improbable combination of two different animals—a tiny bear dangles by its jaws and front paws. Undecorated horizontal bands between the ranges of design and raised vertical flanges give a certain stability to the highly animated surface, and fine spirals of *leiwen*, or "lightning pattern" squared spirals, fill what little space remains.

Both Max Loehr[1] and Robert Bagley[2] have discussed the evolution of the *guang*. Developed by the bronze casters of the Anyang period in the thirteenth century BCE,[3] it has no apparent pottery prototype and appears to be a hybrid of other animal-shaped bronzes and gourd-shaped vessels. A *guang* in the Arthur M. Sackler Museum, Harvard University, represents an early version of this extraordinary form.[4] The lid of that vessel has the head of a tiger at the front, with the tiger's body extending down the entire front half of the vessel, while the back half of both lid and body take the form of an owl. As the *guang* developed through the Anyang period, it kept its uniquely asymmetrical shape but fell more in line with the decoration of other vessels, where ornament was confined to compartments divided by plain horizontal bands and raised vertical flanges.

The Norton *guang* incorporates the full range of Shang bronze casting vocabulary. Animal forms covering the vessel contrast with the structure of horizontal bands and raised flanges. Animals combine various features, transforming real creatures into fantastic beasts. In addition to the dragon on the front, the owl at the back of earlier forms of the vessel persists here as a tiger's head, but retains an owl's square beak below its snout (the beak projects over the handle). The raised ears of the tiger also recall owls' "ears." A late addition to the repertoire of ritual bronze vessels, the *guang* underwent a relatively swift evolution to the exaggerated forms of early Zhou examples. The Museum's vessel exhibits a superb balance between earlier forms and later vessels, epitomizing the best of Shang bronze casting.

PUBLISHED

Umehara, *Inkyo*, pl. 110; Loehr, *Ritual Vessels*, no. 34; Munsterberg, *Art of the Far East*, p. 24; Jayne, *The Chinese Collections*, no. 9; Bagley, *Shang Ritual Bronzes*, p. 415, fig. 73.4 (after Loehr, *Ritual Vessels*, no. 34)

NOTES

1 Loehr, *Ritual Vessels*, no. 34.
2 Bagley, *Shang Ritual Bronzes*, no. 73; see also pp. 31–32.
3 Ibid., p. 25; see also figs. 150, 63.2
4 For a discussion of the evolution of the *guang* form, see Colin Mackenzie's essay in this catalogue, p. 40, and n. 32; for the Sackler *guang*, see Mizuno, *Bronzes and Jades of Ancient China*, pl. 54.

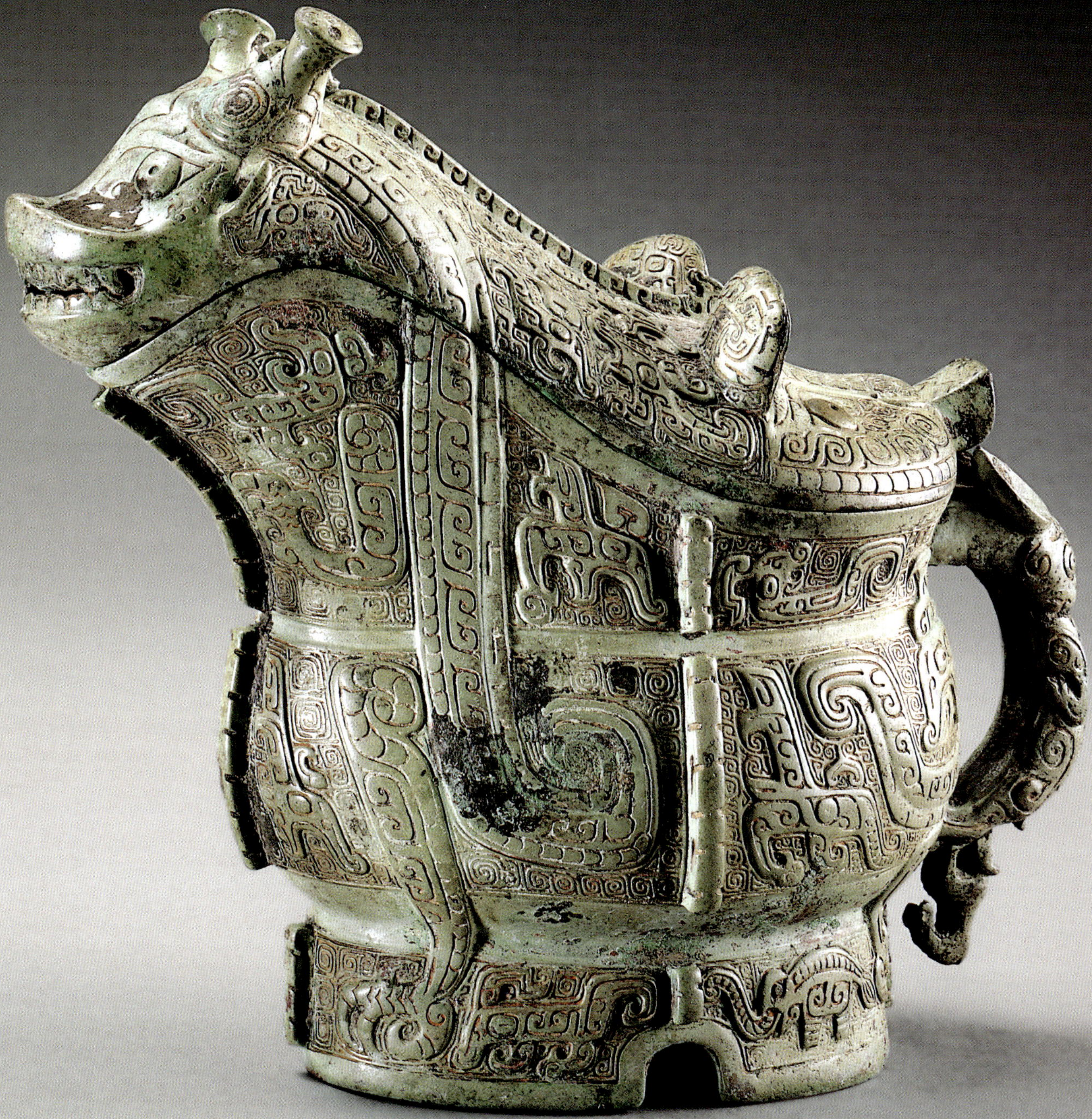

2 RITUAL WINE VESSEL (*HU*)

Shang dynasty, Anyang period, ca. 13th century BCE
Bronze, 15 ½ × greatest diam. 11 in. (39.4 × 27.9 cm)
Gift of R.H. Norton, 52.6

The large size, elegant silhouette, and refined decoration of this *hu*, or ritual wine-storage vessel, make it an extraordinary example of Shang dynasty bronze casting. Deep, undecorated grooves divide horizontal fields of animals and zoomorphic masks called *taotie*;[1] the alternation of narrower and wider fields of animal motifs establishes a dynamic rhythm to the decoration. Narrow vertical flanges divide the surface into right and left halves, and lug handles mark the sides of the vessel. The eyes, as always in Shang bronze decoration, help to focus the viewer's attention on the animal and mask imagery.[2] In the broadest field of decoration around the belly, for example, we see a central raised flange and the large, round staring eyes to the left and right. Above the eyes are S-shaped horns, and below them a snout and open mouth. To the left and right the body of the animal, seemingly split in two, wraps around the sides of the *hu* and ends in raised, spiraling tails. A similar mask with a bifurcated body fills most of the field between the handles, centered, again, on a narrow flange. The top band of this field is filled with a row of birds, four on each side of the vessel. Difficult to make out, they are identified by their oval eyes and squared-off beaks.

The narrower fields of decoration are even more complex. The topmost ring is filled with four dragons whose heads turn back from the central flange and look up toward the rim. The narrow belt around the waist is filled with small dragons whose bodies are formed of flat lines and tiny spirals that are difficult to distinguish from the background design. Finally, the wide foot, which is much corroded, is covered with animals whose bodies are a mass of spirals. A *hu* in the Royal Ontario Museum, Toronto, is close in size and decoration to the Norton bronze.[3] Both vessels have the same inscription on the inside bottom: a rectangle surrounded by four hands, traditionally read as the character *xing*, perhaps the name of a tribe or small state contemporary with Shang.[4]

The narrow flanges, the eyes of the animals and the *taotie* masks, and the two lug handles are the only elements that protrude above the surface. The vertical flanges provide a central focus for the designs, the handles highlight the smoothness of the rest of the design, and the flattened oval form of the *hu* (it is not round, as it may appear in photographs) gives the design a broader field, enhancing the vessel's imposing silhouette, which would have been completed by a dome-shaped lid with a round or pointed knob at the top, as on the Norton's Shang ceramic *hu* (cat. 55).

PUBLISHED

Loo, *Exhibition of Chinese Arts* (1941), no. 43; Jayne, *The Chinese Collections*, no. 2

NOTES

1 The term *taotie*, used to describe the mask-like decoration on bronzes is useful but problematic. It appears in this usage in the *Lü Shi Chunqiu*, the Spring and Autumn Annals of Lü [Buwei] (d. 235 BCE), almost a millennium after the end of the Shang dynasty. Scholars do not know what the Shang called this image, and its meaning is the subject of much speculation.

2 The eyes of Shang animals—real and imaginary—often take the form of a smooth, raised circle with a dot for the center. Around this is drawn a stylized eye with pointed corners. One corner, which turns sharply down, indicates the center of the face or the direction in which an eye in profile is looking.

3 Royal Ontario Museum, *Chinese Art*, cat. 53. See also Royal Ontario Museum, *Homage to Heaven*, cat. 43, and Colin Mackenzie's discussion in this catalogue of a *hu* from Xiaotun tomb YM238, pp. 41–42 and fig. 9.

4 See Bagley, *Shang Ritual Bronzes*, no. 7, p. 165, for vessels with the same inscription; see Royal Ontario Museum, *Chinese Art*, cat. 53, for the probable reading.

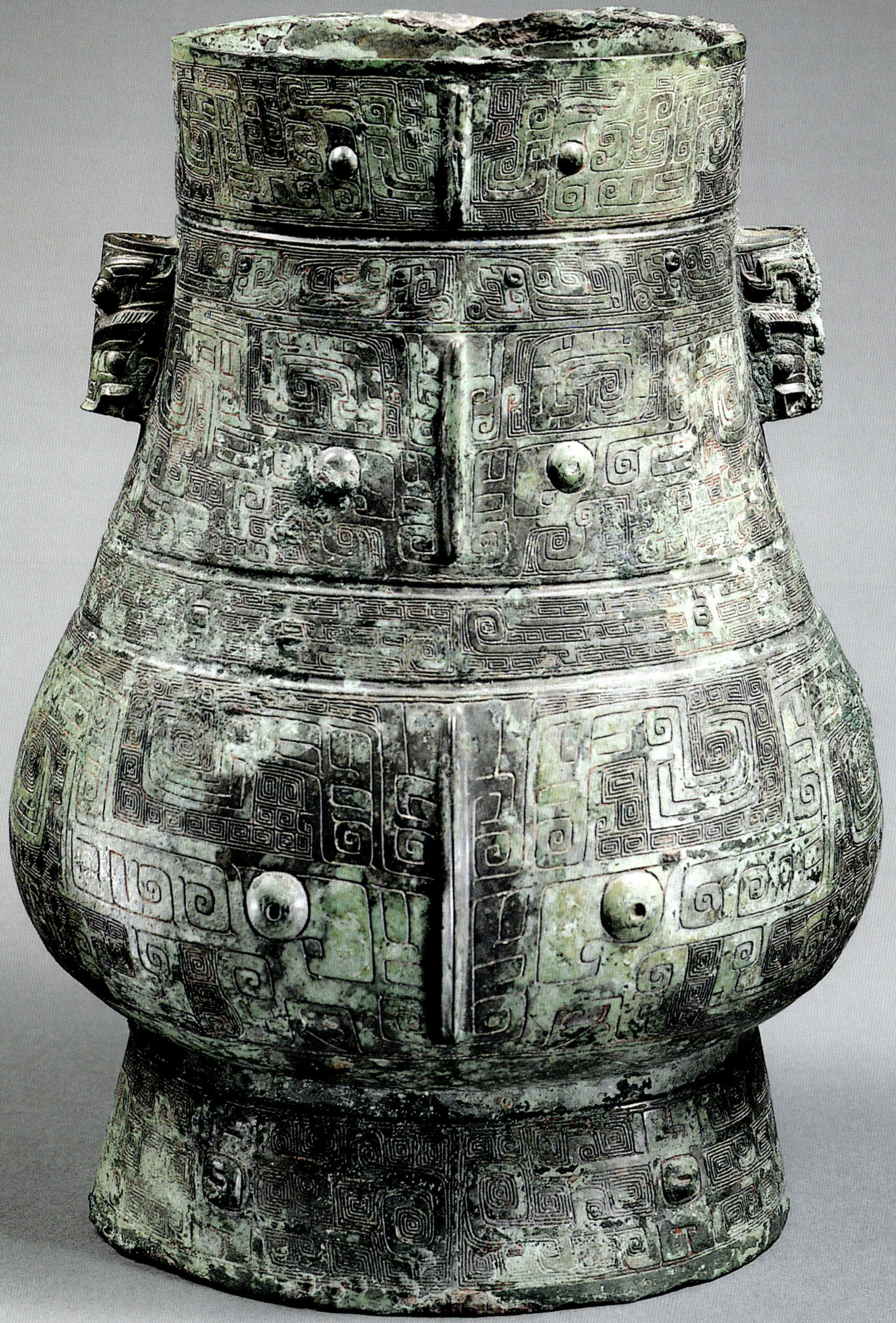

3 **RITUAL WINE BEAKER** (*GU*)

Shang dynasty, ca. 14th–13th century BCE
Bronze, 6 5/8 × mouth diam. 4 1/2 in. (16.8 × 11.4 cm)
Purchase, the R.H. Norton Trust, 69.15

4 **RITUAL WINE BEAKER** (*GU*)

Shang dynasty, Anyang period, ca. 12th–11th century BCE
Bronze, 11 11/16 × mouth diam. 6 7/8 in. (29.7 × 17.5 cm)
Purchase, the R.H. Norton Trust, 62.1

Both Norton wine beakers exhibit the basic form of all *gu*: a wide, trumpet-shaped mouth; narrow, banded waist; and flaring foot. The decoration on the shorter Norton *gu* (the earliest bronze in the collection) consists of two bands, bordered above and below by lines of small circles, a decoration typical of early *gu*. The remaining decoration consists almost completely of dense, spiraling lines, and only the round, raised eyes and the outlines around them are readily identifiable. The design on the foot seems to represent four separate animals, while around the waist two halves of the masklike *taotie* are centered on an undecorated vertical strip that forms the nose. Parts of the design represent the nostrils, lower jaw, and a schematic body wrapping around the sides of the vessel, but all these features are completely subordinated to the dense massing of tight spirals.

The taller *gu* shows the refinement in silhouette and decoration of this vessel toward the end of the Shang dynasty. The design consists of *taotie* in which the elements of the face appear to be scattered on a densely patterned background. In the succeeding Western Zhou dynasty this process would continue until the features and limbs of *taotie* and other animals became seemingly independent, abstract motifs. Still, the features here form coherent faces on the flaring foot and on the band around the waist. The vertical flange forms the nose between two staring eyes. Spirals below the eyes outline the snout and jaw, and there are C-shaped eyebrows and spiraling or curving horns above the faces. On the mouth of the vessel are pointed, bladelike panels decorated with inverted *taotie* whose eyes and eyebrows are easily located. On all of the raised elements there are designs of spirals, dots, parallel lines, and even shallow-relief copies of the raised flanges.

The earlier *gu* (left) has one very unusual feature—a single-stroke mark or inscription on the underside of the foot. As Colin Mackenzie notes in his essay in this volume (see page 39, fig. 6), pre-Anyang inscriptions are very rare, and this is one of the few that can be reliably dated to an earlier period. Interestingly, the same type of mark (a vertical line with one wider, rounded end) appears on a late Anyang period *gu* that is remarkably similar to the Museum's own later vessel (right).[1] Anyang bronze casters took the sturdy form of the *gu* and developed it into a slender, highly sophisticated wine cup that still retained the essential form of the earlier vessels. In the evolution of Shang bronze decoration, the two Norton *gu* clearly illustrate an early, robust style and its very late, highly evolved descendant.

PUBLISHED

3: Parke-Bernet, *The Richard Bryant Hobart Collection*, lot. 38; Jayne, *The Chinese Collections*, no. 1.
4: Jayne, *The Chinese Collections*, no. 10

NOTE

1 Li Ji and Wan Jiabao, *Yinxu chutu qingtong gu xing qi*, pl. XXIII. They suggest no reading for the mark or character.

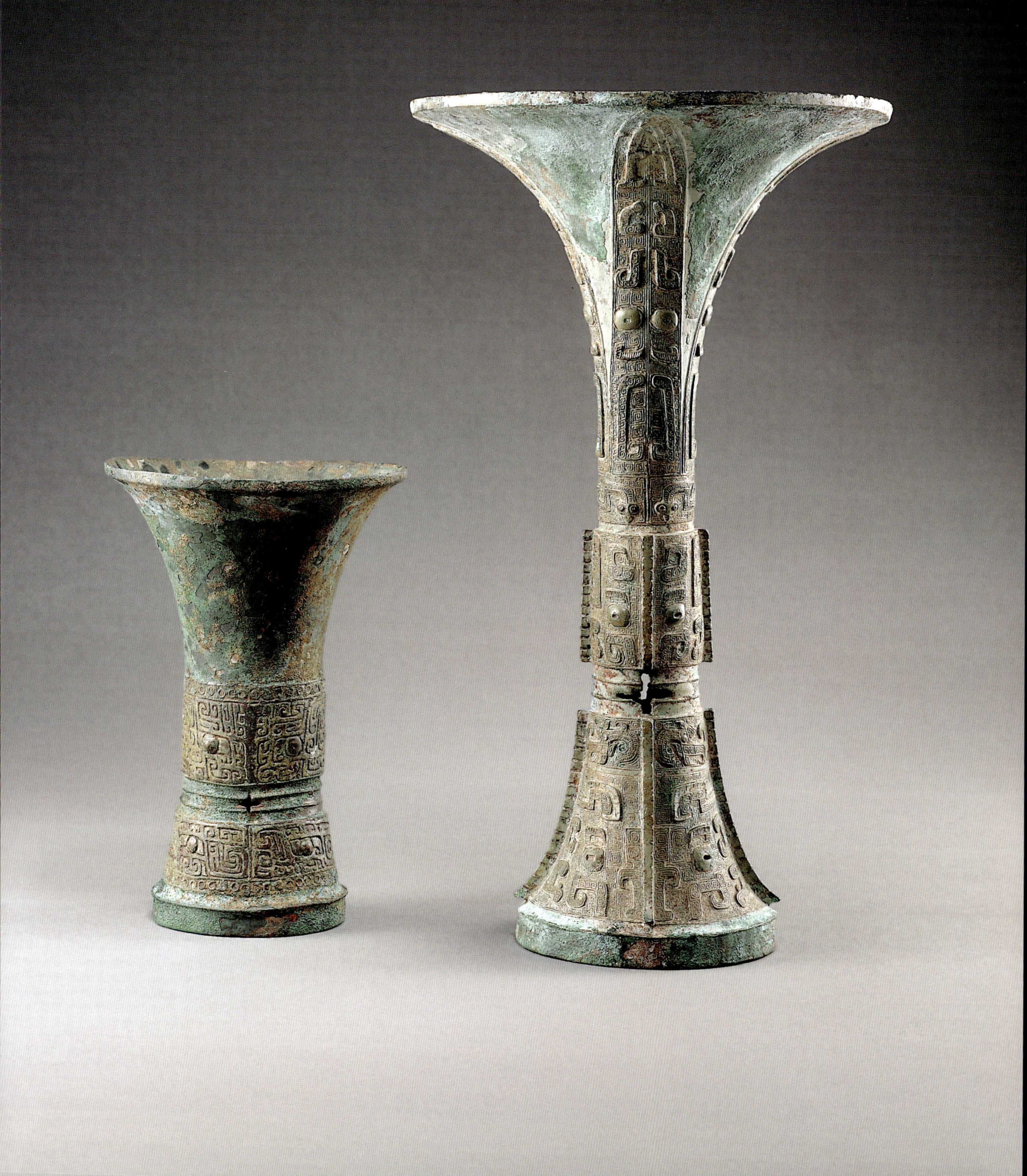

5 TRIPOD RITUAL FOOD VESSEL (*DING*)

Shang dynasty, Anyang period, ca. 12th century BCE
Bronze, 9 7/8 × diam. 7 1/2 in. (25.1 × 19.1 cm)
Gift of R.H. Norton, 52.3

A *ding* is a food vessel, probably used to cook and serve meat or grain. Derived from pottery prototypes, a *ding* has three legs, which would hold the bowl steady over a fire, and two large handles that would make it easy to lift. The earliest bronze *ding* have conical legs open to the inside of the vessel, a feature directly related to their pottery ancestors. Later vessels, like this one, have more architectural, solid or solid-appearing legs. The decoration on this *ding* fills two ranges, both of which are divided into six compartments by raised flanges. The narrow upper band consists of long-tailed dragons, face-to-face and tail-to-tail around the top of the vessel. The dragons have open mouths, pointed horns, and long thin bodies that end in curled tails. The body of the vessel is decorated with three large *taotie* masks, each of which is centered over the space between the legs. The face and small bodies of the *taotie* are organized around large, staring eyes, above which are broad, curving horns. The nose is partly formed by the raised flange that divides each face in half. At the bottom we can see the nostrils and the open, hooklike jaws. There is a pointed ear behind each eye, and diminutive bodies with raised, spiraling tails and short legs fill the rest of the space in each panel. Like the design on the Norton's *hu* (cat. 2), two bodies share one large, central face. The elements of the design are raised in high relief above the background, which is filled with a dense pattern of spiraling *leiwen*. This is a bold version of the same style that appears on the Museum's *guang* (cat. 1). The bronze foundries of Anyang developed this particular style approximately 1200 BCE,[1] and the presence of long-tailed dragons on the upper band of decoration helps to date the vessel to the somewhat later in the twelfth century BCE.

An inscription on the inside of the vessel consists of two graphs. One, formed by two figures kneeling on either side of a ritual vessel or small sacrificial altar, is partially visible in the photograph, near the center of the back wall. The other graph, below the kneeling figures, is a rectangle with horizontal lines extending from the sides. The combination of the two, which has been only tentatively identified as a name or clan sign, appears on a large number of bronzes. Although other graphs sometimes appear between them, the figures with the ritual vessel and the rectangle always appear together.[2]

PUBLISHED

Karlgren, "Marginalia," p. 299, and pl. 16; Barnard, *Bronze Casting*, p. 262; Jayne, *The Chinese Collections*, no. 6

NOTES

1 Bagley, *Shang Ritual Bronzes*, p. 28.
2 Ibid., no. 88, pp. 473–75.

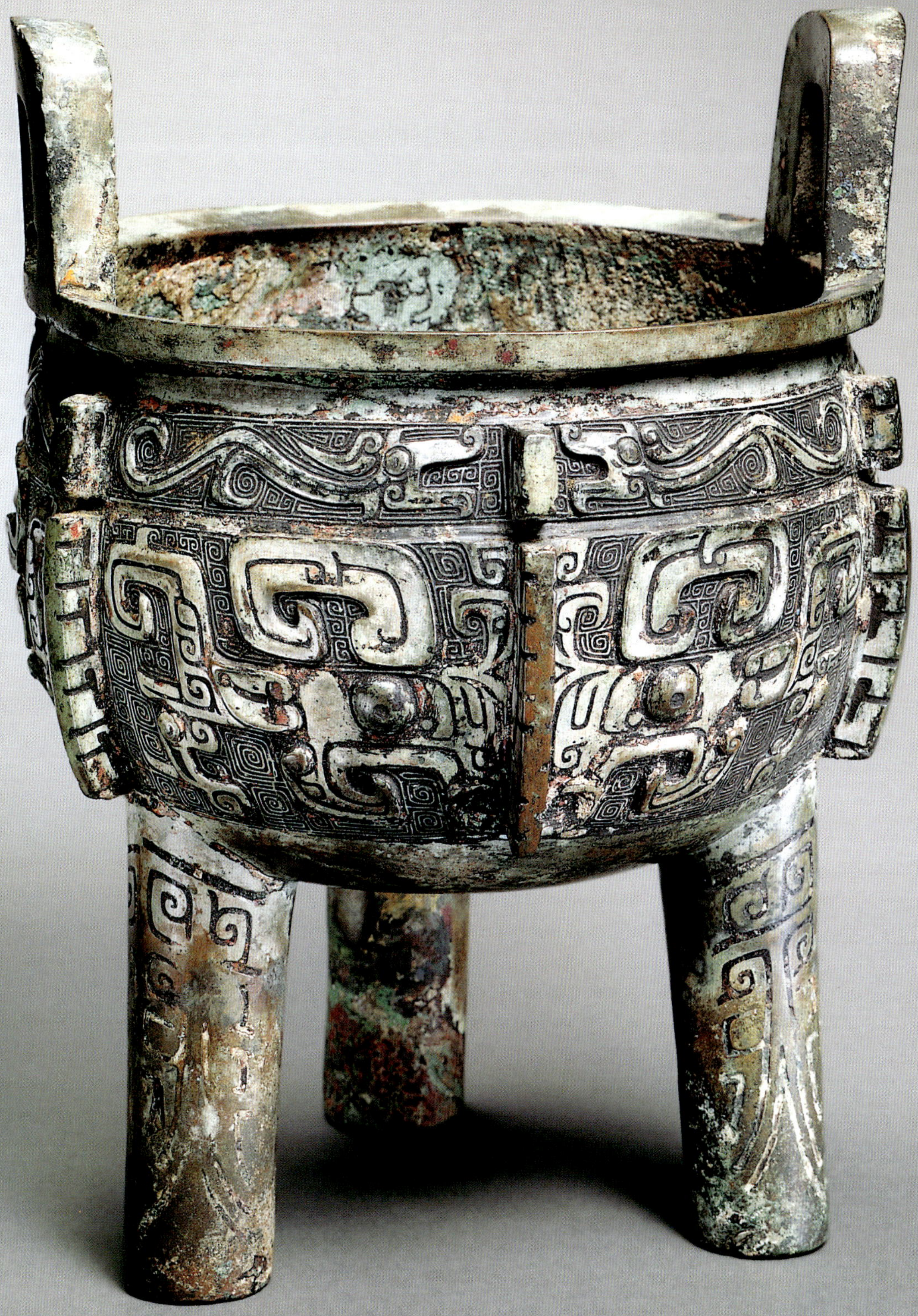

6 LOBED DING

Late Shang–early Western Zhou dynasty, ca. 12th–11th century BCE
Bronze, 9 1/4 × diam. 7 1/2 in. (23.5 × 19.1 cm)
Gift of R.H. Norton, 52.1

A tripod vessel for holding or cooking food, this *ding* has three large lobes decorated with staring *taotie* masks, each appearing to be biting the leg below it. The eyes and snouts of the masks stand out in high relief while other elements of the design are raised only slightly above the surface. The band below the rim is filled with a line of small dragons arrayed face-to-face and tail-to-tail. Most of the design consists of short, hooked spirals, with only the eyes standing out in relief from the surface. Where these dragons meet head on—above the center of the lobes and above the spaces between the lobes—their faces are joined in an ambiguous image that can be read as two animals in profile or one face sharing two bodies. (A version of the same design appears on the *hu*, cat. 2.) All of the design here is subtly modeled, and the elements in relief show superb control of the curving, undulating surfaces and an ability to render them in a strikingly rich manner. Even the tight spirals that fill the background spring from the relief elements, uniting the entire surface in one animated whole.

The lobed *ding* vessel form was popular in the late Shang and early Western Zhou dynasties.[1] Most published examples, however, do not have the extra band of *taotie* under the rim that enhances the decorative richness of this vessel. The lobed *ding* is often referred to as a *liding* because its shape falls between the more emphatic shape of the three-lobed vessel called a *li* and the round *ding* (cat. 5).[2] What distinguishes the lobed from the round *ding* is the orientation of the decoration: on the round vessel the masks are centered between the legs, while on the lobed version they are centered over the legs. What links the two forms is the position of the inscription,[3] which almost inevitably appears on the inside wall of the vessel over the leg centered between the handles. That is, if one positions the vessel so that the inscription is visible on the inside of the "back" wall, one is facing the side with two legs. As a result, on a round *ding* a single *taotie* mask stares from the center of the vessel toward the viewer, while on the lobed *ding* two masks face obliquely left and right, lessening, perhaps, the dramatic impact. The side with the single, centered leg was apparently considered the back of the *ding* in the Shang and Zhou dynasties. Later conventions for viewing *ding* vessels, appearing in Han dynasty pictorial reliefs, put the centered leg on the front.[4] That orientation in the photograph here reveals more fully the remarkable artistry of the decoration.

PUBLISHED

Barnard, *Bronze Casting*, p. 279; Jayne, *The Chinese Collections*, no. 8

NOTES

1 See, for example, Bagley, *Shang Ritual Bronzes*, nos. 93, 94, 95, and esp. figs. 93.2–93.7.

2 See ibid., p. 481, for a discussion of the interrelation of these three types.

3 The Museum's *Lobed ding* has a three-graph inscription, which Jayne believed to be a later addition. It consists of a banner inside a rectangle with notched corners followed by the characters *Fu Ding* or "Father Ding," with the cyclical character *ding*, not the vessel name. The inscription has been aggressively cleaned, and the results of this treatment cast it in some doubt.

4 See, for example, Bagley, ed., *Ancient Sichuan*, fig. 17.

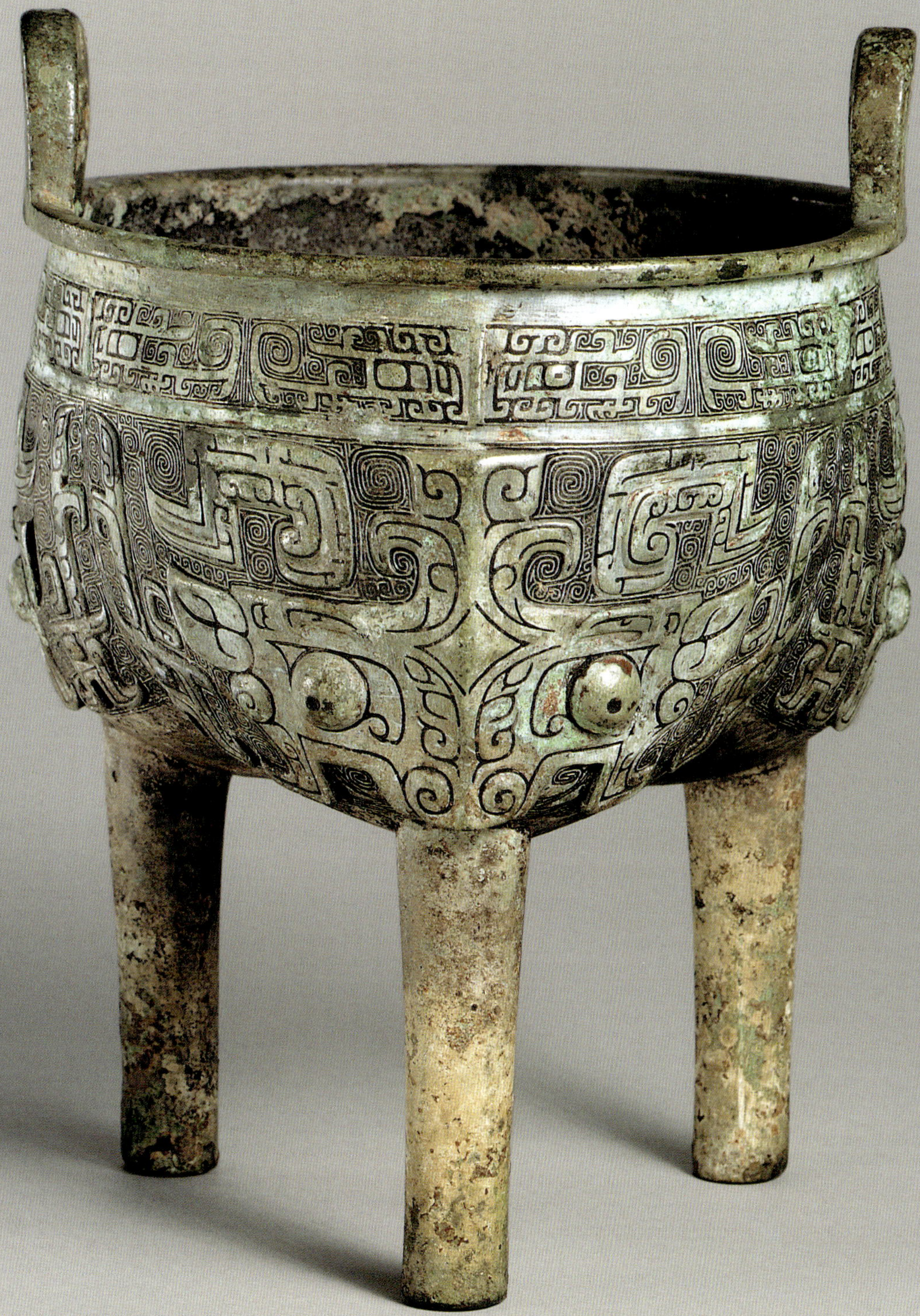

7 TRIPOD WINE VESSEL (*JUE*)

Shang dynasty, ca. 12th–11th century BCE
Bronze, 8 × 6 ½ × 3 ½ in. (20.3 × 16.5 × 8.9 cm)
Purchase, the R.H. Norton Trust, 62.2

8 TRIPOD WINE VESSEL (*JUE*)

Shang dynasty, ca. 12th–11th century BCE
Bronze, 8 ⅛ × 6 ⅞ × 3 ½ in. (20.6 × 17.5 × 8.9 cm)
Purchase, the R.H. Norton Trust, 62.4

Cast bronze ritual vessels first appear in China in the Erlitou culture of the Yellow River valley between approximately 2000 and 1500 BCE. Interestingly, among these earliest bronzes are the relatively complex wine vessels called *jue* and *jia* (cat. 9). Although the form evolves significantly over the centuries, all *jue* share the same basic elements: an oval cup supported on three legs; a loop handle; a long pouring spout on one side balanced by a pointed tail on the other; and a pair of posts rising from the rim. The earliest known *jue* were cast from multipart piece molds. It is likely that the tips of the posts, and perhaps the handles as well, were cast first, then mounted in the mold for the body and captured in the final bronze pouring.[1] The sophistication of technique seen in the earliest well-documented vessels suggests that bronze casting began at an even earlier date.[2]

The two Norton *jue* are similar in form and decoration, but there are important differences. The decoration on cat. 7 (left) consists of animals standing nose-to-nose across a narrow flange on the back of the cup, their bodies wrapping around the vessel but separated on the front by the handle. The eyes are clearly visible, but the horns, mouths, legs, and bodies are filled in with small spirals that are indistinguishable from the background pattern. The decoration of cat. 8 (right) also consists of facing animals separated by a notched flange and the handle. The style of the decoration here is closely related to that on a late Shang *gu* (cat. 4). The elements of the faces are similarly independent, and there are similar bladelike motifs and notched flanges reaching up under the spreading spout and tail. On both *jue*, the handle is anchored by a horned animal head, and each has an undeciphered inscription in the space behind the handle, the usual location for inscriptions on *jue*.

The form of the *jue* vessel is complex, and the lack of symmetry is relatively unusual among ritual bronzes. Unlike other tripod food and wine vessels, the three legs of the *jue* are not evenly spaced around the bottom; instead, the two legs opposite the handle are a little closer together and a little more vertical. To balance the handle visually as well to support its weight, the leg under it is slightly longer and sticks out at more of an angle. The artistic qualities of a *jue* are embodied in this dynamic balance as well as in its surface decoration, and these two *jue* are fine examples of this surprisingly intricate vessel type.

PUBLISHED

7: Jayne, *The Chinese Collections*, no. 4
8: Jayne, *The Chinese Collections*, no. 5

NOTES

1 Chase and others, *Ancient Chinese Bronze Art*, p. 31, n. 32, citing a 1990 symposium paper by Noel Barnard, "Thoughts on the Emergence of Metallurgy in Pre-Shang and Early Shang China," p. 27.
2 On the *jue* see Childs-Johnson, "The *Jue*-Vessel and Its Ritual Use in the Ancestor Cult of Shang China."

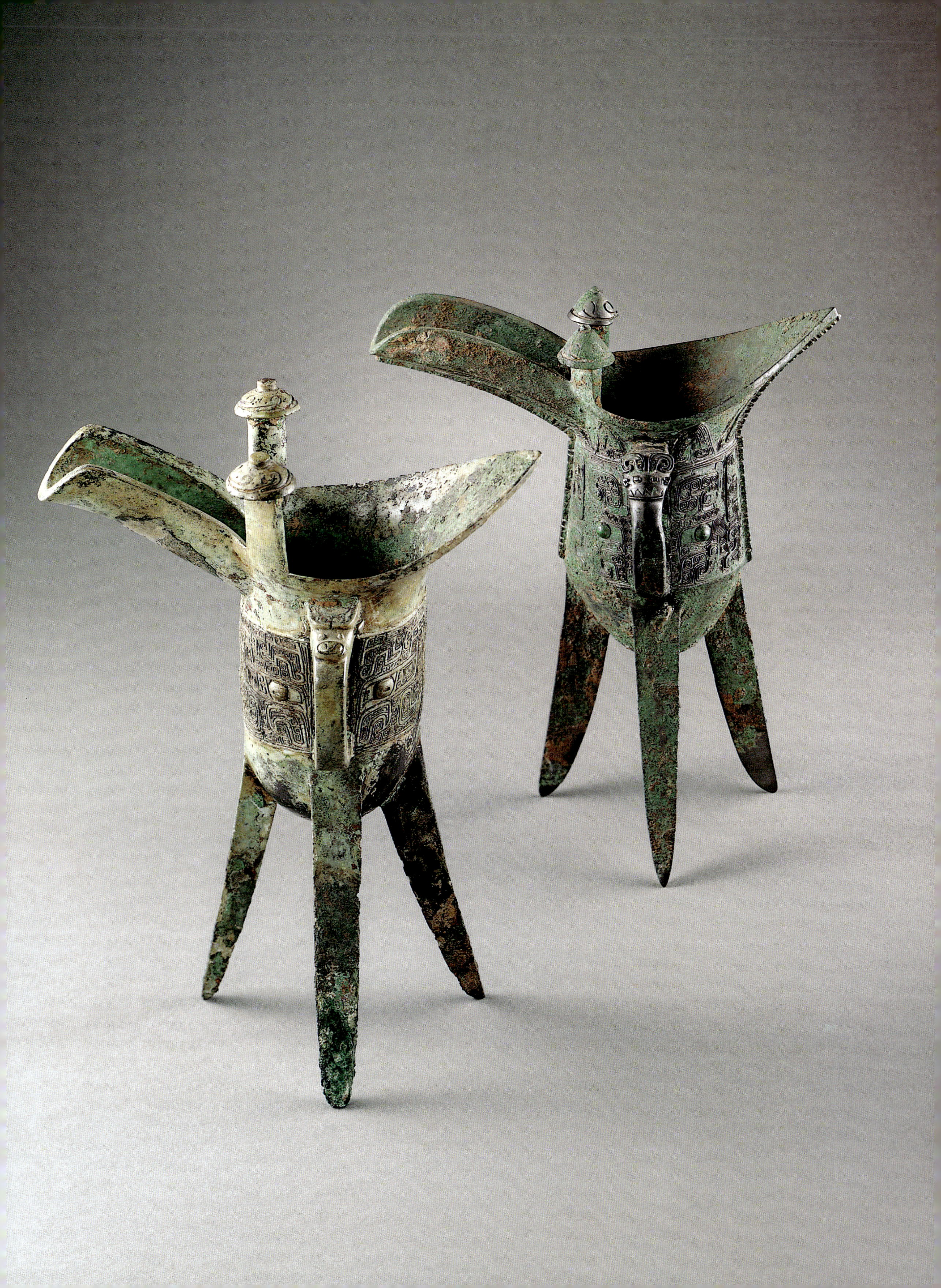

9 TRIPOD RITUAL WINE VESSEL (*JIA*)

Shang dynasty, Anyang period, ca. 13th–12th century BCE
Bronze, 13 × 7¾ × 8⅛ in. (33 × 19.7 × 20.6 cm)
Gift of R.H. Norton, 52.4

A three-legged vessel for heating and dispensing wine, this *jia* is very close in style and date to the Museum's *hu* (cat. 2). Both vessels emphasize monumental form and a simple, powerful silhouette. The more complex shape of the *jia* is comparable to the wine vessel *jue* (cats. 7, 8), with which it shares the configuration of three legs (although there are *fang jia*, or square *jia*, with four legs), a single loop handle on one side, and two large posts mounted on the rim.

Starting at the rim, the decoration of the Norton *jia* consists of triangular panels with spiral motifs most likely derived from images of cicadas. Farther below the rim is a narrow band of small birds alternating with low-relief bosses decorated with spiraling whorl designs; similar whorls also appear on top of the large, decorated posts. The main body of the vessel displays three *taotie* masks, which serve to emphasize the tripartite division of the vessel's decoration. The handle is topped with a bovine head, while the design on the outside of the long, pointed legs is an almost entirely abstract animal with tiny eyes about halfway down the leg. A *jia* of similar size and with very similar decoration on the body but without a lid or the bovine head at the top of the handle was excavated at Anyang, the site of the last Shang capital.[1] The similarities between these two vessels help date the Norton example to the thirteenth or twelfth century BCE.

Indeed, the Norton *jia* is unusual in having a lid, which rarely survive intact with their vessels. The handle on the lid is formed by a pair of small birds standing back-to-back; not all *jia* originally had lids, but it is interesting to note that the handles of extant *jia* with lids are often bird-shaped.[2] The lid further displays unusual decoration of dense spirals with four distinct eyes consisting of flat circles surrounded by a ring of small scalelike designs (not visible in the photograph). This is a Shang convention for depicting owls' eyes, and the design indeed represents four highly schematic owls. Owls are usually associated with other vessel types, specifically *you*, *zun*, and early *guang* (see cat. 1), all of which are covered wine vessels. The lid of the *jia* also has an inscription, cast in the inside center under the double-bird handle, which consists of one graph, the drawing of a *ce* or section of a bamboo-slip scroll supported by two hands. The large size of the Museum's *jia*, its rich but sober decoration, and the presence of the original lid signal its importance as a ritual bronze.

PUBLISHED

Loo, *Exhibition of Chinese Arts* (1941), no. 41; Barnard, *Bronze Casting*, p. 267; Jayne, *The Chinese Collections*, no. 3

NOTES

1 Li Ji and Wan Jiabao, *Yinxu chutu qingtong jia xing qi*, pl. 16.

2 See *Yinxu Fu Hao mu*, pl. XXXIV:1 for a *fang jia* with a very similar double-bird handle; see also Loehr, *Ritual Vessels*, nos. 31, 32, for two *fang jia* with bird knobs on the cover, including an example in the Albright-Knox Gallery, Buffalo (no. 31) with two back-to-back birds. Finally, see *Yinxu qingtongqi*, color pl. 61, for a *jia* very similar to the Norton example, which has a cover (stuck between the two posts) with an unidentified quadruped for a handle.

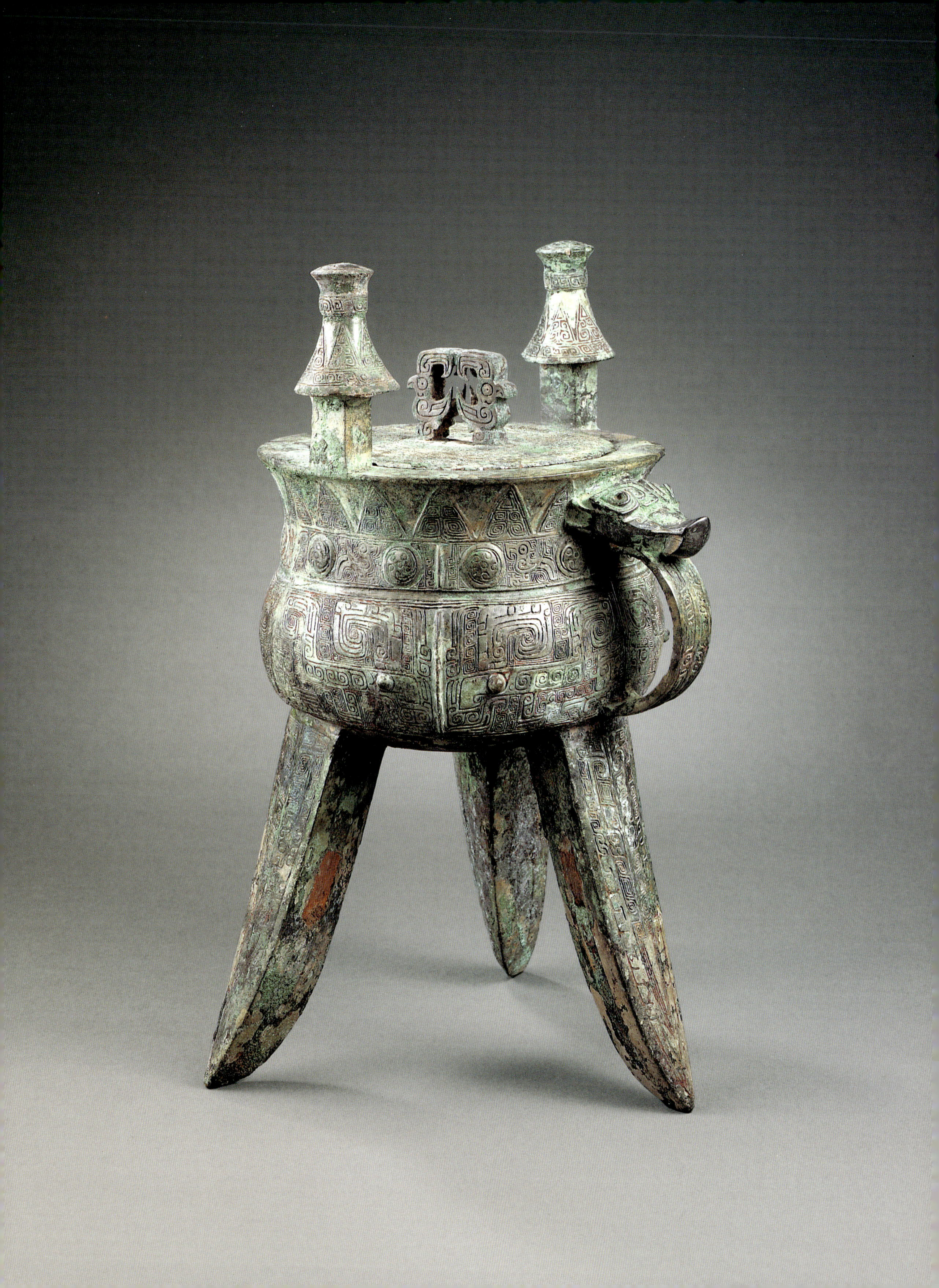

10 AX HEAD (*YUE*)

Shang dynasty, Anyang period, ca. 13th century BCE
Bronze, 7 11/16 × 4 7/8 × 9/16 in. (19.5 × 12.4 × 1.4 cm)
Gift of Mr. and Mrs. Bartlett Richards, 70.8

The Shang dynasty kings who reigned at Anyang from approximately the thirteenth to the eleventh century BCE practiced human sacrifice, sometimes on a massive scale.[1] A royal tomb might have numerous victims buried in the tomb proper, on the ramps leading down into the tomb, or in sacrificial pits arranged nearby.[2] Large bronze axes, some over one foot wide,[3] could easily have served to behead sacrificial victims. This ax head, decorated on both sides, is a small-scale version of a type called a *yue*, and was most likely a symbolic weapon. On the tang (the wide tab inserted through the vertical wood handle) there is a *taotie* mask on one side (shown in the photograph) and the character *ge*, meaning "dagger-ax," on the other side.[4] The mask and the character are formed of shallow recessed areas that retain a fill or inlay of unidentified composition.

The decoration on the blade is surprisingly complex. It consists in general of a mask that represents a tiger's head with its open mouth and sharp fangs facing toward the cutting edge. There are two raised eyes and two C-shaped ears just in front of the two slots that would have been used to tie the blade to its handle. The mouth, eyes, and ears stand out in high relief. The pointed outlines around the eyeballs, however, conventionally indicate that the eyes are facing out toward the edges. Other details of the design also imply that it may be read as two faces set back-to-back with their profiles facing the top and bottom edges of the blade. *Taotie* masks on bronze vessels sometimes embody a similar ambiguity: a design that can be read as one face seen from the front or two faces in profile. The same face transformed in two other faces also appears on cat. 20, a jade blade with a bronze handle, where the two halves of the face on the handle also form two stylized birds.

This Norton ax is smaller but remarkably close in style to two *yue* found in the tomb of Fu Hao, consort of the Shang king Wu Ding, who was buried about 1200 BCE.[5] Those two examples also have an inscription on one side of the tang and a *taotie* mask on the other. Also like the Norton ax, they have a complex design of double faces or masks on the blade, with the eyes, ears, and mouth in high relief. The subtly balanced and dynamic curves of the blades of these small axes, their very similar proportions, and even the *taotie* and characters formed in shallow recessed areas on the tangs clearly indicate that they were manufactured at approximately the same time and perhaps in the same foundry.

PUBLISHED

Archives of Asian Art 25 (1971–72), p. 102, fig. 34; Jayne, *The Chinese Collections*, no. 11

NOTES

1 See Chang, *Shang Civilization*, pp. 228–30, for the sacrifice of war captives in Shang ancestral rites.
2 For a brief statement of Shang burial sacrifices, see Keightley, "The Shang," pp. 266–67.
3 See Fong, ed., *The Great Bronze Age of China*, cat. 23, for one exceptional example.
4 This single-character inscription is one of the most common on bronzes of all types.
5 *Yinxu Fu Hao mu*, p. 105, fig. 66:2, pl. LXIX:1.

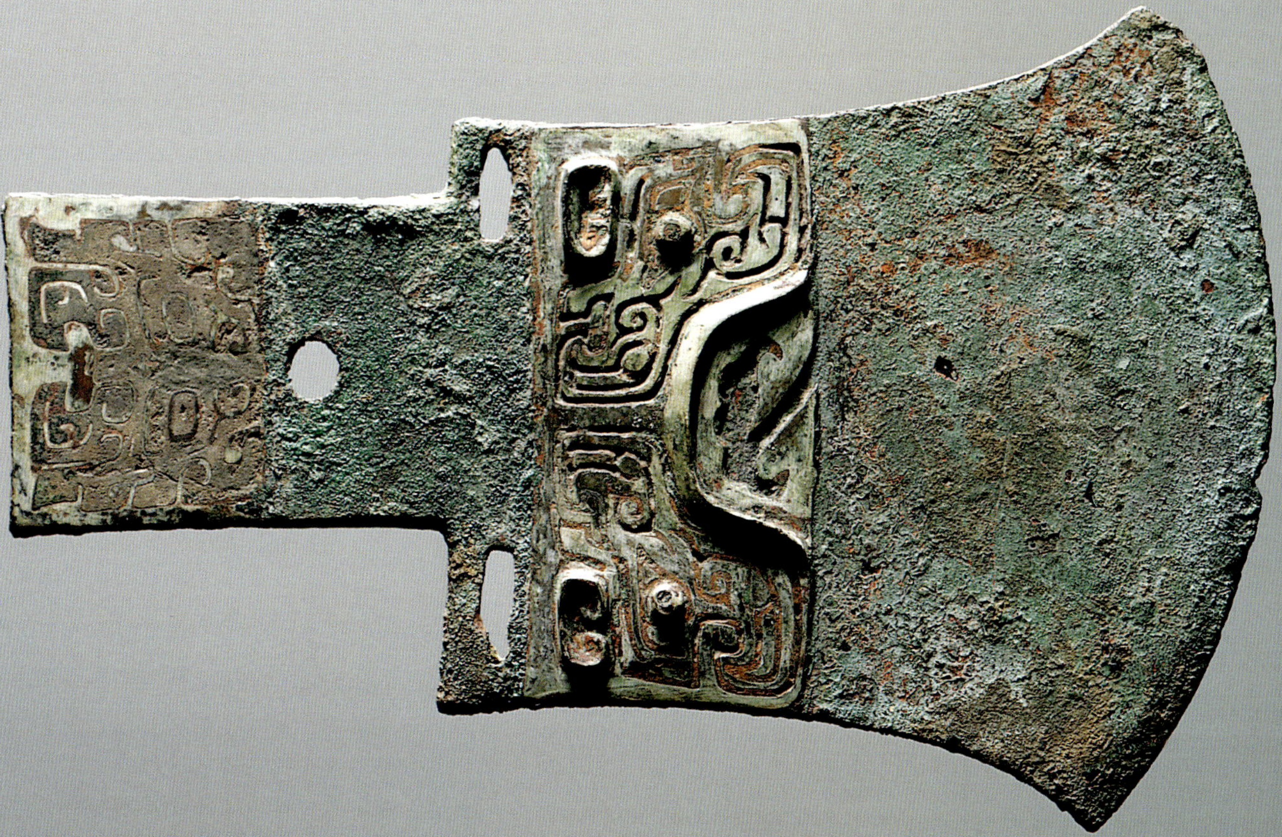

11 STAND OR MOUNT IN THE FORM OF A WATER BUFFALO

Eastern Zhou dynasty, 6th–3rd century BCE
Bronze, 4¾ × 9¼ × 4 in. (12.1 × 23.5 × 10.2 cm)
Gift of R.H. Norton, 51.1

Purchased from the dealer C.T. Loo in 1951, this animal figure was the first Chinese bronze to enter the Norton collection. In 1972 Horace H.F. Jayne wrote that the piece was possibly associated with the Dong Son culture, which extended across southeast Asia and into the Indo-Malaya archipelago during the first millennium BCE. His opinion was based on the relatively high zinc content of the bronze, the iron chaplets or spacers used in its casting, and other, unspecified evidence.[1] Excavations carried out from 1957 to 1965 at Houma, a major bronze-foundry site in southern Shanxi province, have provided examples of sixth- to early-fifth-century BCE casting models and mold fragments that might help place this quadruped in a Chinese context.[2] While it appears a plain and distant cousin, it shares with the sumptuous Houma finds certain stylistic features. Among these are the application of decorative patterns to the whole surface of relatively naturalistic animals, and shoulders and haunches modeled as low-relief spirals overlaid with a decoration of incised S-scroll-and-hook designs.[3] In addition, Houma animals frequently exhibit two other features we see here: snouts stylized as a kind of flat scroll rolled back from the upper lip, and horns anchored by a decorated disk with linear decoration continuing up the horn.

In particular, two very fine and elaborate quadruped bronzes associated with the Houma foundries, one a buffalo-shaped vessel and one a stand with a tray,[4] have proportions generally similar to this water buffalo, with the same distinctive stout legs and smooth cloven hooves. On the latter piece, a pin on the bottom of the tray fits into a spoutlike opening on the animal's back—a socket very similar to that on the Norton piece. As Jayne and other writers have noted, the Norton animal is the mate to or closely similar to various examples.[5] All of them are stoutly modeled and stand foursquare on sturdy legs, and most of them have a tube- or spout-shaped opening on the back. All of them are hollow and open on the underside, some with the head turned to the left, some to the right, and all have similar designs of curves and spirals on their bodies. It appears that these animals make up sets of mounts or stands, although what they may have so placidly supported remains a mystery.

PUBLISHED

Loo, *Exhibition of Chinese Arts* (1941), no. 69; Jayne, *The Chinese Collections*, no. 15

NOTES

1 *The Chinese Collections*, no. 15. Jayne cites no sources for his reference. The heavily oxidized remains of several iron chaplets are visible on the exterior of the bronze. One appears in the photograph between the tail and the decorative spiral on the haunch.

2 See *Art of the Houma Foundry*. See also *Houma zhutong yizhi*.

3 See especially *Art of the Houma Foundry*, pp. 330–31, figs. 710–13.

4 Ibid., pls. 16:2, 19:1; see also fig. 835.

5 The earliest publication is the "Object of Uncertain Use," cat. 8, pl. XXXIX, in the 1915 Burlington Fine Arts Club's *Catalogue of a Collection of Objects of Chinese Art*. Jayne mistook the buffalo in Tch'ou and Pelliot, *Bronzes antiques*, p. 37, pl. XIX, for the Norton animal. A buffalo very similar to the Norton example is in the Morse collection (see Thorp and Bower, *Spirit and Ritual*, no. 22). The buffalo in Umehara (*Shina kōdō Seikwa*, vol. 3, part 1, no. 1) came from C.T. Loo and appears to be the one now in the Kunstindustrimuseet, Copenhagen (see "The Exhibition of Early Chinese Bronzes," *Bulletin of the Museum of Far Eastern Antiquities* 6 [1934], pl. XX). The buffalo from the Stoclet collection, Brussels, was most recently sold by Christian Deydier in 1993. A slightly stockier animal is in Minneapolis (see Karlgren, *Pillsbury Collection*, no. 90, pl. 105).

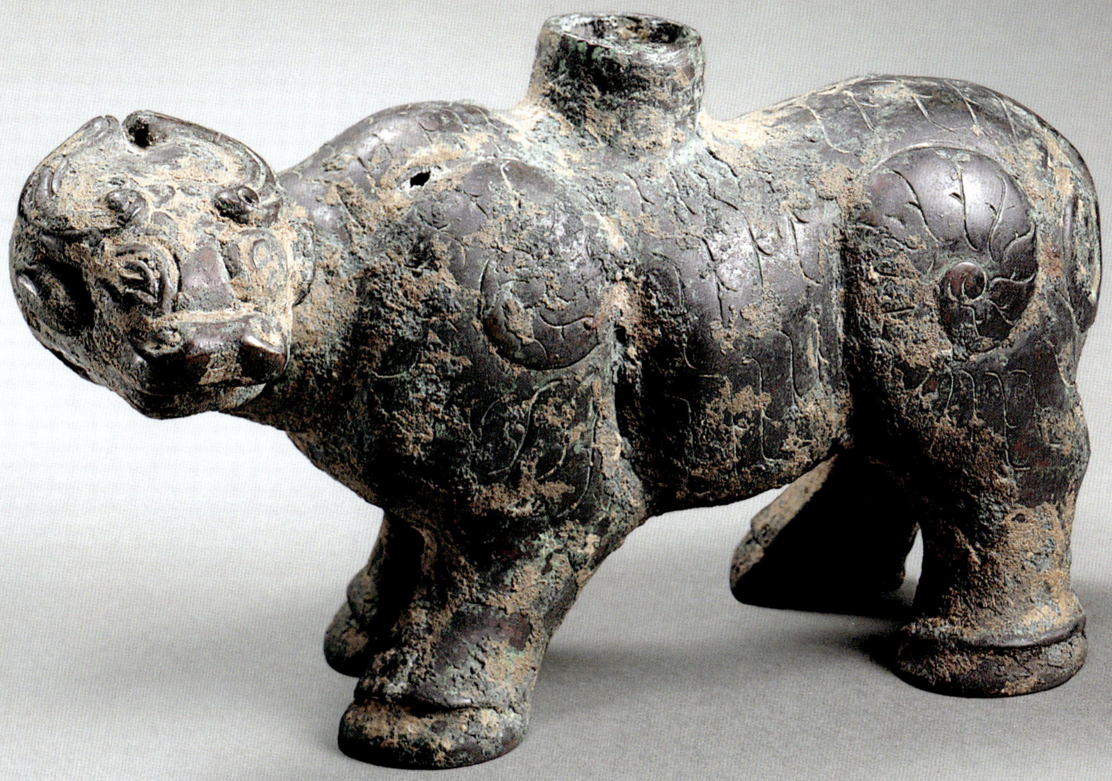

12 GARLIC-HEADED HU

Qin–Western Han dynasty, ca. 4th–2nd century BCE
Bronze, 14 ½ × diam. 7 ¾ in. (36.8 × 19.7 cm)
Gift of Dr. Gerald Shepps, 99.152

The so-called garlic-headed *hu* is a bronze bottle with a flaring foot, a wide, round body, a long neck encircled by a ring, and a mouth ornamented with six lobes, which give the vessel its modern name. This type of bottle is associated with the state of Qin (8th century-221 BCE)[1] on China's northwest frontier, and it is possible the shape was adapted from a hammered metal type from farther west in Central Asia. The ring around the neck, for example, would help support the seams of a bottle made from thin sheets of metal but is mostly decorative on a cast bronze vessel such as this.

Garlic-headed *hu* are found in Qin tombs in Shaanxi and Hubei, the Qin heartland, and they also appear in tombs in territory seized by the Qin during their long conquest of China.[2] A very fine garlic-headed *hu* was discovered in the tomb of the King of Nanyue, a vassal of the Western Han who died around the year 122 BCE.[3] His sumptuous tomb, located in the modern city of Guangzhou (Canton) in southern China, included jades from many parts of China as well as the garlic-headed *hu*, which must have been a relatively exotic object.[4]

Five examples of garlic-headed *hu* are included in the *Xuanhe bogu tulu* (Xuanhe [Hall] illustrated record of the connoisseurship of antiquities), compiled at the beginning of the twelfth century[5] to record the collections of the Northern Song Huizong emperor (r. 1101–25). The text carefully noted the size, weight, and often the volume contained in ancient bronzes, illustrating each with a woodcut print. One garlic-headed *hu*, titled "Han mountains and dragons warm-water *hu*," is covered with an extraordinary decoration of dragons flying among mountains.[6] Like the four undecorated garlic-headed *hu*, it is referred to in the *Bogu tulu* as a bottle for hot water for warming the hands and feet. The mountains in the decoration are likened to the stable forms of energy in the earth and the dragons to changing energy, making the design appropriate for holding warm water, whose energy is transferred to the hands and feet.

Interestingly, a 1924 C.T. Loo sale catalogue included a garlic-headed *hu* with an inscription identifying it as a "hot-water bottle" (*wen hu*) belonging to a Princess of Quyang and giving the weight and number of the bottle.[7] The inscription, cast in large, elegant characters around the outside of the foot, has a good chance of being authentic, but it is difficult to make a final judgment based on the rubbing reproduced in the 1924 catalogue. Nevertheless, the twelfth-century assessment of this exotic vessel type and the appearance of at least one inscribed example point toward a very practical function for these well-known bronze bottles.

NOT PREVIOUSLY PUBLISHED

NOTES

1 On dates, see Li, *Eastern Zhou and Qin Civilizations*, p. 223: Qin from the "early Spring and Autumn Period," i.e. ca. 770 BCE.

2 See ibid., p. 229, citing the reports of excavations of Qin-period tombs in former Chu territory at Shuihudi in Hubei; see also p. 262 for garlic-headed *hu* as typical products of Qin tombs in general.

3 On this death date, see *Xi Han Nanyue wang mu*, English abstract, vol. 1, p. 3.

4 Ibid., vol. 1, fig. 185:2.

5 See Poor, "Notes on the Sung Dynasty Archaeological Catalogs," pp. 35–36, for the origins of the *Bogu tulu*, and pp. 39–40 for a list of early editions. References here are to the *Chongxiu Xuanhe bogutu* contained in the *Siku quanshu*, reprint vol. 840, pp. 371 ff. See also Watt, "Antiquarianism and Naturalism," esp. pp. 220–21.

6 *Chongxiu Xuanhe bogutu*, in the *Siku quanshu*, reprint, vol. 840, pp. 632–33.

7 Tch'ou and Pelliot, *Bronzes antiques*, pl. XXXII.

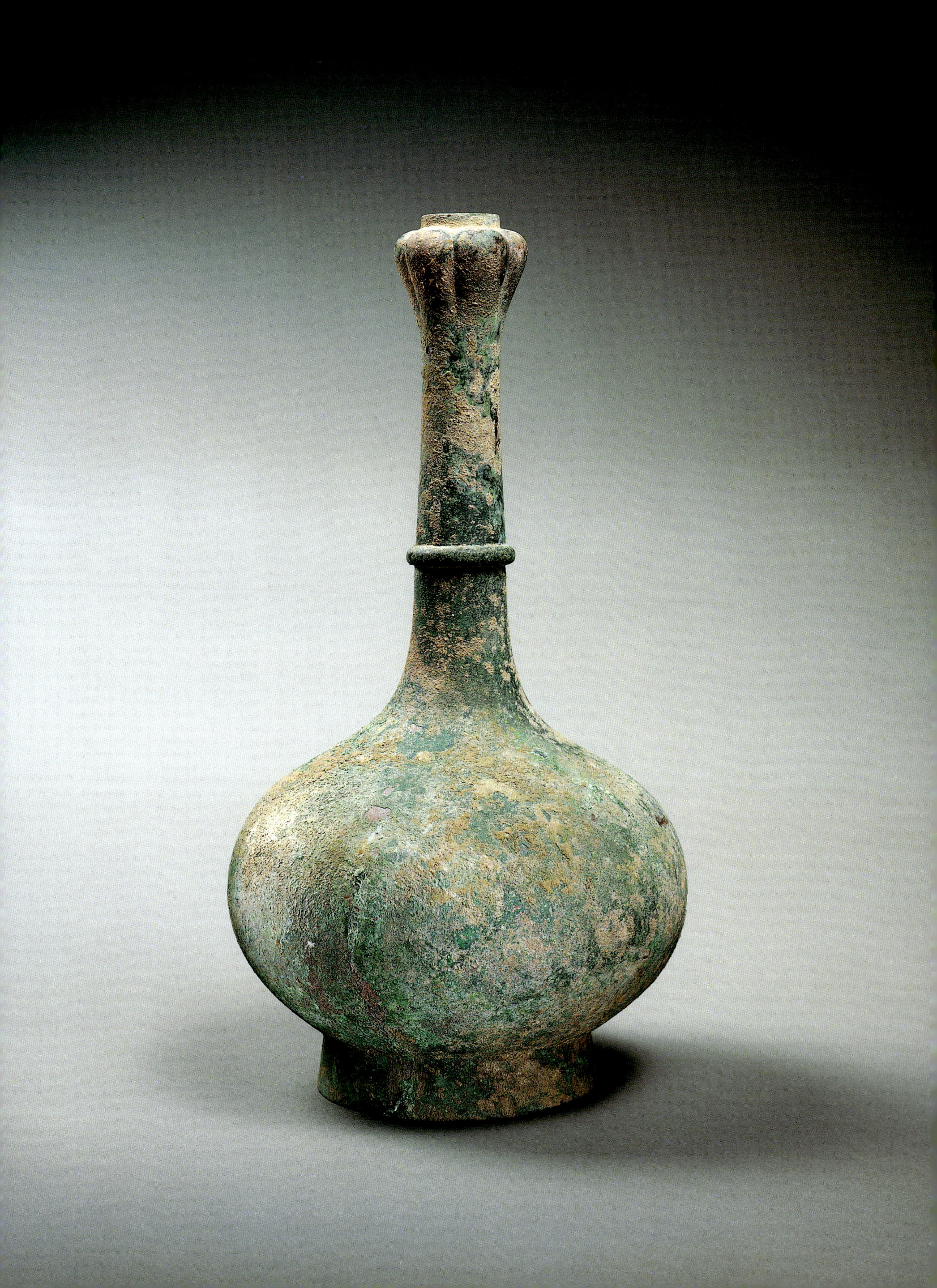

13 LION-AND-GRAPEVINE MIRROR

Tang dynasty (618–907)
Bronze, $^{11}/_{16}$ × diam. 9 $^{3}/_{16}$ in. (1.7 × 23.3 cm)
Purchase, the R.H. Norton Trust, 2001.4

Bronze mirrors have been produced in China since at least the Shang dynasty, and most have the same basic form: a round disk with a flat, reflective front and a highly decorated back. In the center of the back is a perforated knob that would have been threaded with a cord or tassel to lift the mirror. This mirror is a particularly large and elaborately decorated version of a well-known Tang dynasty type. Here, a crouching animal forms the central knob while twisting and turning around it are six more mythological creatures, many with the bushy tails, grinning jaws, and sharp claws of *shizi*, or "Buddhist lions." The outer broad band of decoration is filled with an extraordinary variety of animals, from winged horses and additional leonine creatures to ducks, pheasants, and even insects—all interspersed among scrolling vines and lush flowers. The combination of mythological, lionlike animals and scrolling vines have led such bronzes to be dubbed "lion-and-grapevine" mirrors.[1]

Since the Warring States period real and mythological animals have been a feature of mirror decoration, but the addition of exotic grapevines is a Tang innovation. The vogue for exotic foreign fruit parallels Tang exoticism in fashion, music, and even sports—this is the time of the introduction of polo from Central Asia into China. The appearance of scrolling grapevines, derived from Western classical prototypes, reflects this burgeoning exoticism and signals Tang China's contacts with other cultures on the Eurasian continent. Annette L. Juliano has summed up the complex sources of lion-and-grapevine mirrors in discussing two excavated examples from Gansu province.[2] Their exotic qualities were noted as early as the early twelfth century, when the compilers of the *Xuanhe bogu tulu* (see cat. 12) associated them with the arrival of grapes in China in the Han dynasty and dated the mirrors to the Han.[3]

Chou Ju-hsi has recently sketched the stylistic development of the animal-and-grape design in the early Tang, dating this important group to the last half of the seventh and the first decade or so of the eighth century.[4] Early versions of the decorative scheme were relatively restrained, but animal-and-grape designs become elaborate as more and more creatures, real and imagined, were crowded onto the mirrors. Notably, the outer band of decoration, which in earlier examples had often contained a poetic or auspicious inscription, came to be filled with a second range of animals and flowers. In later examples, too, the scrolling vines begin to encroach on the raised borders between the ranges of design, and on the Norton *Lion-and-Grapevine Mirror* the designs are barely contained within their frames. Finally, the scrolling floral motifs repeated in miniature on the raised edge of the mirror back represent a final elaboration of the lion-and-grape style. All these elements point to a date somewhere around the beginning of the eighth century for this sumptuous, massive mirror.

PUBLISHED

Priestley & Ferraro Chinese Art, *Chinese Art 1998*, n.p.

NOTES

1 See Avril, *Chinese Art in the Cincinnati Art Museum*, cat. 11, for the link between lion-and-grapevine mirrors and Persian lionlike mythological *simurvs*.
2 Juliano and Lerner, *Monks and Merchants*, cats. 116, 117.
3 For a detailed discussion of the scholarly history and thematic development of such mirrors, see Thompson, "The Evolution of the T'ang Lion and Grapevine Mirror." Alexander Soper's "Addendum" in the same issue of *Artibus Asiae* (1967) provides intriguing literary evidence for the meaning of the so-called "lions."
4 *Circles of Reflection*; see esp. pp. 10–11 and cats. 50–56.

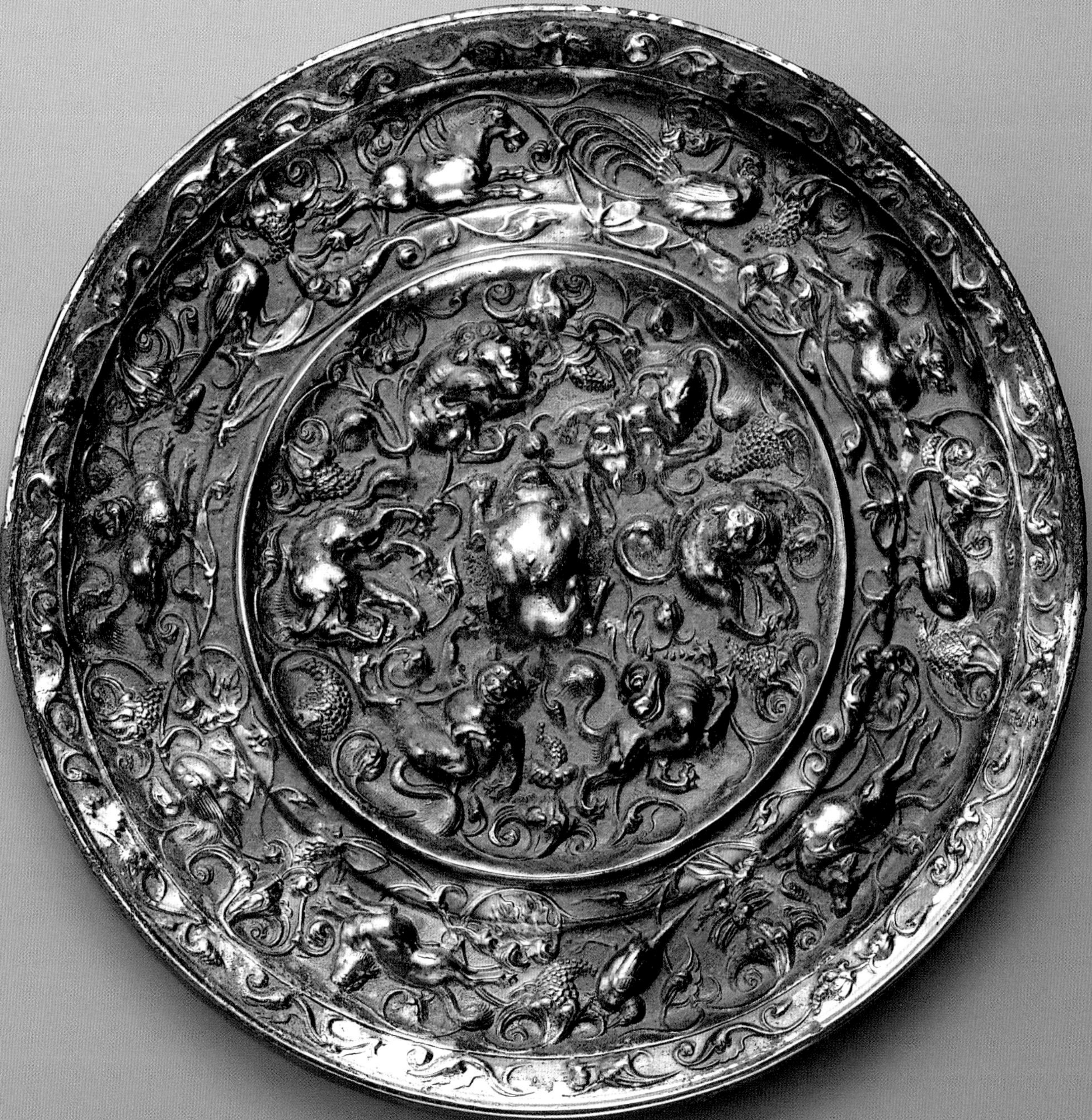

14 SECTION OF A RITUAL OBJECT (*CONG*)

Neolithic period, Liangzhu culture, ca. 3500–2000 BCE
Jade, 1 15/16 × 1 1/16 × 3 1/16 in. (4.9 × 2.7 × 7.8 cm)
Gift of R.H. Norton, 50.13

15 THREE-PRONGED ELEMENT OF A HEADDRESS

Neolithic period, Liangzhu culture, ca. 3500–2000 BCE
Jade, 2 3/4 × 1 3/4 × 7/16 in. (7 × 4.4 × 1.1 cm)
Gift of Mr. Bartlett Richards, 91.30

These creamy tan jades with darker veins are the oldest in the Norton collection. It was not until the mid-1970s that extensive excavations identified these and similar jades as products of the Liangzhu people, who lived in the region around the modern cities of Shanghai and Hangzhou approximately 3,500 to 2,000 years BCE.[1]

The *Section of a ritual object* (right) is only part of what was originally a tube-shaped jade with a circular opening down through the center and projecting square corners. The highly stylized decoration on each corner depicts two faces, one above the other, which together form what is probably the most important motif in Liangzhu culture. The upper face represents a man wearing an elaborate headdress formed of three horizontal bands. The face has lightly incised circular eyes and a bar that angles around the corner of the jade to represent the mouth. The lower face is an animal with round, staring eyes set on wide ovals that are raised slightly above the surface. A broad, angled bridge connects the eyes above another bar-like mouth. Both faces are engraved with patterns of extraordinarily fine lines. The headdress on the upper face has bands of parallel lines surrounding a range of tiny, swirling spirals, and the same design—which appears on many Liangzhu jades—almost completely covers the lower face. Although recent excavations of unfinished jades and fragments of tools have suggested some of the highly sophisticated techniques used by Liangzhu jade workers,[2] the creation of such superbly controlled surfaces and the almost microscopic detail are remarkable artistic achievements.

The Museum's *Three-pronged element of a headdress* (left) is very similar to another excavated Liangzhu jade, a W-shaped ornament from Fanshan, Yuhangxian, Zhejiang province, close to the Liangzhu type-site, and just northwest of Hangzhou.[3] Both are plain, three-pronged objects, with a single large hole drilled from the bottom up through the central prong, and a hole drilled only part of the way down into each side prong from the top. When Liangzhu three-pronged jade ornaments are found in burials, they are most often at the top of the head of the body, with the prongs pointing upward.[4] They have thus far been interpreted as parts of a headdress, perhaps a type of feathered headdress represented on other Liangzhu jade artifacts. The beautifully polished surfaces of these undecorated pieces are a brilliant counterpoint to finely decorated companion jades. In sum, Liangzhu jades are among the most astonishing artistic achievements of Neolithic China.

PUBLISHED

14: Loo, *An Exhibition of Chinese Archaic Jades* (1950), pl. XXXV (2); Jayne, *The Chinese Collections*, no. 55
15: Not previously published

NOTES

1 Sun, "The Liangzhu Culture," pp. 117–20, cats. 29–36.
2 Ibid., p. 119, n. 9, citing Wang Zunguo, "Liangzhu wenhua yulianzang shulue," *Wenwu* 1984.2, pp. 23–35; and Zhou Xiaolu and Zhang Min, "Zhiyu shuo—Changjiang xiayou xinshiqi shidai sanjian yuzhipin feiqiwu de yanjiu," *Nanjing bowuyuan jikan* 1984.7, pp. 46–50.
3 *Liangzhu wenhua yuqi*, nos. 124, 125. The Museum's *Section of a cong* is remarkably similar to a complete *cong* excavated in 1987 at Yaoshan, Yuhangxian, Zhejiang province, differing only by a millimeter or so in size.
4 Ibid., no. 18.

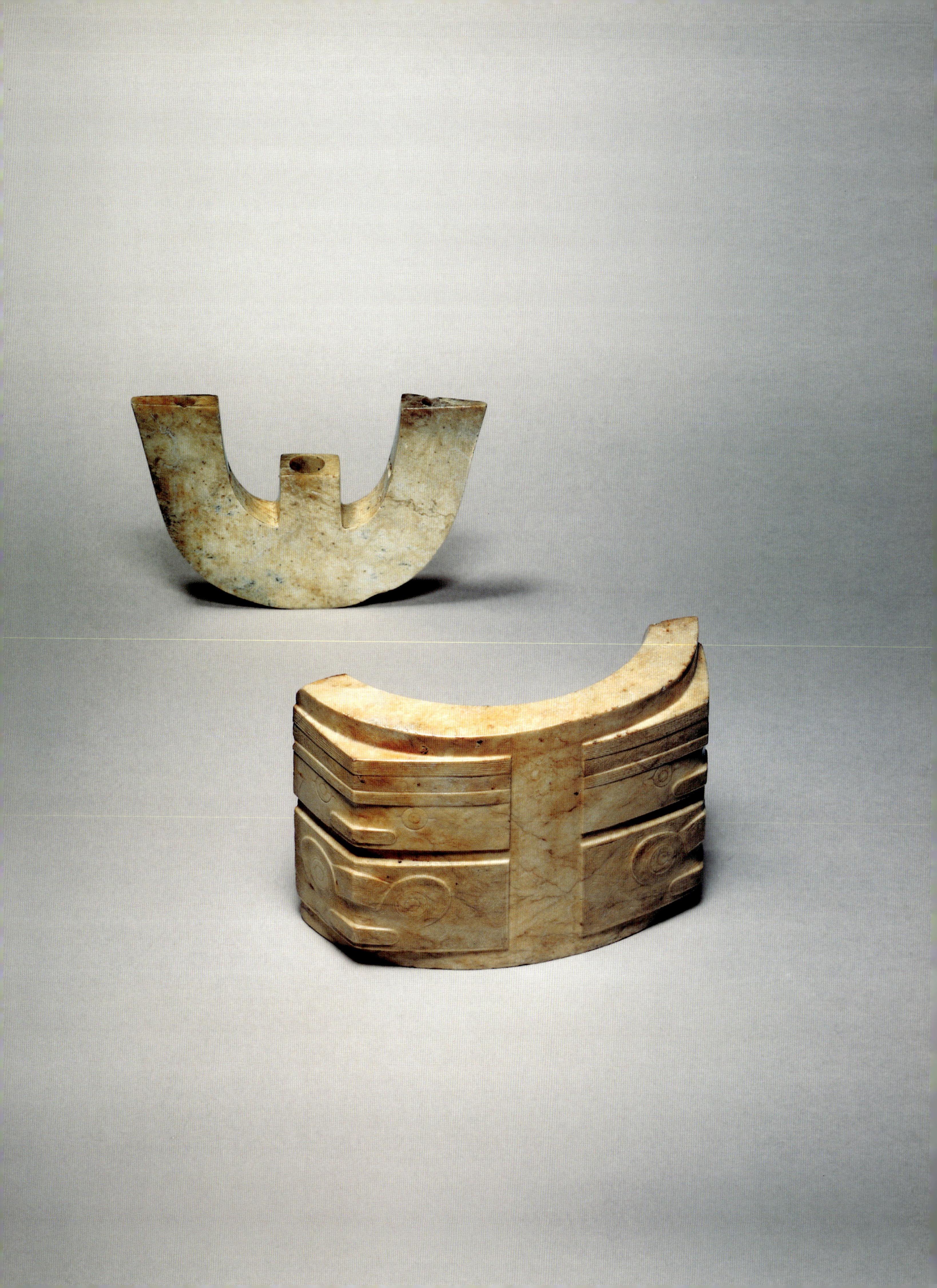

16 RITUAL OBJECT (*CONG*)

Late Neolithic period–early Shang dynasty, ca. 1600–1300 BCE
Jade, 4¾ × 3 × 3 in. (12.1 × 7.6 × 7.6 cm)
Gift of R.H. Norton, 50.31

17 RITUAL OBJECT (*CONG*)

Eastern Zhou dynasty, late 6th–5th century BCE
Jade, 1⅝ × 1¾ × 1¾ in. (4.1 × 4.4 × 4.4 cm)
Gift of R.H. Norton, 50.11

Other cultures in Neolithic China as well as later historical dynasties adopted the form of the *cong*, the tubular jade with square corners of the Liangzhu culture (see cat. 14), and invested it with it new forms and new meanings. While *cong* jades could be undecorated, many repeated in some form the faces that appeared on the corners of Liangzhu jades.[1] On the tall, late Neolithic–early Shang dynasty *cong* (left), the faces are reduced to an almost completely abstract design of three long parallel lines over two shorter lines (some Liangzhu *cong* also show a similar abbreviation of facial features), and there are a total of four faces, one above the other, on each corner of the jade. Possibly produced in northwest China,[2] this *cong* preserves one additional Liangzhu trait: it tapers slightly toward the bottom.

The small Eastern Zhou *cong* (right) is even farther from its Neolithic model. Here the decoration consists of typical Zhou designs of densely packed, interlocking spirals. There are small faces at each of the corners, one at the bottom (rightside up) and one at the top (upsidedown). With their curled snouts, tiny round eyes, and spreading horns, they are distantly related to animals that appear on Eastern Zhou bronzes. The rims at the top and bottom of the *cong* are decorated with fine lines that imply a gently twisting spiral. A group of jades with closely comparable decoration was excavated in 1979 from a group of Chu tombs at Xiasi, Henan province, datable to the sixth or fifth century BCE.[3]

While the *cong* form may have evolved from a bracelet decorated with four faces,[4] Liangzhu *cong* and later examples seem rarely if ever to have been used as personal ornaments. The Norton's Eastern Zhou *cong* has holes in three of the four square shoulders, suggesting that the *cong* was attached to something. However, it seems unlikely that such a blocky object would have been worn as a personal ornament.

Although the basic form of the *cong* has persisted throughout Chinese history, it disappears as a shape for long periods of time to be rediscovered and reinterpreted over the centuries (cat. 66). Our knowledge of Neolithic examples comes mostly from interpreting their location in burials, but we have only tentative ideas about what this object may have meant to the ancient Chinese.

PUBLISHED

16: Loo, *An Exhibition of Chinese Archaic Jades* (1950), pl. XXXV (4); Jayne, *The Chinese Collections*, no. 54; Hayashi, *Chūgoku kogyokuki sōsetsu*, p. 244, fig. 5–96
17: Loo, *Exhibition of Chinese Arts* (1941), no. 252; Loo, *An Exhibition of Chinese Archaic Jades* (1950), pl. XXXV (1); Jayne, *The Chinese Collections*, no. 53

NOTES

1 On the relation of Liangzhu faces to Shang *taotie* masks, see Li, "Liangzhu Culture and the Shang Dynasty *Taotie* Motif."
2 Hayashi identified the Norton's jade as a product of the Longshan culture, once situated in Shandong province on China's east coast; see *Chūgoku kogyokuki sōsetsu*, p. 244, and fig. 5–96. See also Yang Boda, "Gansu Qijia yu wenhua chutan," p. 15, fig. 3.
3 *Xichuan Xiasi Chunqiu Chu mu*, fig. 177. For color images, see *Zhongguo yuqi quanji*, vol. 3, pls. 77, 81, 83–85.
4 Yang, ed., *The Golden Age*, cat. 30.

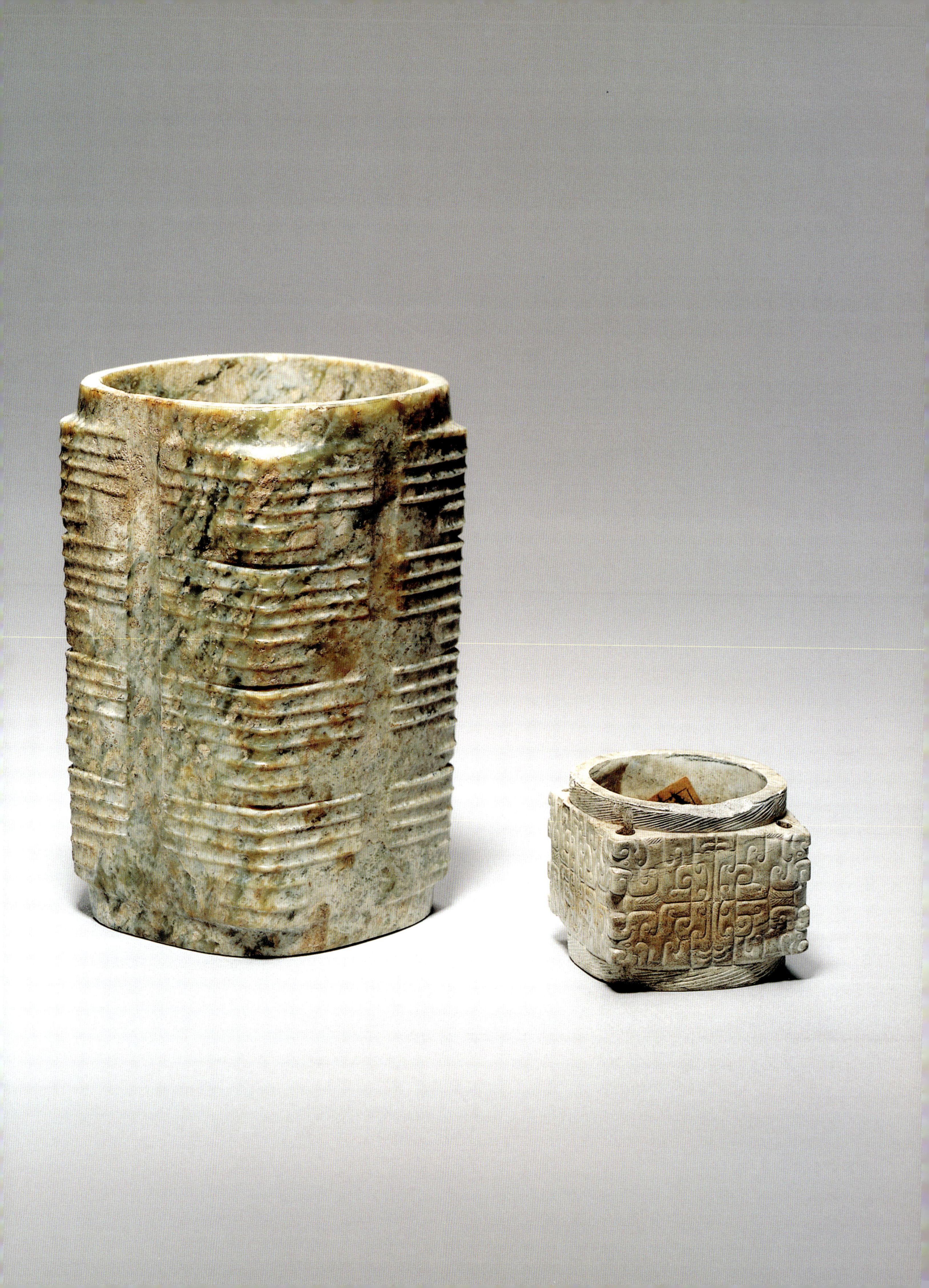

18 FORKED BLADE

Late Neolithic period, ca. 1700–1500 BCE
Stone (unidentified), 15 3/8 × 5 × 1/4 in. (39.1 × 12.7 × .6 cm)
Gift of R.H. Norton, 50.34

Originally catalogued as a jade, this impressive blade is actually carved from a flat slab of fine-grained gray stone. The surface appears to have been coated with a reddish brown substance that has degraded into a pattern of small lines and open areas. The long blade has a plain, rectangular tang pierced with a hole drilled from the back. Between the tang and the wider, gently curving sides of the blade are rows of small projections cut by narrow notches that are symmetrically arranged on either side of the blade. The complex silhouette of projections and notches, joined by fine, parallel lines, is a distinctive feature of this particular type of ritual blade. The blade ends in a broad, shallow curve beveled from one side only, which distinguishes the front from the back.

Long blades with crescent or forked ends are well known, and their large numbers and wide distribution, often remarkable size, and apparent ritual power are the subject of much scholarly research. While they seem to replicate a specific type of weapon, their precedents are unclear, and even Neolithic bone plowshares have been suggested as the prototype.[1] Archaeologically excavated examples have been found throughout the range of Neolithic cultures, but the blades seem to be concentrated in a few areas.[2] Among these are finds at Shenmu, Shaanxi province, on the upper reaches of the Yellow River, the sacrificial pits at Sanxingdui in Sichuan province, as well as a very few, isolated finds at Erlitou and other sites near Zhengzhou in Henan on the Central Plain. Where the blades first appeared is a matter of conjecture. Some Chinese scholars see their beginnings in Shandong on the east coast or in Shaanxi province, from where they were adapted by Neolithic predecessors of the Shang in Henan and spread further to Sichuan on China's southwest borders.[3] On the other hand, the forked blade may have developed on the periphery of the Chinese Neolithic cultural range, a view supported in part by the technical similarities between blades found in Sichuan and in distant Shaanxi province.[4] It is possible that the blades in Henan were exotic imports—occasionally copied locally—from centers to the north or southwest.

Forked blades closest to the Norton example are linked to both the Erlitou culture of Henan province, the Neolithic predecessor to the Shang, as well as to the spectacular discoveries at Sanxingdui in Sichuan. While Erlitou examples have been found in burials, evidence at Sanxingdui shows forked blades with a very different use (see pp. 21–25, figs. 3, 4, in Jenny So's essay in this catalogue). A miniature kneeling bronze figure "holding a blade before its chest has attracted scholarly attention all out of proportion to its tiny size."[5] Holding the blade upright by the tang, the little figure may represent only one ritual peculiar to this particular time and place, and Erlitou burials certainly seem to testify to a very different concept of ritual purpose. Still, the few verifiable facts we have provide dramatic evidence of the power and importance of these very compelling forked stone blades.

PUBLISHED

Loo, *An Exhibition of Chinese Archaic Jades* (1950), pl. V (3); Jayne, *The Chinese Collections*, no. 46

NOTES

1 Rawson and Michaelson, *Chinese Jade*, cat. 10:21, n. 1, citing among others Teng Shu-p'ing, "Ye tan Huaxi xitong de yuqi," part 2, *Gugong wenwu yuekan*, no. 126 (Sept. 1993), pp. 62–71.
2 See the map in Deng Cong, ed., *Nan Zhongguo ji linjin diqu gu wenhua yanjiu*, endpapers.
3 Rawson and Michaelson, *Chinese Jade*, p. 168, cat. 10:21.
4 So, "Jade and Stone," pp. 159–60.
5 Xu, "Bronze at Sanxingdui," no. 51.

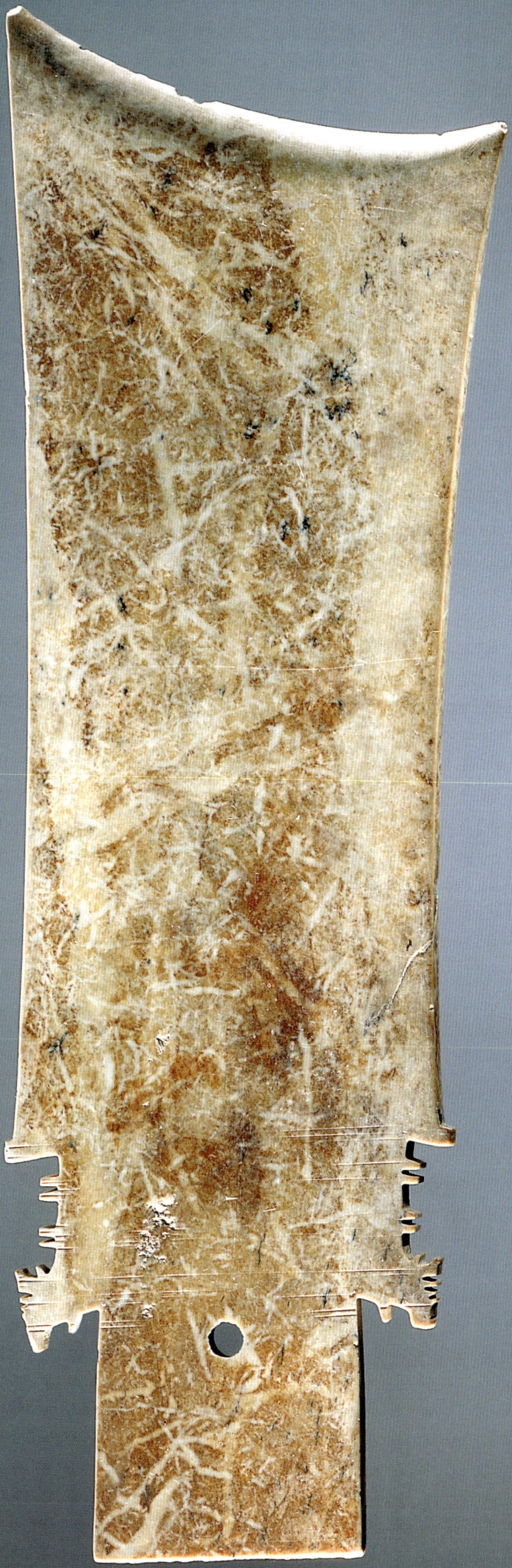

19 **CEREMONIAL BLADE WITH BRONZE BUTT** *(GE)*

Shang dynasty, Anyang period (ca. 1300–1050 BCE)
Jade, bronze inlaid with turquoise, 13 1/8 × 3 3/4 × 5/16 in. (33.3 × 9.5 × .8 cm)
Gift of R.H. Norton, 50.1

20 **CEREMONIAL BLADE WITH BRONZE BUTT** *(GE)*

Shang dynasty, Anyang period (ca. 1300–1050 BCE)
Jade, bronze, 8 1/8 × 2 7/8 × approx. 1/2 in. (20.6 × 7.3 × 1.3 cm)
Gift of R.H. Norton, 50.16

These ceremonial dagger-axes replicate in jade a common bronze weapon of the Shang dynasty called a *ge*. The larger piece (top) copies a typical bronze *ge* type: the wide blade, hafted into a bronze handle, rises to a ridge in the center, its sharp point and distinctly beveled edges mimicking an actual blade. Two holes, one in the blade and one in the handle, would have helped secure the blade to a wooden pole or mount. The rounded, curving portion of the handle is decorated with small pieces of turquoise. Although there are substantial remnants of the turquoise decoration on both sides of the handle, it is not possible to decipher the design. The handles of many *ge*, both bronze and jade, present images of birds, and that may be the case here as well. However, there are indications that both blade and handle, while certainly authentic Shang dynasty objects, may have undergone subsequent restoration. For example, a minute, brass-colored pin that helps to secure the blade to the handle is not appropriate to Shang working methods. Both a turquoise-inlaid bronze and jade *ge* from the ca. 1200 BCE tomb of Fu Hao and another, even closer in style to the Norton's blade, excavated at Xiaotun, Anyang, have an additional bronze section between the projecting guards of the handle and the visible end of the jade blade. This deeper socket must have helped to affix the jade to the handle more securely.[1] Nevertheless, the silhouette of the Norton's blade is roughly identical to numerous all-bronze *ge*.[2]

The smaller blade (bottom) is an example of the frequent reuse of jade, so highly valued in ancient China. From its abbreviated proportions, it appears to be the point of a longer blade that was broken, then refashioned and remounted in a bronze handle. The extensively corroded but elaborate decoration of the handle is formed of raised ridges, with the deep blade socket taking the form of a tiger's face, its jaws clenching the jade. Although the circular eyes are immediately recognizable, the lines that form the face also delineate two highly stylized birds standing back to back, and the features of the two motifs allow simultaneous readings. The pointed corners forming the tiger's ears, for example, also represent the beaks of the birds. (See cat. 10, *Ax head* (*yue*), where two back-to-back faces similarly form a snarling tiger head.) The decoration of the end of the handle is another bird, highly simplified in design and facing upward. Such stylized, overlapping decoration is difficult for us to decipher. Perhaps in Shang times familiarity with the underlying animal designs made these abstract images more easily legible.

PUBLISHED

19: Loo, *An Exhibition of Chinese Archaic Jades* (1950), pl. III (2); Jayne, *The Chinese Collections*, no. 42
20: Loo, *An Exhibition of Chinese Arts* (1941), no. 93; Loo, *An Exhibition of Chinese Archaic Jades* (1950), pl. II (1); Jayne, *The Chinese Collections*, no. 41

NOTES

1 *Yinxu Fu Hao mu*, color pl. XVII (3). See also Watt and Knight, *Chinese Jades from the Collection of the Seattle Art Museum*, cat. 5, for a similar jade blade with inlaid bird-shaped handle. The Xiaotun blade is reproduced in Hayashi, *Chūgoku kogyokuki sōsetsu*, figs. 7–14.
2 See, for example, *Hebei sheng chutu wenwu xuanji*, fig. 59, for a selection of typical bronze *ge* excavated at Yueyao, Wu'an county, Hebei.

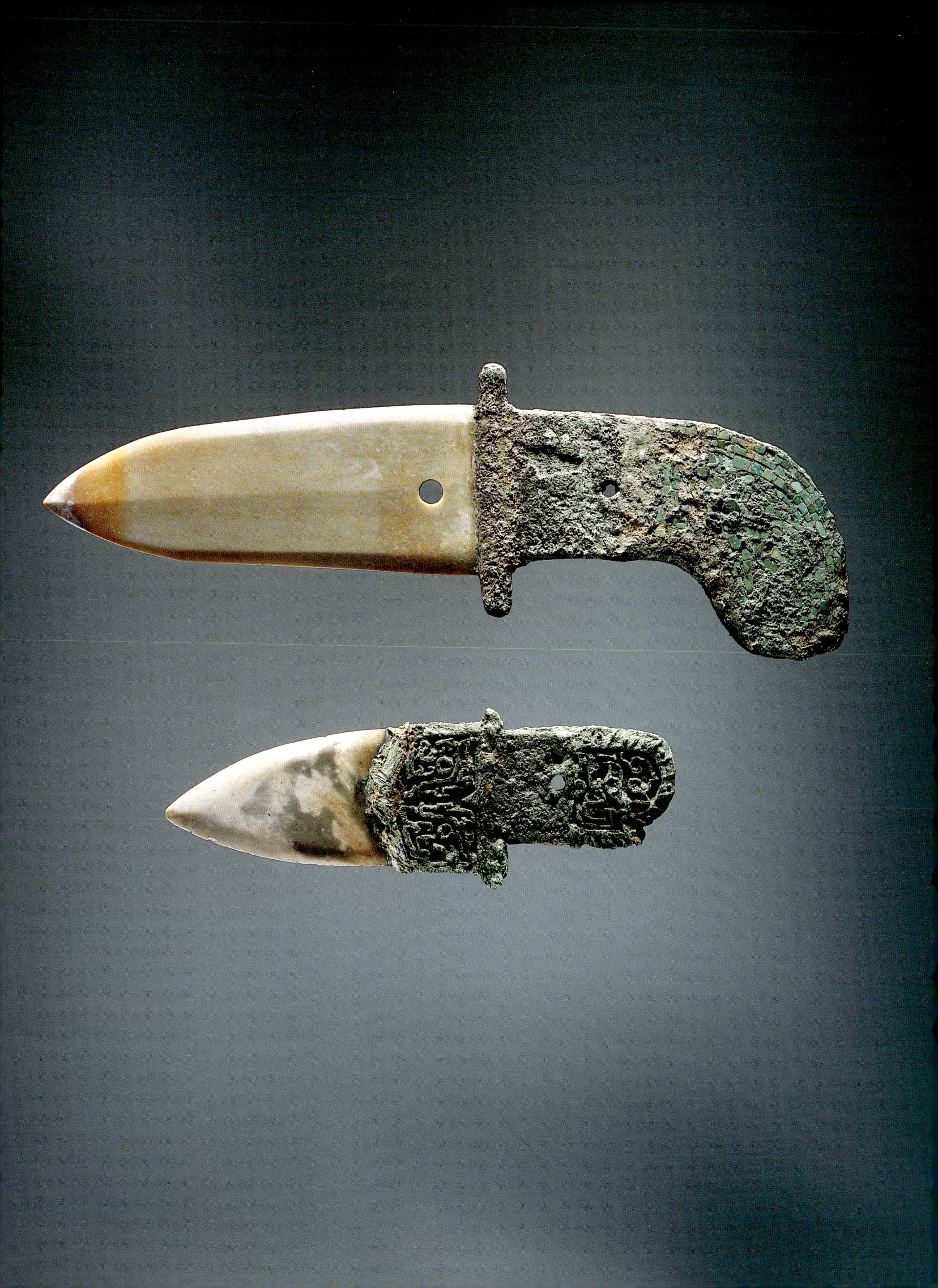

21 CEREMONIAL AX HEAD *(QI)*

Shang dynasty, ca. 13th–11th century BCE
Jade, 5 5/16 × 3 5/8 × 3/16 in. (13.5 × 9.2 × .5 cm)
Gift of R.H. Norton, 50.28

22 CEREMONIAL AX HEAD *(QI)*

Shang dynasty, ca. 13th–10th century BCE
Stone, 4 3/8 × 2 1/2 × 5/16 in. (11.1 × 6.4 × .8 cm)
Gift of R.H. Norton, 50.26

Jade ax heads are modeled after stone tools for actual use, although their precious material, fine workmanship, and extreme thinness mark them as ritual objects. Stone axes and their jade counterparts are often elegantly simple rectangles with curved, sharpened edges, but these examples have a symmetrical pattern of six prongs and notches ornamenting the top and bottom sides. Jessica Rawson has discussed the evolution of these distinctive notches, which most likely further emphasize the ceremonial function of the objects.[1] Such prongs and notches appear on Neolithic jades, and adaptation and experimentation in the Erlitou period resulted in a significant number of jade forms, including axes and rings, with this six-prong design. This enigmatic decoration continues intermittently, most likely as copying and revivals, through the Shang into the early Western Zhou (see cat. 23).[2]

The larger *Ax head* (top) is cut from a very thin slab of green jade that is translucent in many places. Areas of the surface are colored bright red, most likely from the cinnabar, or red mercuric oxide, sprinkled in Shang dynasty burials. The red accretions show a distinctive woven pattern, indicating that the ax head was wrapped in a textile at the time of burial. Two large holes—one toward the center and one at the very edge—are drilled from one side only. The butt end is straight, and the sides, while appearing straight, curve almost imperceptibly. The front edge has a narrow bevel, and the entire blade is extremely thin, no more than three-sixteenths of an inch at the thickest part. The prongs are symmetrically arranged in groups of three around a narrow central notch, and are slightly curved, giving the impression of flaring out from the center. Comparable ax heads were excavated in the ca. 1200 BCE tomb of Fu Hao at Anyang.[3]

The smaller *Ax head* (bottom) was originally catalogued as jade, but it actually is a type of veined hardstone, not true jade (that is, nephrite). The stone is beautifully mottled with areas of dark green, almost black, and areas of lighter gray green. There are also distinctive veins radiating through the stone. The blade is thickest at the butt end and center, tapering smoothly toward the cutting edge, which has a very narrow bevel. While the front and back of the blade are finely polished, revealing the beauty of the stone, the edges and the prong-and-notch pattern are unpolished. It appears that the butt end has been slightly recut and polished at some point. (Since the tang of a stone ax was intended to be fitted into a wood handle, there was little need to finish the end, and even ritual blades typically have a rough edge where the blade was snapped from the original slab of stone or jade.) The large hole in the center of the blade was drilled from both sides. Both ax heads exemplify the precious materials, fine workmanship, and distinctive notch-and-prong design that is characteristic of an important group of ancient ritual objects.

PUBLISHED

21: Loo, *An Exhibition of Chinese Archaic Jades* (1950), pl. VI (4); Jayne, *The Chinese Collections*, no. 48

22: Loo, *An Exhibition of Chinese Archaic Jades* (1950), pl. XXXVIII (5); Jayne, *The Chinese Collections*, no. 47

NOTES

1 Rawson and Michaelson, *Chinese Jade*, cat. 10:13.

2 For a variety of jade and stone axes of this general type, see Loehr, *Ancient Chinese Jades*, nos. 17–21.

3 *Yinxu Fu Hao mu*, color pls. XIX (1), CXV (1,3), CXVI (1–4).

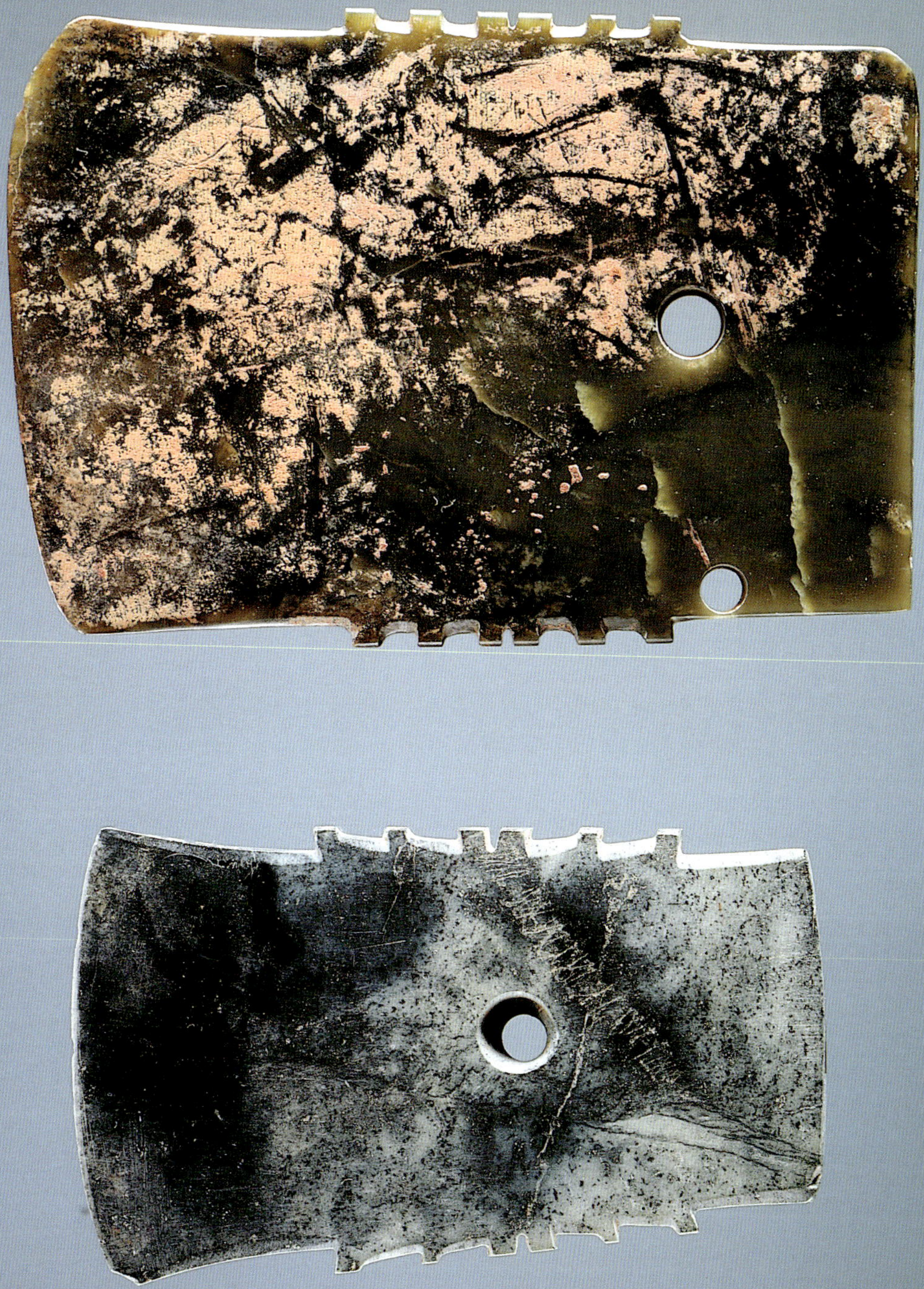

23 NOTCHED RING

Western Zhou dynasty (ca. 1100–771 BCE)
Jade, 3/16 × diam. 4 7/16 in. (.5 × 11.3 cm)
Gift of R.H. Norton, 50.12

This flat ring is carved from pale green jade with areas of pale brown and dark brown veins; its surface and edges are all carefully polished. Like the jade and stone *Ceremonial ax heads* (cats. 21, 22), the *Notched ring* has distinctive groups of raised prongs around the outer edge. Here there are five groups, each consisting of six prongs symmetrically arranged with three each on either side of a central notch. The square points are almost imperceptibly curved to give the impression that they are radiating outward from the center.

These enigmatic ring forms first appear in the Neolithic Hongshan culture in Liaoning in northeastern China as small three-lobed ornaments with a central hole.[1] Such ornaments were both preserved and reinterpreted by later Neolithic cultures as well as by the Shang and Zhou. As the type evolved further from its origins, it retained the three lobes, while the disks became larger and the central hole much broader, most likely in response to the evolution of the disks conventionally called *bi* (cat. 41). In the late Neolithic period, the distinctive pattern of notches and square prongs was added to the silhouette of the disk, probably at about the same time it appeared on ax heads and larger ritual stone blades. The reason for the addition of the notches—or their meaning in any of the cultures that adopted them—remains a mystery, although it is likely they helped distinguish ritual objects from functioning stone blades and tools. In the final evolution of the form, the three-lobed shape disappeared, and only the distinctive pattern of notches remained on the outer edge of the disk, as we see here.

PUBLISHED

Loo, *An Exhibition of Chinese Archaic Jades* (1950), pl. XL (1); Jayne, *The Chinese Collections*, no. 49

NOTE

1 See Rawson and Michaelson, *Chinese Jade*, pp. 160–62, citing Yang Meili, "Pu an cheng daojue, yabi qi xuanji," *Gugong wenwu yuekan* 129 (Nov. 1993), pp. 68–76, for the likely history of this jade type.

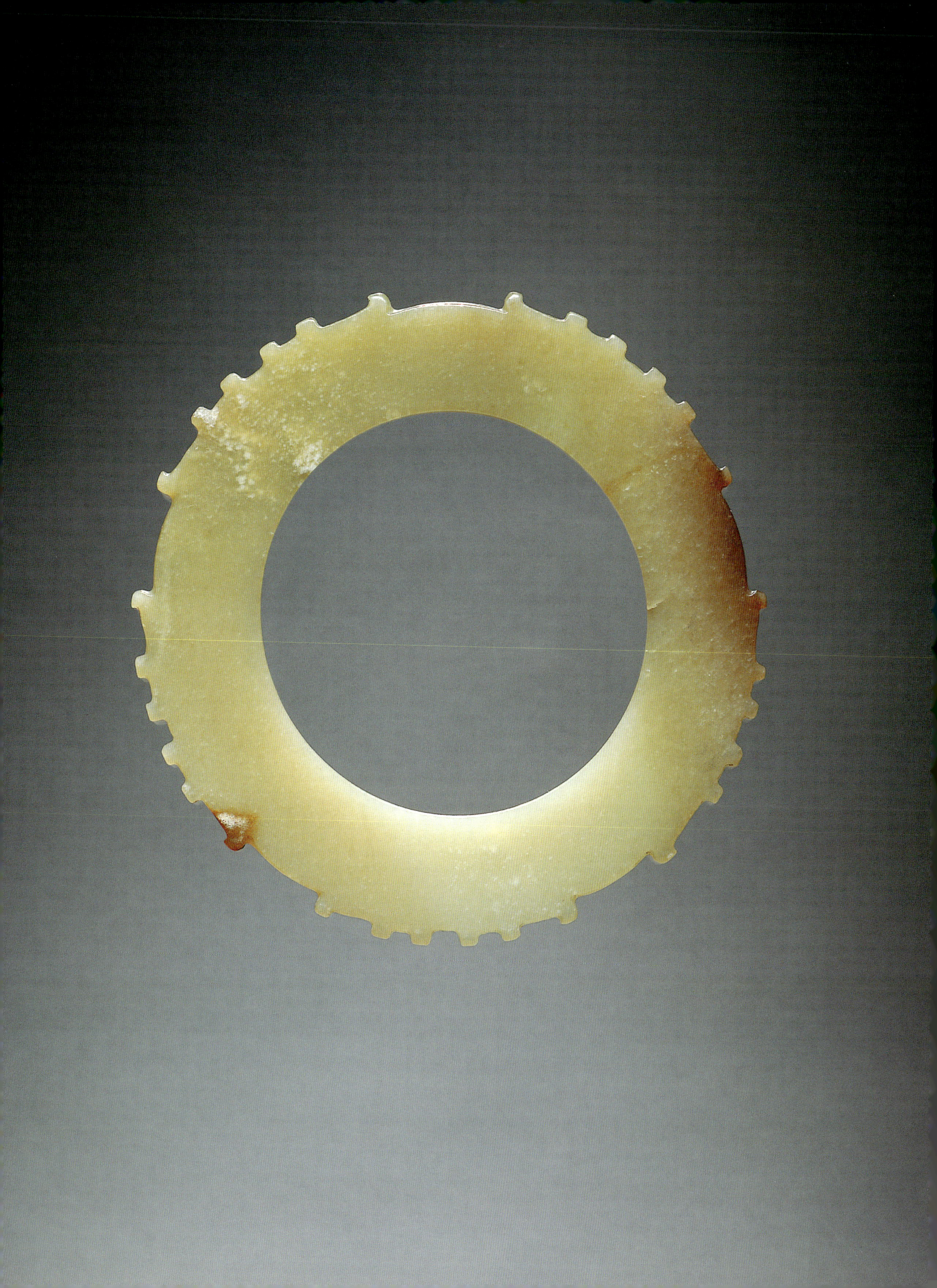

24 CRESTED BIRD

Shang dynasty, Anyang period, ca. 1200 BCE
Jade, 5 1/2 × 2 7/16 × 3/8 in. (14 × 6.2 × 1 cm)
Gift of R.H. Norton, 50.21

This large, fine bird has a tall two-part crest decorated with notched flanges. It has a prominent hooked beak, staring eyes, and folded wings depicted as a spiral on the shoulder that extends into the bird's back as a series of parallel lines. The body is supported by a squared-off tail and a thick leg with broad claws and a small spur on the back side. A small hole is drilled through the foot, the bottom edge of which has a narrow, straight flange. Originally catalogued as a pendant or a plaque, the *Crested bird* may have originally stood upright, with the tab and hole securing it to another object.[1]

Drilling and cutting were the main techniques used to produce the elaborate silhouette; the carver first drilled holes at the bottom of the beak as well as inside of the spirals of the crest, wing, and tail, and then cut from the hole to the edge of the jade to create hook-shaped points. The notched flange that surrounds much of the silhouette is ground down as a thinner edge, and various overlapping cuts formed the sawtooth details. Great care has been taken to produce dynamic, curving lines, with the surface carefully ground and polished to give the threadlike details the appearance of standing out in shallow relief. The jade itself is not a flat slab, as most Shang objects of this type, but is slightly thicker in the center and tapers almost imperceptibly toward the edges, suggesting that the jade was possibly part of a blade that was broken and recut (see cats. 19, 20).

Among the many jades in the ca. 1200 BCE tomb of Fu Hao are twenty-one crested birds.[2] The type was previously well known, and the Fu Hao tomb provides an important archaeological context for them. Jessica Rawson has succinctly outlined the development of these birds and their relationship with Shang human figures with similar crests and theorizes that the birds most likely follow the precedent of human figures with elaborate crests or headdresses (see cat. 25)[3]. The crested-bird jades in the Fu Hao tomb are remarkably varied in form, but most of them combine the essential features we see here: the tall crest, prominent beak, folded wing, thick legs, and short tail. Moreover, a bird-shaped bronze *zun* in the Fu Hao tomb embodies the crested-bird image in three dimensions.[4] Each of these remarkably diverse Shang objects demonstrates the power of the crested-bird image that we see superbly represented in this Norton jade.

PUBLISHED

Salmony, *Carved Jades &c.*, pl. XVII (1)[5]; Loo, *Exhibition of Chinese Arts* (1941), no. 224; Loo, *An Exhibition of Chinese Archaic Jades* (1950), pl. XV (7); Na Zhiliang, *Yuqi tongshi* vol. 1, p. 57; vol. 2, pp. 164–65, fig. a (after Loo, *An Exhibition of Chinese Archaic Jades*, 1950); Jayne, *The Chinese Collections*, no. 62

NOTES

1 Jenny So, in a personal communication, pointed out this combination of a small tab and holes, which is common among Shang crested birds ornaments and suggests they were intended to be mounted standing up.
2 See, among others, *Yinxu Fu Hao mu*, figs. 86–87, pls. 141–145. The Chinese archaeologists catalogued these as parrots, probably because of their beaks, but their features are distinctly un-parrotlike.
3 Rawson and Michaelson, *Chinese Jade*, cat. 12:14.
4 *Yinxu Fu Hao mu*, color pl. 7. See also Rawson and Michaelson, *Chinese Jade*, pp. 206–8, for the likely exotic, southern sources for such animal images in the Anyang period.
5 The reference comes from Jayne's 1972 catalogue, which does not provide a bibliography. It may refer to Alfred Salmony, *Carved Jade of Ancient China*, or to a sales catalogue.

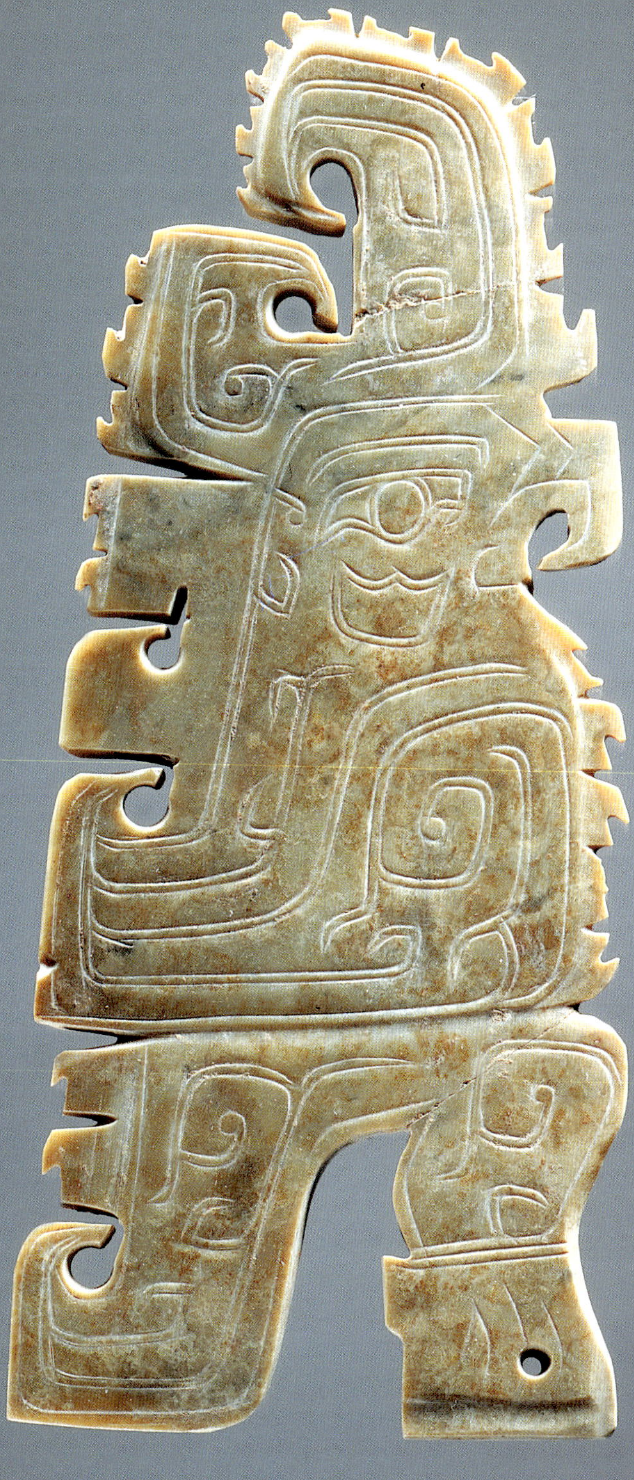

25 PENDANT WITH A HUMAN FIGURE

Shang dynasty, Anyang period, ca. 1200–1100 BCE
Jade, 3 5/8 × 7/8 × 1/4 in. (9.2 × 2.2 × .6 cm)
Gift of R.H. Norton, 50.3

Although there are striking Shang dynasty carvings of human figures in jade and stone, as well as in bronze, they are extraordinarily rare compared to animal and bird images. Jade pendants with human figures often follow the format we see here, curving as if the figure were part of a circle. The crest on top of the head of the Norton *Pendant* has a raised flange that is slightly thinner than the rest of the jade, and there is a hole drilled through the top of the *Pendant*. The large head has prominent features, including a wide eye and pointed ear rendered in thread relief. The nose, mouth, and chin are carefully modeled in low relief, and these features continue around the edge of the jade. There is a flange with diagonal lines along the upper back, the arms are shown bent at the elbows, and the hands and fingers curl up under the chin. The legs are folded below the body with the knees bent under the stomach and the stylized feet under the buttocks. There is a prominent mark in the shape of an X inside a circle on the hips. Fully carved on both sides, the stone is a translucent green with light brown veins with areas that have become opaque light tan from burial.

There are good reasons to believe that Shang images of humans with elaborate crests are the source of crested-bird images (see cat. 24).[1] It would appear that the elaborate high crests on Shang figures are descended from jades produced by the Neolithic cultures of China's east coast. Jades depicting human figures with elaborate crests have also been found at Neolithic Liangzhu sites in southeastern China, and Shang figures with elaborate crests perhaps represent a later reinterpretation of Neolithic examples. The connections between human and bird images are intriguing, and a comparison of the Norton's *Pendant with a human figure* and the *Crested bird* helps to illustrate this phenomenon. The high crest is an obvious link, but examples of birds and human figures can share other features,[2] such as the rectangular ears. In addition, the position of the arms—bent at the elbow with the stylized hands and fingers curled back under the chin—follows the outline of a bird wing, which is often depicted as a spiral on the shoulder with parallel lines sweeping toward the bird's back. Read in one direction, the design can be a wing; in the other direction, an arm. On the Norton pendant the feet are very close in style to the claws on jade birds, and some birds have thick legs and prominent bent knees (the tail notably absent) making them appear to be a bird's head and wings placed on a human lower body.[3] The circled X on the hips appears on other jade human figures,[4] while a bird in the Fu Hao tomb also has this distinctive emblem on its hips,[5] where, along with the bent knees and long toes, it may represent a composite bird-human.

PUBLISHED

Loo, *An Exhibition of Chinese Archaic Jades* (1950), pl. XXXI (7); Na Zhiliang, *Yuqi tongshi*, vol. 1, pl. 54.2 (after Loo, *An Exhibition of Chinese Archaic Jades*, 1950); Jayne, *The Chinese Collections*, no. 71

NOTES

1 Rawson and Michaelson, *Chinese Jade*, cat. 12:14.
2 See *Yinxu Fu Hao mu*, fig. 86 (1, 2, 3, 6, 10, 11, 16), fig. 87 (12, 13), among others.
3 See the rubbing in *Yinxu Fu Hao mu*, p. 166, text fig. 86 (3).
4 See, for example, Loo, *An Exhibition of Chinese Archaic Jades* (1950), pl. XXXI (9), opposite the jade purchased by the Norton.
5 *Yinxu Fu Hao mu*, p. 166, text fig. 86 (6).

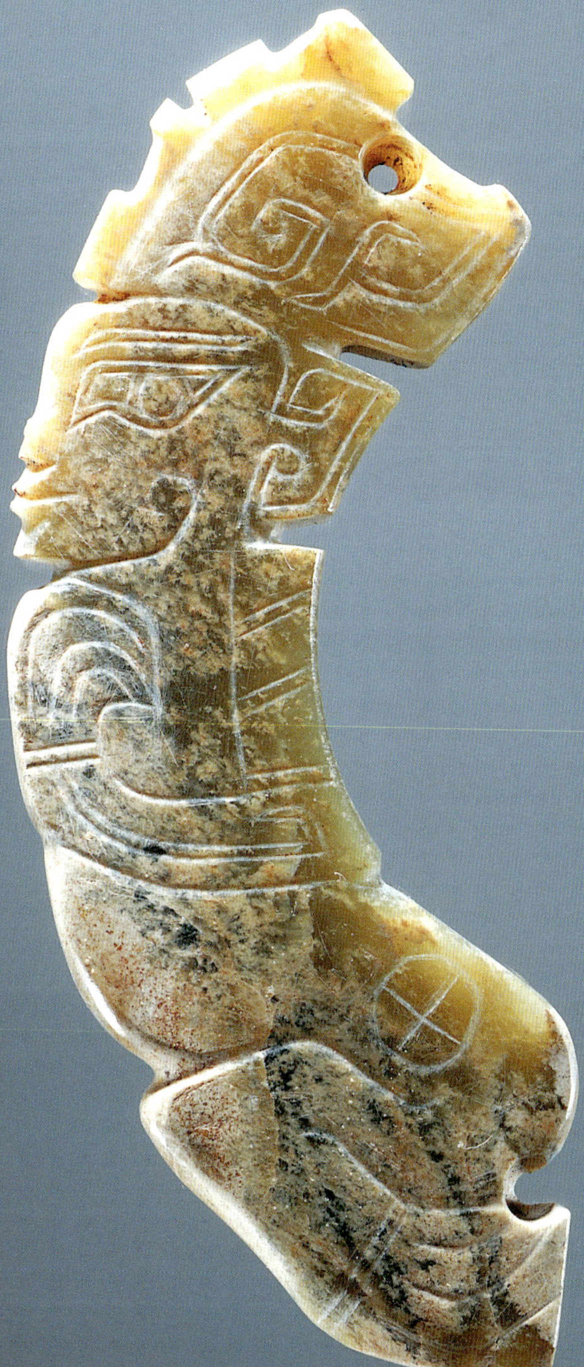

26 **DRAGON PENDANT**

Shang dynasty, Anyang period, ca. 1200 BCE
Jade $2\frac{5}{16} \times 2 \times \frac{1}{4}$ in. (5.9 × 5.1 × .6 cm)
Gift of R.H. Norton, 50.23

27 **DRAGON PENDANT**

Shang dynasty, Anyang period (ca. 1300–1050 BCE)
Jade, maximum diam. $1\frac{1}{4} \times \frac{5}{16}$ in. (3.2 × .8 cm)
Gift of Mr. Bartlett Richards, 91.29

The Museum's larger *Dragon pendant* (top) is carved from a particularly fine slab of translucent green jade. Remains of burial material, probably red cinnabar, fill some areas of the design, but most of the surface is clean and finely polished, revealing the quality of the stone. The jaws of the dragon are opened wide, as if swallowing the tip of the tail. Behind the eye, to the left, is a prominent ear or horn, with a hole for suspending the pendant just behind that. The pendant is carved on both sides, and a shallow groove between the ears is the only detail on the outside edge. The relatively large size of the piece and the thickness of the jade slab it was carved from both indicate the superior quality and value of this superb ornament.

The smaller *Dragon pendant* (bottom) is more three-dimensional in its modeling, and its carved details continue around the back and sides. The head is shown with the jaws grasping the end of the rather thick tail, and the eyes and other features are carved on the outside of the jade. Two bottle-shaped horns laid flat against the back of the head are the key feature identifying the animal. Diagonal parallel lines form a diamond pattern on the back of the dragon, and while this pattern is more often associated with Shang images of snakes, bottle-horn dragons in the ca. 1200 BCE Fu Hao tomb also have this diamond pattern covering their bodies.[1] The jade here is slightly yellow in tone, and there is one prominent natural vein as well as a network of tiny veins throughout the stone. In several places the very fine scratches of the Shang jade carver's tool are visible in the grooves that delineate the features and diamond design, giving us a faint glimpse of Shang jade-carving technology.

These two circular *Dragon pendants* are Shang dynasty adaptations of Neolithic jade dragons.[2] The animal generally classified as a dragon appears in a number of Neolithic cultures,[3] but the most striking examples come from the Hongshan culture (ca. 3500–2500 BCE) of China's northeastern Liaoning province.[4] Several Hongshan-type jades were found in the Fu Hao tomb,[5] and some may be Neolithic examples rediscovered in the Shang. Their circular form, with the head appearing to bite the tail, was likely the inspiration for dragons cut from flat plaques of jade in a more typically Shang style.[6] The Museum's two circular *Dragon pendants* illustrate the apparent attempt on the part of the Shang to recreate and reinterpret what must have already appeared to be an ancient artifact.[7]

PUBLISHED

26: Loo, *Jades Archaïques de Chine* (1925), pl. XVII (3); Loo, *An Exhibition of Chinese Archaic Jades* (1950), pl. XXVIII (7); Willetts, *Foundations of Chinese Art*, pl. 46; Jayne, *The Chinese Collections*, no. 67
27: Not previously published

NOTES

1 See among others *Yinxu Fu Hao mu*, fig. 83 (2–4).
2 See Rawson and Michaelson, *Chinese Jade*, pp. 205–8 and nos. 12:1–12:4, for circular dragon pendants in the Fu Hao tomb and the probable Shang revival of the Hongshan Neolithic dragon; for dragon pendants similar to the Norton example, see no. 12:4 and fig. 1(a), p. 211.
3 One of the earliest examples is from Anhui province. See *Lingjiatan yuqi*, no. 1.
4 Yang, ed., *The Golden Age*, cat. 10.
5 *Yinxu Fu Hao mu*, pl. 105.
6 Ibid., pl. 104.
7 See note 2, above, for references to this phenomenon.

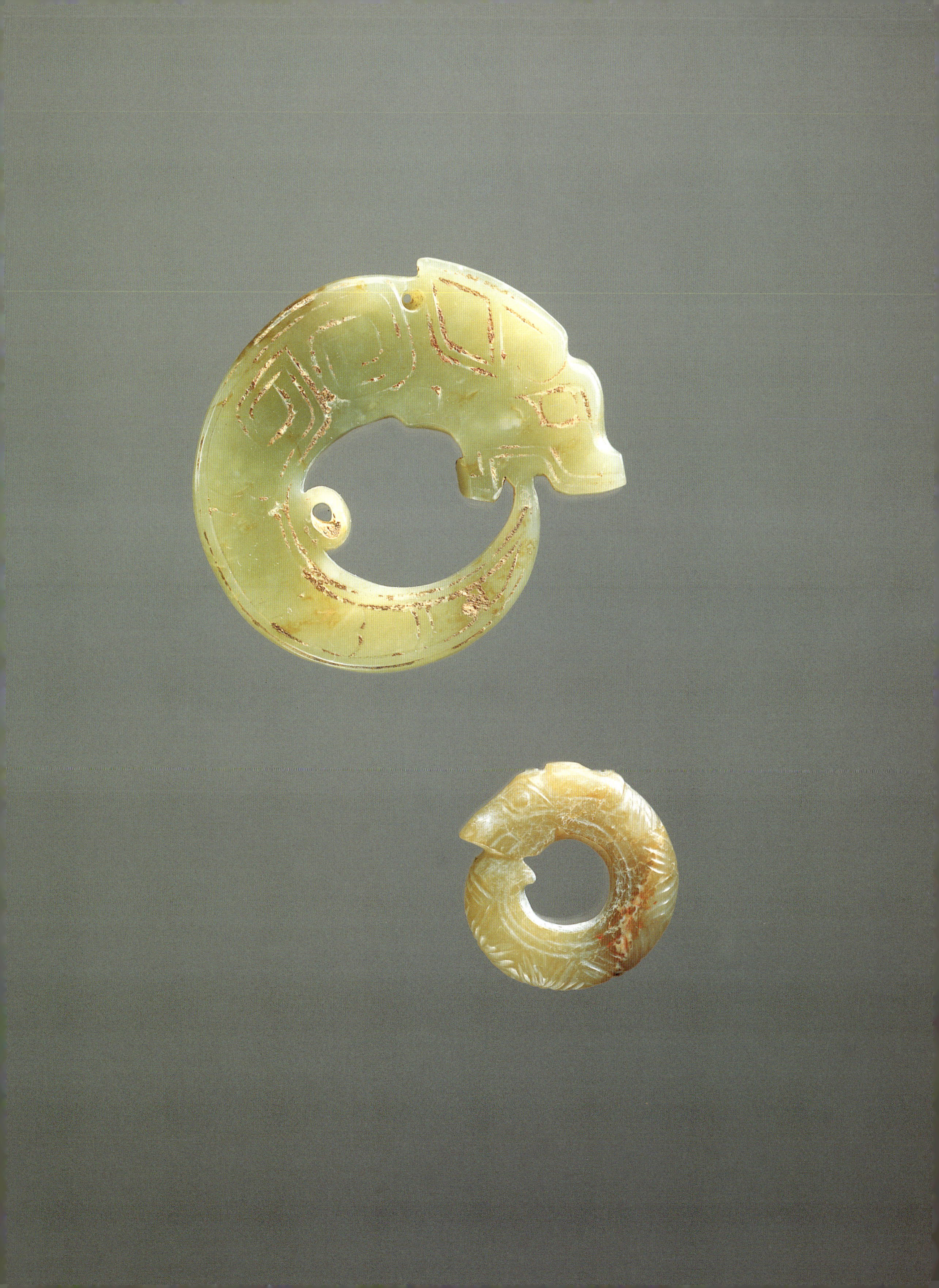

28 TIGER PENDANT

Shang dynasty, Anyang period, ca. 1200 BCE
Jade, 2 3/8 × 3/4 × 3/4 in. (6 × 1.9 × 1.9 cm)
Gift of R.H. Norton, 50.29

The Museum's *Tiger pendant* has a monumental presence that belies its miniature size. It is skillfully carved in the round from a piece of translucent gray-green jade whose surface has become almost completely opaque white from burial. Significant amounts of burial material, some bright red, adhere to the surface. The tiger is crouching with all four legs tucked under its body, the head held low, ears cocked back, and mouth open with sharp fangs clearly evident. The shoulders and the hips are subtly modeled and the end of the thick tail curves upward—all surprisingly lifelike details that portray a powerful feline predator crouched and about to strike.

Tiger-shaped jades in the Shang dynasty take many forms, from completely flat pendants to fully three-dimensional carvings. In some cases the tail ends in a beveled, bladelike appendage (see cat. 30), and a few examples have tails that loop to form a second hole for suspension.[1] At least two jade tigers closely comparable to the Museum's *Tiger pendant* were discovered in the ca. 1200 BCE tomb of Fu Hao,[2] although neither has quite the expressive power of the Norton example. A rather large—4 5/8 inches in length—malachite tiger from the Fu Hao tomb, however, is very close to the present example, including such details as the drilling that defines the mouth and fangs.[3] Jessica Rawson has noted that images of tigers in late Shang are most likely an exotic import from southern China, and probably arrived at the Shang capital at Anyang as elements of southern bronzes that were then replicated in jade.[4] One of the most impressive Shang tiger images decorates a flat stone chime, excavated at Anyang, that is almost 33 inches long.[5] Tigers seem to have seized the imagination of Shang jade carvers, and this *Tiger pendant* provides ample evidence of their skill in compressing the power of this great animal in a compact carving.

PUBLISHED

Catalogue of the International Exhibition of Chinese Art, no. 280; Loo, *An Exhibition of Chinese Archaic Jades* (1950), pl. XI (4); Jayne, *The Chinese Collections*, no. 64

NOTES

1 See Watt and Knight, *Chinese Jades from the Collection of the Seattle Art Museum*, cat. 16, for a tiger pendant dated late Shang to early Western Zhou. See also Yang, *Chinese Archaic Jades from the Kwan Collection*, cat. 83.
2 *Yinxu Fu Hao mu*, color pl. CXXXV (1,2).
3 Ibid., pl. CLXXV (4).
4 Rawson and Michaelson, *Chinese Jade*, p. 206; see also cat. 12:8.
5 See Rogers and others, *China 5,000 Years*, cat. 9.

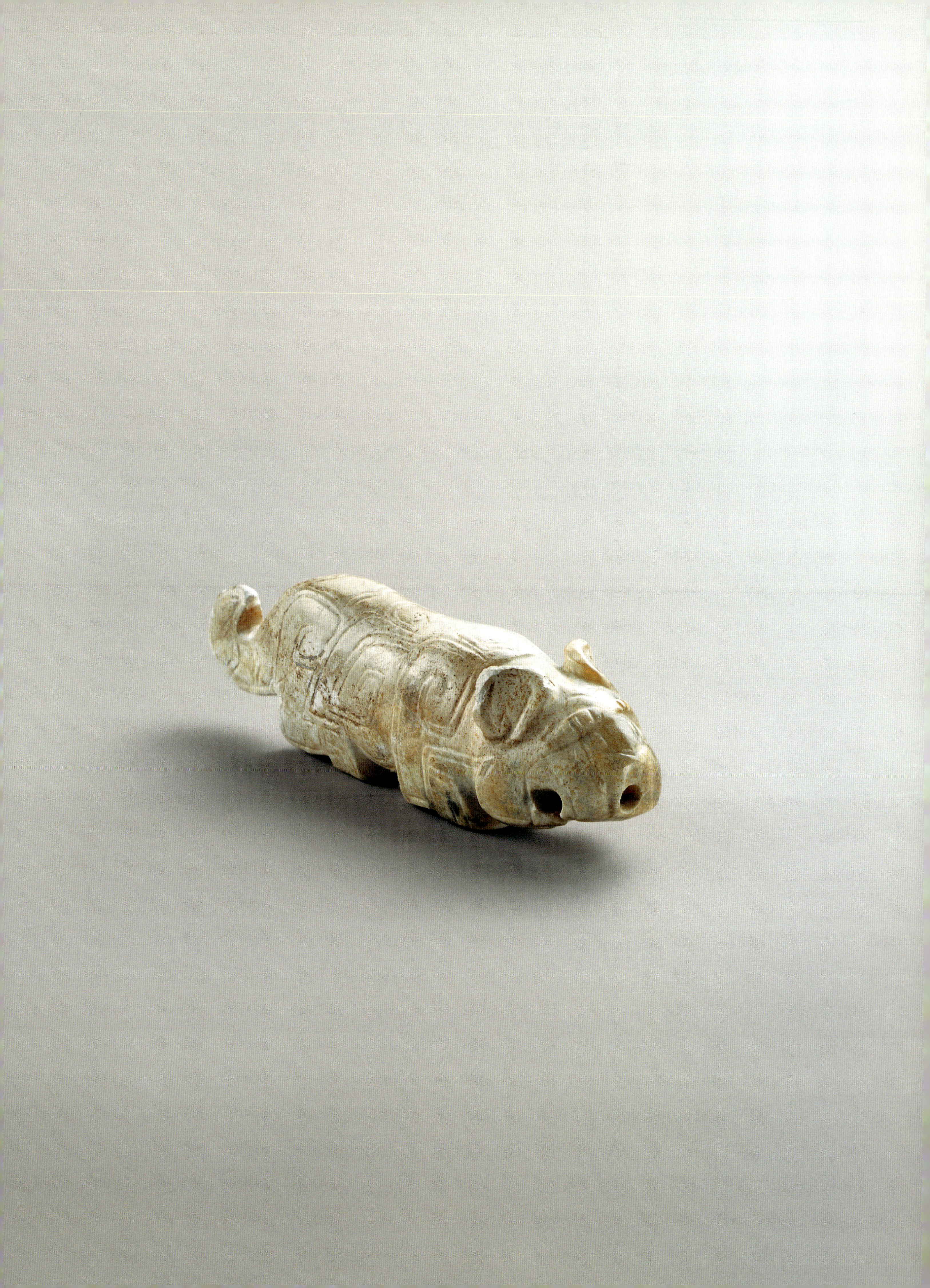

29 **DRAGON PENDANT**

Shang dynasty, Anyang period, ca. 1200 BCE
Jade, $3\frac{3}{16} \times \frac{7}{16} \times \frac{3}{16}$ in. (8.1 × 1.1 × .5 cm)
Gift of R.H. Norton, 50.24

30 **TIGER PENDANT**

Shang dynasty, Anyang period, ca. 1200 BCE
Jade $4\frac{1}{16} \times 1\frac{1}{8} \times \frac{1}{8}$ in. (10.3 × 2.9 × .3 cm)
Gift of R.H. Norton, 50.25

Carved with fine-line details on both sides, the *Dragon pendant* (top) has a head with the mouth wide open, a slanting eye, and a stylized bottle-shaped horn lying along the back of the neck. The features are similar to other dragon-shaped jades (see cats. 26, 27). The head is set off by a tiny notch behind the chin, and there is a hole drilled through the mouth as well as another hole at the base of the scraperlike tail. The body is decorated with a pattern of spirals, and the short parallel lines behind the chin are probably a stylized foot. The jade is a translucent pale gray-green that has become mostly opaque through alteration caused by burial. All the details of the surface design are softly rounded, as if they had been worn down.

The *Tiger pendant* (bottom) is vividly carved on both sides as a crouching tiger. It has an open mouth and large, square ears. There is a hole drilled through the eye and a second hole in the tail. The legs are tucked under the body and have stylized, angled claws. The whole body is covered with a design of wave-shaped marks cut at a flat angle into the thickness of the jade to render the tiger's stripes. The tail is very wide and ends in a slightly flaring beveled tool or blade of unknown use. The jade is very thin, only one-eighth of an inch thick, and is generally translucent gray-green with a network of fine, light tan veins throughout the stone. Small amounts of bright red burial material adhere in the details on one side of the tiger's head.

These two pendants are part of a group of jades, including tigers, fish, and other animals, that have flat, beveled, scraperlike tails. Although they seem to be tools for some specific purpose, there is no consensus on how the shape evolved or what it might have been used for. These toollike pendants appear in the Anyang period of the Shang dynasty (ca. 1300–1050 BCE) and continue into the early Western Zhou, when they seem to fall out of fashion.[1] The Museum's two pendants represent the range of such jades, and the large numbers of surviving examples strongly suggests that they had an intended use, one that is now unknown.

PUBLISHED

29: Loo, *An Exhibition of Chinese Archaic Jades* (1950), pl. XXVIII (7); Willetts, *Foundations of Chinese Art*, pl. 46; Jayne, *The Chinese Collections*, no. 66
30: Loo, *An Exhibition of Chinese Archaic Jades* (1950), pl. XXVIII (10); Willetts, *Foundations of Chinese Art*, pl. 461; Jayne, *The Chinese Collections*, no. 65

NOTE

1 See Rawson and Michaelson, *Chinese Jade*, cats. 12:11 and 12:13.

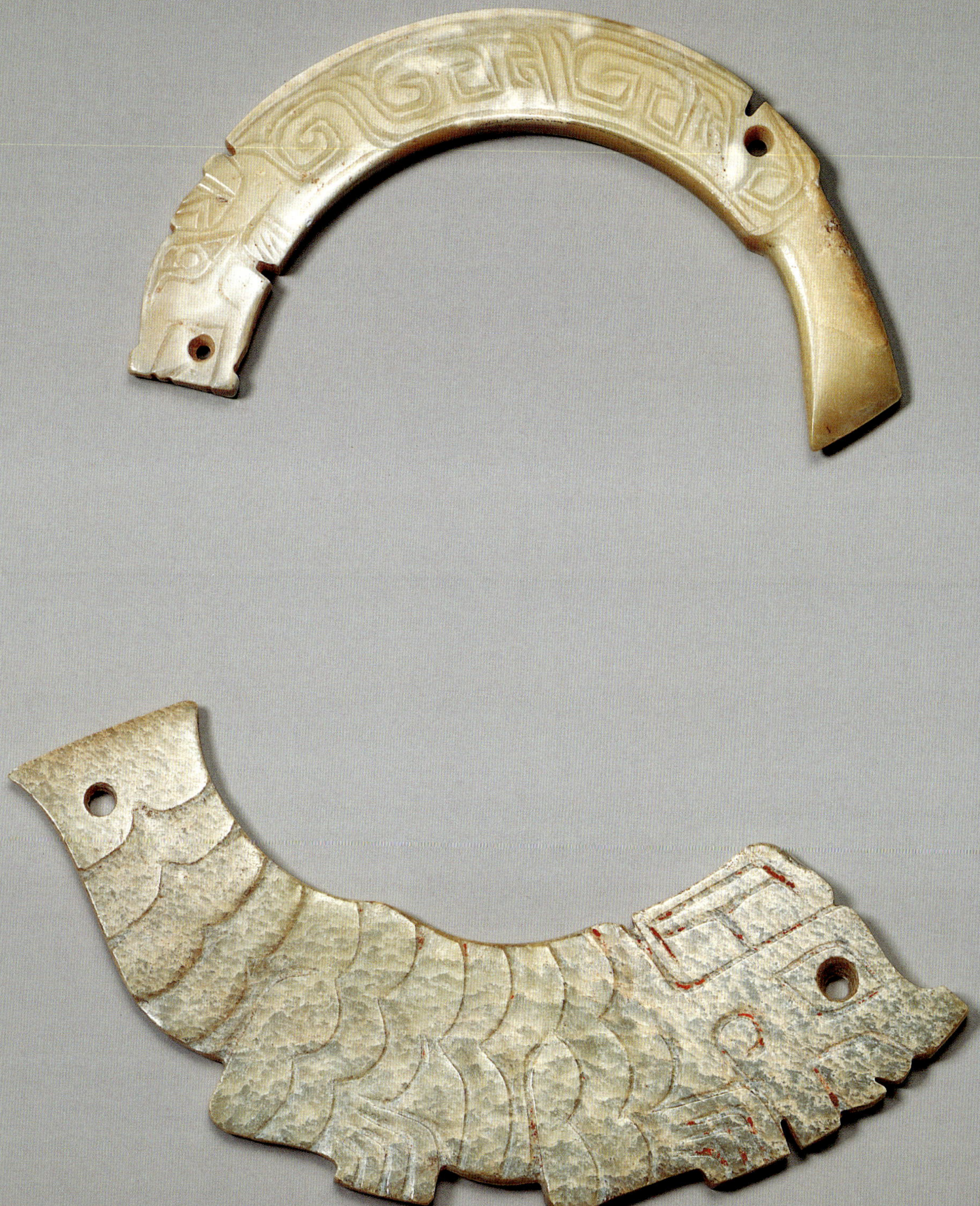

31 BOVINE-HEAD PLAQUE

Late Shang–early Western Zhou dynasty, ca. 1300–1000 BCE
Jade, 3 3/16 × 3 1/4 × 3/16 in. (8.1 × 8.3 × .5 cm)
Gift of R.H. Norton, 50.19

This relatively large plaque is carved from a thin sheet of pale gray jade suffused with a fine network of brown veins. The surface retains significant amounts of red material, most likely cinnabar or mercuric oxide, adhering from burial. Most of the design is carved in so-called pseudo-thread relief, that is, areas on both sides of the lines are almost imperceptibly beveled, so that they appear raised above the surface. The animal is most likely an ox or some other bovine. It has a broad snout and flaring nostrils, spreading cheekbones, small pointed ears and large horns—now partially missing—that probably curled inward over the top of the head. The small diamond shape in the center of the forehead and the prominent oblong crest incised with fine parallel lines in a chevron pattern are closely related to the mythological monster mask called a *taotie*, which occurs more frequently on bronzes than jades (see cat. 6). The back of the plaque is largely undecorated, and there is a large hole drilled from the back through the jade on the right-hand side. Invisible from the front, two small holes are drilled to meet each other through the edge of the jade at the point of the snout. These small, hidden holes and the undecorated back strongly suggest that this jade was intended to be attached to another object or article of clothing.

A number of Shang and early Zhou dynasty animal-head plaques have features similar to this piece, although most are smaller and have a large hole drilled through the center of the face. A white jade *taotie* mask in the Brundage collection, San Francisco, has a similar square snout with flaring nostrils.[1] A zoomorphic mask in the Kwan collection, Hong Kong, is more clearly a bovine head with long, pointed horns and a prominent diamond-shaped motif in the center of the forehead.[2] And a third plaque in the Hotung collection has a broad snout and nostrils, small pointed ears, and a dragon's bottle-shaped horns with a rectangular crest between them decorated with two rows of chevron patterns rendered in fine lines.[3] The jade plaque most comparable to the Norton piece in proportions and details was excavated in 1956 from a Western Zhou site near Chang'an in Shaanxi province.[4] It has a long, square snout, tiny ears, and horns that spiral over the top of the head. Both pieces have distinctive, wide-set eyes where the line of the inner corner of the eye continues down to form the center of the snout, and both have a prominent raised crest between the horns as well. A hole drilled through the tip of the nose of the Chang'an jade parallels the hole in the back of the Norton plaque. The editors of the original archaeological report noted specifically that this large group of jades perpetuated Shang styles into the early Western Zhou dynasty.

PUBLISHED

Jayne, *The Chinese Collections*, no. 63

NOTES

1 Lefebvre d'Argencé, *Chinese Jades in the Avery Brundage Collection*, pl. VI, lower right (accession no. B60 J805).
2 Yang, *Chinese Archaic Jades from the Kwan Collection*, cat. 71.
3 Rawson and Michaelson, *Chinese Jade*, cat. 12:17.
4 Hansford, *Chinese Carved Jades*, pl. 19, p. 100, citing Institute of Archaeology, comp., *Xin Zhongguo de kaogu shouhuo* (*Archaeology in New China*) (Beijing: 1961), p. 54, pl. XXXV (2).

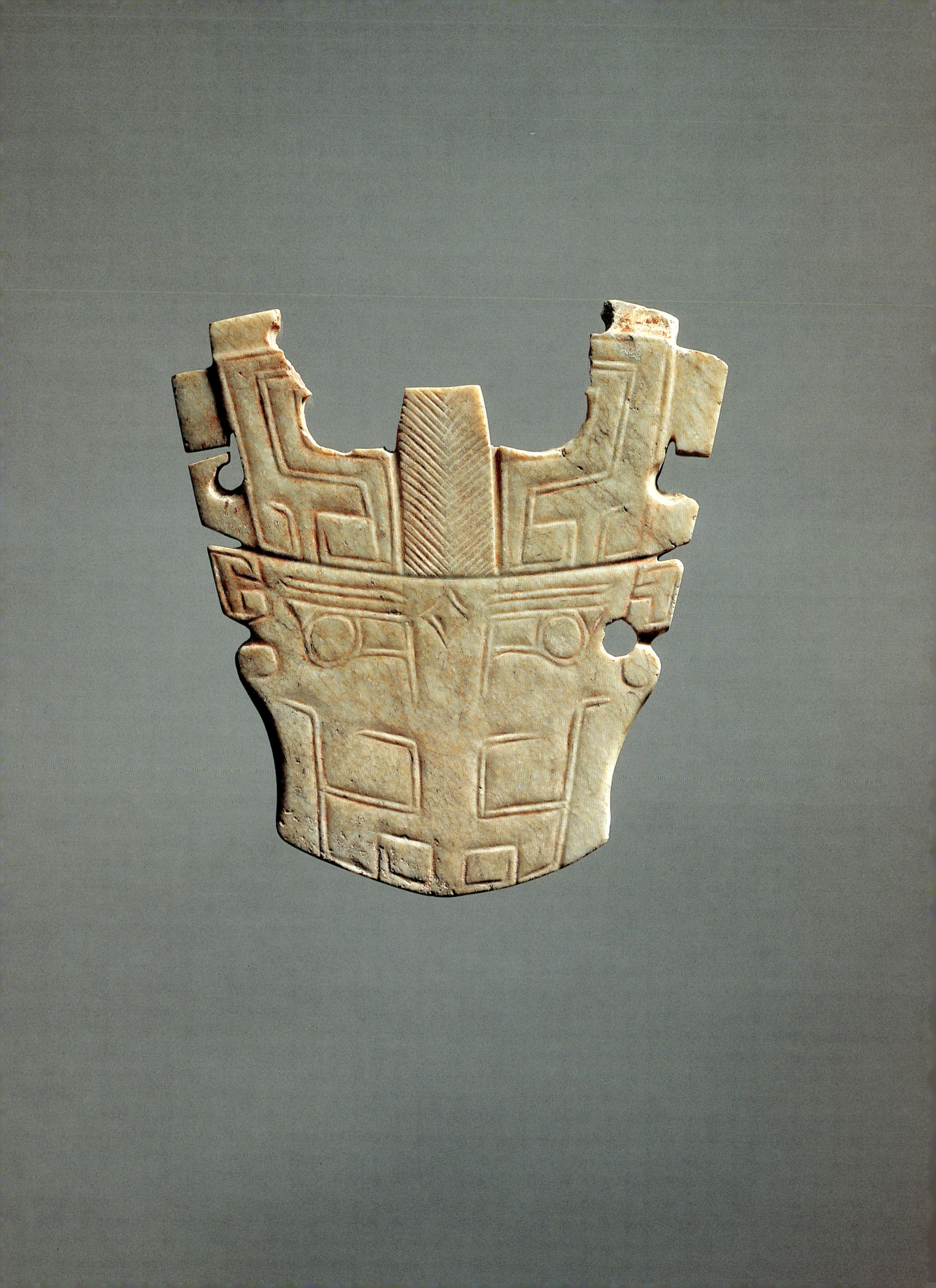

32 OBJECT IN THE FORM OF THREE BIRDS

Late Shang dynasty, ca. 1300–1000 BCE
Jade, 1 3/16 × 1 9/16 × 1 1/8 in. (3 × 4 × 2.9 cm)
Gift of R.H. Norton, 50.33

This small object is perhaps the Norton's most mysterious jade. Carefully carved on all sides, it is formed of two short-tailed birds perched on the outspread wings of a third bird that forms the base. The bottom bird—possibly an owl—has a wide head, large round eyes, and a short beak, which appear in low relief on the front edge of the jade; its broad outspread tail splits into two short plumes. The two perching birds have thick legs, deep breasts, and rounded heads with small pointed beaks and prominent round eyes. They are depicted with their squared-off tails pointing down toward the back edge, and both have bodies that curve slightly outward. Each perching bird has a hole drilled through the center of the breast, and a large hole is drilled down through the center of the bottom bird. Significantly, the lower end of this hole on the bottom of the jade (not visible in the photo) has a raised collar around it. The stone is a translucent, gray-green jade with a few veins of darker brown material. Much of the surface has become a powdery opaque white, most likely due to the conditions of burial, and significant amounts of reddish-brown burial material adhere to the surface.

Although individual birds are common in the Neolithic period and succeeding Shang dynasty, there are no examples comparable to this composite object. A jade owl from the Neolithic Hongshan culture shows relatively naturalistic details, such as the head and outspread wings, rendered in the characteristically rounded, soft-edged forms of Hongshan jade animals.[1] Hongshan and other Neolithic jades were found in the ca. 1200 BCE Shang dynasty tomb of Fu Hao,[2] and Hongshan dragon pendants were certainly the inspiration for Shang pendants (see cats. 26, 27). Knowledge of Hongshan birds may have helped perpetuate the style of carving we see in many Shang birds, which contrasts with Shang jades more typically cut from flat slabs. A Shang dynasty bird with outspread wings in the Kwan collection, for example, seems to replicate the round Hongshan bird form, emphasizing the head with disk-like eyes and the schematic, spreading tail feathers.[3] Yang Boda's description of that jade bird notes specifically the "short tube-shaped protuberance on the abdomen," which seems comparable to the raised collar surrounding the hole on the bottom of the Norton jade. Birds with stout legs, short beaks, round eyes, folded wings and long tails are relatively common among Shang jades,[4] and it is this general type that provides the proposed date for the Museum's puzzling *Object in the form of three birds*. The several holes indicate that it was indeed attached to something else, perhaps as a finial or an ornament or even a pendant, but for the present its intended function remains a subject of conjecture.

PUBLISHED

Loo, *An Exhibition of Chinese Archaic Jades* (1950), pl. XXVII (5); Jayne, *The Chinese Collections*, no. 59

NOTES

1 Yang, ed., *The Golden Age*, cat. 16.
2 See *Yinxu Fu Hao mu*, pls. CLXII (1) and CLXIV (1). See also Rawson and Michaelson, *Chinese Jade*, pp. 205–8 and nos. 12:1–12:4.
3 Yang, *Chinese Archaic Jades from the Kwan Collection*, cat. 97, dated late Shang (ca. 14th–11th centuries BCE).
4 See Hansford, *Chinese Carved Jades*, pl. 12 (2, 3), for examples excavated at Anyang. See also *Yinxu fajue baogao*, pl. LXV (2), for another excavated Shang example.

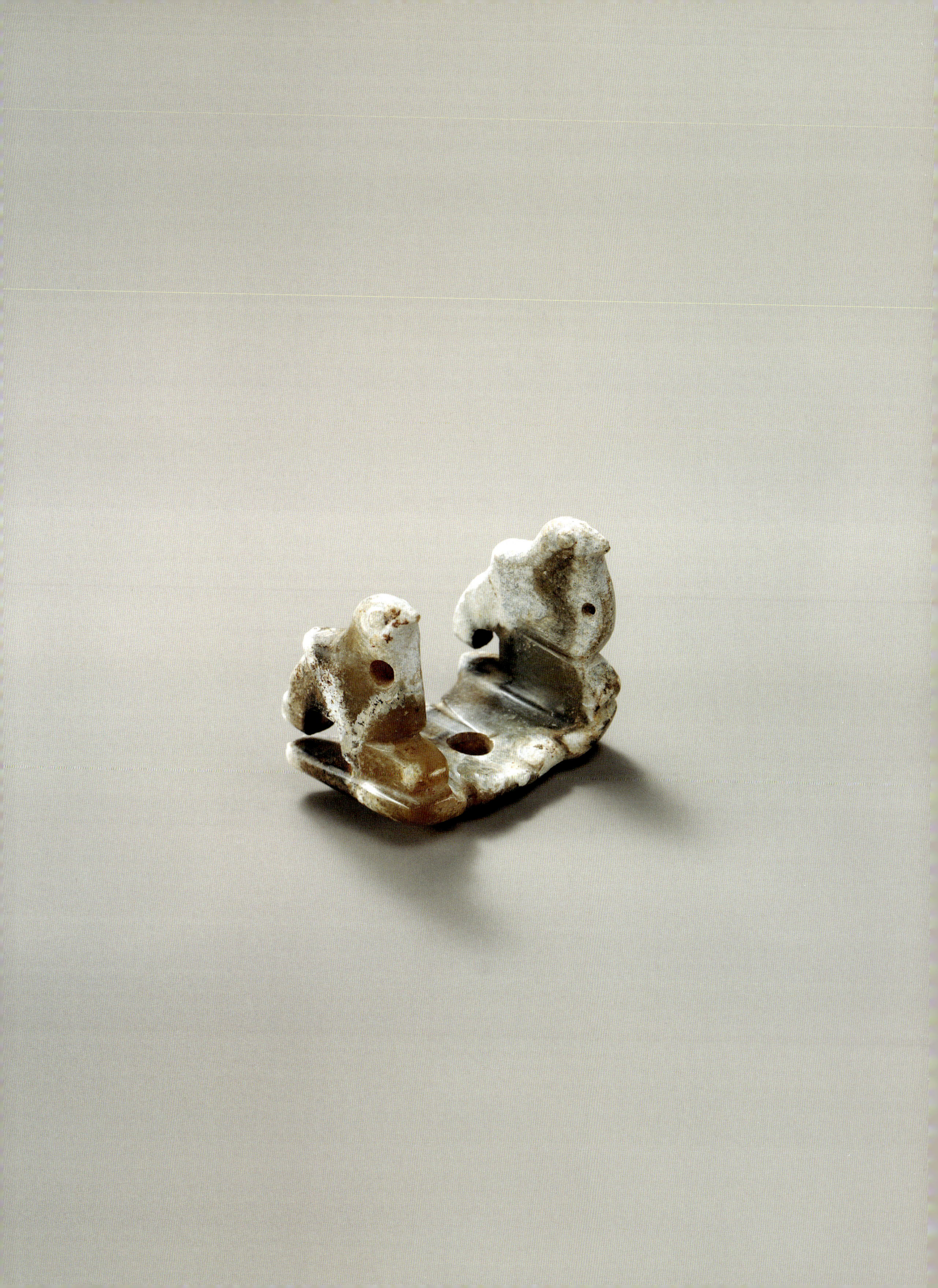

33 PENDANT OR AMULET WITH A HORNED BIRD

Western Zhou dynasty (ca. 1100–771 BCE)
Jade, 4 × 1 1/4 × 3/16 in. (10.2 × 3.2 × .5 cm)
Gift of R. Norton Richards, 91.36

34 LONG-TAILED BIRD PENDANT OR AMULET

Western Zhou dynasty (ca. 1100–771 BCE)
Jade, 3 × 1 3/16 × 1/8 in. (7.6 × 3 × .3 cm)
Gift of R.H. Norton, 50.4

Jade birds in the Western Zhou represent the continuation of Shang traditions as well as new designs borrowed from bronzes. The *Pendant* or *amulet with a horned bird* (top) is in many ways the Western Zhou descendant of Shang jades like the *Crested bird* (cat. 24). It retains the sharply hooked beak, wings drawn as spirals with parallel lines, thick tails, and solid legs of Shang prototypes. The elaborate crest, in contrast to Shang birds, has been changed into a pair of branching bottle-shaped horns. The jade has been almost completely altered by burial to an opaque tan with only a few scattered translucent areas. Significant amounts of bright red cinnabar, the result of burial practices, adhere to the surface.

The smaller *Long-tailed bird pendant* (bottom) is carved from a piece of light green jade that has not been much altered by burial and remains relatively translucent, although it also has accretions of red burial material. This bird, too, repeats the Shang convention of representing the wing as a spiral with parallel lines extending out from it. The design is so stylized, however, it might be difficult to recognize it as a wing without knowing the tradition from which it springs. The bird has a hooked beak, large round eye, and a spiraling crest—elements that represent new features of Western Zhou bird forms. The carver has focused his energy on the long tail, which extends to an unusual length, helping the jade to fill out the general shape of a section of a ring or circle.

Birds were an increasingly important motif on bronze ritual vessels of the late Shang and early Western Zhou,[1] and it is to those that we turn for the sources of the two Norton jades. Birds had long filled the minor ranges of bronze decoration, and as they became more prominent, they took on more fantastic forms. A covered *you* from the early Western Zhou in the Freer Gallery, Washington, D.C., has an exuberant decoration that includes birds (and other animals) with bottle-shaped horns that have sprouted radiating points.[2] The horned bird here is a not-too-distant cousin of those birds. A covered *gui* in the Arthur M. Sackler collection, Smithsonian Institution, has birds with boldly hooked outlines that extend to fill the various available spaces,[3] and the hooked prongs of the long-tailed bird here recreate those bronze forms. On the Norton *Long-tailed bird*, the two bands with central oval panels that stretch across the tail are an unusual element, most likely reflecting yet another bronze precedent. While Shang jade birds may have had a life of their own, Western Zhou birds seem to take their inspiration from the growing vitality of bronze birds.

PUBLISHED

33: Not previously published
34: Loo, *An Exhibition of Chinese Archaic Jades* (1950), pl. XXX (6); Jayne, *The Chinese Collections*, no. 61

NOTES

1 On the evolution of Western Zhou bird motifs, see Rawson, *Western Zhou Ritual Bronzes*, pp. 75–83.
2 See Bagley, *Shang Ritual Bronzes*, fig. 220, Freer Gallery of Art (acc. no. 30.26).
3 Rawson, *Western Zhou Ritual Bronzes*, cat. 38, an early Western Zhou *gui* (acc. no. S-870003a,b).

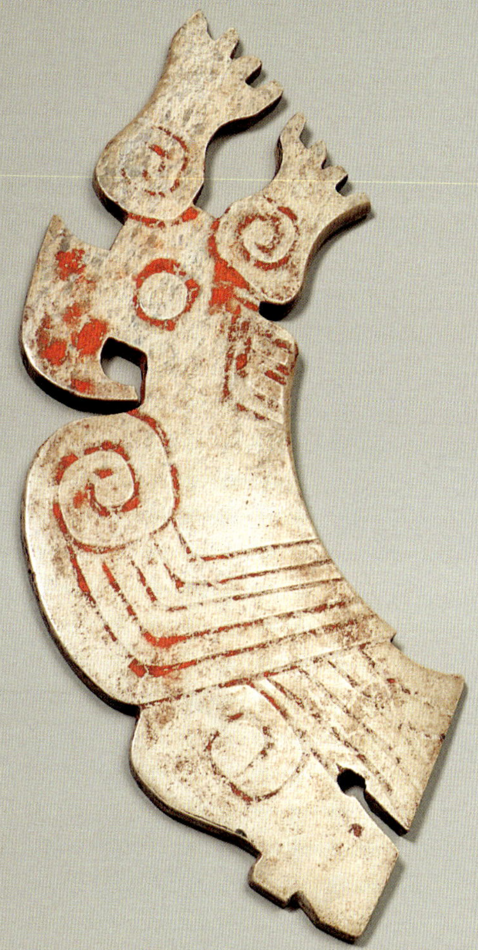

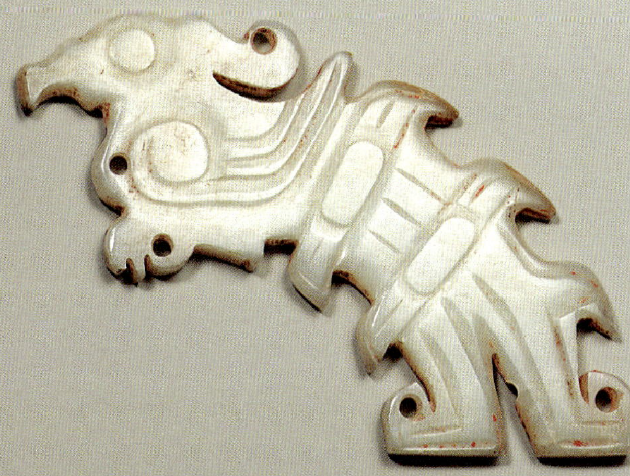

35 PENDANT IN THE FORM OF A WATER BIRD

Late Shang–early Western Zhou dynasty, ca. 1200–1000 BCE
Jade, 2 1/4 × 1 1/8 × 3/16 in. (5.7 × 2.9 × .5 cm)
Gift of R.H. Norton, 50.7

36 RABBIT AMULET OR PENDANT

Western Zhou dynasty (ca. 1100–771 BCE)
Jade, 1 11/16 × 2 × 3/16 in. (4.3 × 5.1 × .5 cm)
Gift of R.H. Norton, 50.9

37 PENDANT IN THE FORM OF A STAG

Western Zhou dynasty (ca. 1100–771 BCE)
Jade, 1 7/16 × 2 3/16 × 3/16 in. (3.7 × 5.6 × .5 cm)
Gift of R.H. Norton, 50.8

The *Pendant in the form of a water bird* (top) may represent a duck or cormorant, with a slightly hooked bill, large round eye, and broad wings, which are rendered in a familiar convention as a spiral at the shoulder and parallel lines continuing to the back. The short legs are tucked up under the body, and the broad tail is split in two plumes. A small hole is drilled through the breast, and the tail is beveled at the edge. Similar water birds are known from Shang and Western Zhou sites.[1]

The surprisingly naturalistic *Rabbit amulet* or *pendant* (left) has long, concave ears, which are divided by a narrow groove around their outside edge, a long neck, and taut, crouching body. Rabbits of this type appear to be a Western Zhou innovation,[2] and examples have been found in Zhou tombs at Baoji, in Shaanxi province.[3]

The *Pendant in the form of a stag* (right) is perhaps the most intriguing of these three animal-shaped jades. The carving shows close attention to detail: the alert ear is slightly concave, and the legs end in tiny, pointed hooves. The broad spirals that outline the haunches of both legs are an unusual detail, a design element that is closer to Shang jades.

The image of an animal turning its head appears occasionally in early China.[4] The Western Zhou site at Baoji mentioned above yielded jade stags turning to look over their backs that are close to the Norton *Pendant in the form of a stag* as well as bronze chariot ornaments with images of stags.[5] Some of these ornaments show a Chinese-style mythological animal-head gripped by a small human figure that is tattooed with pairs of deer turning their heads. Chinese archaeologists identify these figures as non-Chinese, perhaps members of the Western Rong or Qiang peoples,[6] who lived on the northwestern frontiers of Zhou China and had extensive contacts with it.[7] The appearance of jade stags with this distinctive posture—and their use as emblems literally tattooed on foreigners—points to a compelling image adapted by Chinese artists looking beyond China's borders.

PUBLISHED

35: Loo, *An Exhibition of Chinese Archaic Jades* (1950), pl. LVIII (5); Jayne, *The Chinese Collections*, no. 58
36: Loo, *An Exhibition of Chinese Archaic Jades* (1950), pl. XXIX (5); Jayne, *The Chinese Collections*, no. 56
37: Loo, *An Exhibition of Chinese Archaic Jades* (1950), pl. X (2); Jayne, *The Chinese Collections*, no. 57

NOTES

1 See Rawson and Michaelson, *Chinese Jade*, cat. 12:28, for a bird with a similar silhouette but a hole for the eye.
2 Ibid., cats. 12:37, 12:38.
3 *Baoji Yu guo mudi*, vol. 2, color pl. 28 (4), and pl. 185 (4, 5).
4 For animals in this distinctive attitude, see *Yinxu Fu Hao mu*, color pl. XXX (4), identified as a "deer" but perhaps a newborn calf; color pl. XXXI (2) and pl. CXXXVI (2) for recumbent bovines; and fig. 84 (3) for a dog.
5 *Baoji Yu guo mudi*, vol. 2, pls. 183–84, jade stags; and pls. 213, 216, among others, for chariot ornaments.
6 Ibid., vol. 1, p. 448.
7 Hsu and Linduff, *Western Chou Civilization*, pp. 55–56, 58, 211, 225, 258, among others.

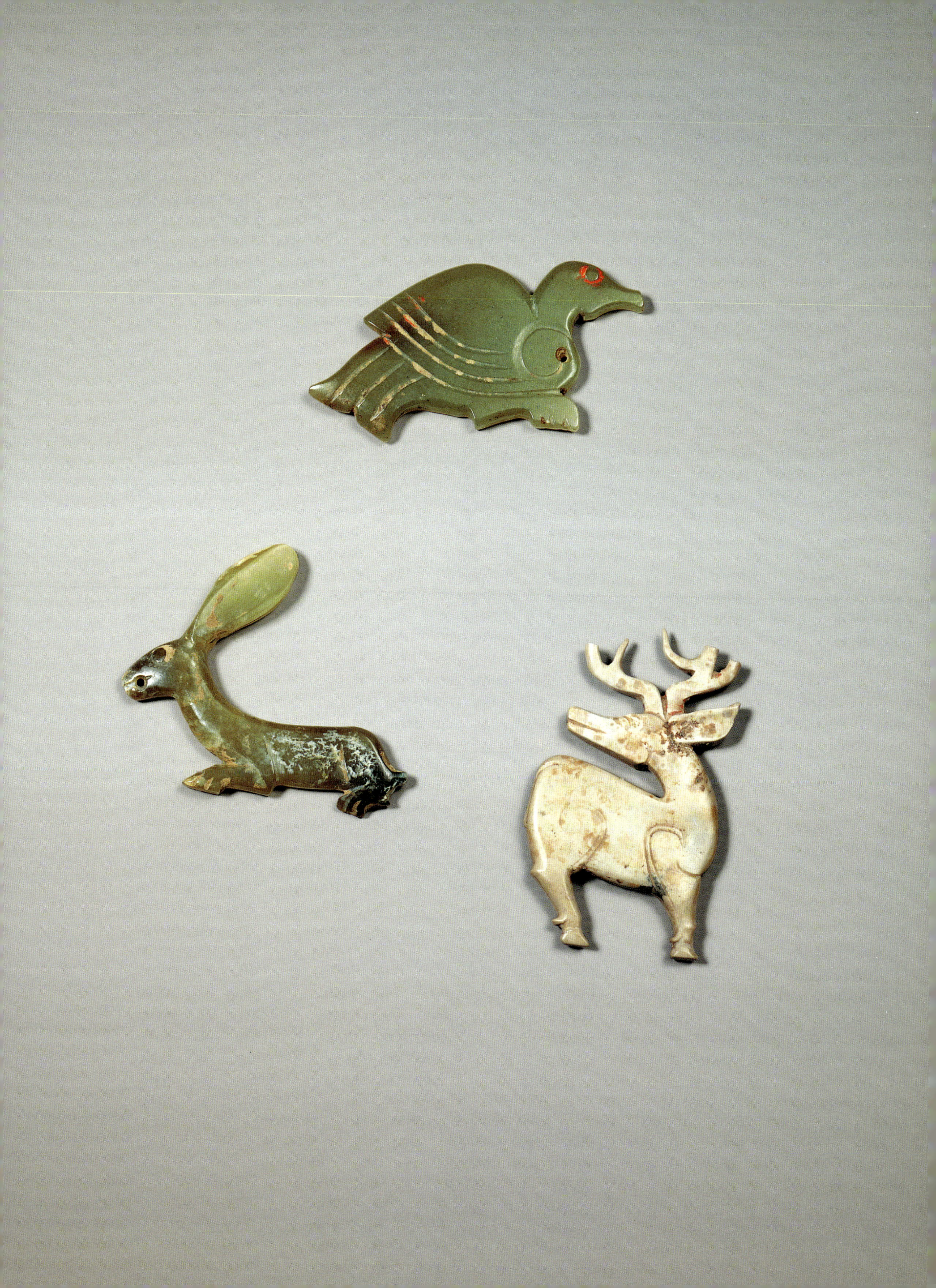

38 PAIR OF DRAGON PENDANTS

Eastern Zhou dynasty, early Warring States period, ca. 5th century BCE
Jade, each 5 × ¾ × 3/16 in. (12.7 × 1.9 × .5 cm)
Gift of R. Norton Richards, 91.33, 91.34

39 DRAGON PENDANT

Eastern Zhou dynasty, Qin State, ca. 6th–5th century BCE
Jade, 3 ½ × 7/8 × 1/8 in (8.9 × 2.2 × .3 cm)
Gift of R.H. Norton, 50.30

These pendants represent just two of the many forms that dragons could take in early Chinese art. Each of the *Pair of dragon pendants* (top) has a long snout that turns back to form the nostrils. Bordering the nose and mouth is a band engraved with fine lines that gives the impression of spiraling or twisting. The eye is a tiny, nearly imperceptible oval just behind the snout, and the horns that appeared on Shang dragons have here been reduced to a narrow bar on the back of the head. A raised border outlines the animals. Their simplified S-shaped bodies are covered with an overall design of tiny raised spirals derived from the designs on a Zhou jade *bi* disk (see cat. 41), where their alignment along three axes that intersect at 60-degree angles can be more clearly seen. From the evidence of unfinished pairs of jade ornaments, we know that the rough outline was sometimes cut first from a slab of jade, after which the piece was carefully sliced in two matching halves. Individual finishing of each piece produces minor variations between pairs. Although great varieties of dragon pendants appear in the Eastern Zhou, one excavated example is quite close to the Norton pair. Discovered tomb at Qufu, in Shandong province, the city that was the capital of Confucius's home state of Lu, it has a very similar compressed head, turned-back nose, and body with only two small hooks to represent the legs.[1]

Like the *Pair of dragon pendants*, the single *Dragon pendant* has a small hole carefully drilled in the center of the back so that it could be worn as a personal ornament. There is also a small hole drilled part way through the crook of the tail but left unfinished. The *Dragon pendant* has a relatively large head on which the features are very distinctly squared off. The slit that represents the mouth comes down from the top of the snout and turns at a right angle to spiral into the center of the head. Again, the eye is an almost imperceptible oval lost among the raised and engraved spirals. The head and body are covered with a design of thick spirals that fill all the available space. The square head and somewhat random spiral designs are typical of jades from the state of Qin on China's northwestern frontier, as is the tail that is bent back over the body.[2]

PUBLISHED

38: Not previously published
39: Loo, *An Exhibition of Chinese Archaic Jades* (1950), pl. LIV (4); Jayne, *The Chinese Collections*, no. 70

NOTES

1 *Zhongguo yuqi quanji*, vol. 3, no. 184. There is a closely comparable pair in the Grenville L. Winthrop Collection, Harvard University; see Loehr, *Ancient Chinese Jades*, no. 436.
2 Yeung, *Zhongguo guyu yanjiu lunwenji*, vol. 1, p. 173, fig. 5 (9–10).

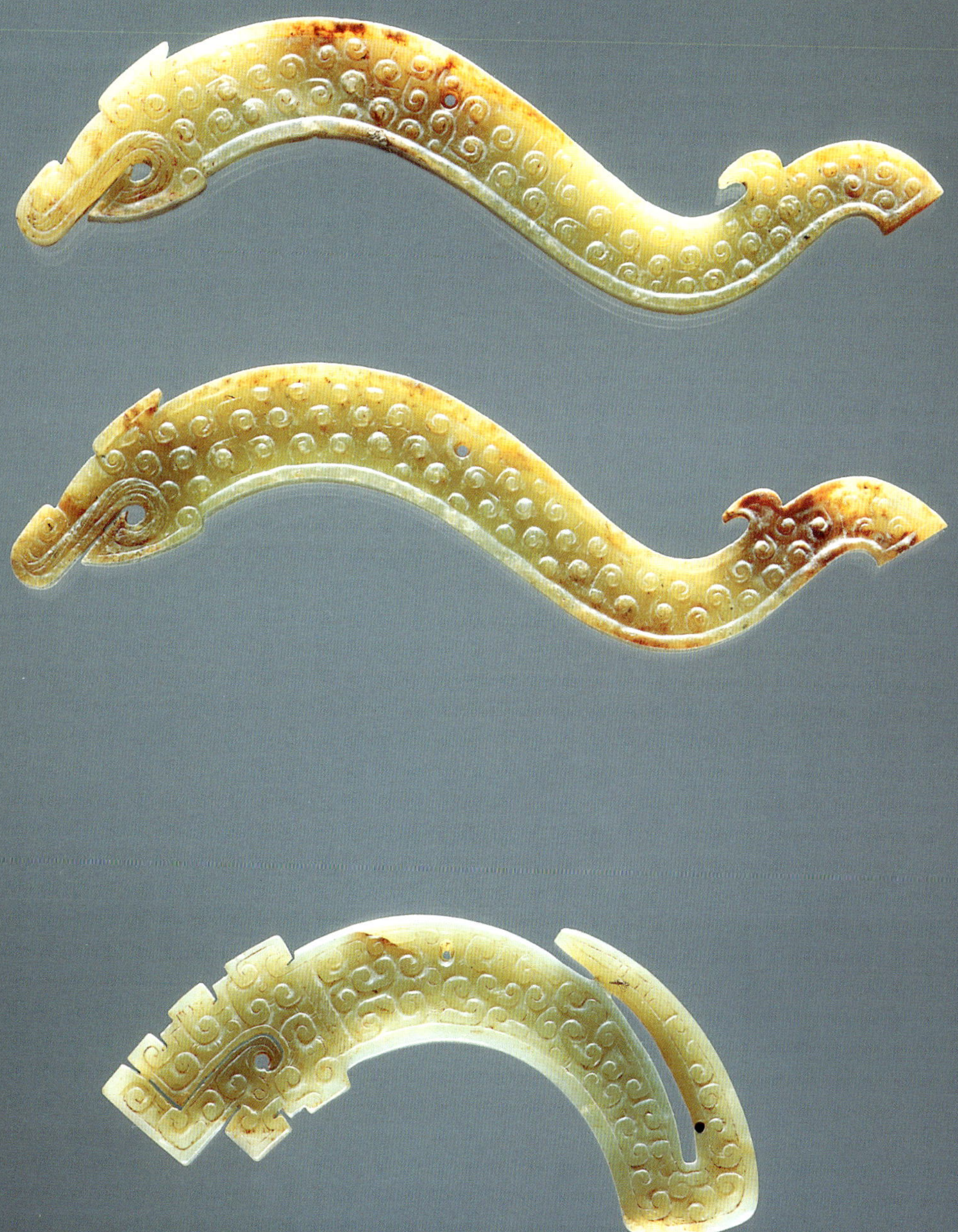

40 RING-SHAPED ORNAMENT

Eastern Zhou dynasty, Spring and Autumn period, ca. 6th century BCE
Jade, 3/16 × diam. 2 1/2 in. (.5 × 6.4 cm)
Gift of R.H. Norton, 50.2

The decoration on both sides of this small *Ring-shaped ornament* consists of eight dragon-heads in four pairs, one pair positioned face-to-face in each quadrant. The highly stylized faces can be identified by the round eyes with tiny raised pupils in the centers. Behind each eye are two squared spirals turning toward the eye, while in front of each eye a squared spiral nose turns upward and, on a few of the heads, a thin curving tongue hangs down. Note the spacing between the two back-to-back heads at the bottom of the ring, where the jade worker appears to have slightly miscalculated the layout of the design, so that the two back-to-back heads at the bottom have less space than the others. The spirals behind the eyes have been joined as a C-shaped curl clearly visible in the whitish patch along the very bottom edge. The design is highly abstract, difficult to make out, and many elements only suggest actual parts of a face.

Max Loehr has discussed this dragon-head design and its evolution from relatively recognizable images to abstract, geometrically ordered rows of tiny spirals (cat. 41). Although the organization of the design here is not immediately clear, it contains all the elements of a dragon-head seen on a 7th-century BCE plaque from the tomb of the Marquis of Cai, Shouxian, Anhui province.[1] The various bands of the decoration on the Norton *Ring-shaped ornament* are carefully polished and slightly angled in different directions, and, since the whole surface is slightly curved, the cutting and polishing makes the ring sparkle subtly as it moves.

The form of the flattened ring is well known, although most examples are decorated with fine spiraling lines or fluting.[2] Representations of these rings appear on lacquer-painted tomb figures of the Eastern Zhou,[3] where they form part of an assemblage of jades linked by cords and worn as personal ornaments. The Norton *Ring-shaped ornament* is most likely this type of jade, and as such was clearly designed to be appreciated closely by its wearer.

PUBLISHED

Loo, *Archaic Chinese Jades* (1940), pl. I; Loo, *An Exhibition of Chinese Archaic Jades* (1950), pl. LV, 2; Jayne, *The Chinese Collections*, no. 51

NOTES

1 Loehr, *Ancient Chinese Jades*, pp. 25–26, fig. 11.

2 See Rawson and Michaelson, *Chinese Jade*, cat. 17:1, Eastern Zhou; see also Yang, *Chinese Archaic Jades from the Kwan Collection*, cats. 171–173.

3 Rawson and Michaelson, *Chinese Jade*, cat. 17:1, fig. 1. See also *Zhongguo yuqi quanji*, vol. 3, pp. 39–40, figs. 24–27, lacquer-painted tomb figures depicted wearing various combinations of jade ornaments, including small rings. And see Jenny So's essay in this catalogue, pp. 25–26, and fig. 12.

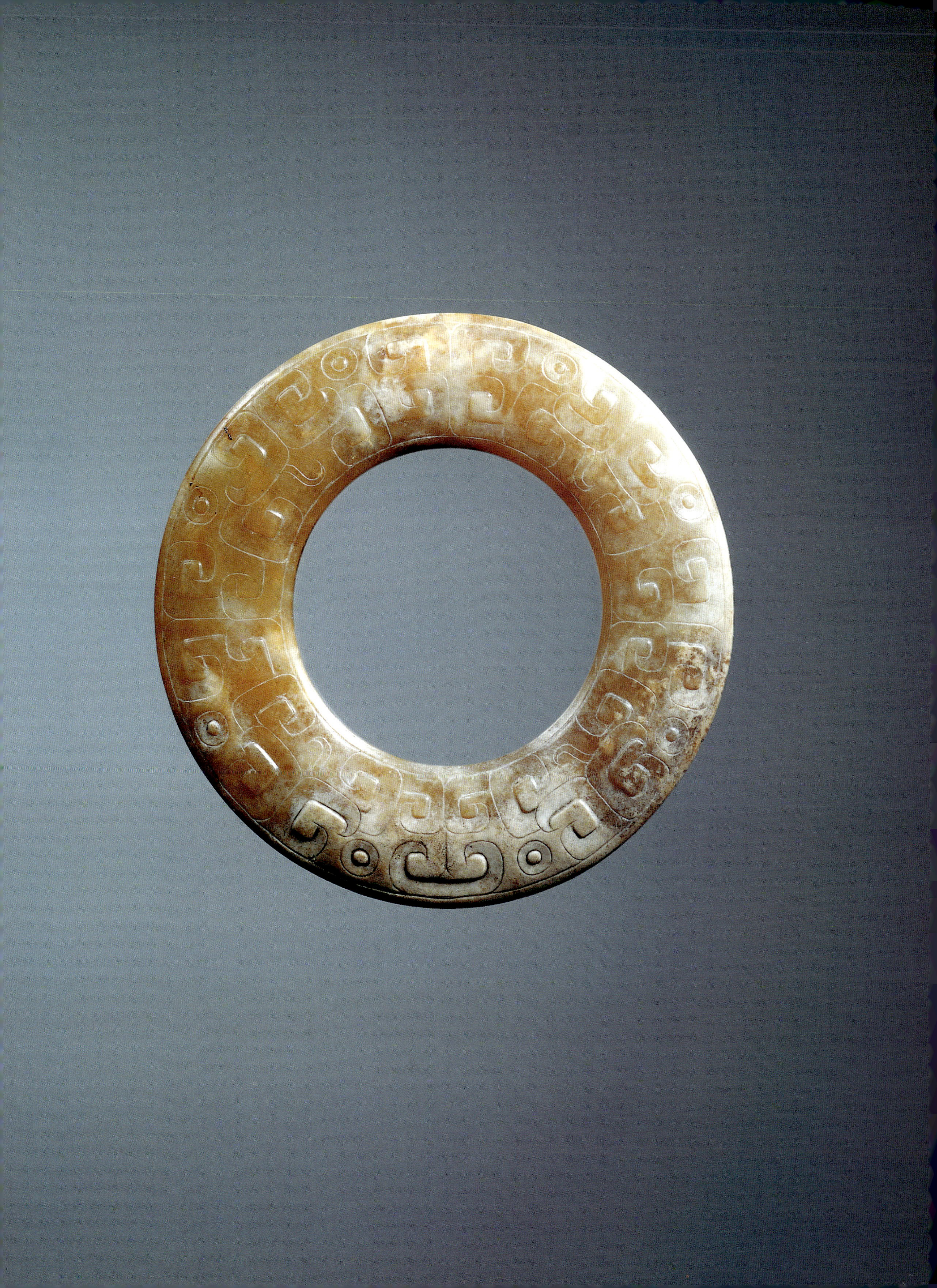

41 DISK (*BI*)

Eastern Zhou dynasty, Warring States period, ca. 4th–3rd century BCE
Jade, 3⁄16 × diam. 5 9⁄16 in. (.5 × 14.1 cm)
Gift of R.H. Norton, 50.15

The form of a large, flat disk with a hole in the center, later designated a *bi* disk, originated among China's Liangzhu culture around 3000–2500 BCE. The Liangzhu also created the squared tubular jade called a *cong*, and although we do not know if their Neolithic originators made specific connections between these two important and long-lived forms, by at least the Eastern Zhou they had come to be paired as complementary ritual objects.[1] Jades of the Neolithic *bi* form—a large disk with a relatively small hole in the center in contrast with smaller circular pierced jade ornaments that have large central holes—are very rarely found in Shang and Western Zhou dynasty burials. In the Eastern Zhou and Han, however, they appear in much larger numbers, often with decorated surfaces, and seem to be associated with Zhou and Han burial practices.[2]

The Norton *bi* disk is cut from translucent light yellow-green jade with a large area of darker brown along one side. Part of one edge is a more opaque tan, most likely the result of burial conditions. The outside and the central hole are bordered with a narrow frame that is slightly beveled toward the decorated front surface, which is covered with a regular pattern of tiny raised spirals. Although equally spaced to form a grid of lines intersecting at 60-degree angles, each of the spirals is slightly different: they twist clockwise or counterclockwise with no discernible pattern, and their tiny points taper off in various directions. This design, common to Eastern Zhou and later jades (see cat. 38), is conventionally called a "grain pattern," but it is most likely a highly refined, abstract version of dense patterns of spirals and S-curves that originally represented animal-heads.[3] (See cat. 40 for an example of the earlier dragon-head image.) The pleasing variation of the decorative spirals on this particular disk marks it as a relatively early example, since later versions of the same spiraling design tend to have the spirals all turning in the same direction,[4] while Han examples often have rows of hexagonal bumps no longer finished as delicate spirals.

PUBLISHED

Loo, *An Exhibition of Chinese Archaic Jades* (1950), pl. XLIV, 4; Jayne, *The Chinese Collections*, no. 50

NOTES

1 The pairing of *cong* and *bi* as ritual jades, which until recently dominated Chinese discussion of these objects, appears first in the *Zhou Li* (Rites of Zhou), which is based in part on late Zhou practice and was most likely compiled in the late Zhou or Western Han dynasty, almost two millennia after the Neolithic period. For an illuminating discussion of the interpretation of ancient jades in early texts, see Rawson and Michaelson, *Chinese Jade*, pp. 54–60.
2 See ibid., pp. 248–51, for the evolution of Eastern Zhou *bi* disks and their characteristic decoration.
3 See Loehr's perceptive discussion of this stylistic evolution in *Ancient Chinese Jades*, pp. 21–28.
4 See Rawson and Michaelson, *Chinese Jade*, cat. 15:1, for a closely comparable *bi*.

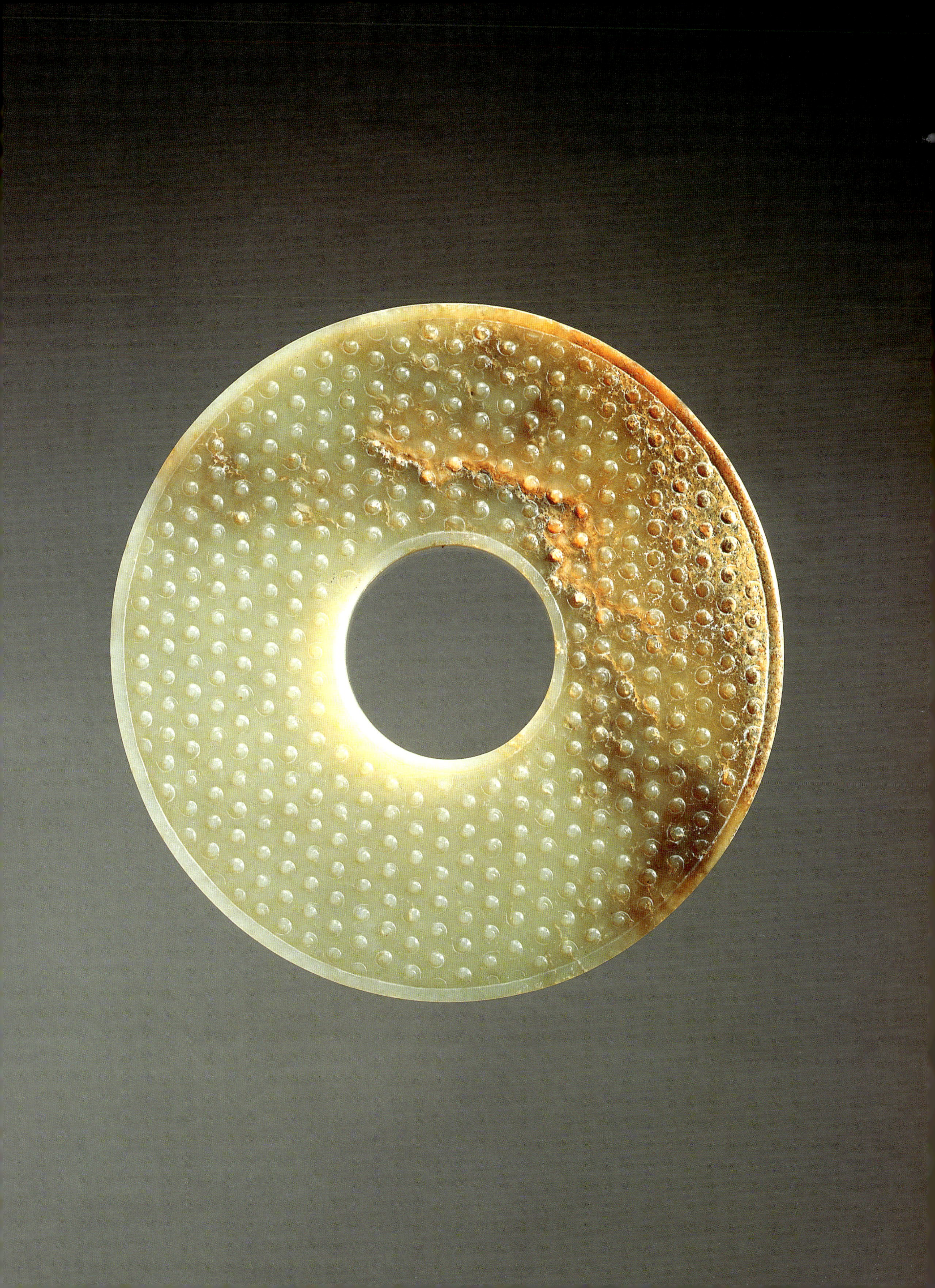

42 DOUBLE-HEADED DRAGON PENDANT

Eastern Zhou dynasty, late Warring States period, ca. 4th–3rd century BCE
Jade, 12¾ × 2½ × ¼ in. (32.4 × 6.4 × .6 cm)
Gift of R.H. Norton, 50.18

This extraordinarily large *Double-headed dragon pendant* is vigorously carved from a slightly translucent dark gray-green jade with significant inclusions of other minerals. Note the irregularly beveled top edge of the central panel, indicating that this area was close to the surface of the jade boulder from which the slab for the pendant was cut. One of the natural veins through the jade has split, and the jagged break is visible here as a dark line through the head on the right end. The break was repaired by drilling two sets of holes into the thickness of the jade very near the top and bottom edges, then inserting pins composed of a copper alloy, probably bronze, to secure the two parts. Microscopic examination reveals that the corrosion on the pins is very deep, indicating that the break and subsequent repair occurred in antiquity, perhaps even at the time of manufacture in the fourth or third century BCE.

The head at each end is composed of a thick jaw and square snout, with a raised band of fine spiraling lines surrounding the mouth and framing the eye. There is a cross-hatched, bracket-shaped brow over the eye and a small, triangular design that represents the ears or horns. The open areas of the face are covered with a dense pattern of small, raised spirals. A raised border decorated with zigzag lines, small whorls, and cross-hatching—a motif adapted perhaps from lacquer or textile designs—frames the panel of raised spirals on the center of the body. A large hole for suspending the jade is drilled through this panel. This particular jade is so large and heavy that it would have been difficult to wear, if indeed it was actually meant to be a personal ornament. It may have been intended for presentation, since a jade of this monumental size would have implied high social or political status.[1] The catalogue of the pioneering 1950 exhibition of ancient jades organized by the dealer C.T. Loo for the Norton included this remarkable *Double-headed dragon pendant*, and the dealer noted that it was one of a pair.[2] Two jades of this scale together would have made a spectacular display of wealth and power indeed.

PUBLISHED

Loo, *An Exhibition of Chinese Archaic Jades* (1950), pl. XL (7); Jayne, *The Chinese Collections*, no. 69

NOTES

1 For another impossibly large personal ornament, see Fong, ed., *The Great Bronze Age of China*, cat. 76, a gold- and silver-inlaid cast-iron belt hook almost 19 inches long and weighing 1 lb. 9 oz.

2 See Mino and Robinson, *Beauty and Tranquility*, pl. 17, for the pair to the Norton's pendant. The authors point out that the details of the dragon-heads are closely comparable to contemporary bronzes.

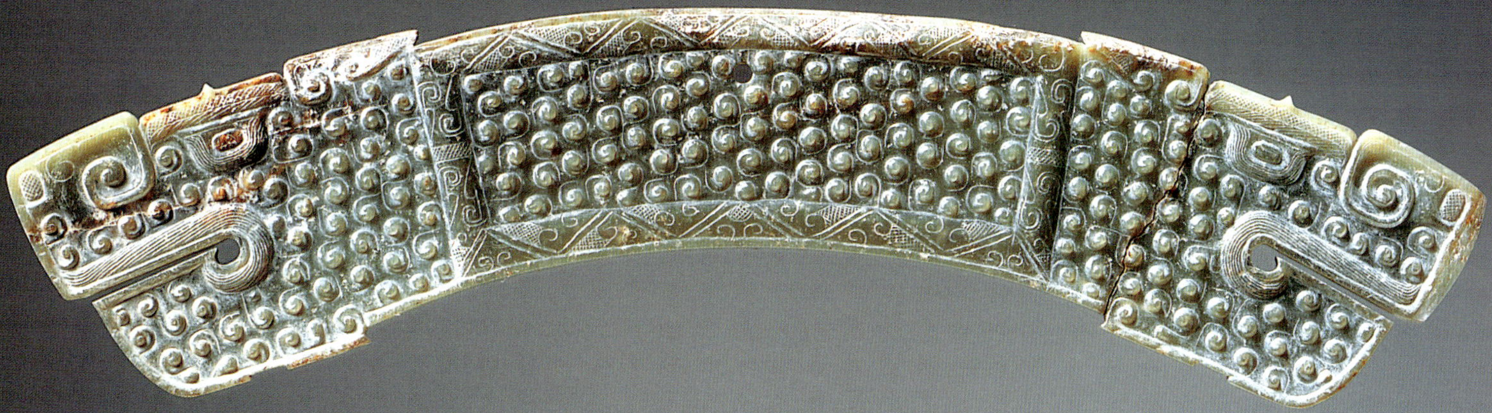

43 **DRAGON PENDANT**

Eastern Zhou dynasty, early Warring States period, 5th century BCE
Jade, 8 1/8 × 4 1/8 × 1/4 in. (20.6 × 10.5 × .6 cm)
Gift of R.H. Norton, 50.27

This wonderful sinuous creature is carved from a slab of translucent gray-green jade with areas of dark brown inclusions. The head turns toward the writhing body, and all the features are depicted in low relief with fine lines delineating such details as the eyes. The jaw and snout are rounded and the face is undecorated, in contrast with the blunt, square faces on the *Double-headed dragon pendant* (cat. 42). A narrow, beveled border frames most of the body, which is covered with a regular pattern of small, raised spirals; the same beveled frame and spiral pattern appear on a jade *bi* (cat. 41) that dates to the fourth or third century BCE. The *Dragon pendant* has a long horn projecting from the back of the head, four short legs with stylized claws set at various points along the body, and two additional spiral projections. Although part of the tail has broken off—a borderless edge cuts through part of the spiral pattern—not too much of the original jade is missing: the piece still balances well when suspended from a line through the single hole in the center of the back.

Dragon pendants of this type appear rather suddenly in the Eastern Zhou, in the fifth century BCE.[1] The S-curves and elaborate silhouettes of these pendants may even be related to metal work in animal forms possibly introduced into China in the sixth or fifth centuries BCE.[2] Whatever the source of this particular fashion, numerous jade pendants share variations of the basic form of an undulating body whose silhouette is embellished with stylized legs and projecting spirals. The Grenville L. Winthrop Collection at Harvard University includes jade pendants that are similar to the Norton example,[3] and Yang Boda refers to a dragon pendant with a similar silhouette excavated from a Warring States tomb in Henan province.[4] The Museum's pendant almost certainly was one of a pair (see cat. 38), and a comparable pair in light green jade (with some variations in design between the two) appears in the early Warring States tomb of the Marquis Zeng of Yi, who died around 433 BCE and was buried near Suizhou, Hubei province.[5] And the most elaborate example of a single dragon pendant, where added spirals begin to obscure the dragon's body, was found in one of the fourth-century BCE tombs of the kings of Zhongshan, a small state of the Warring States period located in modern Hebei province.[6] Other examples are found in tombs of the state of Lu in Shandong.[7] The profusion and wide distribution of these jade dragon-shaped pendants attest to their remarkable popularity in the Warring States period, and the care and skill used to produce jades like this *Dragon pendant* give further proof of their importance.

PUBLISHED

Loo, *Exhibition of Chinese Arts* (1941–42), no. 268; Loo, *An Exhibition of Chinese Archaic Jades* (1950), pl. XXXVIII (4); Na Zhiliang, *Yuqi tongshi*, vol. 2, pl. 28(c) (after Loo, *An Exhibition of Chinese Archaic Jades*, 1950); Jayne, *The Chinese Collections*, no. 68

NOTES

1 Rawson and Michaelson, *Chinese Jade*, pp. 257–62, cat. 17:9.
2 Ibid., p. 65.
3 See Loehr, *Ancient Chinese Jades*, nos. 419–27 for dragon pendants of this general type.
4 See the sketch in Yang, *Chinese Archaic Jades from the Kwan Collection*, no. 181, citing *Dong Zhou Wu Chu yuqi*, Yan Zhiqiang and others, comp. (Taipei: Yishu tushi gongs, 1993), p. 39, pl. 20.
5 *Zeng Hou Yi mu*, vol. 1, fig. 289 (1, 9–10); vol. 2, color pl. XIX (4), pl. CLVII (3).
6 *Zhongguo yuqi quanji*, vol. 3, no. 215, dated to the mid-Warring States period.
7 *Qufu Lu guo gucheng*, pl. 105 (2–5, 7).

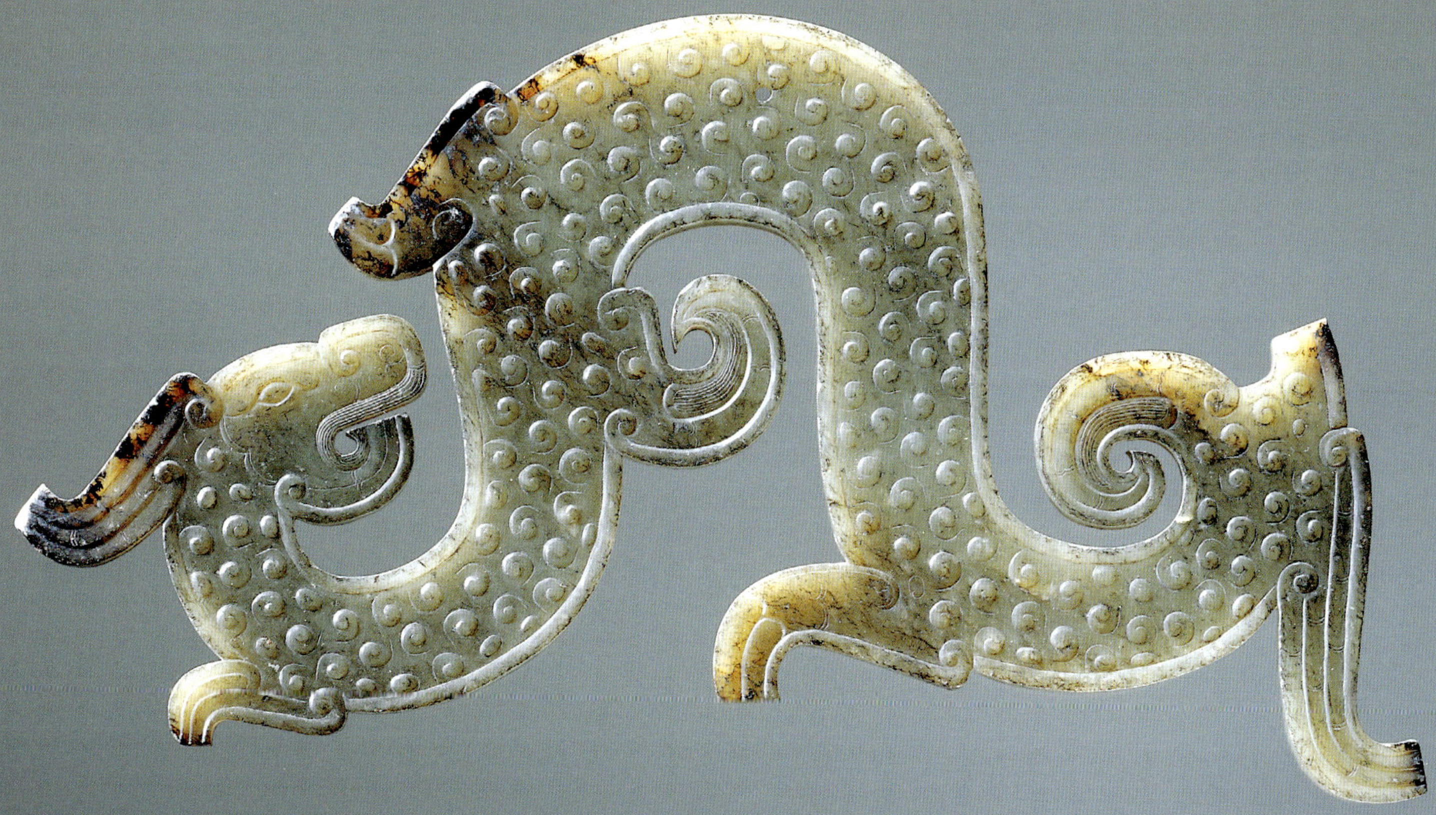

44 PENDANT OR KNOT-OPENER

Late Eastern Zhou–Western Han dynasty, ca. 4th–2nd century BCE
Jade, 3 5/16 × 5/8 × 3/16 in. (8.4 × 1.6 × .5 cm)
Gift of R.H. Norton, 50.20

45 PENDANT IN THE FORM OF A THUMB RING

Eastern Han dynasty (25–220 BCE) or possibly later
Jade, 2 1/8 × 1 × 3/16 in. (5.4 × 2.5 × .5 cm)
Gift of R.H. Norton, 50.22

Beautifully carved in jade, these small personal ornaments reward close inspection. The long, pointed *Pendant* or *knot-opener* (top) is made of a translucent gray-green jade that has been greatly altered by burial: much of the surface is chalky, opaque white with rust red splotches, possibly the result of interment near an iron object. It is carved in low relief with details rendered in fine lines on both sides; its shape is that of a fabulous composite animal with the head and sharp beak of a bird of prey. A hole has been drilled through the back of the head, which has broken, and a small part of the jade is missing. The body twists and turns, and just below the head is a short leg with a clawed foot grasping a thick spiral element. Other spirals spin out from the body, while a second, longer leg with tiny claws grasps the base of the curving pointed tail. Chinese writers conventionally identify this well-known type of jade as a *xi*, a bodkin or knot-opener. The 1983 excavation of the tomb of the King of Nanyue (died ca. 122 BCE) has revealed that such pieces may have commonly been part of a set of jade ornaments.[1]

The smaller pendant (bottom) carries the style of the *Knot-opener* to an extreme of miniature decoration. It has a dramatically cut and drilled silhouette, and the various spiraling and overlapping elements are rendered in subtle low relief and fine engraved lines. It is carved on both sides, but the details on each side are slightly different. One looks in vain for the head of an animal or feet or wings that might identify a specific creature; the entire design seems to be composed of abstract elements. The identification as an archer's thumb ring comes from the large hole in the center and the slightly concave area to the left. A larger, more three-dimensional jade identified as an archer's thumb ring was found in the ca. 1200 BCE Shang dynasty tomb of Fu Hao.[2] That jade probably simulates a leather or bone ring in the shape of an irregular tube that slipped over the thumb to protect it and help pull the bowstring.[3] These rings, however, soon evolved into decorative objects: they became flattened out, so that only the central holes and concave areas recalled that they had once been functional. In addition, the hook that might have pulled the bowstring metamorphosed into a series of decorative spirals. The Norton pendant represents a stage in this evolution when the original form and function may have been entirely forgotten.[4] The "thumb ring" proper has become an odd, concave oval with a circular hole, while the carver has lavished most of his attention on the sumptuous ornamentation.

PUBLISHED

44: Loo, *An Exhibition of Chinese Archaic Jades* (1950), pl. XXXI (7); Jayne, *The Chinese Collections*, no. 72
45: Loo, *An Exhibition of Chinese Archaic Jades* (1950), pl. LI (4); Jayne, *The Chinese Collections*, no. 73

NOTES

1 *Xi Han Nanyue wang mu*, vol. 1, p. 244, illustrating a set of jades that includes two so-called knot-openers. See also vol. 1, fig. 134, for other jades of this type; and see vol. 2, pl. 152, for a set of five jades found together.
2 See *Yinxu Fu Hao mu*, p. 195, figs. 97, 98; pl. 164 (3,4).
3 See So essay in this catalogue, fig. 15 and page 28.
4 For a comparably elaborate ring, with a matching pointed pendant, now in the British Museum, see Rawson and Michaelson, *Chinese Jade*, p. 287, fig. 3.

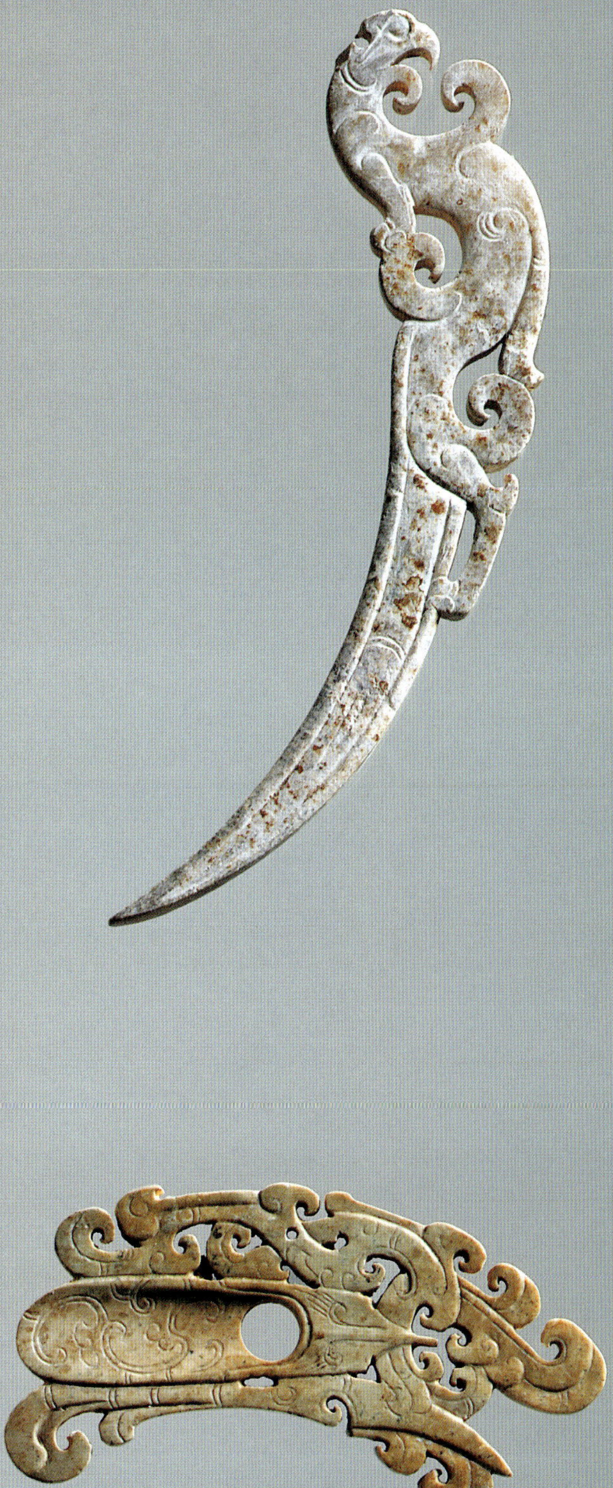

46 SWORD GUARD WITH SECTION OF BLADE

Western Han dynasty (206 BCE–9 CE)
Jade, bronze; sword guard 1 × 2 1/2 × 1 1/4 in. (2.5 × 6.4 × 3.2 cm);
blade: 4 5/16 × 1 1/4 × 1/4 in. (11 × 3.2 × .6 cm)
Gift of R.H. Norton, 50.6

This translucent, light yellow-green sword guard would have been one of four ornamental jade fittings of a sword and scabbard set. The end of the sword handle would have been mounted with a thick, disk-shaped pommel, and a guard such as this would be positioned between the handle and blade. A cliplike jade tied to the side of the scabbard would allow the sword be held on a belt or sash. Lastly, a hoof-shaped sword chape would be fixed at the bottom of the scabbard both as decoration and to prevent the sharp point from piercing the end of the scabbard. Typically all four pieces would be fashioned in the same style with the same decorative motifs, forming an important set of jade personal ornaments.[1]

The Norton *Sword guard* is particularly well carved. Its decoration consists of a fabulous animal with small, round ears like a tiger's set on either side of the face and connected by arched ridges over the top of the head. The neck and the body twist and turn, giving the impression of a powerful creature in mid-stride. There is a spiral decorative element attached to the long tail, and the tail itself curls all the way to the edge of the guard, where a smaller feline is chewing or playing with the tip of the tail. The front of the sword guard, seen here, is carved in such high relief that the animals are worked almost completely in the round. On the back of the sword guard is a similar feline carved in much shallower relief so that the guard would not catch on the clothing of the person wearing the sword. The resemblance of these feline creatures to a type of dragon has led some writers to mistakenly describe them as *chilong* or hornless dragons (see cat. 105 for an archaistic jade rhyton with felines derived from Han prototypes).

A large number of jade sword fittings, including at least eight complete sets of four jades each, were discovered in the Western Han dynasty tomb of the King of Nanyue (died ca. 122 BCE) in the modern city of Guangzhou (Canton).[2] Several of these are close in style to the Norton guard, showing the same type of feline creature superbly carved in high relief.[3] Many of the King of Nanyue's swords had iron blades, and the Norton jade is unusual in being mounted on the remains of a bronze blade.[4] Regrettably, the bronze blade was shortened in modern times, perhaps by a dealer who wanted to emphasize the superb quality of the jade *Sword guard.*

PUBLISHED

Loo, *An Exhibition of Chinese Archaic Jades* (1950), pl. LVIII (3); Jayne, *The Chinese Collections*, no. 44

NOTES

1 Loo, *An Exhibition of Chinese Archaic Jades* (1950), pl. LVIII (4, 7), included two sword clips whose style is close enough to the present jade that either one might have come from the complete set of four.
2 *Xi Han Nanyue wang mu*, vol. 2, color pl. 13; pls. 70, 73–74, 101, 103.
3 See the discussion of the tomb's jades in Rawson and Michaelson, *Chinese Jade*, pp. 71–75.
4 Colin Mackenzie, personal communication.

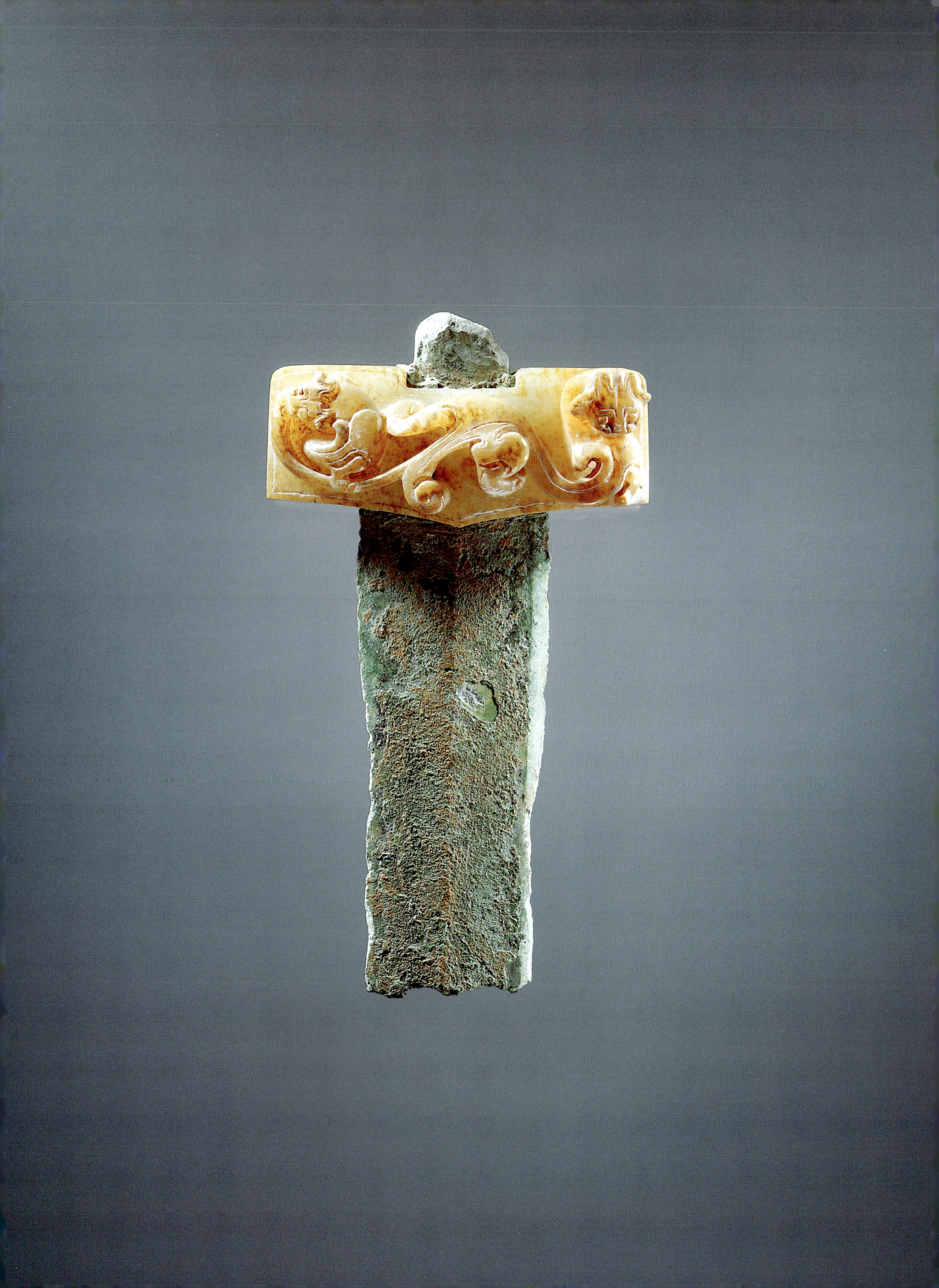

47 KNEELING WORSHIPER

Northern Wei dynasty (386–535), mid- to late 5th century
Sandstone, 21¼ × 12½ × 3⅛ in. (54 × 31.8 × 7.9 cm)
Bequest of R.H. Norton, 53.237

The rough sandstone figure of a *Kneeling worshiper* is typical of images carved in relief in the cave-temple complex at Yungang. The Yungang caves are cut into the cliffs along the Wuzhou River in northern Shanxi province just outside at the modern city of Datong, site of the Northern Wei capital from 398 to 494. The tradition of carving images and cave-temples from the living rock follows Indian practice, and spread with the Buddhist religion along the trade routes through northern India and the Silk Road into northwestern China. The Buddhist sculptures at Yungang show affinities with rock-cut images farther to the west in Central Asia, including the now-lost colossal Buddhas at Bamiyan, in north-central Afghanistan. The earliest caves at Yungang, begun in 460, contain five gigantic Buddha images, each associated with the first Northern Wei emperors as embodiments of the historical Buddha.[1] The great majority of caves were excavated and decorated between 460 and 494, when the Northern Wei capital was moved south to Luoyang (see cat. 48).

The Yungang sandstone is light buff in color with a coarse texture that we see clearly in the *Kneeling worshiper*. With the exception of the most important images, the majority of the sculptures at Yungang are carved in high relief. The friable stone did not permit fine detail, and the Northern Wei sculptors organized their figures in architectural frameworks, giving them clearly defined, deeply rounded forms with details cut in strong, graphic lines. All were stuccoed and brightly painted, and a few traces of the original coating remain here. Wearing long robes that wrap around the body and drape over his left arm, the worshiper leans forward with one knee on the ground and his elbow resting on the other. His softly rounded features are carefully modeled to give a surprising sense of volume and depth. His eyes are drawn as a single curved line, with a similar curve outlining the brow and bridge of the nose. The head, originally set off against a round halo, has thick curls pulled up into a tall chignon.

Édouard Chavannes's 1909 publication on the Yungang site shows rows of half-figures of worshipers remarkably close in detail to the Norton example,[2] and Osvald Sirén's 1925 photographs of Cave II show similar figures kneeling in the arched panel over a seated Buddha.[3] In his 1972 catalogue, Horace H.F. Jayne identified this figure as one that appeared in a 1932 illustration.[4] Despite many early photographic records of the site, however, it is not possible to positively locate this particular figure. Large numbers of smiling worshipers fill the Yungang caves, crowding around Buddhas and bodhisattvas, sometimes as individual figures, sometimes as overlapping ranks of devotees or musicians. They are visual testimony to the piety of the Northern Wei patrons of Buddhism, and, as an ensemble, are among the great masterpieces of early Buddhist art in China.

PUBLISHED

Jayne, *The Chinese Collections*, no. 101

NOTES

1 Ch'en, *Buddhism in China*, pp. 166–67. See also *Yungang shiku*, English supplement, pp. 2–3, 5–6, citing the "Records of Buddhism and Daoism" in the *History of the Northern Wei*.
2 Chavannes, *Mission archaéologique*, plates vol. I, pl. CXIII, nos. 215, 216.
3 Sirén, *Chinese Sculpture*, reprint, vol. 1, pl. 23.
4 See Mullikin and Hotchkis, *Buddhist Sculptures at the Yun Kang Caves*, drawing, p. 30. The identification is most likely incorrect.

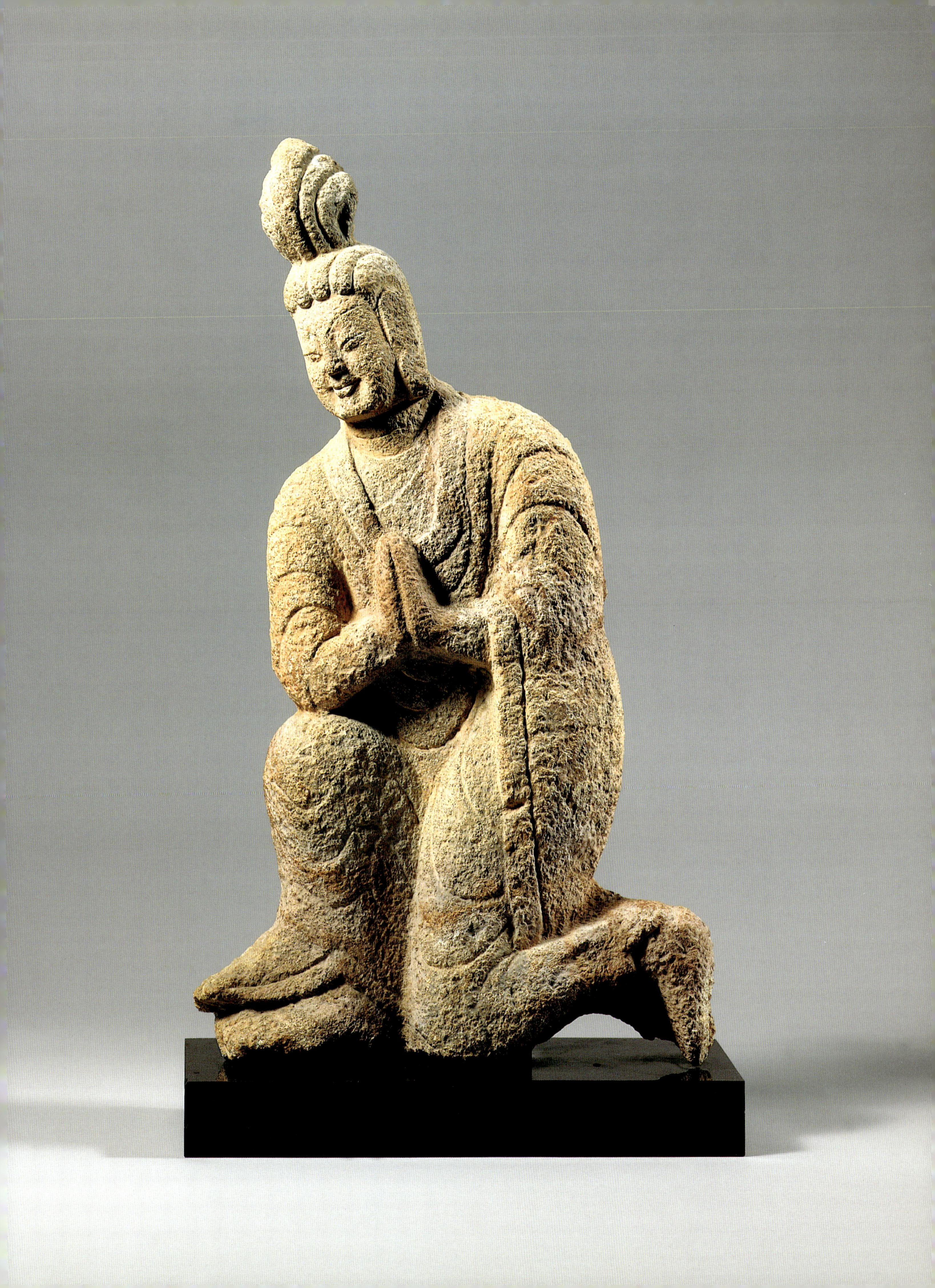

48 SEATED BODHISATTVA MAITREYA

Northern Wei dynasty (386–535)
Gray limestone, 22 5/8 × 14 1/2 × 3 1/2 in. (57.5 × 36.8 × 8.9 cm)
Purchase, the R.H. Norton Trust, 62.5

The Norton *Maitreya* closely resembles sculptures from the walls of the so-called Guyang cave, the oldest and one of the most richly decorated shrines at Longmen. When the Northern Wei rulers moved their capital south from Datong to Luoyang in 494, they almost immediately began to commission the same type of rock-cut temples that they had sponsored at Yungang (see cat. 47). For the new site they chose the dramatic cliffs along the Yi River; in the Sui dynasty (589–618) this complex was renamed Longmen, literally "Dragon Gate," the name by which it is known today.

The crown of the *Seated Bodhisattva Maitreya* (which has been slightly trimmed along the top edge), the sweetly smiling face and arched eyebrows engraved with a single line, the robe draped over the shoulder with the ends pulled through a ring at the waist, the crossed legs and pointed toes, and the elaborate cascade of draperies are all details shared by the earliest Northern Wei images at the site. Numerous early photographs document images with stylistic parallels.[1] Although we should be cautious in view of the large number of detached sculptures associated with the Guyang cave, close identification with sculptural styles represented there securely dates the Norton figure to the late fifth to early sixth century.

When the Museum acquired this sculpture in 1962, it was identified as the Bodhisattva Avalokitesvara (Guanyin in Chinese), but it most likely represents Maitreya, the Buddha of the Future. The confusion is understandable. Avalokitesvara as Padmapani, the "lotus bearer," is conventionally depicted in similar fashion: youthful, dressed in flowing princely robes, and wearing a five-leaf crown with a tiny image of Amitabha Buddha.[2] Worship of Maitreya, however, was far more popular at the time this figure was created, and consideration of its gestures in particular, as well as its costume and seated posture, help to determine its probable identity. The right arm and hand of the Norton *Bodhisattva* make a gesture identical to that of several figures that are identified by inscriptions as Maitreya.[3]

Indeed, the *mudra*, or hand gestures, of the Norton *Bodhisattva* are particularly distinctive. A Longmen figure of Maitreya from the von der Heydt collection, Zurich,[4] exhibits identical hand gestures, as does a seated Maitreya in the Cincinnati Art Museum,[5] though both figures lack any emblem on the crown. Considering iconographical details and the religious climate in which the Norton sculpture was produced, it can probably be identified with some confidence as Maitreya, the bodhisattva who will descend from his Tushita Heaven and become the Buddha of the Future.

PUBLISHED

Jayne, *The Chinese Collections*, no. 103

NOTES

1 Among others, see Chavannes, *Mission archaéologique*, plates vol. 1, pls. CCLV, CCLVII. See also Sirén, *Chinese Sculpture*, pl. 80 and others, depicting the Guyang cave; and see Tokiwa and Sekino, *Shina Bukkyō shiseki*, vol. 2, pls. 89, 92.
2 Getty, *The Gods of Northern Buddhism*, p. 61. A similar seated stone bodhisattva in San Francisco is identified as Guanyin; see Lefebvre d'Argencé, *Chinese, Korean, and Japanese Sculpture*, cat. 38.
3 See, for example, *Longmen shiku*, fig. 21. The head is missing, but the left hand rests palm down on the knee, a common gesture for images identified specifically as Maitreya. See ibid., figs. 15, 23.
4 Museum Rietberg, *Chinesische Skulpturen*, no. 12.
5 Avril, *Chinese Art in the Cincinnati Art Museum*, cat. 17.

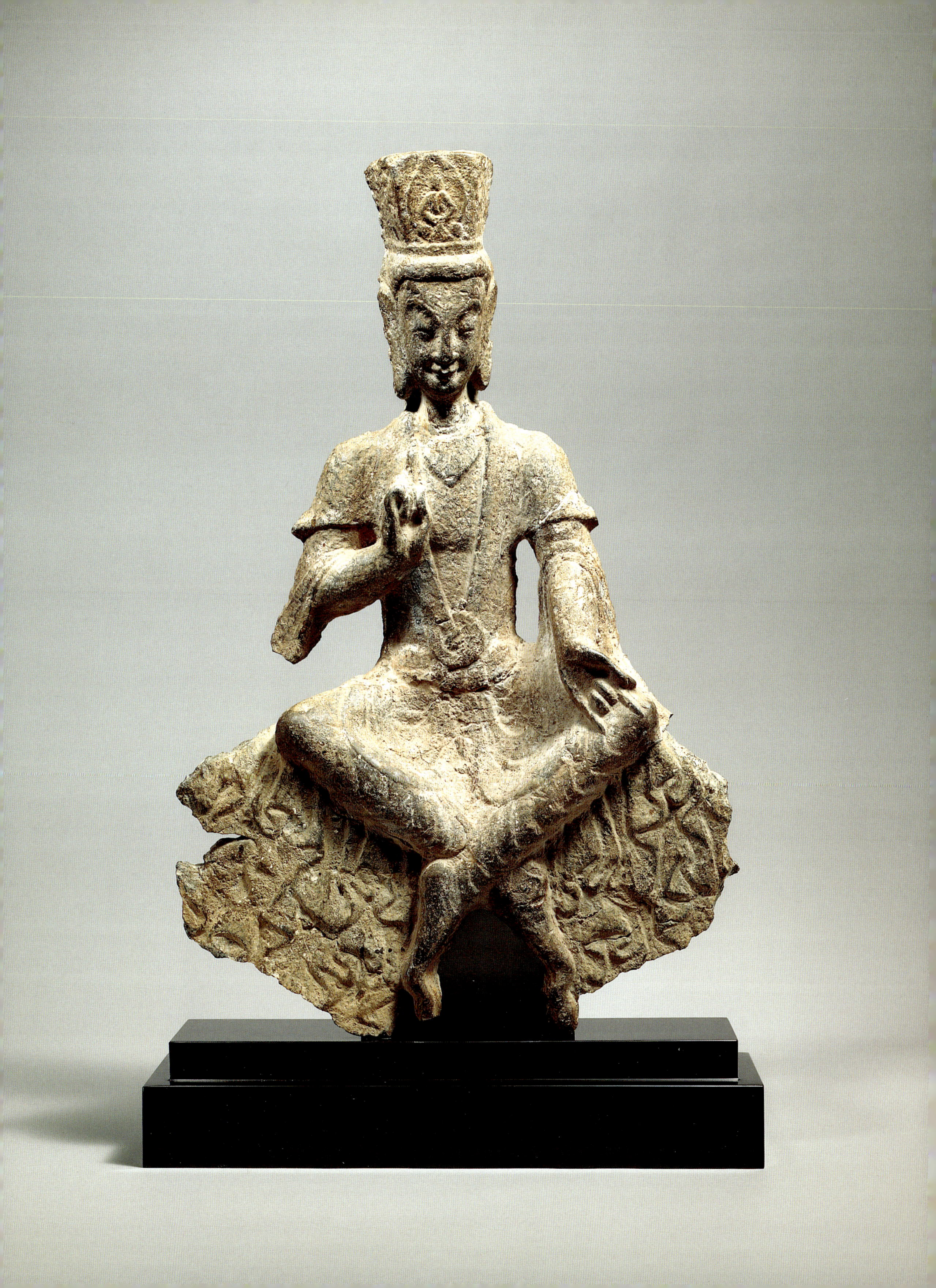

49 HEAD OF A COLOSSAL BUDDHA

Tang dynasty (618–907), late 7th century
Limestone, approximately 30 × 16 × 16 in. (76.2 × 40.6 × 40.6 cm)
Purchase, the R.H. Norton Trust, 61.14

The carving of Buddhist cave-temples and the myriad images at Longmen, near Luoyang, the Northern Wei capital (see cat. 48), generally came to a halt in the mid-sixth century, but during the Tang dynasty there was a renewed period of intense imperial patronage from about 640 to 720.[1] The *Head of a colossal Buddha* is the product of that great period of excavation of cave-temples and carving of monumental images. Tang imperial commissions, sponsored for the most part by the Empress Wu, consort of Emperor Gaozong but later ruling independently as Wu Zetian, included the largest image at Longmen, a Vairocana Buddha standing over 56 feet tall and flanked by attendant bodhisattvas, monks, and guardians. The preaching of Pure Land Buddhism during the Tang led also to the carving of images of Amitabha Buddha, who presides over the Western Paradise, or Pure Land. The great majority of Buddha images carved after 650 are those of Amitabha,[2] and the Museum's *Head of a colossal Buddha* may possibly come from such a figure, although firm identification is not possible. From comparisons of stone samples, however, we know that the sculpture does comes from Longmen,[3] and stylistic comparisons can help place it in the development of the monumental images there.

In general, among the Longmen images there is an evolution in the treatment of the hair, from a rendering as rhythmic waves seen in earlier images—based ultimately on Indian styles and generally reflected in examples on the west bank of the Yi River that flows through the Longmen site—to tight curls, which appear more frequently among images on the east side of the river. An example of the former type is the seated Amitabha in the Qianji Si cave, carved in the reign of Tang Taizong (r. 627–49).[4] The curls of the head are wavy, and the facial features, especially the eyes, are shallowly carved, giving the face a schematic and less spiritual cast. The Norton head, by contrast, has tight, snail-like curls. The face is round and full, and the very large features are highly stylized, conveying the impression of an other-worldly being. The eyes are deeply set behind half-closed lids, as if the Buddha is looking inward as much as down at the worshiper. The image would originally have been painted, and a few traces of a fine coat of a light-colored ground remain on the surface of the stone.

During the brief period of Tang imperial patronage, Buddha images seemed to reach a moment of extraordinary balance between oversize, stylized features and the sense of an immensely powerful deity. The great Longmen Vairocana Buddha, carved between 672 and 675, gazes down in awe-inspiring majesty.[5] Like this enormous image of Vairocana, a seated Maitreya Buddha of about 673 has a slightly square face suffused with a spiritual presence.[6] The Museum's *Head of a colossal Buddha* probably dates to this period, and exhibits a similar spiritual expression.

PUBLISHED

Jayne, *The Chinese Collections*, no. 106

NOTES

1 Ch'en, *Buddhism in China*, pp. 170–73, summarizing the work of Tsukamoto Zenryū, *Shina Bukkyō shi kenkyū: Hokugi hen* (Tokyo: Shimizu Kobundo, 1942, reprint, 1969).
2 Ibid.
3 Jayne, *The Chinese Collections*, no. 106, n. 1. Dr. I.M. Drew of Columbia University analyzed a sample from the Norton head; comparison with a known sample from Longmen confirmed the identification.
4 *Longmen shiku*, 1980, fig. 127.
5 See, among many images, ibid., fig. 148.
6 See Sirén, *Chinese Sculpture*, vol. 4.1 (plates), pl. 461(B); Longmen cave J, which has an inscription dated 673, probably close to the date of the sculptures.

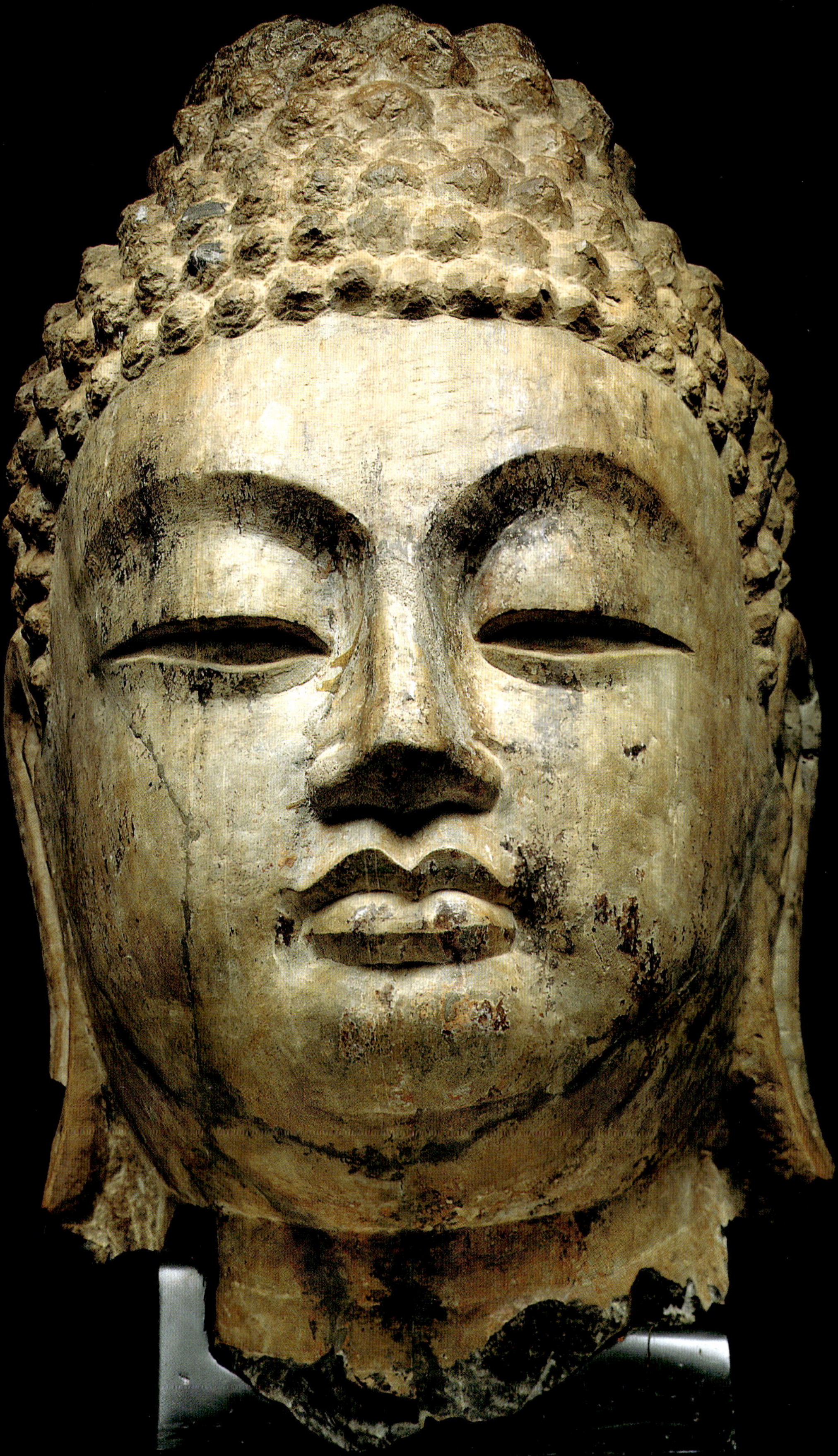

50 SEATED BODHISATTVA

Song dynasty (960–1279)
Wood, 14¾ × 10⅜ × 8⅝ in. (37.5 × 26.4 × 21.9 cm)
Purchased with funds from the Col. and Mrs. Frank E. Hart Fund, 66.8

The Museum's *Seated bodhisattva* is one of a large number of wooden figures that present many problems of identification and dating and have received relatively little scholarly attention. Wood is a common medium for sculpture, and in the cool, dry climate of North China more wood construction and associated wooden figures survive than in the South. This *Seated bodhisattva* entered the collection as a Tang dynasty figure, attributed to the mid-eighth century. The attribution is understandable, since Tang sculptural styles represent a high point in Chinese Buddhist art, and in many ways Tang styles became canonical, profoundly influencing the forms of Buddhist images to the present day. Certainly the round face and folds around the neck, the three-dimensional modeling of the body and drapery, and the overall impression of the figure owe a debt to Tang sculpture. The very elaborate robes, however, and the layers of costume and jewelry that are not always clearly distinguished from each other indicate a later date. The sculptor seems to have misunderstood the collar of the figure's inner robe, which should form two lapels where one side of the robe closes over the other.

The figure was carved from several blocks of wood, of which two remain. One, with the grain running vertically, forms the head and body, and the other, with the grain horizontal, the crossed legs. Like the now missing arms, these two sections were joined with square pegs that fit into holes cut into each piece. The surface of the completed figure was brightly painted, as shown by tiny fragments of the original decoration that remain in the folds of the robes. The head once had an elaborate crown that sat on the flat ledge in the hair; the intact crown of a seated wooden bodhisattva in the Victoria and Albert Museum, dated to the Song dynasty, gives some indication of how the Norton figure once looked.[1] The large hole in the forehead once held an inset stone, perhaps rock crystal, representing the *urna*, an emblem of spiritual vision shared by buddhas and bodhisattvas, and the image surely sat on a carved pedestal.

Probably the closest stylistic parallel to the Norton figure is a seated wooden bodhisattva dated to the Song and exhibited at the National History Museum, Taipei, in 1997.[2] It also has a somber face with downcast eyes, an elaborately layered robe with folds gathered at the waist held with a narrow belt, and a ledge around the head that once supported a crown. It is seated with crossed legs, also carved from a separate block, with the left foot concealed under the robe. This last detail led Horace Jayne to identify the Norton image as the Tantric Buddhist Bodhisattva Xukongzang (Sanskrit: Akasagarbha). It is, however, impossible to identify the incomplete figure on the basis of one such detail,[3] leaving many questions about this fine Chinese wood sculpture yet to be answered.

PUBLISHED

Jayne, *The Chinese Collections*, no. 112

NOTES

1 See National Palace Museum, *Haiwai yizhen: Fo xiang (xu)*, cat. no. 143.
2 National History Museum, *Fo jiao zhi mei*, n.p., *Seated Bodhisattva*, wood, Song dynasty, collection of Li Jikun, Taipei.
3 A wooden statue of Akasagarbha, associated with the Tang dynasty, 9th century, now in the Kanchi-in, Tōji, Kyoto, has an elaborate metal crown and hands raised in *mudra* different from the Taipei image. See Wright, *Buddhism in Chinese History*, pl. 5; it is not possible to see both feet in the photo.

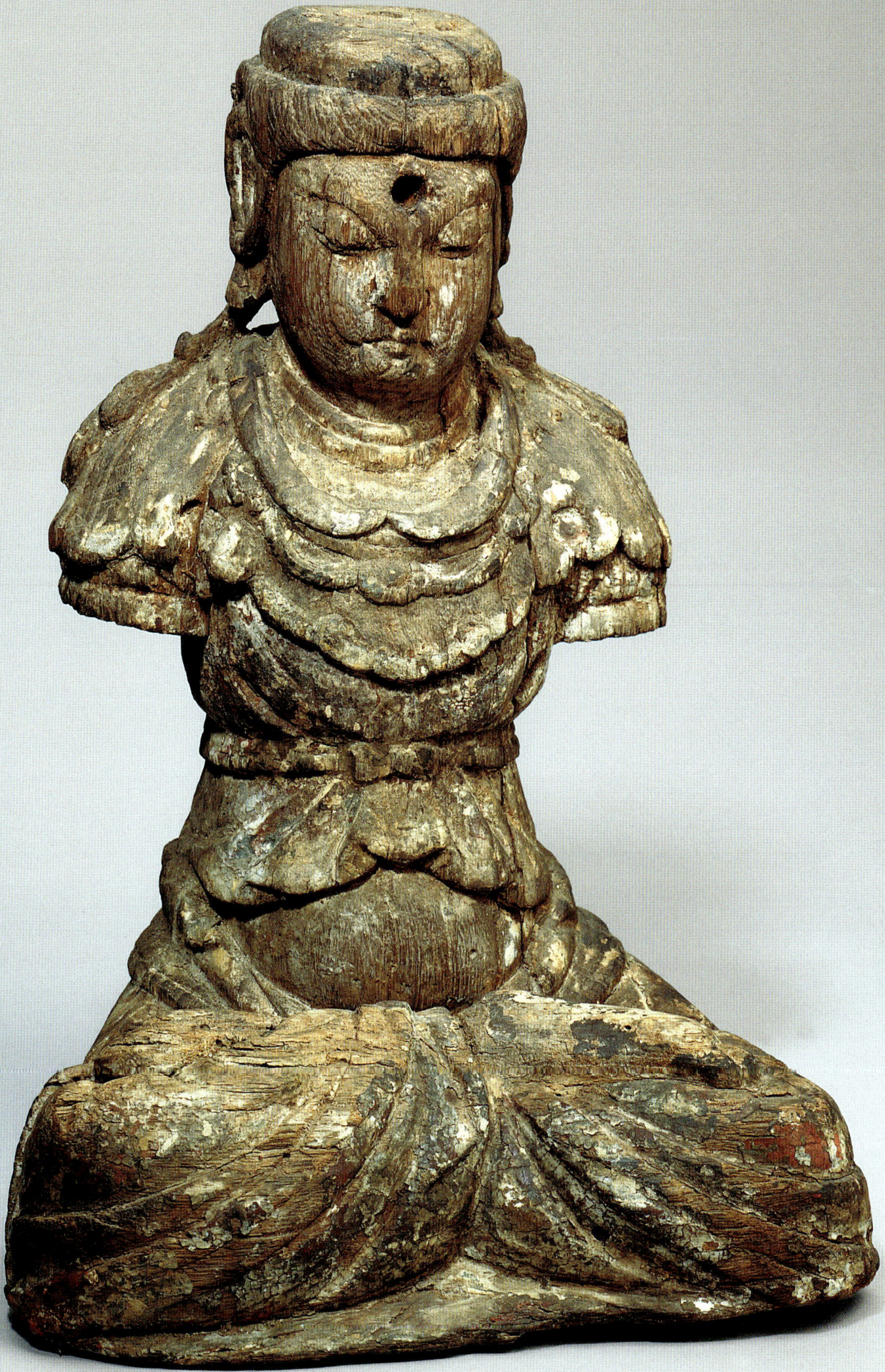

51 GUANYIN, GIVER OF SONS

Ming dynasty, probably 17th century
Ivory, 3 7/8 × 2 5/16 × 1 1/8 in. (9.8 × 5.9 × 2.9 cm)
Gift of Mary Tyack Philpit, 2000.18

This small-scale ivory image represents a specific deity—*Guanyin, the Giver of Sons.* The Bodhisattva Avalokitesvara is known in Chinese as Guanyin, the "hearer of prayers." This compassionate deity is described in chapter 25 of the Lotus Sutra as manifesting itself in the world in thirty-three different forms, old and young, male and female, to help save believers from danger and grant their wishes. One important passage states that a woman who desires a son, after making "worshipful offerings to the Bodhisattva [Guanyin],...shall straightway bear a son of happiness, excellence, and wisdom."[1] The Lotus Sutra, a key text in the Buddhist tradition, had first been translated into Chinese in the third century, and in the succeeding centuries the worship of Guanyin spread throughout China.

Sometime during the late ninth to tenth century, Guanyin, who had previously been depicted as a male, began to appear as a female image, a portrayal that appears only in East Asian Buddhism.[2] Among the most popular of these portrayals is the White-Robed Guanyin, clearly a female figure who wears a long white cloak, often draped from the top of her head. Chinese Buddhist texts tell stories of the White-Robed Guanyin who miraculously granted children, particularly sons to carry on the family name. Stories circulated of miraculous births achieved after chanting a particular sutra, and grateful believers supported the printing and distribution of free copies of the sutra, gaining merit for their souls and helping spread the worship of Guanyin through many levels of Chinese society. During the Ming dynasty these activities were especially popular, and the texts sometimes included woodblock illustrations showing Guanyin holding a baby boy.[3] Called Guanyin the Giver of Sons (*Songzi Guanyin*), this is the portrayal we see here.

The Norton figure is carved from ivory, whose creamy white color, now much mellowed with age, would have been appropriate for a white-robed goddess. Her hands are clasped before her, holding a rosary with a dangling tassel, and her arm supports a little boy grasping a lotus bud. Probably the most important ivory-carving center in China was the city of Zhangzhou in the southeastern province of Fujian. Like other Fujian coastal cities, Zhangzhou had commercial connections with the Spanish colony of the Philippines, and during the Ming dynasty these centers produced Christian images, such as the Virgin and Child, for European markets.[4] The porcelain kilns at Dehua, also in Fujian province, similarly produced many Christian figurines as well as countless images of Guanyin. Dehua white porcelains, called "blanc de chine" in the West, provide stylistic parallels for much rarer ivory carvings. The Norton's ivory *Guanyin* may subtly reflect European influences in the pose of a mother holding her child, and certainly it is a touching expression of Chinese popular devotion to the compassionate Guanyin as the Giver of Sons.

NOT PREVIOUSLY PUBLISHED

NOTES

1 Weidner, ed., *Latter Days of the Law*, cat. 46; the citation is adapted from Hurvitz, trans., *Scripture of the Lotus Blossom*, p. 313.
2 Yü, "Feminine Images of Kuan-yin," especially pp. 71–85. The discussion of Guanyin is based in large part on Yü's article.
3 Although images of Guanyin holding a child were especially popular in the Ming, Yü cites only one earlier image, a stele dated 1084 with such an image accompanying the text of this particular sutra. See Yü, "A Sutra Promoting the White-robed Guanyin," p. 98.
4 See Yü, "Feminine Images of Kuan-yin"; see also Leidy, *Chinese Decorative Arts*, p. 40.

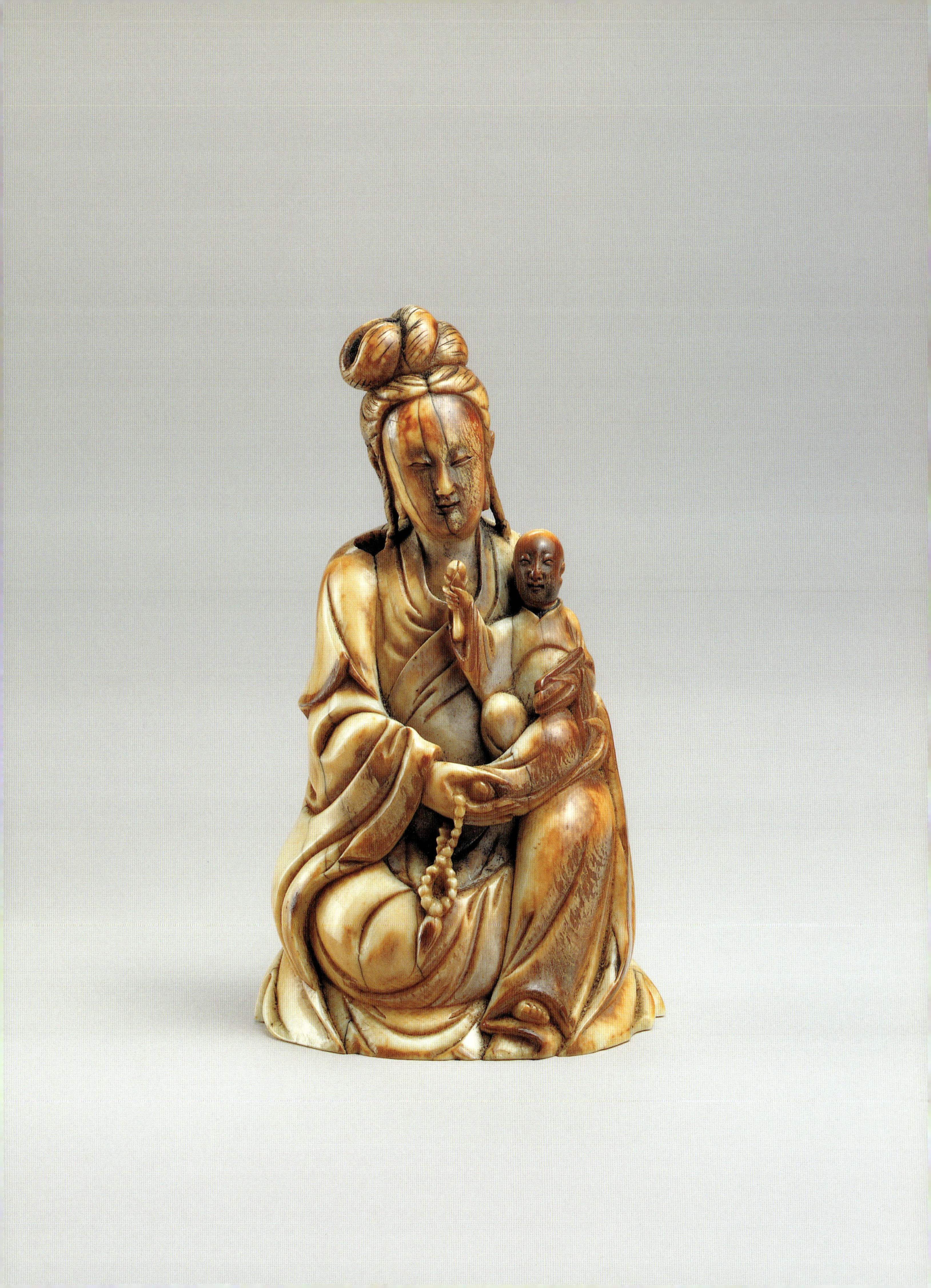

52 SEATED FIGURE OF BUDDHA AMITAYUS

Qing dynasty, Qianlong era (1736–95), dated 1761
Gilt bronze, traces of polychrome decoration, 8 ½ × 4 ⅝ × 3 ¾ in. (21.6 × 11.7 × 9.5 cm)
Purchase, the R.H. Norton Trust, in Honor of The Elizabeth Norton Society and our other Volunteers who serve in Education, the Library, Membership, Museum Store, Office Support, Special Events and Visitor Services, 2000.3

The Buddha Amitayus, whose name means Buddha of Eternal Life, is a form of the Buddha Amitabha, the Buddha of Boundless Light.[1] Prayers to Amitayus were believed to bring long life and rebirth in paradise, and a Dunhuang text dating to the tenth century or earlier attests to such a belief in the deity's powers.[2] Amitayus is almost always shown seated in meditation, with folded hands resting in his lap holding a vase filled with an elixir of longevity. Four strings of pearls, which may represent the magic pills of a Tibetan Lamaist ceremony of long life, drape downward from the lid of the vase.[3] This small, gilt-bronze image was produced for the Manchu Qing imperial clan in Tibetan style, reflecting the clan's longstanding patronage of and belief in Tibetan Buddhism. The corner posts of the pedestal and the traces of color on the image echo Tibetan precedents.

The inscription carefully engraved at the bottom edge of the pedestal reads: "Respectfully made in the *xinsi* year [1761] of the Qianlong era of the great Qing dynasty." That year marked the seventieth birthday of the Qianlong emperor's mother, the Dowager Empress, who was by reputation a devout believer in Tibetan Buddhism. Over a period of eleven days, the emperor presented her with an extraordinary list of birthday gifts.[4] These included large numbers of Amitayus figures — nine sets of nine on the first day, nine more sets of nine on the second day, and additional sets of images, including sculptures, paintings, and Amitayus sutras copied by the Emperor himself on the following days. Nine is both auspicious and the most potent *yang* number, making it appropriate to give birthday gifts in multiples of nine.[5] Although the images alone totaled hundreds, perhaps thousands,[6] we lack specific details on their size or medium, so it is impossible to say if the Norton image was one of them. However, the large number of nearly identical and similarly inscribed small images in Chinese and Western collections is suggestive. An inscription roughly cut on the inside of the model for the pedestal of the Norton *Amitayus* suggests that it was indeed part of a large set. It reads "[illeg.] person [or figure] / 90 / 2," suggesting that this is number 2 or the second type, perhaps, of a group of 90 identical images. Further evidence of this type from similar Amitayus images or the additional publication of the voluminous records of the Qing court, may help positively identify the original purpose of the imperially commissioned Amitayus images that make up this extensive group.

NOT PREVIOUSLY PUBLISHED

NOTES

1 See Getty, *The Gods of Northern Buddhism*, pp. 39–40. The name in Chinese is Wuliangshou Fo.

2 Zwalf, ed., *Buddhism*, cat. 57. The text, the "Incantation of the Sutra of Eternal Life," is written in Khotanese, the ancient language of western Xinjiang.

3 The vase on the Norton's figure is held in place by a small threaded rod that fits into a hole drilled in the hands.

4 See E'ertai and others, *Guochao gongshi*, 1769, reprint, pp. 410–26. See also Clark, *Two Lamaistic Pantheons*, pp. xii–xiii.

5 See Wan Yi and others, *Qingdai gongting shenghuo*, no. 38, for a group of nine gilt-bronze Tibetan-style Amitayus images in the Forbidden City.

6 E'ertai and others, *Guochao gongshi*, reprint, p. 410, give a total of 900 images for the first day and 9,000 for the second, although the text only says that they were presented in "nines," which can be read as sets of nine images, with the sets listed under nine different names for Amitayus.

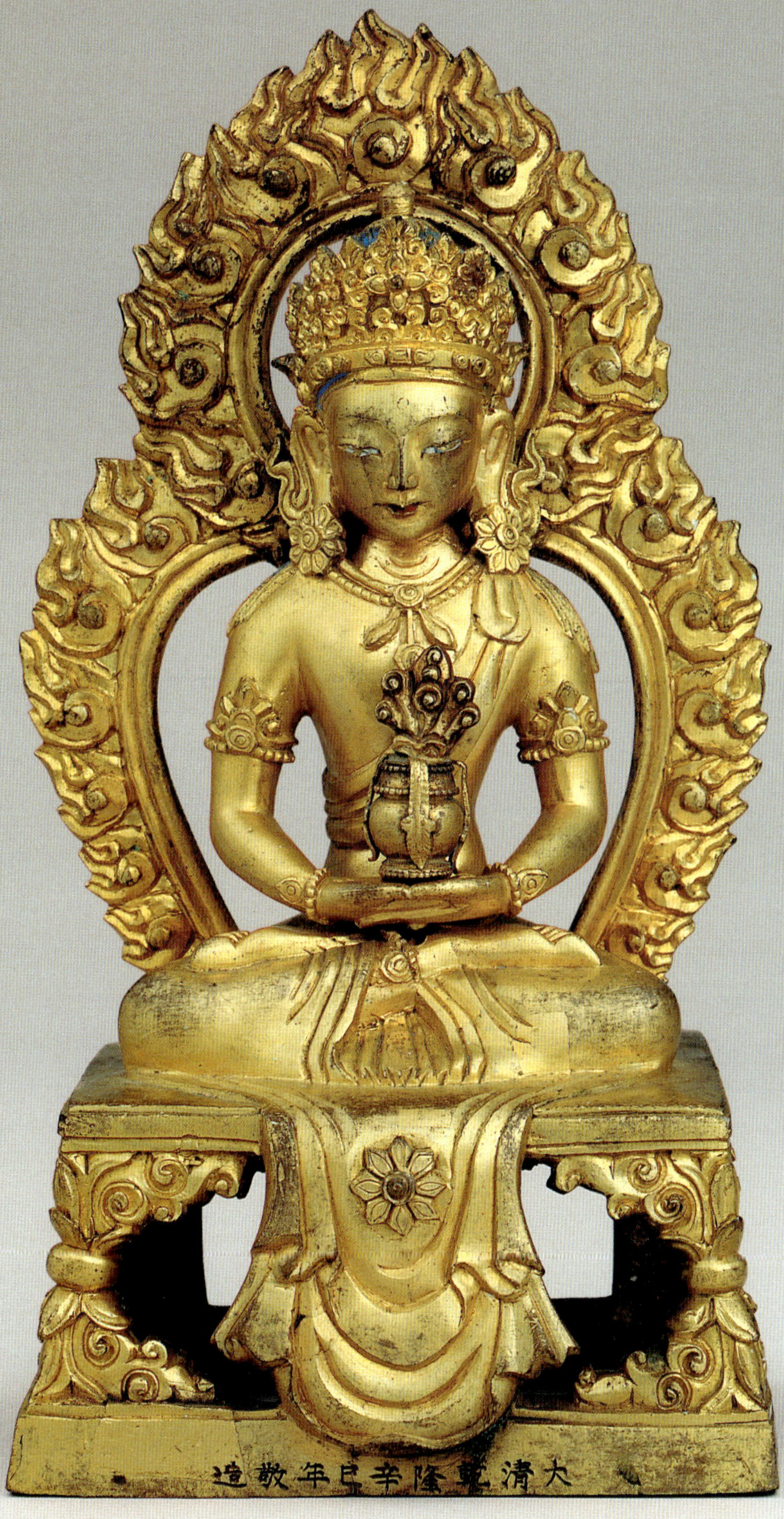
大清乾隆辛巳年敬造

53 PAIR OF AUSPICIOUS ANIMALS (*QILIN*)

Qing dynasty, late 18th–19th century
Copper alloy matrix, cloisonné enamel, gilding,
each 30½ × 20¼ × 12½ in. (77.5 × 51.4 × 31.8 cm)
Gift of Alvin and Helen Zises, 2000.6.1–.2

Auspicious animals called *qilin* (pronounced chee-lin) appear in some of the earliest Chinese written records, and this 19th-century *Pair of qilin* most likely served as guardian images. Descriptions vary, but in general the *qilin* has a body like a horse (a deer by some accounts), round hooves, the tail of an ox, a body covered with multicolored or sometimes white fishlike scales, sometimes with a yellow belly, usually with a single horn, although it can have two horns pointing backward, as we see here. The late Ming illustrated encyclopedia, the *Sancai tuhui*,[1] includes a woodblock illustration of the *qilin* similar to the Museum's pair of cloisonné enamel animals, except that is has a single horn.

The *qilin* is mentioned several times in the Confucian Classics, the earliest reference probably in the *Book of Songs*, compiled some time after the 7th century BCE.[2] It is associated with the Confucian virtue of *ren*, or benevolence toward one's fellow creatures. The Gongyang Commentary to the *Spring and Autumn Annals* explains, "Because flesh covers the point of its horn, it does not harm living animals; and it does not walk on living plants."[3] The Confucian Classics, however, represent only one part of the *qilin* tradition; a widespread body of folk beliefs must have existed as well. One indication of this is a popular print showing a *qilin* ridden by a small boy holding a lotus, the three together forming an auspicious rebus meaning "the *qilin* brings sons."[4]

The Norton's *qilin* are decorated with flaming pearls on their shoulders, five-clawed dragons chasing flaming pearls on their sides, and Chinese phoenixes or *fenghuang* on the haunches. There are bats, a common emblem of good fortune, on the four corners of the bases, which are decorated with large panels with arrangements of flowers in vases and trays, scrolls, lotus roots, and round emblems similar to coins. All of these are part of a popular repertoire of auspicious emblems used to decorate a broad range of objects. The decoration is mostly executed in cloisonné enamel, which covers the creatures except for their heads and tails. These, which are separate, removable parts, and the corner posts on the bases are gilded. Qing dynasty cloisonné workshops mastered the techniques of firing large pieces and assembling monumental objects from separate sections. The bright colors and dramatic effects of large cloisonné objects make them appropriate for use in public settings such as temples and palace buildings, and the Norton pair likely served as auspicious guardian figures.

NOT PREVIOUSLY PUBLISHED

NOTES

1 *Sancai tuhui*, entry on *qilin*, reprint, vol. 6, p. 2,219.

2 The *Shijing* (Book of Songs), traditionally associated with Confucius, contains poetry and lyrics from approximately the 12th through the 7th century BCE, although other dates have been suggested. See Nienhauser, *The Indiana Companion*, pp. 312, 692–94. The poem cited here is no. 11 of the "Zhou Nan" section. See Legge, trans., *The She King*, p. 19.

3 The *Spring and Autumn Annals* of the state of Lu, also traditionally believed to have been edited by Confucius, covers the period from 722 to 480 BCE. The *Gongyang zhuan*, or Gongyang Commentary, probably dates to the late Warring States or early Han. See Nienhauser, *The Indiana Companion*, pp. 313–14. The quotation here is cited in the *Shuowen jiezi zhu*, the annotated edition of the lexicographical dictionary *Shuowen jiezi*, compiled ca. 100 CE by Xu Shen, with extensive annotations by the Qing scholar Duan Yucai (1735–1815).

4 Eberhard, *A Dictionary of Chinese Symbols*, pp. 302–4.

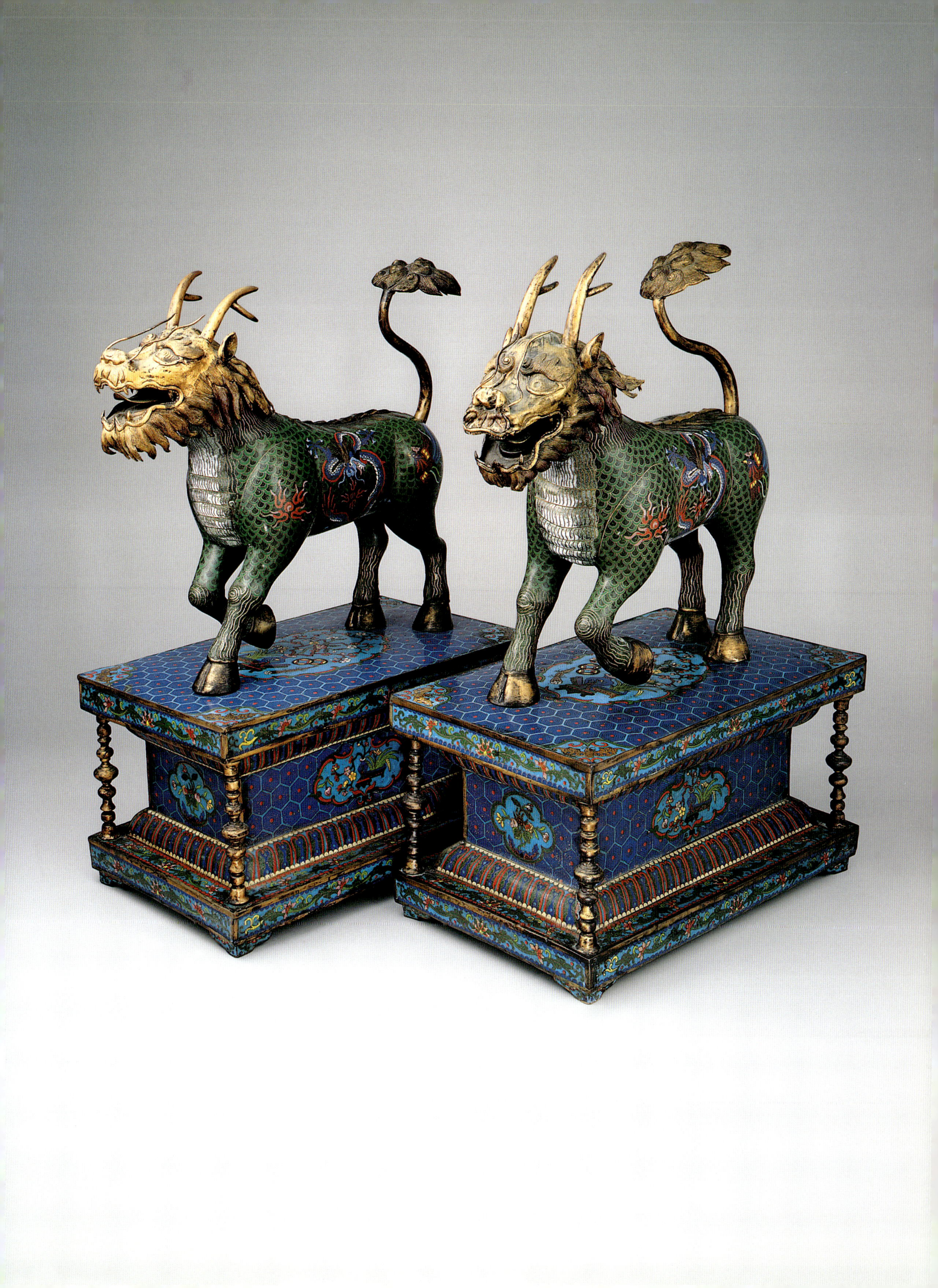

54 BURIAL JAR

Neolithic period, Majiayao Yangshao culture, Banshan phase, ca. 2600–2300 BCE
Earthenware, painted slip decoration 12 ½ × diam. 15 in. (31.8 × 38.1 cm)
Purchase, the R.H. Norton Trust, 62.15

The Neolithic Yangshao culture extended across much of the Wei and Yellow River valleys of north-central China. It was the first Chinese Neolithic culture identified by Western archaeologists and remains the best known.[1] The various phases of Yangshao culture are primarily identified by distinctive types of reddish-brown pottery, and Neolithic potters often painted dramatic designs on pieces intended for burial. Dates for the Yangshao period vary, with 5000 to 3000 BCE generally cited, but adjusted carbon-14 dates indicate a range of dates about one millennium later.[2] One regional phase of Yangshao culture, called Majiayao or Gansu Yangshao, flourished in eastern Qinghai and Gansu provinces, on modern China's western frontier with Central Asia. The late Majiayao phase, named for its type site as Banshan culture, most likely lasted from about 2600 to 2300 BCE.

This wide-bodied Banshan *Burial jar* is typical of the ceramics found at Majiayao sites. It has a flat base, conical lower half, and broad, rounded shoulders. The mouth has a flaring rim, and two small, flat loop handles are attached low on the shoulders. Yangshao painted pottery was made by pressing and shaping coils of clay that contained significant amounts of loess, the friable, wind-blown soil from the Gobi Desert that covers most of northern China. Large jars were formed in sections that were joined together, and the whole vessel was finished by turning and scraping with a tool. The surface of the jar seems to have been carefully smoothed, perhaps by wetting the clay and rubbing it gently, to prepare it for painting.[3] The painted decoration consists of sweeping curves and spirals of black and dark purple-brown slip or a thin solution of clay mixed with colorants. The black slip is rich in iron and manganese oxides, and the purple-brown slip, an innovation of the Banshan phase,[4] is high in iron oxides.[5] The swirling designs are focused on four circles around the shoulder of the vessel, and each circle is filled with a cross-shaped mark. The edges of the curves are hatched with small sawtooth marks, and all of the designs appear to have been applied with a brush or similar tool. This fine example of a well-known Banshan type is the oldest Chinese ceramic in the Norton collection.

PUBLISHED

Jayne, *The Chinese Collections*, no. 301

NOTES

1 See K.C. Chang's brief summary, "Yangshao Culture (5000–3000 BC)," in Loewe and Shaughnessy, *The Cambridge History of Ancient China*, pp. 49–52.

2 Valenstein, *Handbook*, chronological table p. 10, see also p. 6 n. 10, citing Xie Duanju in *Kaogu yu wenwu* 1985.1, pp. 63–74, who provides dates of approximately 4000–2000 BCE.

3 Some writers describe a layer of slip applied to the surface, but chips to the surface of the Museum's jar reveal no discernible difference between the clay body and the smooth surface and no appreciable added layer of slip.

4 Vainker, *Chinese Pottery and Porcelain*, pp. 18–19.

5 Wood, *Chinese Glazes*, p. 12.

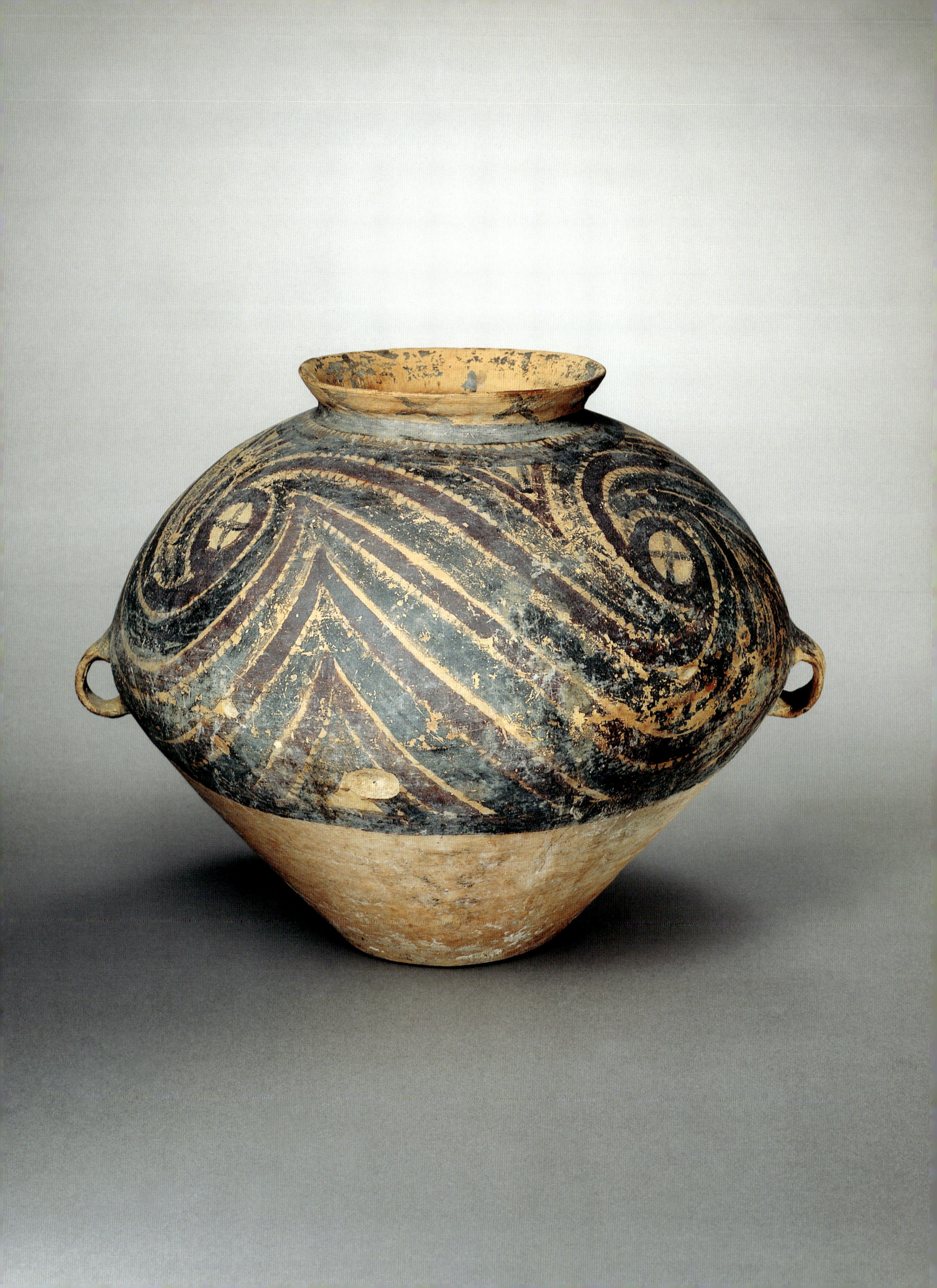

55 VESSEL IN THE FORM OF A RITUAL BRONZE HU

Shang dynasty, Anyang period, ca. 1300–1050 BCE
White kaolinic earthenware, 5 ½ × diam. 4 ¼ in. (14 × 10.8 cm.)
Bequest of R.H. Norton, 53.230

Pure white Shang dynasty stonewares like this *Vessel in the form of a ritual bronze hu* are among the rarest early Chinese ceramics. Composed of almost pure kaolin—one of the two main ingredients of true porcelain—they were fired at temperatures too low, approximately 1050 to 1200°C, to fuse and form into hard, translucent porcelain.[1] They were consequently fragile, and all surviving examples are either shards or, like this vessel, reconstructed from fragments.[2] The decoration on Shang whitewares was usually cut or molded into the surface; upon close examination, the design here appears to have been cut with a sharp tool when the clay was almost dry. The pointed lappets around the shoulder are derived from Shang images of cicadas.[3] Below a narrow band of squared spirals, two typical Shang *taotie,* or monster-mask designs, fill the main range of decoration. The front-facing mask is shared by two bodies, which extend to the left and right around the belly of the vessel. The decoration on the cover, which may possibly be a modern replacement,[4] consists of abbreviated animals sharing *taotie* masks. The knob presents a typical Shang design of whorls.

Almost all Shang whitewares come from Anyang, the site of the last Shang capital, and most seem to be associated with royal burials. The Norton vessel replicates a well-known bronze type of covered *hu,* or wine jar (see cat. 2, which probably once had a cover). However, many Shang whitewares do not copy bronze forms directly. A pedestal bowl in the Asian Art Museum, San Francisco, for example, has a shallow dish on a high foot with no close bronze equivalent.[5] And a round covered jar—again assembled from fragments—in the Asian Art Museum of San Francisco[6] is similar in profile to a covered white marble vessel from the twelfth-century BCE tomb of Fu Hao.[7]

While some writers describe Shang whitewares as mimicking white stone or marble examples (and referring all to bronze prototypes), Nigel Wood has perceptively commented that similar designs are applied to numerous types of Shang "official" objects,[8] many of which are associated with royal burials—bronzes foremost, but also jades, ceramics of various kinds, bone, ivory, or stone objects, and remnants of inlay in turquoise on other media. This *Vessel in the form of bronze hu* should be seen, perhaps, as replicating a ritual bronze in miniature but also existing as part of a broader range of Shang royal burial objects.

PUBLISHED

Jayne, *The Chinese Collections,* no. 304

NOTES

1 Wood, *Chinese Glazes,* pp. 92–93.
2 See Jayne, *The Chinese Collections,* no. 304, where the author notes that a large fragment from the Norton jar—a section of the original neck—apparently exists in a private collection in Kobe, Japan, and together the two parts form an almost complete vessel. For the proportions of a complete jar with cover, see Shangraw, *Origins of Chinese Ceramics,* cat. 31.
3 A fragment of Shang whiteware with a very similar pointed lappet design was excavated at the Miaopu site near Anyang. See *Yinxu fajue baogao,* pl. 28 (5).
4 Extant covers from Shang ceramics, however, are very close to this in profile. See *Yinxu fajue baogao,* fig. 121, nos. 2, 5, 10, for excavated examples from the Miaopu site.
5 Watson, *Pre-Tang Ceramics of China,* fig. 11.
6 Lefebvre d'Argencé, *Chinese Ceramics in the Avery Brundage Collection,* cat. VI.
7 *Yinxu Fu Hao mu,* fig. 98 (1), see also pp. 196, 198. For an indication of the variety of Shang whiteware forms, see Tan, *Zhongguo taoci,* vol. 1, nos. 58–63.
8 Wood, *Chinese Glazes,* pp. 92–93.

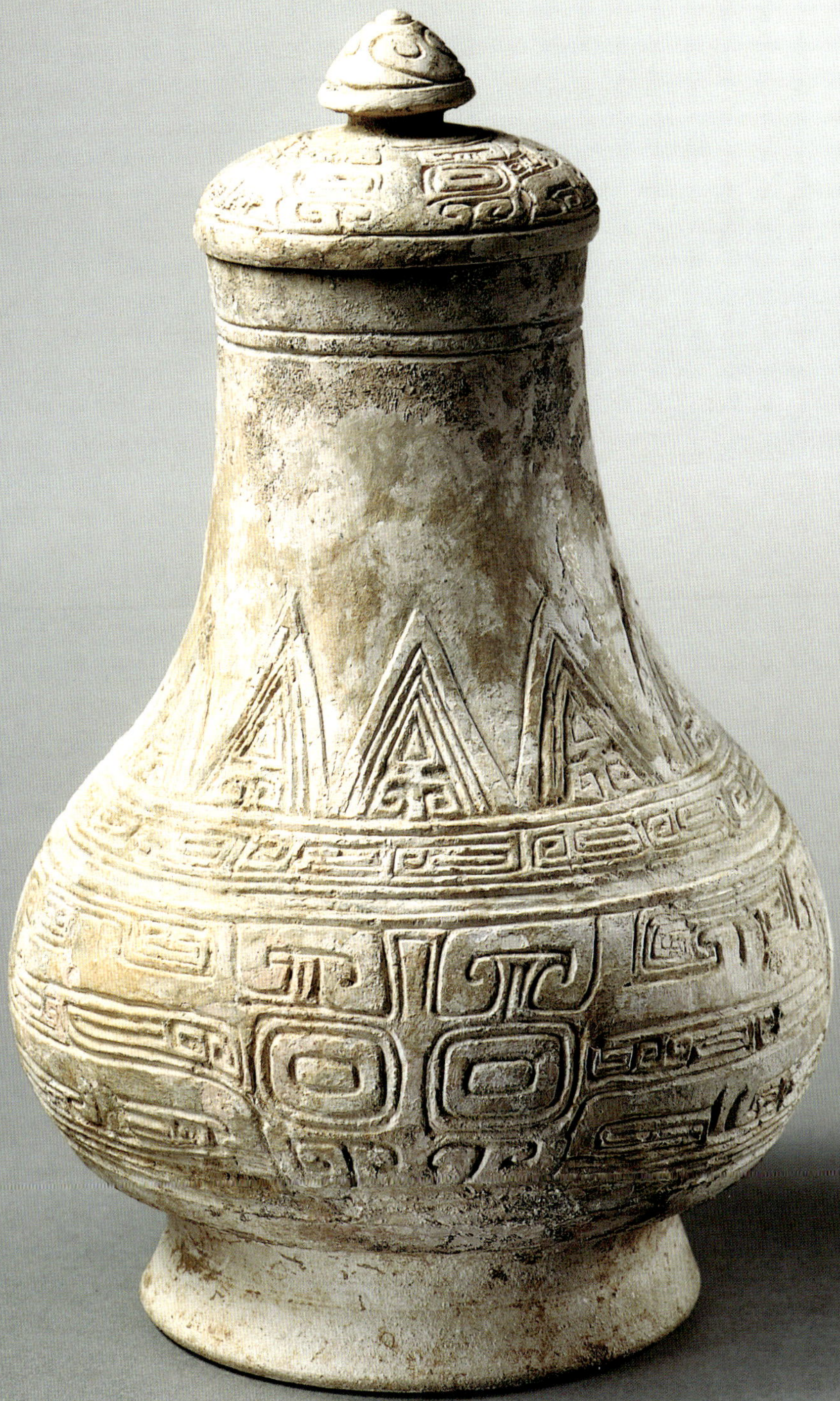

56 STORAGE JAR IN THE FORM OF A POU

Western Han dynasty (206 BCE–9 CE)
Proto-Yue stoneware, ash glaze, 6¾ × 12¼ × 11½ in. (17.1 × 31.1 × 29.2 cm)
Gift of Dr. Gerald Shepps, 95.167

57 STORAGE JAR

Han dynasty (206 BCE–220 CE)
Proto-Yue stoneware, ash glaze, 13 × diam. 14 in. (33 × 35.6 cm)
Gift of Dr. Gerald Shepps, 95.166

The best known early example of deliberate, overall glazing occurs on a jar of the middle Shang dynasty, probably dating to the fifteenth or fourteenth century BCE, excavated at Zhengzhou, Henan province. Decorated with regularly stamped patterns imitating woven textiles, its reddish body is covered with a thin, gray-green glaze.[1] Although the production of glazed ceramics in China does not follow a single, continuous tradition, the larger Norton *Storage jar* (right) demonstrates the reappearance of such techniques almost 1,500 years later. The jar was hand-built and finished by turning, perhaps on a simple turntable, after which the damp clay was stamped with a regular pattern imitating textiles or basketry. The potter most likely used a small wooden paddle with a carved design to tap against the outside while a block was held on the inside. The yellow-green glaze has been thinly applied to the upper surface of the jar, and the glaze on the shoulder is thick enough to fill parts of the stamped design. Where the glaze did not cover the body of the jar, traces of iron in the clay have fired a reddish-tan color.

The smaller *Storage jar in the form of a pou* (left) most likely once had a low, domed lid that fit over the short mouth rim. Its body is also hand-built and finished by turning and scraping—scraper marks are clearly visible on the clay. The design around the shoulders consists of parallel and wavy lines cut with tools into the turning jar. The animal-mask handles, imitating those of contemporary bronze vessels, were first formed in a mold and then attached. The masks have square raised ears, oval eyes, prominent noses, and half-opened mouths. While ceramic versions of this bronze type, called a *pou*, are well known, bronze examples are relatively rare.[2] The glaze is a yellow-green coating applied only to the upper surfaces of the *Storage jar*. Where it is thickest on the top of the shoulders the glaze runs unevenly, but where it is thinner it appears as tiny drops or flakes.

Glazes on Chinese ceramics most likely began as an imitation of the effects of ash falling on pieces during firing. This accidental effect, called "kiln glost," sometimes resulted in a thin layer of fused material on the upper surfaces. No doubt observing this phenomenon, early potters made glaze formulas that blended wood ash with clay.[3] Nigel Wood, noting that the deposits of glaze on vessels similar to the Norton's are thicker than what one might expect from accidental deposits, has theorized that the ash-based glaze was perhaps sifted onto the surface to produce a controlled imitation of what was once a kiln accident.[4] The attractive contrast between the light glaze and the dark purple-brown surface of the unglazed clay appears on a significant number of Western Han ceramics, suggesting that it was indeed a deliberate decorative effect.

NOT PREVIOUSLY PUBLISHED

NOTES

1 See Rogers and others, *China 5,000 Years*, cat. 118; see also Medley *The Chinese Potter*, pp. 40–43 and esp. fig. 20, for a discussion of this frequently reproduced jar and related examples.
2 See Mino and Tsiang, *Ice and Green Clouds*, cat. 14, for four excavated examples and one bronze, citing Trubner, *Arts of the Han Dynasty*, p. 33, no. 38.
3 Vainker, *Chinese Pottery and Porcelain*, p. 46.
4 Wood, *Chinese Glazes*, pp. 21–22.

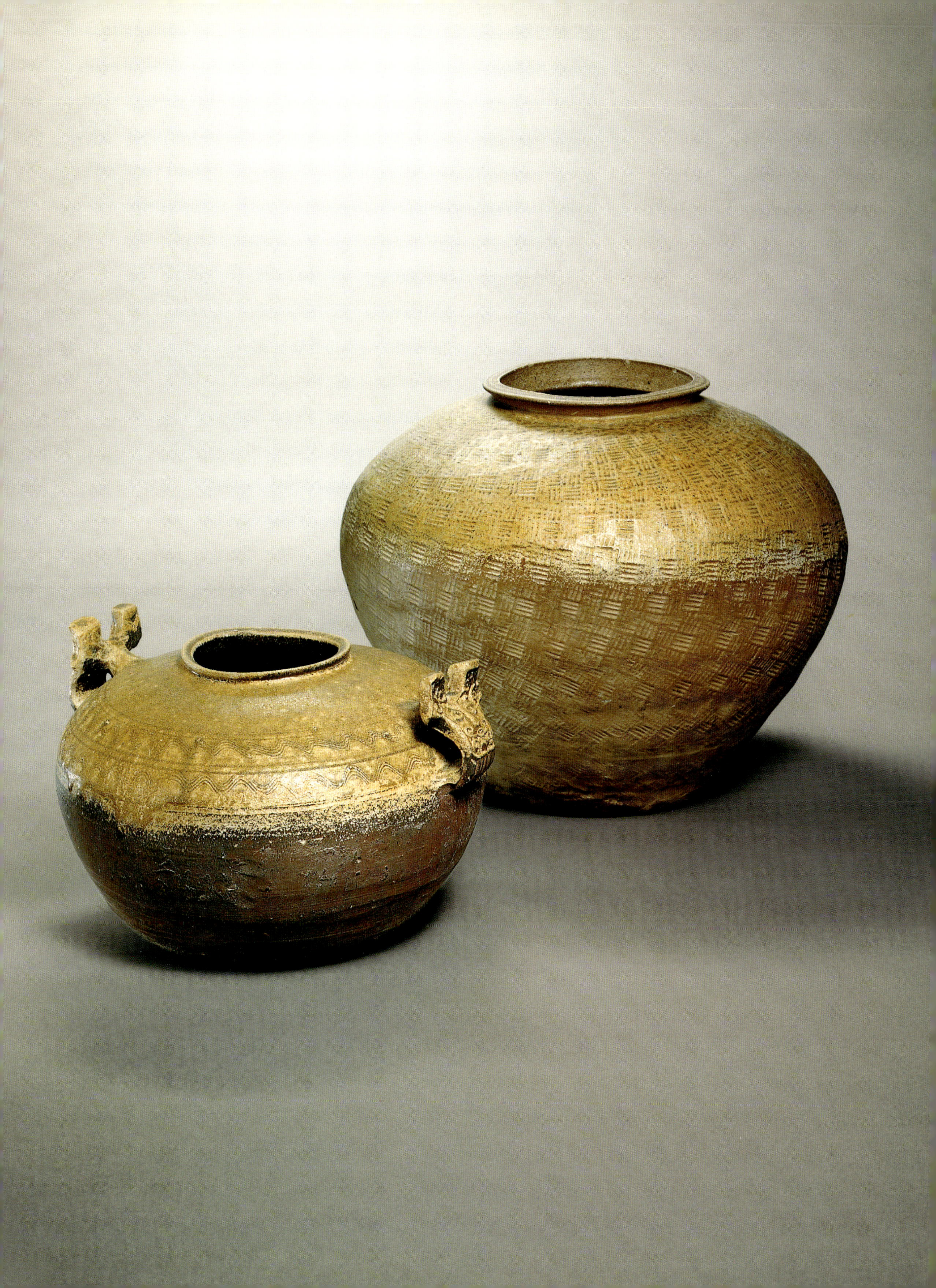

58 BURIAL JAR IN THE FORM OF A HU

Western Han dynasty (206 BCE–9 CE)
Earthenware, green lead glaze, 14¾ × diam. 10¾ in. (37.5 × 27.3 cm)
Purchase, the R.H. Norton Trust, 62.9

Like other early ceramics in the collection (cats. 55, 56), this jar is a ceramic replica of an object in another medium, in this case a bronze *hu,* intended for burial with the dead. The jar has a wide, flaring mouth that tapers seamlessly to the neck and rounded body, presenting an unbroken silhouette that continues to the slightly flaring foot. Decoration consists of a raised band around the mouth and sets of raised ribs on the body. Two moldmade mask-and-ring handles are laid on the surface on opposite sides of the jar. The outside of the jar, including the foot, and the visible part of the inside of the mouth are covered with a translucent dark green glaze. The raised drops of glaze and small breakmarks on the mouth rim indicate that the jar was fired upside down, standing on pieces of kiln furniture.[1]

The familiar dark green glazed burial wares of the Han were first widely manufactured in the metropolitan region of Henan and Shaanxi provinces beginning in the late second century BCE.[2] The glazes are mostly composed of silica with lead oxide as the principal flux, the chemical agent that allows the glaze to melt and adhere to the surface of the vessel.[3] The lead flux lowers the melting point of the glaze to about 700° C, which is sufficient to sinter (or solidify) the clay body and fuse the melted glaze. Such wares were almost certainly fired just once, with the glaze applied to the unfired vessel, cutting down the time and cost of production and making them widely available as burial objects.[4] The earliest example of a lead-based, green-glazed ceramic is a covered jar dating to the early third century BCE, now in the Nelson-Atkins Museum, Kansas City.[5] Interestingly, it is a very close copy of a contemporary bronze vessel, with the crisply molded bands of complex decoration typical of bronzes of the Warring States period. The green glaze recalled the patina of bronzes and no doubt helped make such wares popular as burial objects in the succeeding Han dynasty.

The glaze on the Museum's *Burial jar* has a distinct iridescent sheen, the result of chemical changes in the glaze that occurred on many Han ceramics during their long burial in damp conditions. Green-glazed Han ceramics appeared in Western collections alongside better known blue-and-white and overglaze-enamel porcelains in the late nineteenth century. While they may not have inspired the same admiration as porcelains, iridescent Han ceramics may have caused collectors to think of the glazes on Art Nouveau and later studio pottery. As Hobson and Heatherington commented to collectors of Chinese ceramics in 1923, "the decomposition of the glaze on these wares has given an adventitious beauty to them; ... and a beautiful silvery sheen is generally seen on part or the whole of the object."[6] This accidental effect remains one of their chief attractions.

PUBLISHED

Jayne, *The Chinese Collections,* no. 316

NOTES

1 Many Han burial ceramics were fired upside down. A number retain the small, prism-shaped pieces of clay furniture that were fused to the surface by the melting glaze and never chipped off by the Han potters.
2 Watson, *Pre-Tang Ceramics of China,* pp. 28–29.
3 Valenstein, *Handbook,* p. 45.
4 The lead-based glaze made them unsuitable for daily use.
5 Medley, *The Chinese Potter,* p. 51, fig. 30.
6 Hobson and Heatherington, *The Art of the Chinese Potter,* p. 4.

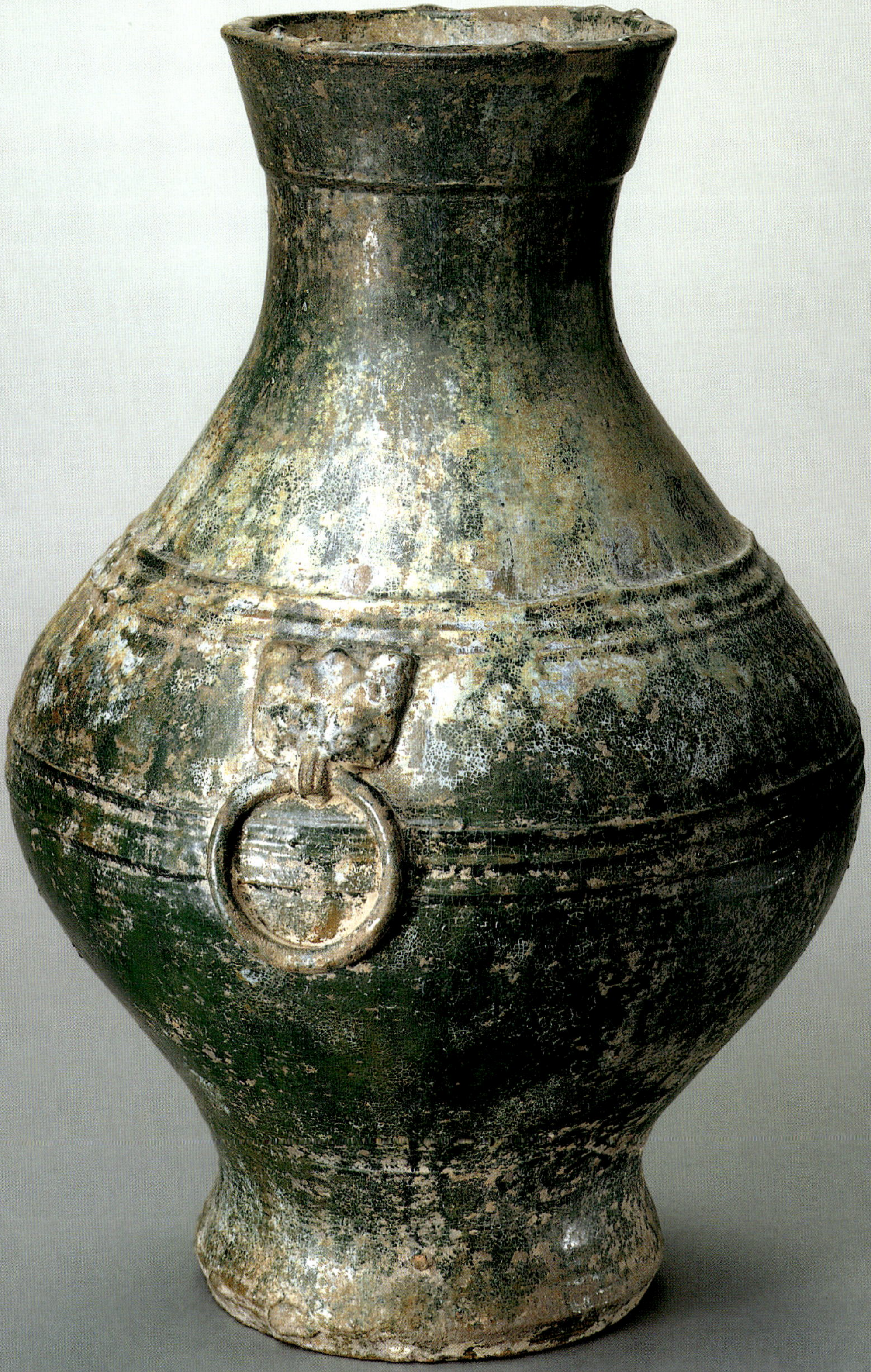

59 HILL JAR AND COVER

Han dynasty (206 BCE–220 CE)
Earthenware, green lead glaze, 10¾ × diam. 9 in. (27.3 × 22.9 cm)
Bequest of R.H. Norton, 53.231a-b

The cover of the *Hill jar* is molded in the shape of a mountain. Small animals are depicted in low relief running among crags and peaks, and a mountain goat with curving horns can be seen dashing into a valley. Like the cover, the cylindrical body of the jar is mold-made. Two slabs of clay were pressed against a flat mold and then shaped and joined together on a flat bottom (a vertical seam is visible at the right-hand side of the jar). On the right-hand side of the jar a figure on horseback, galloping among stylized hills, turns to shoot an arrow at an animal behind him. A large tiger prances on the left-hand side of the jar with its tail raised in the air. The dark green glaze, which has become almost completely iridescent silver from long burial, was intended to mimic the patina of bronze vessels. Large drops of glaze rise from the tops of the mountain peaks, indicating that the cover was fired upside down. Drips and splatters of glaze inside the cover, on the inside and bottom of the jar, as well as small breaks and scars left where vessels touched each other in the kiln, all indicated that hill jars, like other Han burial ceramics, were mass-produced.[1] Han potters packed their kilns as full as possible to make the best use of their fuel.

Like the *Burial jar in the form of a hu* (cat. 58), the *Hill jar* is a ceramic substitute for a costly bronze intended for burial with the dead. While Western collectors call this vessel a "hill jar," it reproduces a covered wine jar called a *zun*.[2] The flat-bottomed *zun*, frequently fitted with a pair of mask-and-ring handles, can have a shallow, domed lid with three short handles that serve as feet when the lid is removed. Other versions have the dramatic, mountain-shaped cover that we see here.[3] The use of small bears for legs on various objects appears rather suddenly in the Western Han, and these animals seem to be a foreign import.[4] (The bear-shaped legs on the Norton jar are simplified almost beyond recognition.) Painted lacquer decoration of elaborate cloud spirals filled with mythological and real animals stretches back to the southern Chu culture (ca. 7th–3rd centuries BCE) that eventually became part of Han China,[5] and stylized mountains seem to be derived from these cloud shapes. Mounted figures—especially the rider turning to shoot his bow and arrow—are an exotic design transmitted from Central or West Asia. In 1909 Berthold Laufer enumerated the value of the then recently discovered Han ceramics as a previously unknown Chinese type that revealed Han burial customs, as examples of Han material culture, and as testimony to Han artistic connections with "Siberian or Turkish art."[6] The themes pioneered in his 1909 catalogue are those that define our approaches to Han ceramics a century later.

PUBLISHED
Jayne, *The Chinese Collections*, no. 318

NOTES
1 An identical example—both the jar and cover are made from the same molds as the Norton's—is illustrated in Laufer, *Chinese Pottery of the Han Dynasty*, pls. LVI (1) and LVIII (4).
2 See Avril, *Chinese Art in the Cincinnati Museum*, no. 51.
3 See *Kaikodo Journal* (Spring 1997), cat. 25, *Bronze Zun with Fu Xi and Nu Wa*, Western Han dynasty, 2nd–1st century BCE.
4 Independent small figures of seated bears appear in the Shang; see *Yinxu Fu Hao mu*, color pl. XXIX (2). Bears with grinning jaws, bulging stomachs and, frequently, a raised paw are a Han innovation.
5 See *Changsha Mawangdui*, vol. 2, color pls. 26–36, for some of the most spectacular examples.
6 Laufer, *Chinese Pottery of the Han Dynasty*, p. 7.

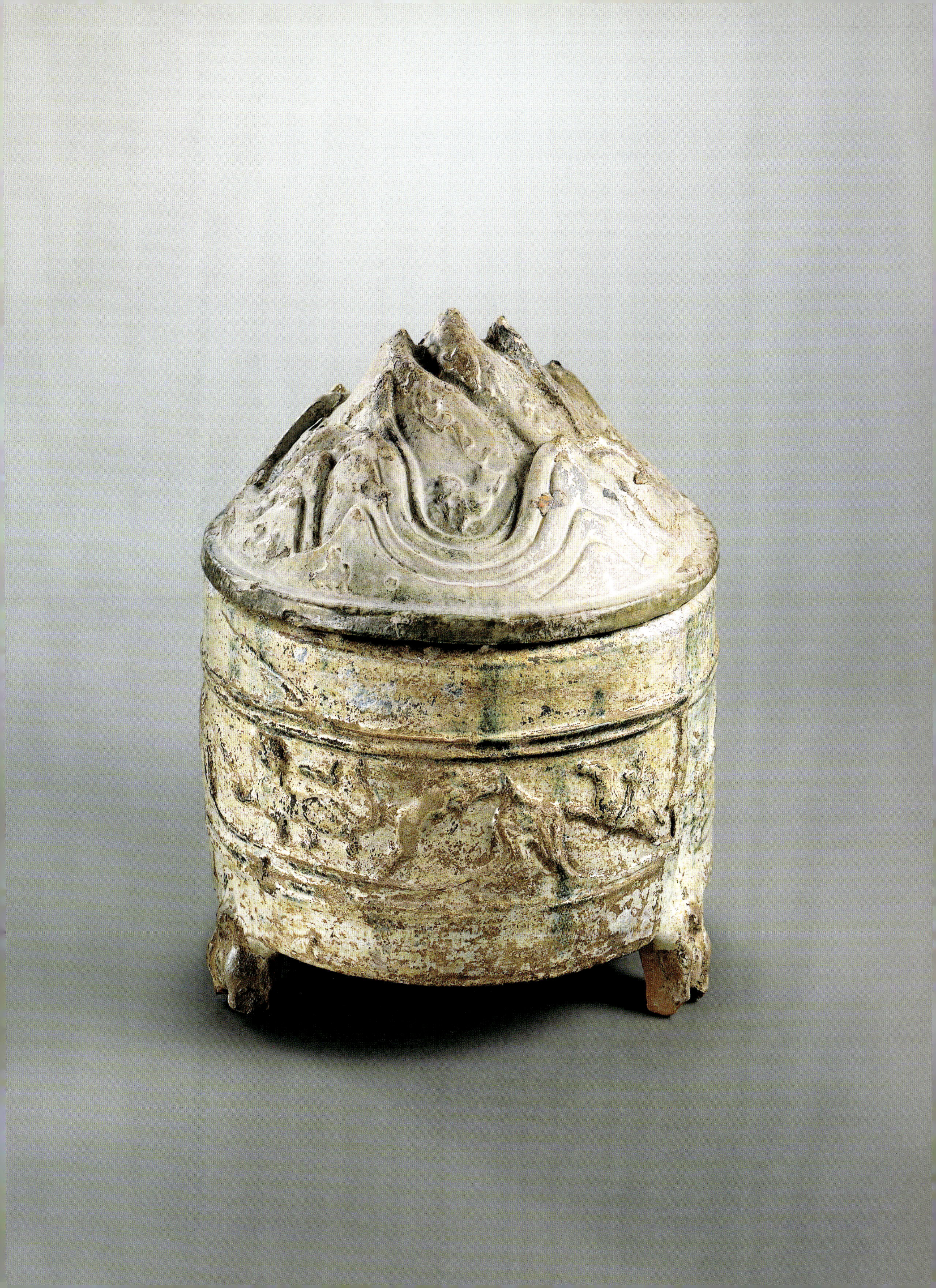

60 TOMB OFFERING STAND

Tang dynasty, 8th century
Earthenware, *sancai* glaze, 2 1/16 × diam. 11 1/4 in. (5.2 × 28.6 cm)
Purchase, the R.H. Norton Trust, 62.11

61 BURIAL JAR

Tang dynasty, 8th century
Earthenware, *sancai* glaze, 10 1/4 × diam. 9 3/4 in. (26 × 24.8 cm)
Purchase, the R.H. Norton Trust, 62.12

Among objects intended for burial with the dead during the Tang dynasty were large numbers of brightly colored vessels as well as the familiar Tang horses (cat. 69). The technique of using lead oxide as the flux—the component that helps the glaze melt and fuse to the clay body—dates to about the third century BCE and provides the technological background for Tang *sancai* wares.[1] Tang potters mixed small amounts of iron oxides with their glazes to produce colors ranging from yellow to dark brown. Copper oxides yielded greens, and costly imported cobalt oxides were added to produce a dark, inky blue.[2] Uncolored glaze over a light-colored slip produced white, and while there were occasional uses of other colorants, such glazes are conventionally called *sancai*, or "three-colored." Despite the large numbers of *sancai* wares, relatively few kiln sites have been identified, and these are mostly in central China's Shaanxi, Hebei, and Henan provinces.[3]

The *Tomb offering stand* (left) is a plate raised on three short legs in the form of animal's paws (not visible in the photo). The decoration consists of a central roundel with a flying goose among stylized clouds. The roundel is surrounded by designs that can be interpreted as clouds or *lingzhi* fungus and framed by eight large lotus leaves, which evoke perhaps the Buddhist image of souls reborn in paradise from the buds of lotus plants. The outlines of the design are stamped into the clay, and colors pooling in the lines help control the colors and accent the design. Stands decorated with lotus, clouds, and geese are well known, and slight variations and overlaps in the designs indicate that they were made with various separate stamps. One stamp produced the circle, another the goose, and one made the small comma-shaped clouds inside the circle. Other stamps made the outer cloud or *lingzhi* design, and a final stamp impressed lotus leaves, one at a time.

Like the decoration of the offering stand, derived from the engraved designs of far more expensive silver platters and stands, the vertical stripe, dot, and lozenge patterns of the *Burial jar* (right) reflect Tang styles in other media. The connections between Tang tie-dyed textiles and *sancai* ceramics have long been recognized, but the use of free-flowing lead-glaze colors and the technique of resists to produce designs that successfully evoke the vitality of textiles testify to the visual inventiveness of Tang potters.

PUBLISHED

60: Jayne, *The Chinese Collections*, no. 327
61: Jayne, *The Chinese Collections*, no. 329

NOTES

1 Lead is occasionally a component in Shang and Zhou glazes; see Vainker, *Chinese Pottery and Porcelain*, p. 42. Han dynasty lead-based green glaze formulas are essentially identical to those used on Tang, Liao, and even Ming tomb models, although the tradition is not a continuous one. See Wood, *Chinese Glazes*, pp. 192–93.
2 Vainker, *Chinese Pottery and Porcelain*, p. 76.
3 Valenstein, *Handbook*, p. 64 and n. 2. Most of the kilns are in the region of the Tang primary capital at Chang'an (modern Xi'an) and the city of Luoyang, the secondary Tang capital.

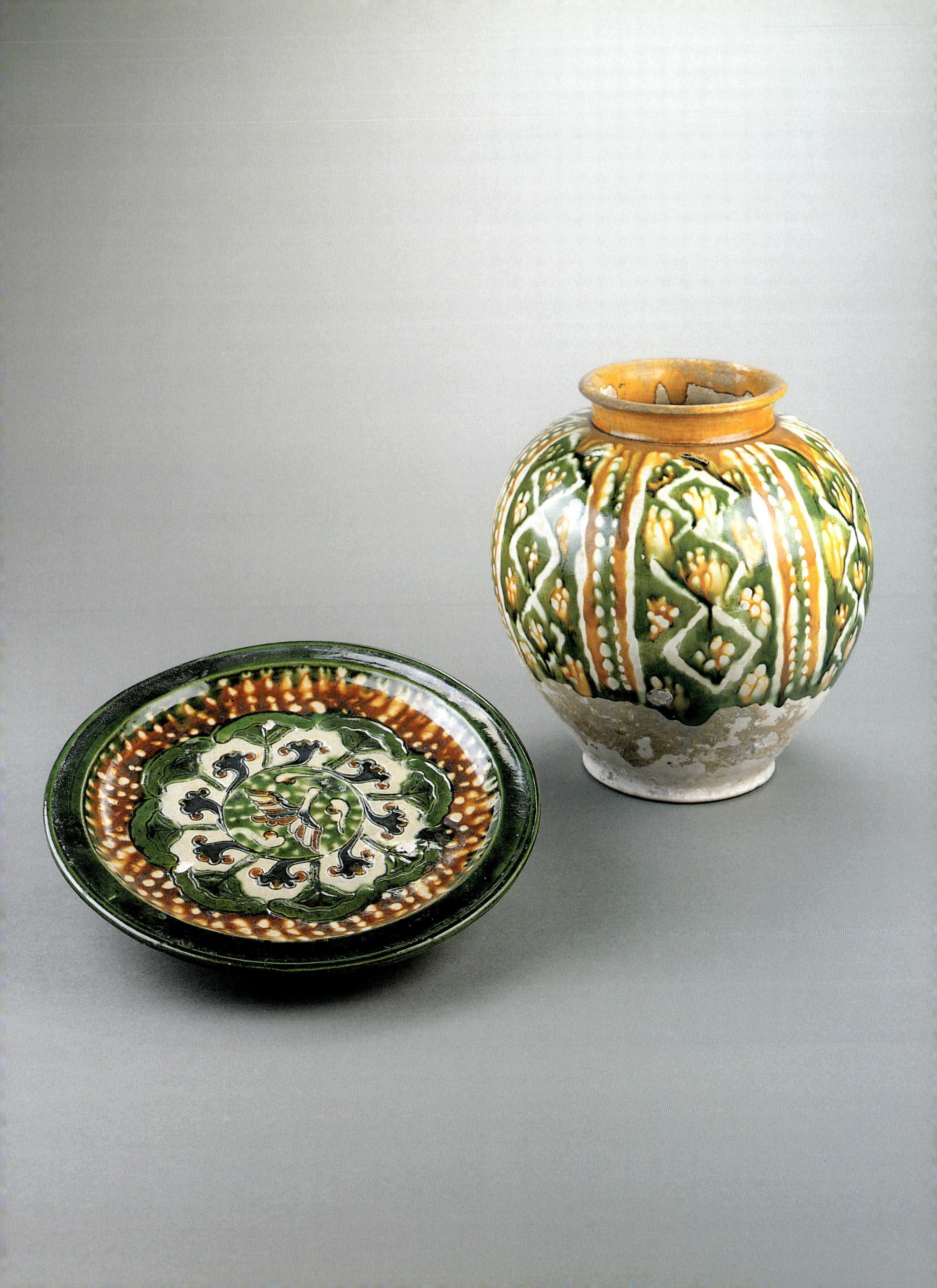

62 EWER WITH PAINTED UNDERGLAZE DECORATION

Tang dynasty, mid-9th century
Changsha ware, underglaze brown and green decoration,
8 1/2 × diam. 5 3/8 in. (21.6 × 13.7 cm)
Gift of Mr. John J. McCarthy, III, 98.760

63 EWER WITH INCISED DECORATION

Five Dynasties to early Song dynasty, 10th–early 11th century
Yue ware, semi-opaque gray-green glaze, 7 1/2 × diam. 5 3/8 in. (19.1 × 13.7 cm)
Gift of Mr. and Mrs. Bartlett Richards in memory of Patricia Norton Hendershot, 74.2

The city of Changsha in Hunan province gives its name to a variety of ceramics manufactured in south-central China during the Tang dynasty, and the best known kilns flourished at Tongguan, north of Changsha on the Xiang River. Fragments of Changsha wares have been found as far away as Korea and Japan, Iran, the east coast of Africa, and Egypt.[1] The Changsha-ware *Ewer with painted underglaze decoration* (left) is typical of the products of the Tongguan kilns at the height of their production in the mid-ninth century. Solidly potted of gray stoneware, the vessel has a flaring mouth, wide neck, short polygonal spout, and sturdy handle (not visible in the photo).

It is the underglaze decoration that makes Changsha ware so important in the history of Chinese ceramics. The design—here a bird and plant motif— is painted directly on the clay body using iron oxides for the reddish brown lines, copper compounds for the green wash, and on occasion a manganese-iron purple brown. A thin glaze, rich in clay with lime as the flux,[2] covers the surface of the ewer inside and out, including the painted decoration, which shows through the clear glaze after firing. Although a few isolated examples of painted decoration under a clear glaze had appeared in the third and fourth centuries,[3] mass-production and marketing of underglaze decorated ceramics begin with Changsha wares.

The tenth- to eleventh-century stoneware *Ewer with incised decoration* (right) is a part of a surprisingly large group of vessels that share the same general form. Related to earlier Tang dynasty ewers, they are distinguished by the addition of decorated loop handles or lugs between the neck and shoulder, which may have secured a cord or handle to help lift them. This vessel has a particularly subtle profile and decoration: a high, rounded handle echoes the flare of the mouth, the body has a crisply defined shoulder, and the elegant spout continues the curve of the body up from the foot. The lugs are press-molded in the form of small trefoils, and the surface decoration consists of a faintly incised floral ornament in lobed medallions set in panels marked off by vertical lines. A subdued gray-green, translucent glaze covers the whole surface

This ewer is an example of Yue ware, a term that broadly defines green-glazed ceramics from northern Zhejiang and southern Jiangsu provinces.[4] Like Changsha wares, Yue wares were widely traded; one superb tenth–eleventh century ewer, with raised ribs evoking a melon shape, was recovered from Butuan, on north-central Mindanao in the Philippines.[5] The understated elegance of the Norton Yue-ware ewer may help explain why this particular shape, in addition to being eminently practical, endured for at least four centuries and was produced by so many widely separated kilns.

NOT PREVIOUSLY PUBLISHED

NOTES

1 See Li Jian, *Changsha Ceramics* (n.p.).
2 Wood, *Chinese Glazes*, pp. 41–45.
3 Li Jian, *Changsha Ceramics* (n.p.).
4 The precise definition of Yue ware (the name is an ancient designation for the region) is the subject of discussion among specialists. See Ho, ed., *New Light on Chinese Yue and Longquan Wares*, preface, p. x; see also Ruan Ping'er, "Yue Ware: The Distribution of Manufacturing Sites and Markets," in ibid., pp. 3–20, esp. p. 3.
5 See Ronquillo and Tan, "Yue-type Wares in Butuan," in ibid., p. 263 and pl. 2(A).

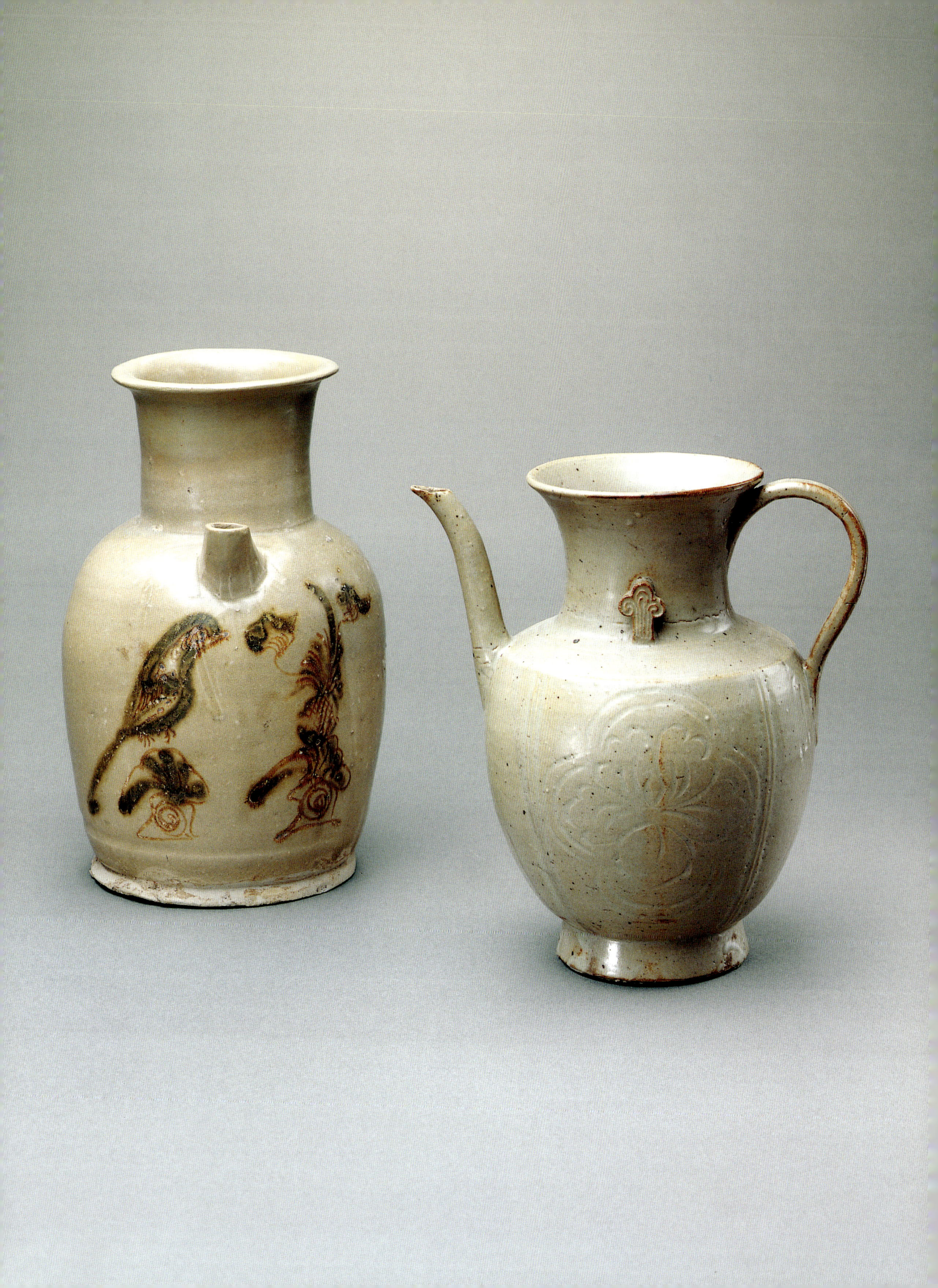

64 BOTTLE VASE WITH A FLARING MOUTH

Song dynasty, beginning of the 12th century or possibly later
Cizhou-type stoneware, white slip, clear glaze, 10¾ × diam. 5 in. (27.3 × 12.7 cm)
Purchase, the R.H. Norton Trust, 70.2

The *Bottle vase with a flaring mouth* poses intriguing questions of interpretation and dating: its manufacturing techniques identify it as Cizhou ware from northern China, but its shape is unprecedented—the wide, flaring mouth appears to be unique—and the decoration is also highly unusual.

Cizhou and Cizhou-type wares take their name from Cizhou, the modern city of Cixian, in northern Hebei province, which was the most important market center for a large group of kilns that stretched across Henan, Hebei, and parts of Shanxi provinces. One characteristic of Cizhou wares is the use of slips—mixtures of clay laid over the gray clay body to provide a smooth surface. Decorating techniques exploited the contrast between different colored slips or between the slip and the body, and cutting through the white slip to expose the gray clay underneath became common by the early tenth century.[1] While such designs are usually cut with tools, paper resists or stencils were used on a small number of Cizhou wares, producing a positive gray design against the colored slip background. The paper pattern would be applied to the surface of the vessel, a slip applied over the entire surface, and the paper removed to expose the body and create the design. Small pieces of paper were most likely used to produce the design on the Norton *Bottle vase*.

Cizhou floral designs are almost always flat stylizations, emphasizing the characteristic silhouettes of flowers and leaves. The Norton *Bottle vase* is unusual in this respect as well, for it attempts to render the motif in three dimensions: the petals of the lotus flower wrap around the seed pod in the center, while the tips of the petals are outlined in a convention that makes them appear curled, thereby revealing their undersides. Moreover, the whole design of the flower turns slightly to the left, suggesting perhaps a gentle breeze bending the flower slightly on its stem. The design seems to be more closely related to painting on paper or silk than to the typical two-dimensional floral decoration of Cizhou stoneware. An important body of Cizhou pillows or headrests is indeed decorated in direct imitation of ink painting, but treating the surface of a round vessel as a field for painting is almost entirely unknown.

One piece of physical evidence may help to date the Norton vase more accurately. In 1108 the market town of Juluxian in northern Hebei province was inundated by a change in course of the Yellow River.[2] Cizhou ceramics recovered from this site exhibit a characteristic staining caused by burial, which is consistent with what we see here: pale purple and brown water stains in the white slip under the clear glaze.[3] While the water stains provide one clue, many questions remain unanswered about this vessel. It would appear to be an experiment, consistent with the known materials, techniques, and general history of Cizhou ceramics, but perhaps one that did not find favor with the usual customers for such wares.

PUBLISHED

Jayne, *The Chinese Collections*, no. 335

NOTES

1 Wood, *Chinese Glazes*, pp. 130, 132.
2 Riddell, *Dated Chinese Antiquities*, pp. 51–55, notes that digging by farmers at the site brought it to the attention of the Tianjian Museum in the 1920s. A Juluxian-type Cizhou pillow with a Qianlong imperial inscription dated 1768 demonstrates, however, that the ceramics with this distinctive staining were known in earlier centuries. See *Oriental Ceramics*, vol. 9, pl. 63.
3 Valenstein, *Handbook*, pl. 86, p. 92.

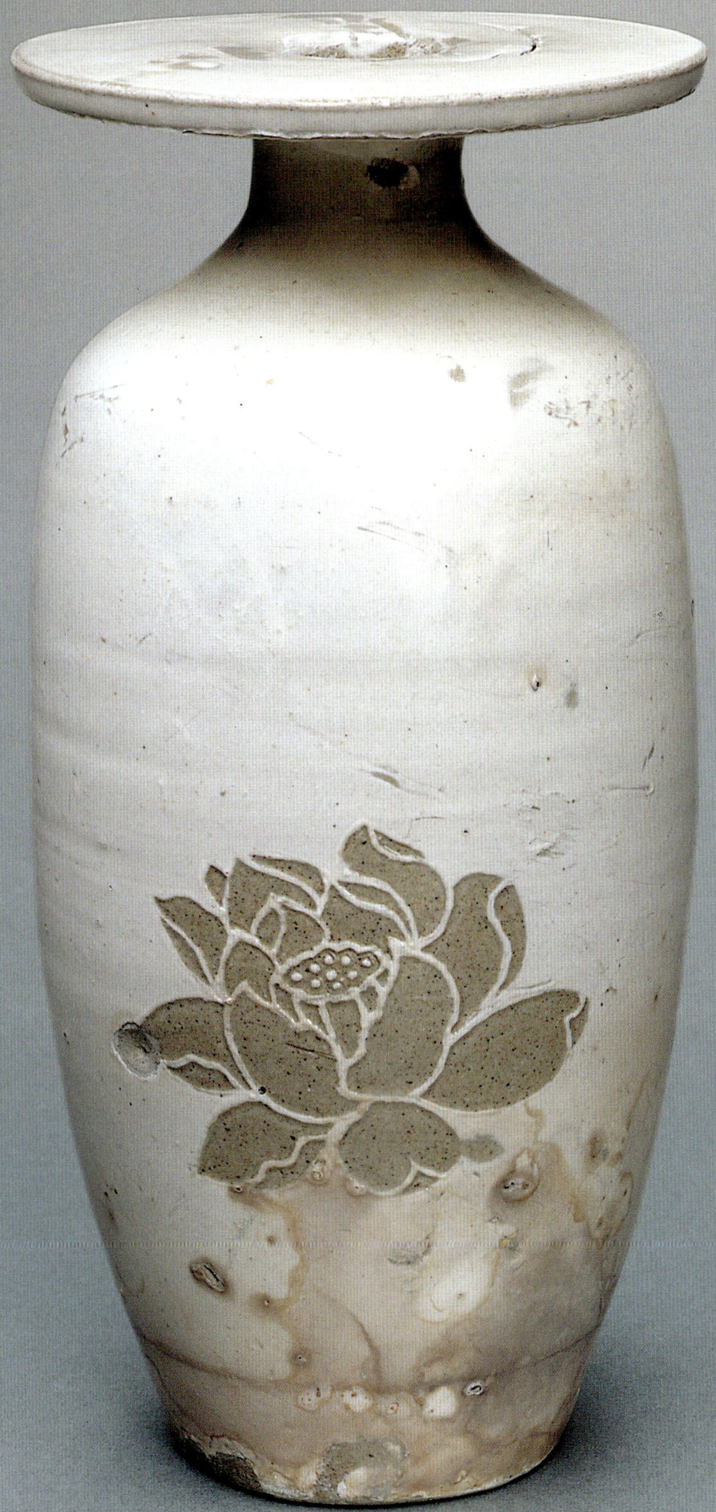

65 DRAGON JAR AND COVER

Southern Song dynasty, 12th–13th century
Longquan stoneware, celadon glaze, 10¾ × diam. 5¾ in (27.3 × 14.6 cm)
Gift of R.H. Norton, 50.38a-b

The jadelike green-glazed wares of the Southern Song dynasty—dubbed celadons by Western collectors—are among the great achievements of Chinese ceramics. Produced in the Longquan district of southern Zhejiang province, they attest to extraordinary skill in combining a clay body similar to porcelain with a subtle and complex glaze on carefully constructed and fired vessels. This *Dragon jar and cover* is one of a large group that perhaps copy ceramics in daily use but were intended as burial goods. The jar was carefully formed on a wheel, and faint horizontal undulations from the potter's hands or tools decorate the lower half.[1] The jar was almost certainly made of parts thrown separately and joined together. The shoulder, with three rounded bands in relief, and the short neck were probably a second, separately formed segment. The lively dragon that wraps around the shoulder is made of hand-formed and press-molded pieces, such as the legs and head, that were then joined together. Details such as scales are barely visible through the thick, translucent glaze. The small rooster that sits on the cover is also a press-molded element.

Jars with dragons wrapped around them have a long history in southern China. A particularly large Tang dynasty Yue-ware gray-green example, excavated in the mid-1990s, is datable to the ninth century.[2] In addition to subtle celadon versions, more exuberant variations appear in *yingqing* ware, light clear-blue glazed stoneware covered jars also produced for burial in southern China in the Song dynasty.[3] These jars occur in pairs and often are decorated with large numbers of hand-modeled and press-molded animals and Daoist or Buddhist images. And at least one northern version of the type is known—a particularly animated thirteenth-century Cizhou-ware covered jar with black-slip-painted flowers on the body, a rudimentary bird for the knob, and a dragon that looks more like a spotted dog wrapped around the neck and shoulder.[4] Like their *yingqing* counterparts, Longquan celadon jars also occur in pairs, traditionally one with a dragon and one with a tiger. One such intact pair is in the collection of the Percival David Foundation of Chinese Art, London.[5]

It is the mysterious depth of the glaze on the Norton *Dragon jar* that makes it such an important object. For a period in the twelfth and thirteenth centuries, the Longquan potters were able to control the firing temperature and atmosphere that helped produce this particular soft, glowing green.[6] While the effect is often attributed to the minute bubbles that suffuse the glaze, the presence of tiny crystals, formed by complex glaze chemistry and firing techniques, is equally crucial to its success. The vast amounts of kiln wasters (ceramics that failed during firing) around all the Longquan kilns testify to the difficulties of the process, while the *Dragon jar* attests to its outstanding success.

PUBLISHED

Jayne, *The Chinese Collections*, no. 344

NOTES

1 Other examples often have stylized lotus petals cut into the lower part of the body.
2 See Lu Minghua, "Newly Discovered Ceramics in the Shanghai Museum," in Pierson, ed., *Collecting Chinese Art*, p. 90.
3 Production was greatest in Jiangxi kilns in the Southern Song. See Peng Shifan, ed., *Song Yuan jinian qingbai ci*, esp. cats. 68, 70, 76.
4 *Oriental Ceramics*, vol. 10, color pl. 87.
5 See Medley, *Illustrated Catalogue of Celadon Wares*, no. 36.
6 See Kingery and Vandiver, *Ceramic Masterpieces*, pp. 69–91, for an extended discussion of the technology of Southern Song celadons.

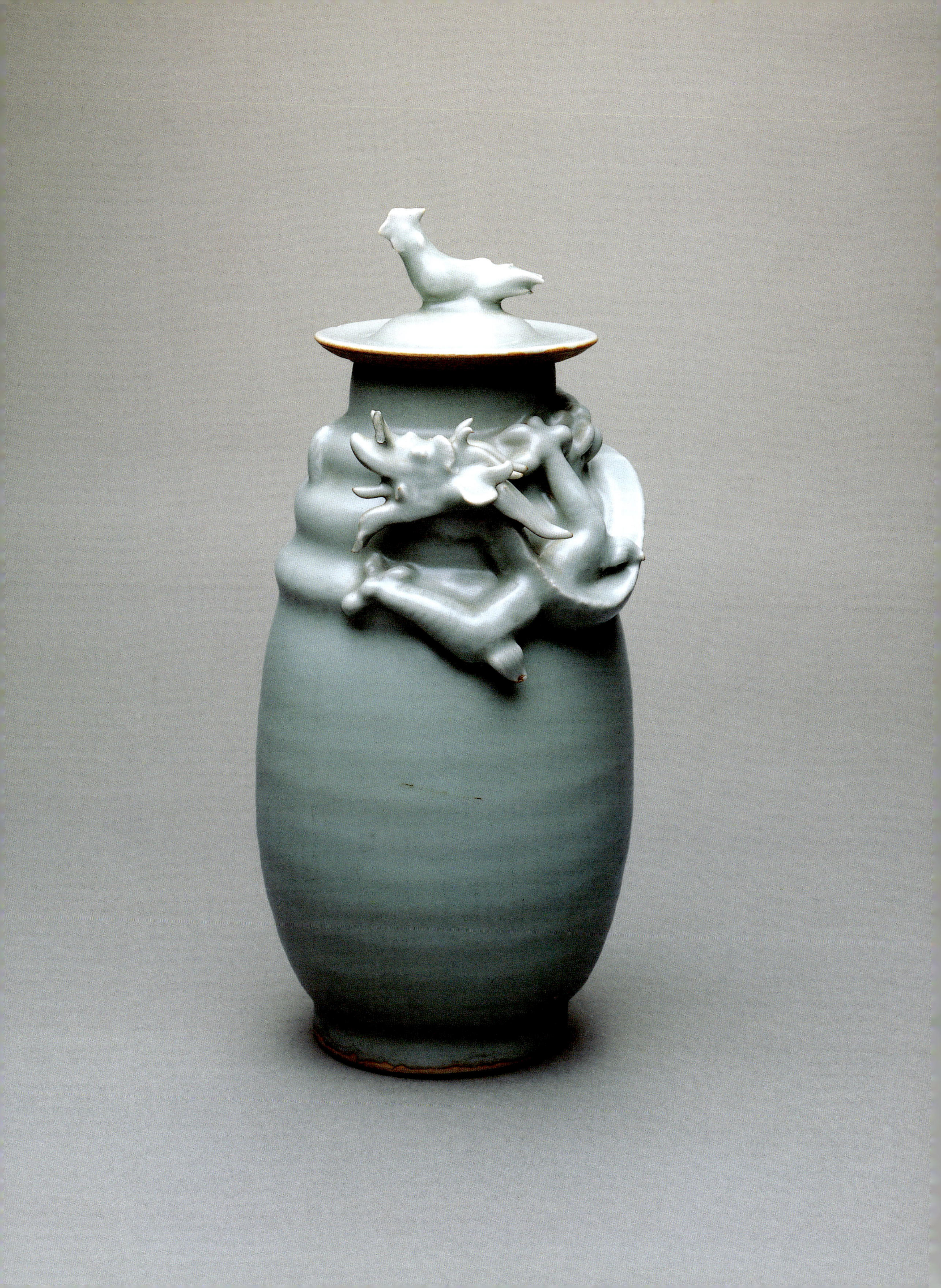

66 VASE IN THE FORM OF A CONG

Southern Song dynasty, 12th–13th century
Longquan stoneware, celadon glaze, $10\frac{3}{8} \times 4\frac{1}{8} \times 4$ in ($26.4 \times 10.5 \times 10.2$ cm)
Gift of R.H. Norton, 50.39

Like the *Dragon jar and cover* (cat. 65), this *Vase in the form of a cong* is an example of Longquan celadon ware from Zhejiang province. In the eleventh century Longquan potters developed high-fired stonewares using a porcelain body nearly identical to the white porcelain formulas used at Jingdezhen. In this case, however, they chose to mix a small amount of iron-rich clay with the porcelain stone to produce a warm gray body that would effectively set off the jade-green color of the celadon glaze.[1] Changes in the kiln atmosphere during firing, especially a slight oxidizing during the last stages, caused parts of the body to reoxidize a pale reddish brown, just where the glaze stops at the edge of the exposed clay (barely visible here on the foot). In other Southern Song celadon pieces, this effect can be seen as well through the thinnest areas of the glaze, producing soft, warm highlights on fine details. The *Vase in the form of a cong* is almost entirely mold-made, although the foot was attached as a separate, tooled ring, and the mouth may have also been finished by turning.

The Longquan potters applied their translucent jadelike green glaze not only to contemporary forms but also to those derived from ancient jades. The *cong* was a ritual jade in the form of a squared cylinder with a round opening at each end and highly stylized images of faces on the square corners (see cats. 14, 16, 17). While the jade *cong* was revived and imitated at various periods, reinventing this form as a ceramic vase most likely began in the Northern Song dynasty. Interest in antiquities in the late eleventh to early twelfth century led to the production of imperially sponsored catalogues that included illustrations and descriptions of bronzes and jade artifacts.[2] Although antiquarianism seemed to be confined to a small elite in the Northern Song, the move of the Southern Song court to Hangzhou and the economic resurgence of southern China in the twelfth and thirteenth centuries helped spread this taste more broadly through Chinese society.[3] Extant examples of jadelike *cong*-shaped vases form a distinct group, and one particularly large piece is in the Minneapolis Institute of the Arts.[4] All seem to represent the same Song dynasty interpretation of a *cong*, since all have the same open panel down the center of each side, with frames and bars replicating what was already a highly stylized design on the jade originals. And almost all extant celadon examples, too, seem to have eight "faces" on each corner, no matter how tall the vase.[5] Clearly these vases answered to a particular taste in Southern Song China, invoking China's ancient past (at a time when the northern half of China was ruled by the Jurchen Jin dynasty) through the medium of incomparable Chinese ceramics.

PUBLISHED

Jayne, *The Chinese Collections*, no. 345

NOTES

1 Wood, *Chinese Glazes*, pp. 76–77.
2 The most important are the *Xuanhe bogu tu* and the *Kaogu tu*; see Poor, "Notes on the Sung Dynasty Archaeological Catalogs."
3 See Mary Ann Rogers, "Mechanics of Change: The Creation of a Southern Song Imperial Ceramic Style," in Kuwayama, ed., *New Perspectives*, pp. 75–76, fig. 23.
4 See Mino and Robinson, *Beauty and Tranquility*, pl. 76.
5 One exception is an example of Southern Song *guan* ware, not celadon, in the Tokyo National Museum, which has five repeats of the design on each corner. See Gompertz, *Chinese Celadon Wares*, no. 58B.

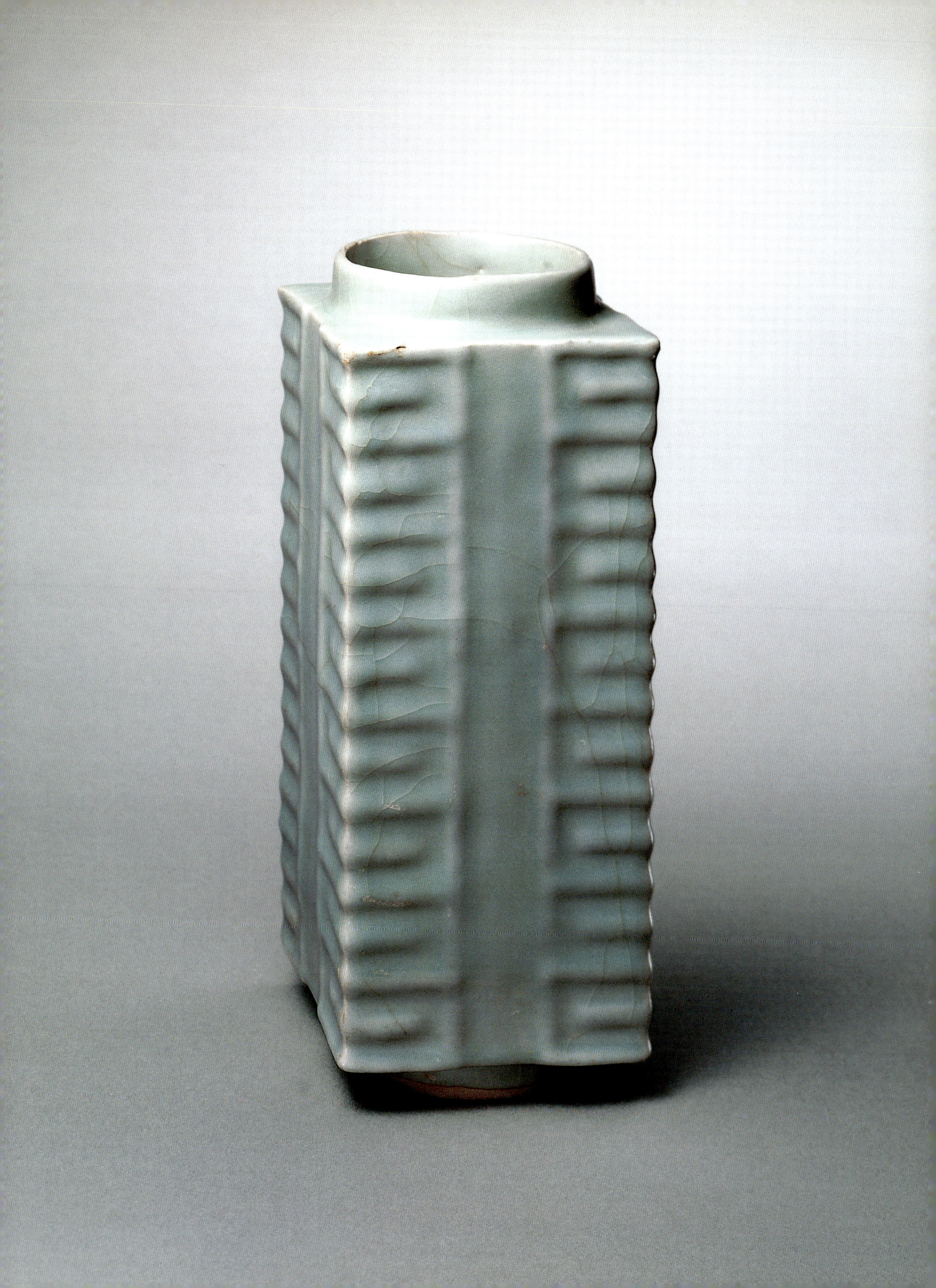

67 STANDING FIGURE OF AN ATTENDANT

Western Han dynasty, ca. 135 BCE
Earthenware, traces of polychrome decoration, 22 ½ × 7 × 4 ½ in.
(57.2 × 17.8 × 11.4 cm)
Gift of Mme. Zalstem-Zalessky, 75.60

For all their apparent individuality, Chinese ceramic tomb figures represent generic types rather than particular individuals.[1] Produced in large quantities from mold-made parts, they were assembled and finished by hand, with the size and number of the figures to be buried, as well as their level of artistry and decoration, determined perhaps as much by economics as by the social status of the deceased. By far the most famous examples are the thousands of ceramic warriors, horses, and other figures buried in pits around the tomb of the First Emperor of Qin (d. 210 BCE) outside Xi'an in Shaanxi province. Popularly described as sculptural portraits, the figures are sophisticated combinations of modular elements—heads, bodies, hands and feet, even fingers—with specific details added to depict rank within the imperial army.[2] The rulers of the succeeding Western Han dynasty continued the practice of burying large numbers of figures in the vicinity of their tombs, but the figures were smaller. The tomb complex of the Han emperor Jingdi (reigned 156–142 BCE), also near Xi'an, likewise included structures associated with the emperor's burial, including a large area of pits containing at least 1,600 tomb figures approximately 24 ½ inches tall.[3] Anatomically correct, the mostly male figures are nude, with elongated, stylized bodies. The hair and facial features are carefully painted on the unglazed figures, which have a remarkable variety of features, giving again the impression of representing individuals. The original wooden arms and textile robes, however, are now lost; these missing elements would have identified the ranks and functions of the various soldiers, courtiers, and attendants represented.

The Norton *Standing figure of an attendant* almost certainly comes from a similar imperial burial, most likely one associated with the tomb of the Empress Dou (d. 135 BCE), the wife of the Han emperor Wendi (reigned 180–157 BCE).[4] Published figures from this site, usually described as female, are remarkably similar, with hair parted in the middle and pulled back behind the head, gently smiling (or almost expressionless) faces, and wearing layered robes with thick collars on the inner garments. The figures' robes hang well below the knee, exposing trousers and large, rather square feet. The Norton *Attendant* has holes in the soles of her shoes, which were perhaps used to help hold the figure upright.[5] These standing court attendants have their hands clasped in front, the left over the right, with the fingers grasping a now-missing object, perhaps a wooden handle or pole. Although their makers imparted a subtle and appealing feeling of humanity in the finishing process, these tomb figures were nonetheless fashioned with strict regard to details appropriate to their rank and function; for the human occupants of Han tombs they would still fulfill their carefully fixed, ideal roles in the afterlife.

NOT PREVIOUSLY PUBLISHED

NOTES

1 See David Keightly, "The Quest for Eternity in Ancient China," in Kuwayama, ed., *Ancient Mortuary Traditions of China*, pp. 12–13, for an intriguing statement of this phenomenon in pre-Han burial practice.

2 See Ledderose, *Ten Thousand Things*, especially ch. 3, "A Magic Army for the Emperor."

3 See *Zhongguo Han Yangling caiyong.*

4 See Los Angeles County Museum of Art, *Quest for Eternity*, cat. 18, color plate on p. 73. The excavation was published by Wang Xueli and Wu Zhenfang, "Xi'an Renjiapo Han ling congzang keng de fajue," *Kaogu* 1976.2, pp. 129–33, 75. An identical figure from the site, now in the Sackler Museum, Peking University, is published in Hasebe, ed., *Chūgoku no tōji*, vol. 2, no. 14.

5 One of the figures exhibited in Los Angeles has the same detail. See Los Angeles County Museum of Art, *Quest for Eternity*, cat. 18.

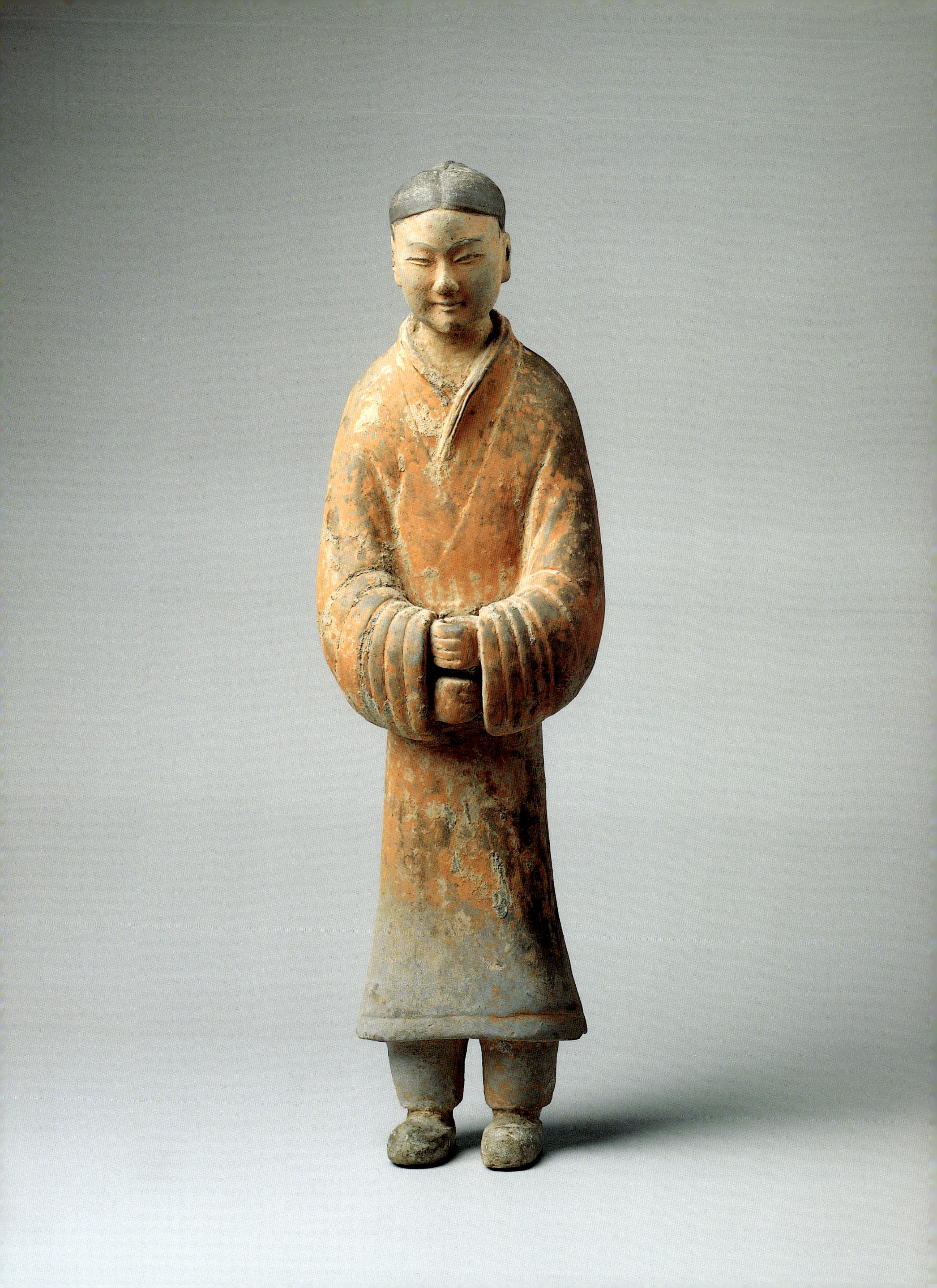

68 TWO HORSES AND TWO GROOMS

Sixteen Kingdoms period (304–439) or Northern Dynasties (386–581)
Earthenware, polychrome decoration; groom: 11 ½ × 5 ½ × 4 in. (29.2 × 14 × 10.2 cm); horse: 15 ⅝ × 8 × 16 in. (39.7 × 20.3 × 40.6 cm); armored groom: 12 ¾ × 5 ¾ × 3 ½ in. (32.4 × 14.6 × 8.9 cm); armored horse: 14 ⅝ × 6 ½ × 16 ¼ in. (37.1 × 16.5 × 41.3 cm)
Purchase, the R.H. Norton Trust, 2000.4.1–.4

These four figures depict, from left to right, a groom with a round cap, a horse with an elaborate harness and low-hanging saddle blanket, a soldier wearing a helmet and carrying a sword, and a horse covered entirely in armor. Both horses and grooms are unusually large, sturdily built, and vigorously modeled.[1] The soldier's armor consists of front and back sections of overlapping plates, the two sides secured by straps over the shoulders. This *liangdang*, or "two-sided" armor, is associated with innovations of the Six Dynasties period (220–589).[2]

It is the full-body horse armor, however, that is the most striking feature of this group. After the fall of the Han dynasty in 220, China broke up into a series of short-lived kingdoms and local dynasties. During this long period of frequent warfare, the invention of the stirrup in about the fourth century permitted, first, heavily armored cavalrymen and, soon after, fully armored horses.[3] A horse's armor would have been made of separate sections secured by straps, with the armor likely consisting of lacquered leather plates tied with cords to a cloth underlayer, shown as a wide, red hem on the present figure. The separate head-covering (or *chanfron*) with its high crest and the funnel-shaped holder for a large decorative plume on the horse's rump (just visible in the photograph) exemplify the most elaborate form of early horse armor.[4]

In 1988 an almost complete set of iron and gilt-bronze saddles and horse armor was excavated at Shi'ertai township, Chaoyang, Liaoning province.[5] The head-cover and elaborate saddles are remarkably similar to those on the Norton armored horse. The most striking parallel to the Norton group in its entirety, however, appears on a relief-modeled brick, part of the mural decoration of a tomb at Dengxian, Hebei province, datable to the early sixth century.[6] The sharply cut image shows two grooms leading spirited, prancing horses,[7] one with an intricate harness incorporating many hanging ornaments and the other wearing a full armor with a wide hem and huge feather plume. The appearance of such elaborate trappings and armor reflects the unsettled period of the fourth to sixth centuries, and its representation in tomb figures signals the crucial importance of warriors and armored horses to the ruling elites of both North and South China.

PUBLISHED

Priestley & Ferraro Chinese Art, *Out of Wind and Dust,* cat. 3 (armored figure and horse only)

NOTES

1 For figures with similar concentration on facial features but disproportionate, even "rubbery," arms, see *Zhongguo meishu quanji, diaosu bian 3: Wei Jin Nan-Bei chao diaosu,* nos. 11, 12.
2 See Dien, "A Study of Early Chinese Armor," pp. 25–26. See pls. XIIa–b, for the figure of an archer wearing *liangdang* armor and a helmet with a short point over the forehead and a knob on top.
3 See Juliano and Lerner, *Monks and Merchants,* cat. 23a–d, and n. 2, Dien's reference to his 1986 article, "The Stirrup and its Effect on Chinese Military History."
4 See Dien, "A Study of Early Chinese Armor," pp. 37–40 and fig. 45, a diagram of the parts of horse armor.
5 Archaeology Institute of Liaoning, "Chaoyang Shi'ertai xiang zhuanchang 88M1 fajue jianbao."
6 The most important English-language study of this tomb is Annette L. Juliano's *Teng-hsien: An Important Six Dynasties Tomb.*
7 For the tile, see *Zhongguo meishu quanji, diaosu bian 3: Wei Jin Nan-Bei chao diaosu,* no. 67.

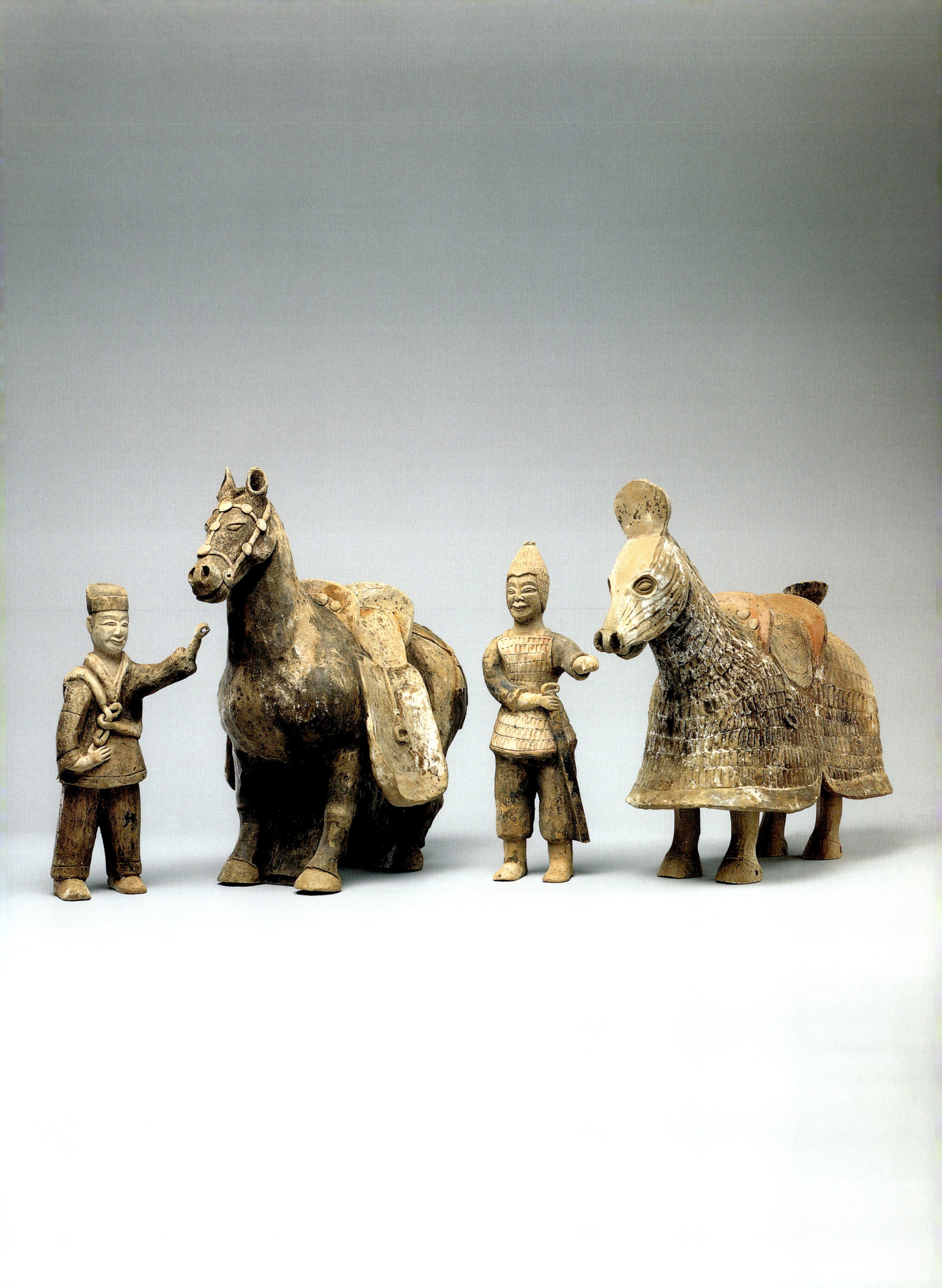

69 TOMB FIGURE OF A HORSE

Tang dynasty (618–907), first half of the 8th century
Earthenware, *sancai* glaze, 17 ¾ × 5 ¾ × 18 ¼ in. (45.1 × 14.6 × 46.4 cm)
Gift of Mr. and Mrs. Robert Carney, 78.16

In the Tang dynasty, horses, especially the swift, long-legged mounts of Central Asia, were key to the empire's military success. Images of horses and mounted cavalry appear in Chinese tombs as early as the Warring States period (475–221 BCE) of the Eastern Zhou,[1] but in the Tang they take on an unparalleled importance. The great majority of Tang figures of horses are magnificent, idealized animals, many accompanied by figures of foreign grooms, reflecting their origins outside China.

The Norton *Tomb figure of a horse*, like many tomb models, is a combination of mold-made parts assembled and finished by hand. A large oval opening in the belly permitted gasses to escape during firing and also allowed the clay to be pressed firmly into the mold. Finger marks are clearly visible inside the horse, and additional fingerprints and brush marks are visible in the thin layer of white slip rubbed on the outside of the figure to give it a lighter color and to make the transparent glaze colors appear brighter. The horse is glazed a deep ocher-yellow over most of the body, with the front of the head covered with a clear glaze and the saddle blanket dark green. The unglazed saddle cloth would have been painted after firing, probably with a tiger-skin design or a fashionably exotic tie-dye patterned Central Asian textile. The mane and tail as well would have been added after firing; there is a slot along the back of the neck for the mane and a hole where the tail should be.

Glazed ceramic tomb figures of horses seem to have been produced for only a relatively short period in the Tang dynasty. Glazed figures appear in large numbers in the Han dynasty, over half a millennium earlier, but they are almost inevitably covered in a monochrome dark green glaze; multicolored figures were fired unglazed and painted after firing. In the early Tang, partially glazed figures had polychrome details added after firing. Colored glazes, still usually applied as all-over monochromes, appear in the later seventh century (although one rare, early blue-splashed tray was found in a prince's tomb dated 664), while the combination of colors dubbed *sancai*, or "three-colors," only appears on figures at the end of the seventh century.[2] Experimentation with the new technique quickly produced startling decorative treatments that exploited the accidental effects of the difficult-to-control, low-fire, lead-based glazes (cats. 60, 61). Production of *sancai*-decorated figures and vessels, however, seems to come to a halt in the middle of the eighth century,[3] at the end of the reign of the emperor Xuanzong (712–56). The turmoil brought about by the An Lushan Rebellion, resulting in the fall of the capital at Chang'an and the emperor's flight to Sichuan, may have helped end the taste for elaborate, sumptuous glazed tomb figures and led to a return to earlier types of painted unglazed images. The Norton *Horse* is part of the early eighth-century fashion for multicolor glazed tomb figures.

NOT PREVIOUSLY PUBLISHED

NOTES

1 See Cooke and others, *Imperial China*, cat. 96, for two painted earthenware cavalrymen excavated from a Warring States period tomb near Xianying, Shaanxi province, now in the Xi'an Institute of Cultural Relics and Archaeology.
2 Karetzky, *Court Art of the Tang*, pp. 35–37.
3 Ibid., pp. 56–58. See also George Kuwayama, "The Sculptural Development of Ceramic Funerary Figures in China," in Los Angeles County Museum of Art, *The Quest for Eternity*, esp. pp. 84–86.

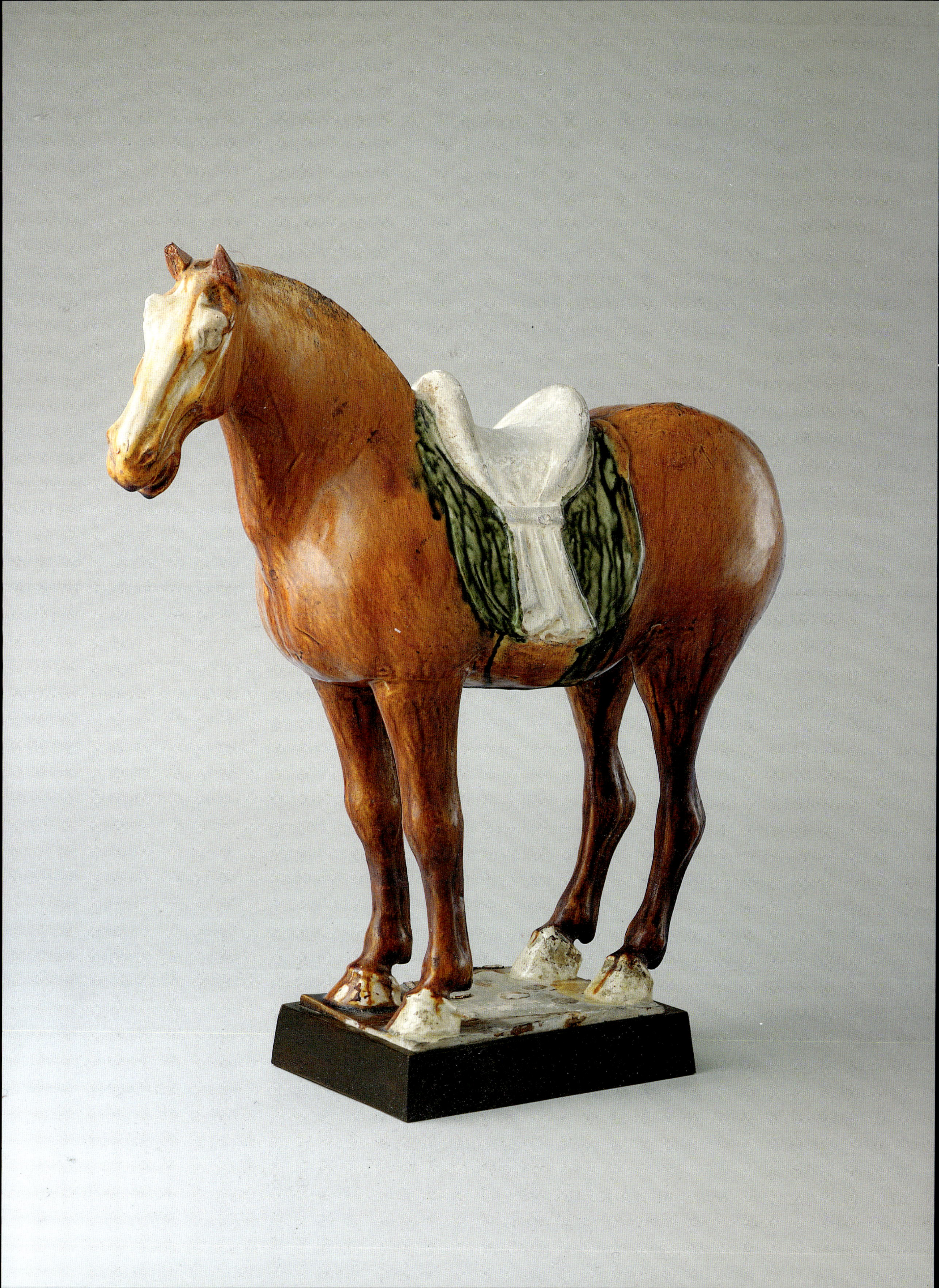

70 PAIR OF HORSES' HEADS

Tang dynasty (618–907) or possibly later
Gray and white marble; one head: 26 × 14 ¾ × 21 ½ in. (66 × 37.5 × 54.6 cm); the other: 23 ¼ × 14 ¼ × 21 ½ in. (59.1 × 36.2 × 54.6 cm)
Bequest of Leonard and Sophie Davis, 2001.158–2001.159

The Museum's massive *Pair of horses' heads* almost surely come from marble sculptures lining the route to a Tang imperial tomb. Starting in the Eastern Han (25–220 CE) changes in imperial burial rituals led to the construction of a ceremonial approach lined with stone sculptures to the southern entrance of the tomb complex.[1] This road is called a *shendao*, or "spirit road." The imperial tombs of the first half of the Tang dynasty set a standard of size and opulence unequaled in Chinese history, and Tang *shendao* were lined with pairs of monumental stone sculptures of winged animals, ostriches, horses, grooms, and officials.

The Norton *Pair of horses' heads* are carved from gray and white marble. Marble sculptures are rare in China, although superb Buddhist images of the Tang are carved from white marble.[2] Although highly stylized, these equine heads are carved with a sure sense of the underlying structure of bone and flesh. The mane parted in two locks across the forehead is typical of Tang stone and ceramic horse sculptures.[3] The elaborate harness is composed of cheek straps that come down the side of the head from behind the ears. These are connected by a strap (or headstall) that passes over the nose, while the cheek strap continues to a ring attached to the bit and the reins. Such complex harnesses are similar to those on Tang ceramic tomb figures of horses.[4] The well-known "Six Chargers of the Emperor Taizong" (r. 626–49) are perhaps the most famous Tang representations of horses.[5] Carved from the designs of Yan Liben (ca. 600–673),[6] renowned for his accuracy in drawing horses in the imperial stud, these too show the same harness and bit configuration.

A similar but simpler harness arrangement appears on a stone horse at the Yong Xiling, the tomb of the Northern Song Emperor Taizong (r. 976–97).[7] Tang dynasty sculptural styles were clearly imitated in the Northern Song, as were the layout of imperial tombs, although with important modifications.[8] Tang styles persist, too, in later Buddhist sculpture (see cat. 50), but the Norton horses' heads are most likely remnants of the great body of Tang imperial marble sculpture.

NOT PREVIOUSLY PUBLISHED

NOTES

1 See Paludan, *The Chinese Spirit Road*, p. 28. The discussion here is indebted to Paludan's pioneering study.
2 See Roger and others, eds., *China 5,000 Years*, cat. 171, for a marble Buddhist image seated on a throne supported by seven winged horses.
3 Among many Tang imperial tomb sculptures of horses, see *Zhongguo meishu quanji, diaosu bian 4: Sui Tang diaosu*, no. 114, one from the Qiaoling, tomb of the Emperor Ruizong (r. 684–90, 710–12), constructed in 716.
4 See, for example, Cooke and others, *Imperial China*, cat. 127, a *sancai*-glazed rider and galloping horse, and cat. 131, a *sancai* horse from the tomb of Prince Yide (d. 701).
5 See Harrist, *Power and Virtue*, figs. 1a, 1b, for the two reliefs in the University of Pennsylvania Museum, Philadelphia. For the six when they were still in place at the Zhaoling, Taizong's tomb, see Chavannes, *Mission archaéologique*, plates vol. 2, nos. 440–45.
6 For the story of Yan Liben's paintings, see Harrist, *Power and Virtue*, pp. 18–20. Interestingly, Yan Liben was the younger brother of Yan Lide (d. 656), architect and builder of early Tang imperial tombs; see Karetzky, *Court Art of the Tang*, p. 14.
7 See Paludan, *The Chinese Spirit Road*, fig. 163.
8 See ibid., pp. 122–23.

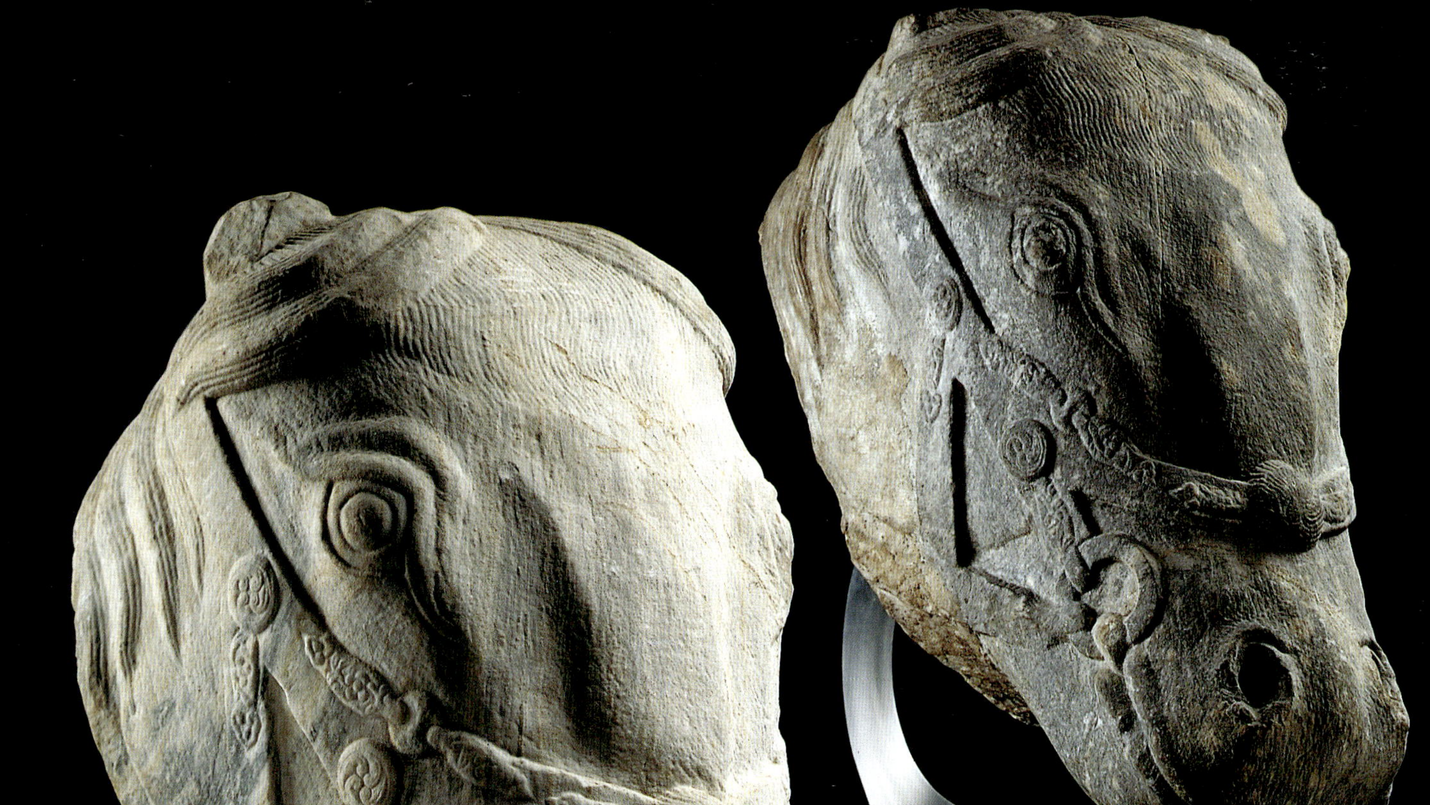

71 TOMB MODELS OF FURNITURE, FOOD, AND UTENSILS

Ming dynasty (1368–1644), probably 17th century
Earthenware, polychrome glaze; table: 6 1/8 × 10 3/4 × 7 1/4 in. (15.6 × 27.3 × 18.4 cm); paneled cabinet: 7 1/4 × 5 1/8 × 2 7/8 in. (18.4 × 13 × 7.3 cm); chairs: each 6 3/8 × 4 1/8 × 3 in. (16.2 × 10.5 × 7.6 cm)
Gift of Dr. Gerald Shepps, 99.154a–q

The Ming dynasty production of *mingqi*, goods made specifically for burial with the dead, continues the ancient tradition of replicating the living world in the precincts of the dead. While imperial tombs of the Ming and Qing contained spectacular luxury goods from the daily lives of the emperors and the imperial courts, they held few if any figures of attendants. Instead, monumental stone sculptures of attendants, officials, and horses stood outside the tomb, lining the ceremonial approach to the tomb complex (see cat. 70). Ceramic figures and models continued to be made, however, for the tombs of high-ranking officials and other members of society able to afford them.[1] Ming dynasty *mingqi* in particular seem to recreate elaborate processions—with musicians, palanquins and bearers, horses, and various attendants—and also include finely detailed models of buildings, furniture, and other utilitarian objects from daily life.

The Museum's Ming dynasty *Tomb models of furniture, food, and utensils* gives a glimpse of Ming material culture. The two horseshoe-back chairs (lower left) represent the most formal type of seating furniture. With only the curving ends of the arms and the footrest visible, such chairs are frequently depicted in the ancestor portraits that were displayed on formal and ritual occasions. The two locked cabinets (on the right) represent a plain-sided storage box with a padlock securing the latch and a paneled strongbox on short legs. The cabinet on short legs (upper left) represents typical hardwood furniture for domestic use. The frame-and-panel doors, front, and sides of the cabinet replicate the assembly techniques that, along with polished fine-grained hardwood, constituted the aesthetic appeal of such furniture. (For the most formal furniture, that with sumptuous lacquer decoration, see cat. 109.) The sturdy table has round legs, a bracketed apron, and a frame-and-panel top. On the table are utensils and plates of food, including one pile of cakes (rear center, glazed deep green) shaped like ingots of gold or silver, as well as the cooked head of a pig. The covered ewer with a curving spout and handle is a type that was first imported into China in the Tang dynasty, and the two oval cups with short projecting knobs on their rims distantly echo ancient bronze *jue* (see cats. 7, 8). As funeral practices changed at the end of the dynastic period, such ceramic models would gradually be replaced by the paper models and substitute currency that are today burned at funerals.

NOT PREVIOUSLY PUBLISHED

NOTE

1 See Los Angeles County Museum of Art, *The Quest for Eternity*, cats. 88–105, for examples of the Song, Jin, Yuan, and Ming dynasties; and cats. 105a–d, for figures from the tomb of a high-ranking Ming eunuch who died in 1510.

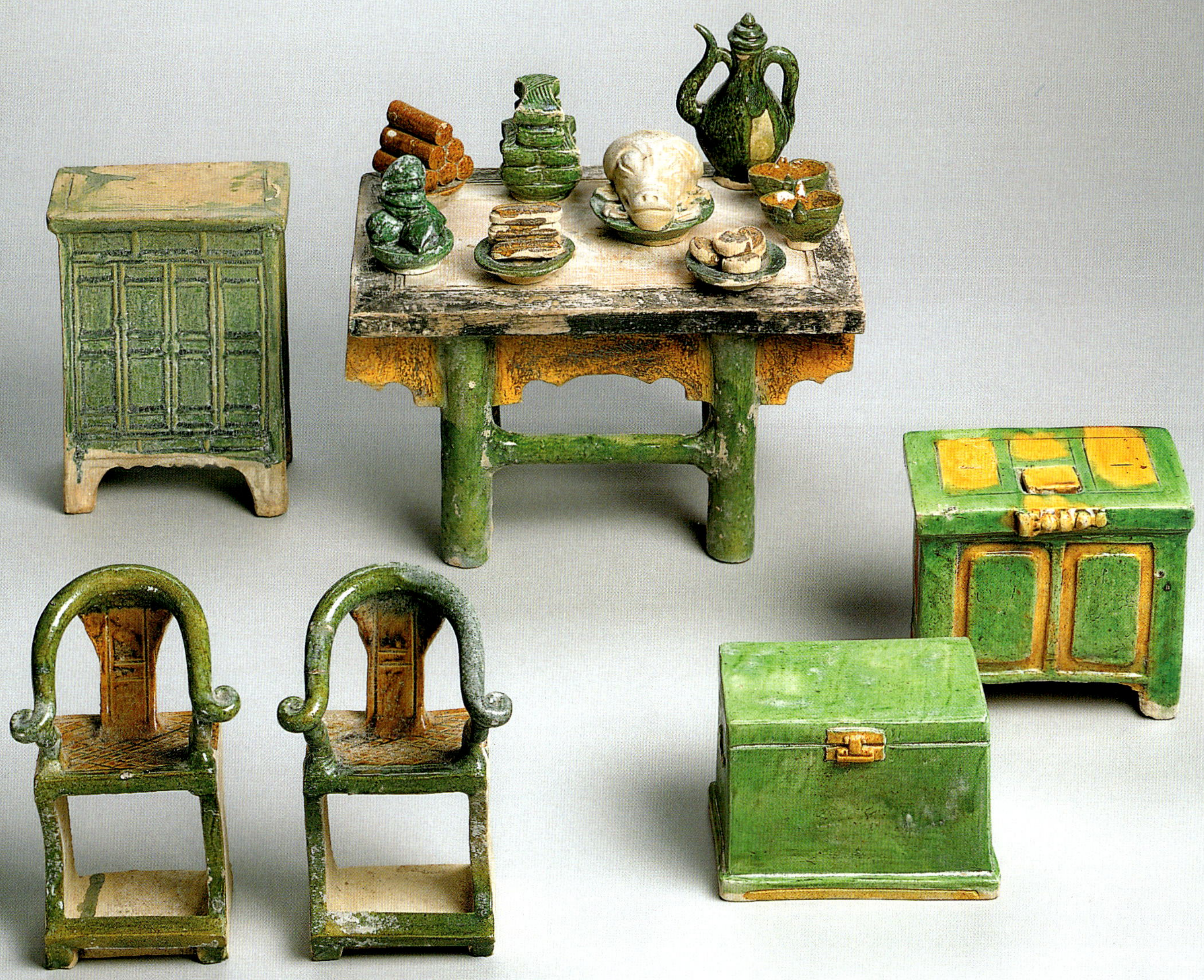

72 THE NINE BENDS RIVER

Tang Yin (1470–1524)
Hanging scroll, ink and traces of color on silk, 86 1/8 × 38 5/8 in. (218.8 × 98.1 cm)
Inscribed and signed by the artist; inscription preceded by partial seal, probably *Nanjing jie yuan*; followed by two seals, *Liu ru ju shi* and *Tao chan xian li*. Seal of C.C. Wang, bottom right
Purchase, the R.H. Norton Trust, 62.8

Tang Yin was a professional painter who lived and worked in Suzhou, a city of prosperous merchants and famous scholars close to the Grand Canal in southern Jiangsu province. Reading from the bottom up, the conventional way to view a Chinese hanging scroll, Tang Yin's landscape *The Nine Bends River* depicts a rocky bank framed by gnarled pine trees. Two servant boys are bringing books to a man wearing scholar's robes who is seated beside a low table. In the middle distance we see a stream that winds in many rivulets down a deep valley. Painted in ink on silk with only slight traces of color, *The Nine Bends River* owes much of its visual style to a revival of the work of Song dynasty Academy painters of the twelfth century.

In Suzhou in the very late 15th and the early 16th centuries, the painter Zhou Chen (ca. 1450–1535) led a revival of the style of the Song Academy painter Li Tang (ca. 1050–after 1130).[1] Zhou Chen was Tang Yin's older contemporary, and, while Tang Yin was deeply influenced by the senior artist's work, he may not have been a formal student of Zhou's; their exact relationship remains unclear.[2] Still, Tang Yin's conspicuous use of so-called "ax cut strokes"—broad sweeps of ink laid on with the side of the brush—to model the foreground rocks and middle-ground hill comes from Zhou's interpretation of Li Tang's painting techniques. The river rendered as many branching streams also follows a convention derived from Song landscape painting.

The Nine Bends River is in many ways the portrait of the man seated at the low table, and his personal qualities are embodied in the landscape. Anne Clapp, in her important study of Tang Yin, lists the Norton's painting as one of nineteen works that constitute a "memorial of house, garden, or estate."[3] Tang Yin's inscription in the upper right-hand corner identifies the figure as a certain Zhixin, an older and respected acquaintance of Tang Yin (we know this from the way the artist's inscription refers to him), who otherwise remains unidentified but who probably commissioned the large painting.[4] The inscription consists mostly of a poem filled with classical allusions and word plays on the name Nine Bends River, which is both an archaic name for the great Yellow River and the name of a smaller river in southern China where Zhixin had probably built his country retreat. The poem implicitly compares Zhixin to ancient scholars who understood true virtue, the Confucian moral quality likened to a stream that flows undiminished without ceasing. Dressed in scholar's robes, Zhixin gazes at this river of knowledge and reflects on the Confucian moral qualities embodied in the landscape. His portrayal as a small figure in the landscape suggests he himself possessed these same qualities. Perhaps the servant boys are bringing him copies of the Confucian classics whose lofty ideals suffuse Zhixin's—and Tang Yin's—view of the landscape.

PUBLISHED

Lowe Art Museum, *Ancient Chinese Painting*, no. 37; Clapp, *The Painting of T'ang Yin*, fig. 68

NOTES

1 On Zhou Chen and the Song Academic revival, see Cahill, *Parting at the Shore*, pp. 189–90. On the scholarly use of style in painting, see cat. 74.
2 On the relationship between the two painters, see Clapp, *The Painting of T'ang Yin*, pp. 127–31.
3 Ibid. The Norton's painting is examined in detail in chapter 7, "Transmitting Hsi-ku: The Late Landscapes," and the discussion here is largely based on Clapp's research. See Appendix 1 "Program Paintings," pp. 239–40, for the list of memorial landscapes.
4 One other of Tang Yin's painting is dedicated to this man.

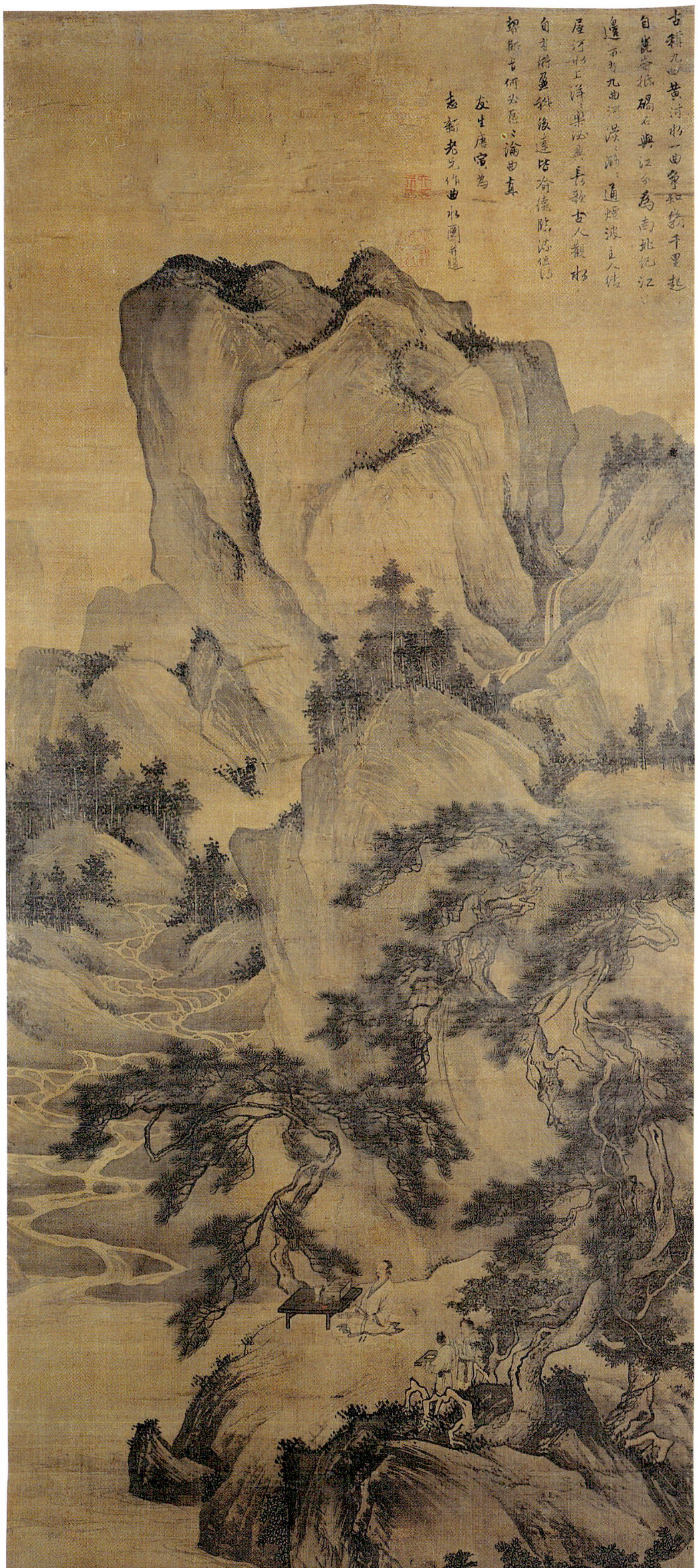

73 WATERFALL IN A BAMBOO GROVE

Zhang Hong (1577–ca. 1652)
Hanging scroll, ink and light color on paper, 128 × 38 ½ in. (325.1 × 97.8 cm)
Inscribed and signed by the artist, with two seals: *Zhang Hong zhi yin*; *Jundu shi*
Purchase, the R.H. Norton Trust, 98.766

Zhang Hong, like Tang Yin (see cat. 72), lived and worked in the city of Suzhou. Late Ming and Qing painting catalogues provide only brief notices of his art, however, describing him as an influential though merely competent painter. In his later life, Zhang explored the representation of naturalistic detail and specific places, perhaps inspired by European paintings and prints brought to China by Jesuit missionaries in the early seventeenth century.[1] Although one Chinese source says "all students in Wu [Suzhou] studied him,"[2] in these experiments he had no followers. As a professional painter, however, Zhang Hong responded to the tastes of his patrons by working in many painting styles.[3]

At the bottom of the Norton's very tall hanging scroll, *Waterfall in a Bamboo Grove*, we see a scholar and his servant boy as they are about to cross a bridge and follow the path leading to a pavilion amid dense bamboo groves. The path continues up among rocky, wooded hills, where we see the gate and one hall of a distant temple set in a mountain valley. The inscription in the upper right consists of a poetic couplet that reads "Among the clouds the color of calyxes fills a thousand flowers; / In the bamboos the sound of a spring flies over a hundred paths." Illustrating and elaborating on the couplet, the various individual elements of the painting reflect classical Chinese painting modes. The bamboos are part of a long tradition of bamboo painting that relies on skillful brushwork. The landscape, composed of rocky humps accented with small dots and modeled by long strokes on the hillsides, vaguely recalls the brush idioms of tenth-century masters Dong Yuan (d. 962) and Juran (active ca. 960–95), a style favored by scholar-painters and their patrons for historical and artistic associations. (On the Dong-Ju style, see cat. 74.) The sense of atmosphere—especially the mists among the foreground bamboos—and the subtle coloration appear in a number of Zhang Hong's other paintings.

The couplet is followed by the artist's signature and two of the artist's seals. The painting is undated, and placing it within Zhang's long career is not easy. The same pair of identical or very similar seals and a similar signature appear on a hanging scroll entitled *Looking at Books and Pictures in Autumn Mountains*, dated 1620. A similar but not identical pair of seals appears on another hanging scroll dated 1652, over thirty years later.[4] The poetry, flowering trees, and spring atmosphere suggests that the Norton *Waterfall in a Bamboo Grove* is part of a set depicting the four seasons, and such sets of large-scale paintings were the stock-in-trade of Suzhou professional painters. Zhang Hong's ability to organize the composition in a very tall, thin format and the variety and skill of his brushwork confirm his standing as one of the most successful Suzhou artists of his day.

NOT PREVIOUSLY PUBLISHED

NOTES

1 Sirén, *Chinese Painting*, vol. 5, pp. 30–32, recognizes Zhang's originality. James Cahill has written about his career and likely contacts with European art; see *The Distant Mountains*, pp. 39–42, 55–58; see also Cahill, *The Compelling Image*, pp. 1–35; and *Paintings of the Zhi Garden*.

2 *Guochao huazheng lu*, compiled by Zhang Geng, preface dated 1739, *juan* 1:6, in Yu Anlan, ed., *Huashi congshu*, vol. 3.

3 For a good selection, see Ho and Smith, eds., *The Century of Tung Ch'i-ch'ang*, vol. 1, pp. 314–36; vol. 2, pp. 258–61.

4 Shanghai Museum, comp., *Zhongguo shuhuajia yinjian kuanshi*, vol. 2, pp. 937–39, nos. 19, 20, 22.

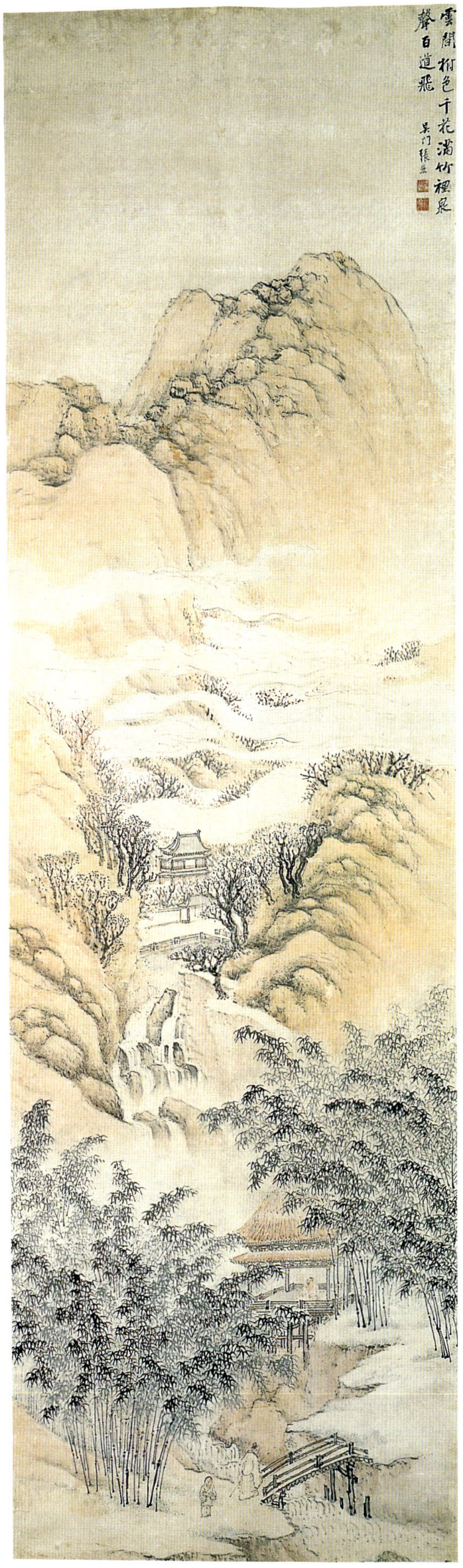
雲間樹色千花滿竹裡泉
聲百道飛
吳門張崟

74 LANDSCAPE IN THE MANNER OF WANG MENG

Wang Jiu (ca. 1715–ca. 1788), dated 1774
Hanging scroll, ink on paper, 53 7/8 × 25 1/4 in. (135.7 × 84 cm)
Inscribed and signed, with two seals of the artist: *Wang Jiu zhi yin*; *Erchi jushi*
Purchase, the R.H. Norton Trust, 2001.25

The history of Chinese painting since the seventeenth century has been dominated by the paintings and critical theories of Dong Qichang (1555–1636). Dong's writings and the masters he chose as models for scholar-painters form the basis of the so-called Orthodox school of painting.[1] Landscape styles were mediated by the followers of Dong Qichang, including Wang Jiu, through paintings they believed to be original works of early masters, through copies after old paintings, and by creative reworkings of the styles of the masters. The strategy of creative imitation lay at the heart of Orthodox painting, a tradition in which Wang Jiu's *Landscape in the Manner of Wang Meng* participates.

The inscription in the upper right begins with three columns of poetry describing the scene and invoking the painter's desire for spiritual retreat among the highest mountains. In the following lines he invokes the spirit and style of the Yuan landscape painter Wang Meng (1308–1385), whose style, as the poem notes, was built on that of the tenth-century masters Dong Yuan (d. 962) and Juran (active ca. 960–95). All three were canonical painters in Dong Qichang's Orthodox tradition. The Dong Yuan style appears in the rounded hills modeled with long parallel brush strokes, which are dubbed "hemp-fiber" strokes in Chinese. The clusters of rocks on the tops of peaks and ridges embody eighteenth-century perceptions of the Buddhist monk-painter Juran. Finally, the Yuan dynasty master Wang Meng, deeply admired by later scholar-artists, had used elements of the Chinese landscape painting tradition to fashion his own expressive style. The grove of pine trees that stands in the lower-right foreground signals the Wang Meng manner in Wang Jiu's painting.[2] The tall pines, with prominent knots and gnarled boughs, and the long needles curling upward, are part of Wang Jiu's effort to actively participate in the transmission of Wang Meng's style as a living tradition.

PUBLISHED

Barnhart and others, *The Jade Studio*, cat. 77; *Kaikodo Journal*, vol. 19, 2001 (*A Natural Selection*), cat. 24

NOTES

1 For just one example of the weight of Dong Qichang in Chinese art history, see Ho and Smith, eds., *The Century of Tung Ch'i-ch'ang*.
2 Wang Meng's style appears in other Orthodox paintings as a particular method of rendering the landscape with dense masses of furry brush strokes, a second visual trope closely associated with Wang Meng. The process of identifying specific styles and motifs is almost endless, given the cross-fertilization of painting styles over the centuries. One might argue here that the overall style—despite Wang Jiu's identification—is more indebted to the achievement of Huang Gongwang (1269–1354).

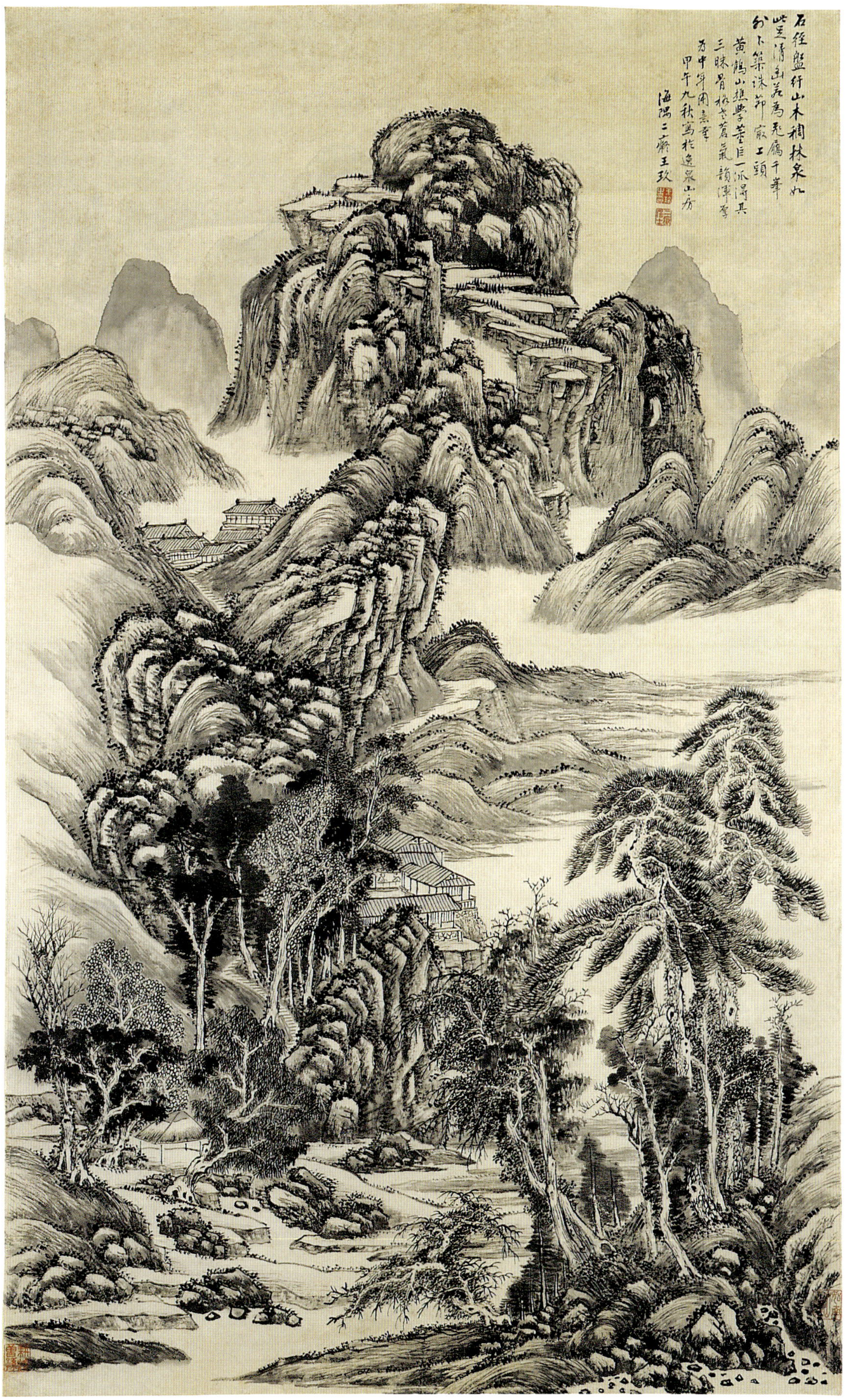

75 FAN DECORATED WITH PAINTING AND CALLIGRAPHY

Qing dynasty, late 19th century
Painting by Gu Yun (1835–1896), inscribed and signed by the artist, followed by one seal of the artist, *Ruobo*
Bamboo frame by Ren Xun (1835–1893), signed by the artist
Calligraphy by Wu Changshuo (1844–1927), inscribed and signed by the artist, followed by one seal of the artist, *Fou*
Ink and color on gold-flecked paper, 12 5/8 × 19 1/2 in. (32.1 × 49.5 cm)
Purchased with funds provided by Marcia and Alan Docter, 2000.153

This painted fan exemplifies some of the complex relationships among artists in and around Shanghai in the late nineteenth century. Most fans decorated by well-known painters and calligraphers have been taken apart and preserved in collectors' albums. In this case the painting and calligraphy are still mounted on their original armature, which preserves two designs by Ren Xun on the polished bamboo end pieces. On the side with the landscape painting is a figure wearing loose robes and standing beside an old pine tree. On the side with the calligraphy are bamboo and banana plants.[1] Ren Xun studied painting with his older brother, Ren Xiong (1820–1857); the brothers were two of the so-called "Four Rens," and all four were important figures in the thriving, innovative Shanghai school of painting of the late 19th and early 20th century.

On one side of the fan (top), Gu Yun's landscape painting depicts a scholar seated in an open building beside a lake. The subject and the painting style, including the slightly amateur quality of the drawing, place Gu Yun well within the so-called Orthodox tradition of Chinese scholar-painters. He is conventionally described as following the Four Wangs, Wu Li (1632–1718), and Yun Shouping (1633–1690), a group of six Orthodox-school painters linked by family and teacher-student relationships.[2]

Wu Changshuo, the artist whose bold calligraphy appears on the other side of the fan (bottom), is the most famous artist represented here. He studied painting in Shanghai with Ren Bonian (also known as Ren Yi, 1840–1896), one of the Four Rens. It is Wu Changshuo's calligraphy, however, that reveals the depth of his scholarship and his skill as an artist. He carefully studied and then adapted as an artistic medium the so-called Stone Drum Script, the large scale archaic characters we see here.[3] Besides their early date, the characters are celebrated for their strength and energy, and they have been enormously important in the history of Chinese calligraphy.

Thus, Gu Yun was a respected painter working in a conservative tradition, Run Xun was one of the more innovative Shanghai artists, and Wu Changshuo literally transformed tradition into innovation, making ancient scripts come alive again. Although we do not know the exact circumstances that brought these artists to work together on one fan, all were present at the end of the nineteenth century in the burgeoning international city of Shanghai, and we know some of the connections between them. The Norton fan was for years part of the collection of the painter Zhu Qizhan, himself an important figure in the Shanghai art world, a teacher and artist who died in 1996 at the age of 104.[4]

NOT PREVIOUSLY PUBLISHED

NOTES

1 Ren Xun probably sketched the very narrow designs, to be cut into the bamboo by a professional craftsman.

2 Gu Yun was born in Suzhou, a more conservative artistic center than nearby Shanghai. On the Orthodox tradition, see cat. 74. For a biographical note on Gu Yun, see Yu, *Zhongguo meishujia renming cidian*, pp. 1547–48.

3 The so-called Stone Drums are a group of ten boulders, shaped somewhat like drums, that were carved with poems celebrating exploits of the dukes of Qin, probably around 422 BCE.

4 For a brief biography and chronology of Zhu Qizhan, see *Unafraid of the Autumn Wind*.

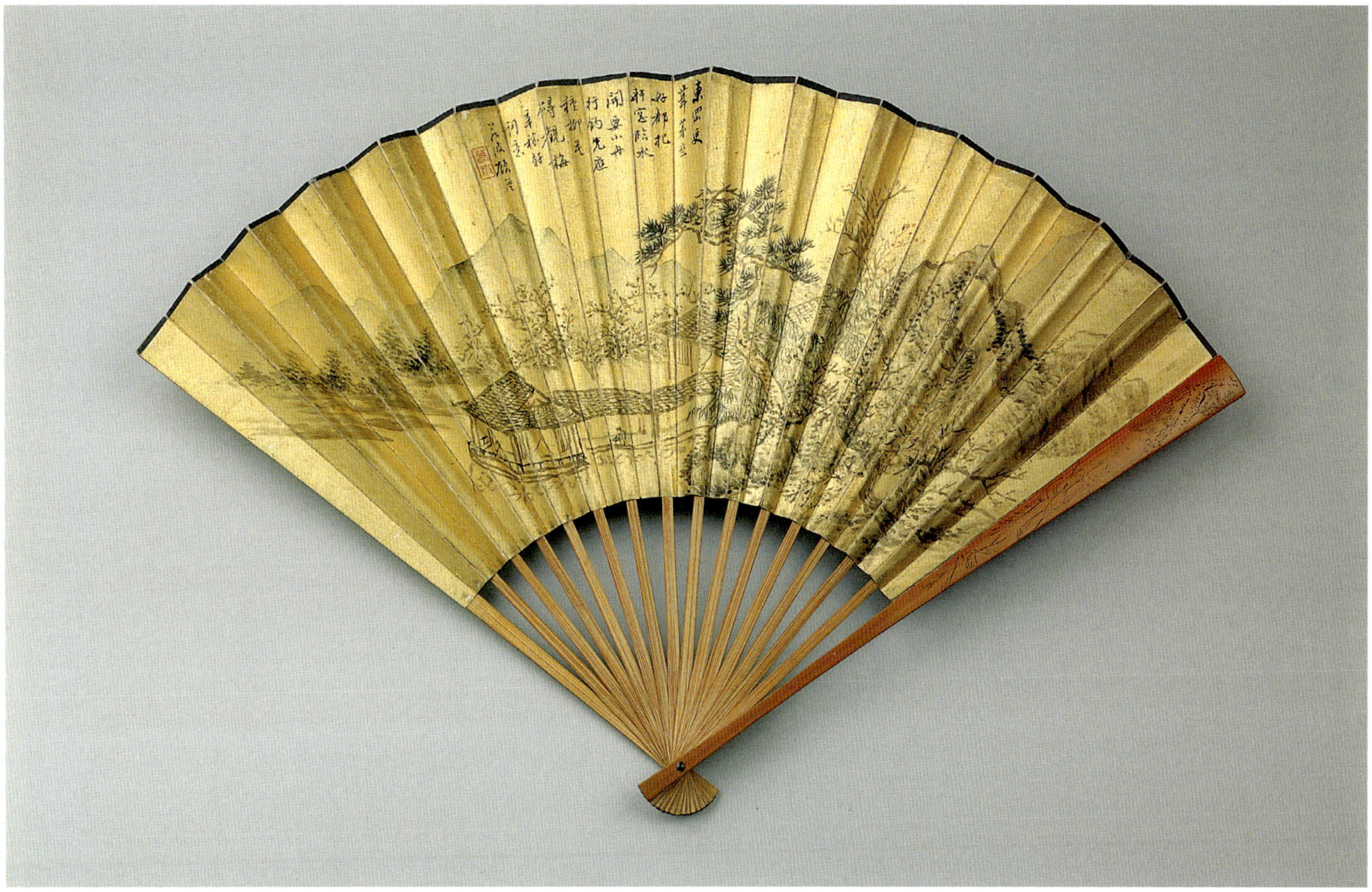

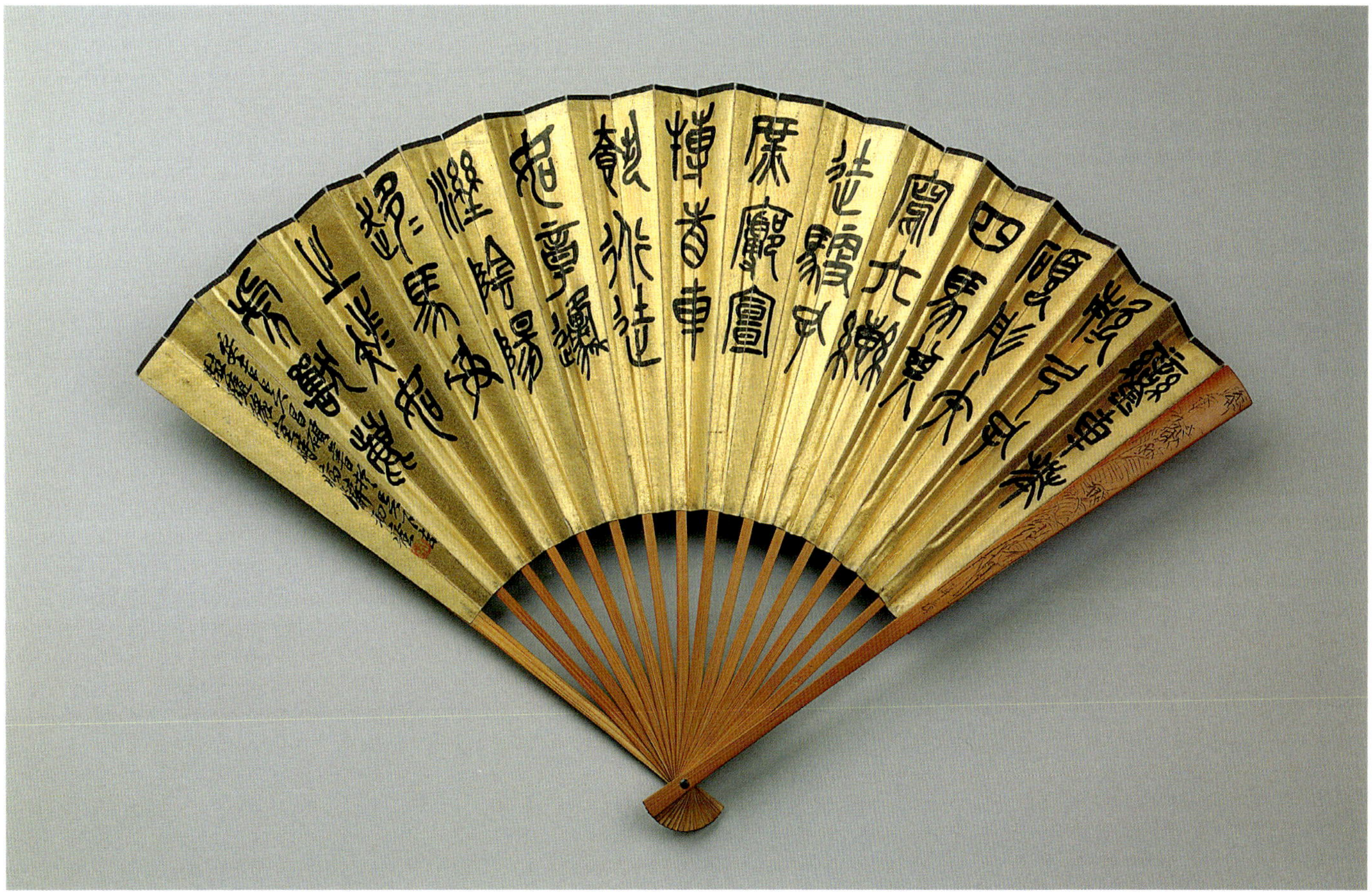

76 LARGE JAR

Ming dynasty, Jiajing imperial mark and period (1522–66)
Porcelain, underglaze blue and white decoration, 19 ½ × diam. 20¾ in. (49.5 × 52.7 cm)
Gift of Mrs. Eugene L. Garbaty, 73.9

This massive jar is stoutly constructed of at least two joined sections. The mixture of white kaolin clay and pulverized porcelain stone that forms the body of Chinese porcelains has the property of remaining stiff without melting or slumping under the very high temperatures (1250°C and higher) needed to fire porcelain. It is not a particularly plastic material, however, and construction in sections and the use of molds are common techniques in the production of porcelains of all periods. The brilliant blue decoration is composed of finely ground cobalt oxide mixed with glaze material[1] and painted on the dried but unfired porcelain body. A clear glaze was applied to the surface of the jar, inside and out, and the jar was fired once to fuse the porcelain into a hard white substance and to melt the glaze into a clear coating that reveals the deep blue painted decoration.

The decoration consists of three ranges of motifs. Around the shoulder are strings of beads or jewels with pendant ornaments in the form of flowers and Buddhist emblems, including conch shells and furled umbrellas. The elaborate beaded design mimics the jewels seen in Buddhist images of paradise or the jeweled canopies over Buddhist temple altars. The body of the jar is decorated with a regular pattern of scrolling stems with small leaves and tendrils framing large lotus flowers. Although closely associated with Buddhism, the lotus is not always a Buddhist emblem. Around the bottom of the jar is a row of stylized palm leaves.

The Museum first catalogued this *Large jar* as a "temple vase," probably on the evidence of the Buddhist decorative motifs and its imposing size, but we do not know its specific function.[2] A large jar in the Hu collection[3] is very similar to that in the Norton. Both have flat, unglazed bottoms with the Ming imperial Jiajing six-character mark written in cobalt blue in a recessed, glazed circle in the center of the bottom. Both jars as well have the deep, intense cobalt blue color that is typical of Jiajing imperial porcelains. Two other jars of this same group—one in Turkey and one in Iran—document the wide dispersal of blue and white porcelains in the Islamic world. One is in the Topkapi Sarayi Museum, the former palace of the Ottoman Sultans in Istanbul.[4] The other is in the collection of the Ardebil Shrine, a Muslim foundation near Teheran,[5] where it was most likely one of the 1,162 Chinese ceramics dedicated to the shrine by Shah Abbas in 1611. Perhaps on the basis of these two jars, T. Misugi suggests that "pendants like strings of pearls were used almost exclusively on export wares."[6] Whatever their intended use, these Ming Jiajing jars are thick and solid enough to survive shipment over long distances.

NOT PREVIOUSLY PUBLISHED

NOTES

1 Medley, *The Chinese Potter*, pp. 176–78.
2 Porcelains with inscriptions dedicating them to temples often imitate archaistic bronze forms. The earliest dated pair (inscribed in accordance with 1351) are in the Percival David Foundation, London. See Medley, *Illustrated Catalogue of Porcelains*, nos. B613, B614. A Ming Hongzhi temple vase, dated 1495 and also in the Percival David Foundation, has a broad band of scrolling lotus flowers similar to the Norton's slightly later *Large jar*. See Medley, ibid., no. 680, and Scott, *Elegant Form and Harmonious Decoration*, cat. 64.
3 Wang and Fan, eds., *Selected Ceramics from the Collection of Mr. and Mrs. J.M. Hu*, cat. 22.
4 Misugi, *Chinese Porcelain Collections*, vol. 2, p. 7, pl. X, noting the jar is 50 cm high.
5 Ibid., vol. 3, p. 205, fig. A.115, including a detail of the Shah Abbas mark engraved in the foot next to the Ming Jiajing mark.
6 Ibid., vol. 1, p. 135.

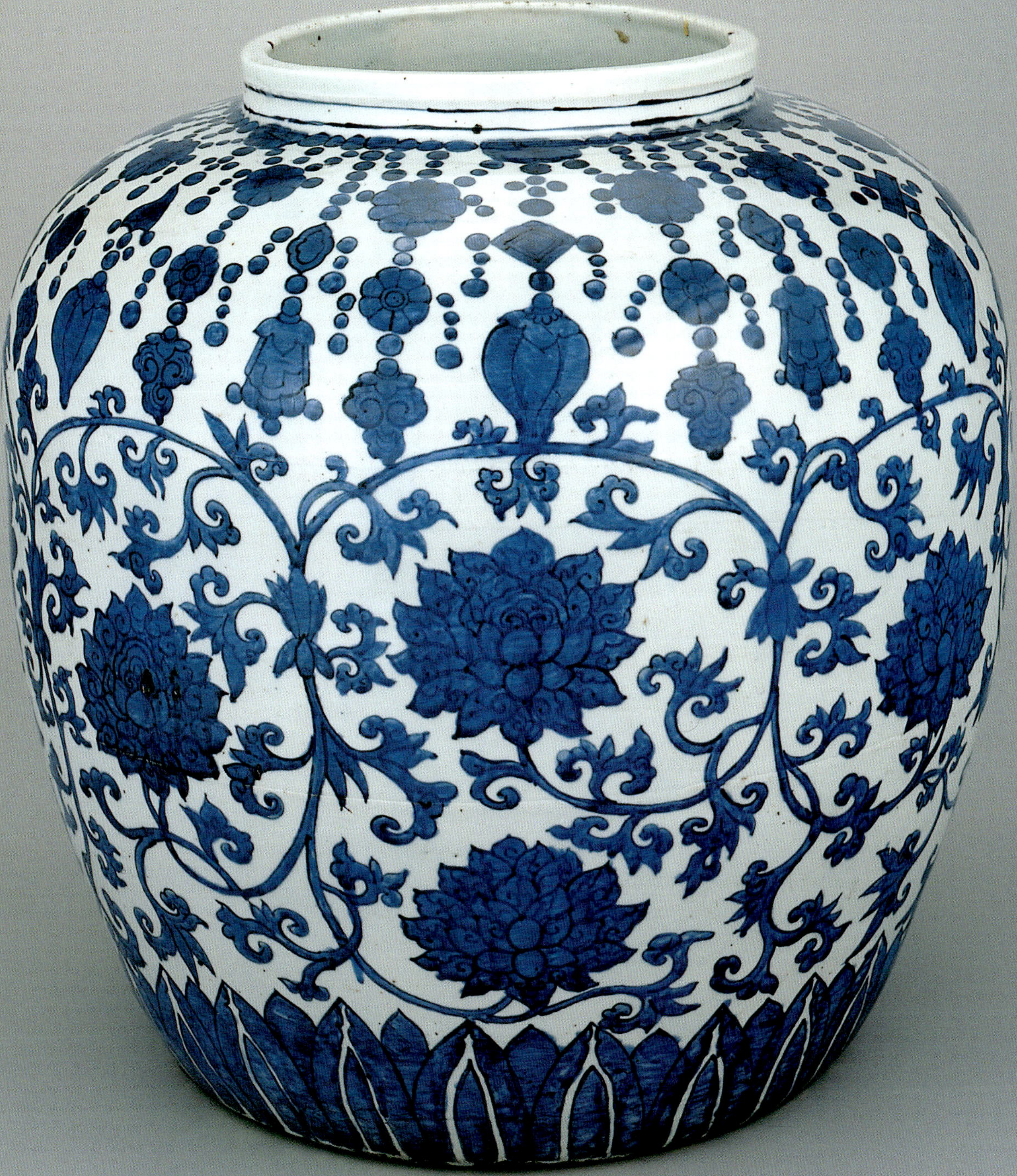

77 DRAGON BRUSHREST

Ming dynasty, Wanli imperial mark and period (1573–1619)
Underglaze cobalt blue and white decoration, 4 × 5 1/8 × 1 5/8 in. (10.2 × 13 × 4.1 cm)
Bequest of Mrs. Eugene L. Garbaty, 94.123

This *Brushrest* takes the form of a mountain with three peaks encircled by dragons. The mountains are similar to miniature scholars' rocks, the fanciful rocks kept on a scholar's desk for contemplation. The base of the *Brushrest* mimics the wood stands for miniature rocks or, indeed, any object of value displayed in imperial China. The dragons twisting and turning around the mountains represent the energy inherent in the landscape, which was conceived of as a living, dynamic force.

The use of molds permitted the mass production of porcelains and other ceramics, and during the Ming and Qing dynasties, when the economy and power of the imperial court were strong, orders for porcelains ran to the tens of thousands, even hundreds of thousands of objects. We know, for example, that in one year alone of the Wanli reign, 1593, orders from the court included 500 brushrests like the present example in blue and white porcelain or porcelain with overglaze enamel colors.[1] Several variations of the *Dragon brushrest* type are known, some with three and some with five mountain peaks, and they seem to be a specialty of the Wanli period, along with porcelain brush handles, and porcelain dishes with two compartments for holding and rinsing brushes.

The mark on the *Brushrest* consists of six characters of standard script which translate "made in the Wanli era of the Great Ming," written in a single line on the underside. Imperial marks or inscriptions designating a new status for porcelains as imperial products appear occasionally in the Ming Yongle reign (1403–25), but become more common and standardized in the succeeding Xuande reign period (1426–35).[2] In the Ming, porcelains can be considered "imperial" by virtue of their quality, even without a reign mark. Officially, Ming porcelains with such marks, like the Museum's *Brushrest*, were for the use of the imperial court, and inferior examples were systematically destroyed and discarded. Reign marks of earlier periods, however, frequently appear on later porcelains. The Ming Chenghua period (1465–87) witnessed an extraordinary revival of porcelain manufacture, and imperial Chenghua porcelains are considered among the finest ever produced. Thus later porcelains may bear Ming Chenghua marks, perhaps not originally meant to deceive but to pay tribute and share in the quality of the earlier porcelains. In the case of the *Brushrest*, other factors help identify it as a Wanli-period porcelain, including the relatively thick material, the vigorous modeling and painting, and faint traces of light red that appear on the unglazed edge of the base or on sharp, raised portions of the mountains. The very thin layer of glaze over these small details could not prevent the oxidation of traces of iron in the porcelain body during firing, and the small reddish areas are one indicator, along with the written mark, of a Ming imperial porcelain object of the late 16th–early 17th century.

NOT PREVIOUSLY PUBLISHED

NOTES

1 Margaret Medley, "Organization and Production at Jingdezhen," in Scott, ed., *The Porcelains of Jingdezhen*, pl. 12 (plate captions contain references to years and amounts ordered).

2 Vainker, *Chinese Pottery and Porcelain*, pp. 186–87.

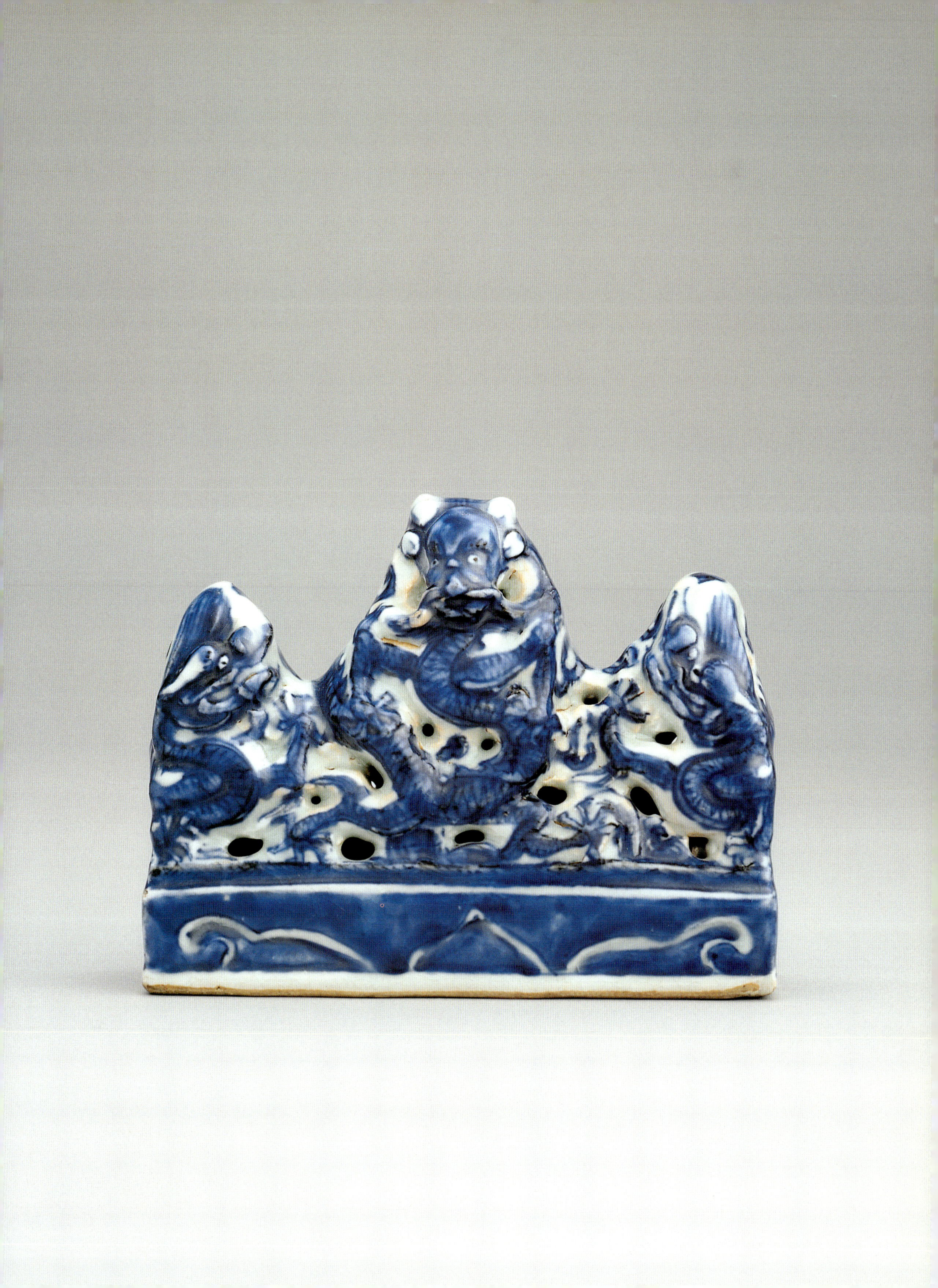

78 **BOTTLE**

Ming dynasty, early 17th century
Porcelain, underglaze cobalt blue and white decoration,
8 3/8 × diam. 2 7/8 in. (21.3 × 7.3 cm)
Purchase, the R.H. Norton Trust, 70.5

79 **INCENSE BURNER**

Ming dynasty, early 17th century
Porcelain, underglaze cobalt blue and white decoration,
2 7/8 × diam. 4 1/4 in. (7.3 × 10.8 cm)
Bequest of Mrs. Eugene L. Garbaty, 94.138

These products of the late Ming dynasty are part of a body of Chinese domestic wares and goods for Asian markets that has not received the scholarly attention given to earlier Ming porcelains or to the Transitional Wares of the late Ming and early Qing that have long attracted Western collectors.[1] The political and economic weakness of the imperial court, especially after the end of the Wanli reign in 1619, led to a falling off of production at Jingdezhen. Late Ming porcelains are sometimes characterized by a coarse body with visible impurities, a pale gray underglaze cobalt blue color, and a less secure "fit" of the glaze, which can cause flaking and other imperfections. A wide variety of shapes and designs were developed to appeal to different tastes and markets to make up for the loss of imperial patronage.

The *Bottle* is the first blue and white porcelain purchased by the Museum. The individual design motifs are Chinese and include floral designs, *fenghuang* phoenixes, and a large variety of auspicious emblems. The shape and the arrangement of decoration, however, are not typically Chinese. The vessel has a relatively thick body and a heavy, slightly flaring rim around the mouth. The decoration is divided into horizontal bands by pairs of parallel lines. The fine-line painted decoration, often called "penciled" decoration (a slightly archaic term for the use of an artist's brush with a fine tip), is another characteristic of late Ming porcelains. Besides exhibiting the porcelain painters' skills, it allows economical use of relatively expensive (and probably increasingly scarce) cobalt oxide. The exotic shape and unusual decoration may possibly have been made to appeal to a non-Chinese Southeast Asian or to a Philippine market.

The *Incense burner* is decorated with the same fine line and pale blue cobalt oxide, with thin washes coloring the dragons and clouds. The form is a simple cylinder with short legs, and such burners were common products for the Chinese domestic market. Like the *Bottle*, the flat base is unglazed. The vessel would have been filled with sand to support burning sticks of incense or smoldering charcoal on which incense, in lumps or ground, was burned. Both porcelains are difficult to date precisely, although a dish in the British Museum[2] offers an interesting parallel with the *Incense burner*. Painted in enamels on the biscuit, the dish has a design of four-clawed dragons that are very close to those on the burner. All have long rubbery snouts, bulging round eyes, and hair that points forward off the head. All have simple, curved bodies and simply rendered scales, spines, and claws. The dish has a Tianqi reign mark, dating it to the brief period of 1621 to 1627 and providing a possible date for the Norton *Incense burner*.

PUBLISHED

78: Jayne, *The Chinese Collections*, no. 352
79: Not previously published

NOTES

1 Scholarship of late Ming–early Qing ceramics often follows collecting and tends to focus on porcelains exported to Europe (see cat. 80). There is also a substantial body of research on Chinese porcelains made for Japan in this period.
2 Hobson, *The Wares of the Ming Dynasty*, pl. 44, fig. 2.

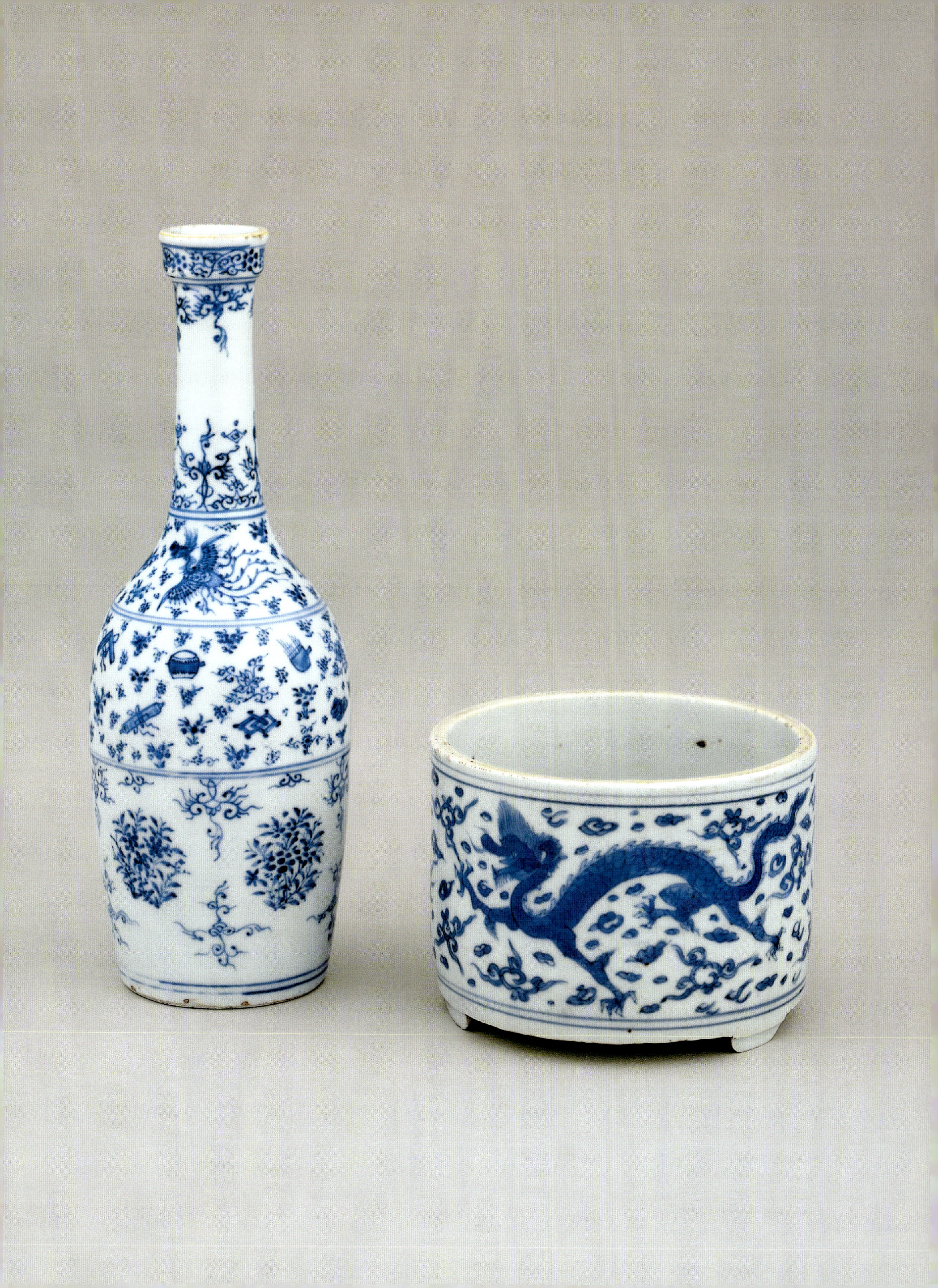

80 CYLINDRICAL VASE

Ming dynasty, probably Chongzhen period (1628–44)
Porcelain, underglaze cobalt blue and white decoration,
18 1/8 × diam. 5 3/4 in. (46 × 14.6 cm)
Bequest of Mrs. Eugene L. Garbaty, 94.125

This *Cylindrical vase* is a well-known type often referred to as a rolwagen, a Dutch word meaning "rolling wagon." This is perhaps a reference to a figure seated in a two-wheeled cart, an element that appears frequently in the decoration of such vases,[1] many of which were imported into Europe in the seventeenth century.

Narrative decoration on porcelains, often scenes from popular novels or plays, was enormously popular during the so-called Transitional Period, the 60 years between the death of the Ming Wanli emperor in 1620 and the reassertion of imperial control over the manufacture of porcelain at Jingdezhen under the Qing Kangxi emperor in 1683. The scene on the Norton vase shows three women in an upper-story room looking down at men on horseback and their attendants. The inscription, written in a deliberately archaistic style, reads: "The red skirts gaze at the green-clothed gentlemen." The scene is taken from the widely popular *Romance of the Western Chamber*, a thirteenth-century play based on the story of a Tang scholar, Zhang Sheng, and the beauty with whom he falls in love, Cui Yingying.[2] Here the heroine, accompanied by her mother and servant, gaze at the young man as he prepares to ride off to the capital for the imperial examinations.

Many details date the *Cylindrical vase* to the mid-seventeenth century, about the year 1640. Invisible in the photograph are a band of lightly incised flowers and leaves around the shoulder and another band of stylized waves just above the foot. Such almost imperceptible decoration is characteristic of the period (see also the *Brush jar*, cat. 81), as is the rich violet-blue tone of the cobalt glaze. Moreover, a significant number of cylindrical vases with dated inscriptions support a relatively precise date. One in particular, decorated with a scene of a man and woman in a garden setting, has a dated inscription corresponding to 1639 that is similar in style to the writing on the Museum's vase.[3] The painting on both vases uses the same tiny V-shaped brushstrokes to indicate grass.

The Norton vase has one unusual detail. While the short necks of most Rolwagen are usually filled with stylized leaves, here the decoration consists of circular whorl designs derived from Shang or early Zhou bronze motifs (see, for example, the bronze *jia*, cat. 9) alternating with a squared, double zigzag emblem called a *fu*, one of twelve ancient symbols officially adopted in the Ming as emblems on imperial robes.[4] A combination of similar whorls and *fu* symbols, along with stylized floral panels, decorates the central range of an archaistic *gu*, or beaker-shaped vase, in the Ashmolean Museum, Oxford, which, interestingly enough, also bears an inscription dated 1639.[5] This vase, too, has a narrative pictorial decoration that is close to the Norton's *Cylindrical vase*.

PUBLISHED

Little, *Chinese Ceramics of the Transitional Period*, cat. 23

NOTES

1 Jörg, *Chinese Ceramics in the Collection of the Rijksmuseum*, cat. 66.
2 See especially Craig Clunas, "The West Chamber: A Literary Theme in Chinese Porcelain Decoration," in *Transactions* 46 (1981–82). The name Zhang Sheng means "Scholar Zhang."
3 Lovell, *Transitional Wares*, color pl. 60.
4 Difficult to interpret precisely, it is a symbol of judgment and the emperor's ability to distinguish right from wrong.
5 Hasebe, ed., *Chūgoku no tōji*, vol. 10, no. 29. Hasebe misinterprets the cyclical date as 1699. See Lovell, *Transitional Wares*, p. 31, fig. 11, for the inscription.

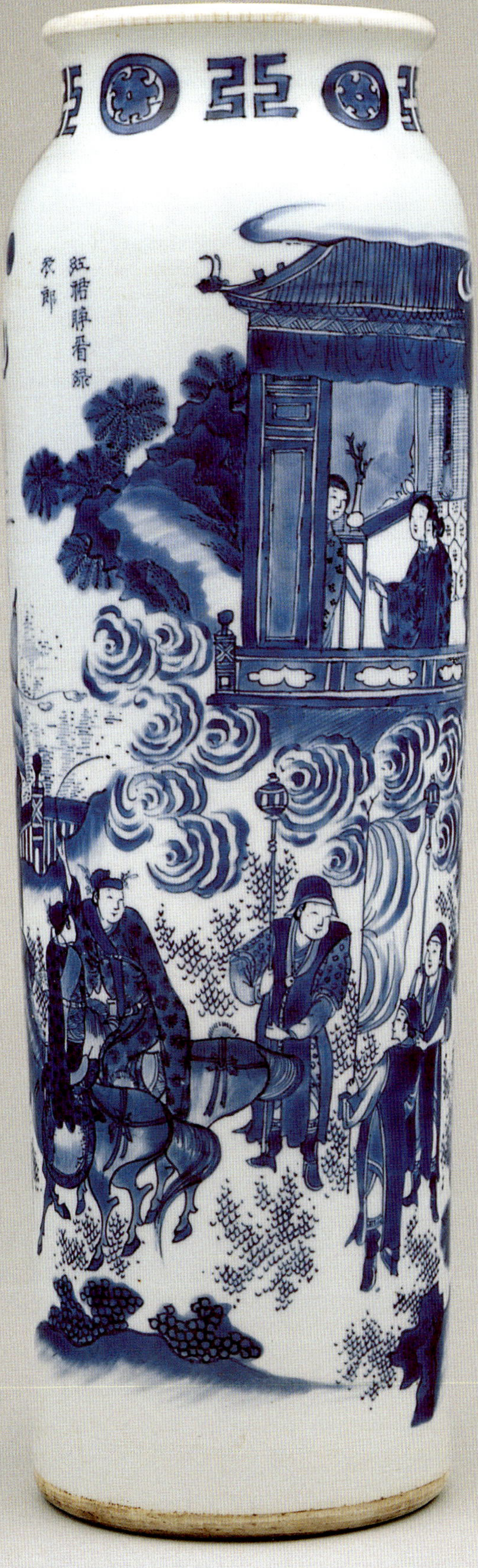
紅袖靜看綠
衣郎

81 BRUSH JAR

Ming dynasty, probably Chongzhen period (1628–44)
Porcelain, underglaze cobalt blue and white decoration,
8 7/8 × diam. 8 5/16 in. (22.5 × 21.1 cm)
Bequest of Mrs. Eugene L. Garbaty, 94.112

This jar with its wide, flaring mouth would have held brushes, rolls of paper, or other objects on a scholar's desk. Like the tall *Cylindrical vase* (cat. 80), it is painted in a style associated with the decades of the 1630s and 1640s. Almost invisible lines are lightly incised in the porcelain just below the mouth and around the base. The color of the cobalt pigment is a deep violet-blue, and the composition is clearly laid out with an effective use of the white porcelain ground. Such details as the skillful drawing, subtle washes, and the small U-shaped strokes to render grass are all typical of the best porcelains of the period.

The breakdown of imperial patronage in the Transitional Period (ca. 1620–83) obliged the potters of Jingdezhen to adapt to new markets and new tastes. Among these were the scholars and wealthy merchants with scholarly tastes of the late Ming dynasty. A contemporary upsurge in the publication of illustrated literature—novels and drama—was echoed in the taste for porcelains decorated with narrative illustrations. As Stephen Little has pointed out in his discussion of this *Brush jar,*[1] the scene represented could be from one of a number of similar moralistic tales in which a mythical ruler of ancient China offers his throne to a sage who has chosen to withdraw from the world and live as a hermit. Here the emperor, distinguished by his elaborate robes and the canopy held by a servant, gestures to the sage-hermit, who is dressed as a farmer and leads an ox. The story represented is probably that of the legendary emperor Yao and the recluse Xu You.[2] Offered the throne, Xu You refused it, arguing that the world was already well governed and would be badly served if men took roles that were not properly their own. As Julia Curtis points out, the story comes from a Daoist source.[3] But for late Ming dynasty audiences, such illustrations also would likely have had Confucian overtones, implying criticism of the weakness and corruption of the last Ming emperors. If the empire were well governed, there would be no need to seek outside the court for virtuous rule. This particular episode is also depicted on another porcelain in the Museum's collection (acc. no. 94.131), a large bottle-shaped vase dating to approximately the same late Ming period.

PUBLISHED

Little, *Chinese Ceramics of the Transitional Period,* cat. 20

NOTES

1 Little, *Chinese Ceramics of the Transitional Period,* cat. 20.
2 See Watson, trans., *Chuang Tzu,* pp. 32–33.
3 Curtis, *Chinese Porcelains of the Seventeenth Century,* cat. 60, a rolwagen in the Butler family collection decorated with a scene very similar to the Norton's *Brush jar.*

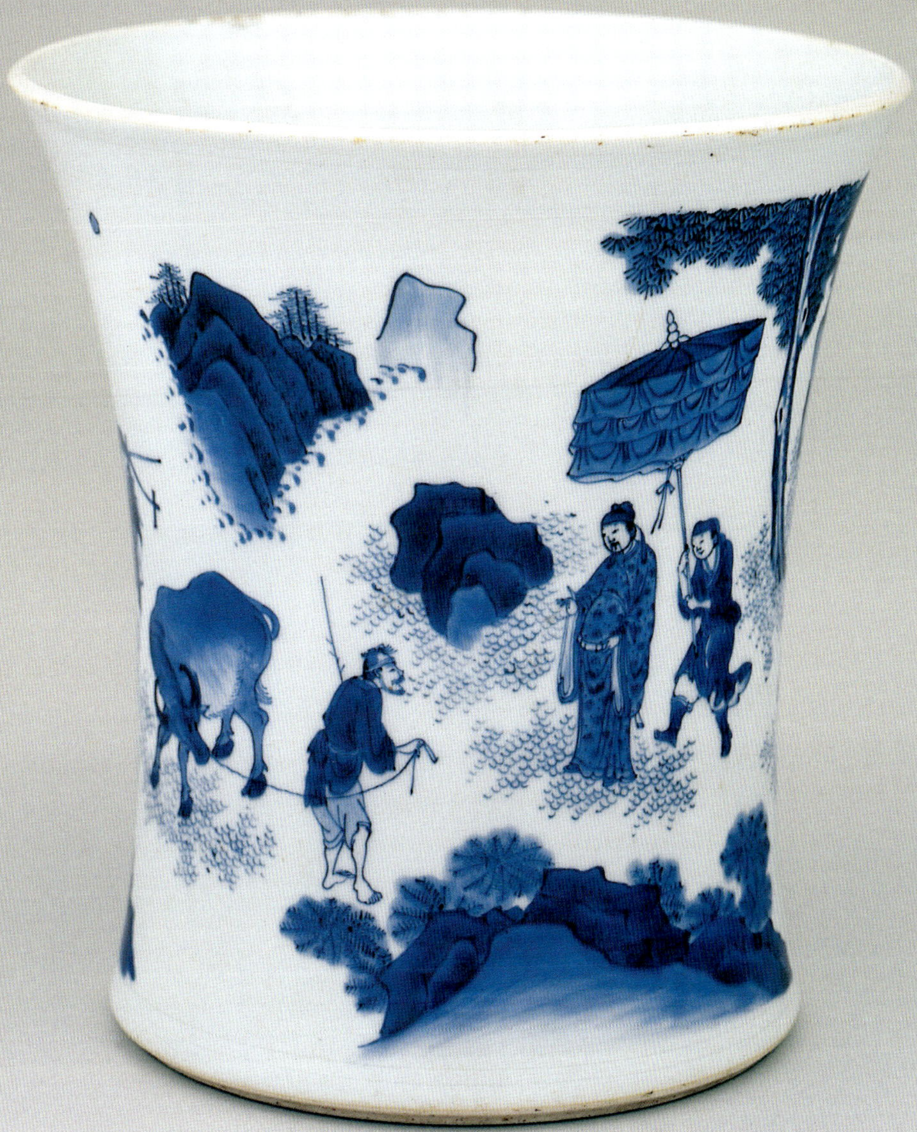

82 PAIR OF JARS WITH WOMEN ENJOYING MUSIC

Ming–Qing Transitional Period, ca. 1620–83
Porcelain, underglaze cobalt blue and *wucai* enamel overglaze decoration, one: 15 1/8 × diam. 12 1/2 in. (38.4 × 31.8 cm), the other: 14 7/8 × diam. 12 3/4 in. (37.8 × 32.4 cm)
Bequest of Leonard and Sophie Davis, 2001.160a-b, 2001.161a-b

This *Pair of jars* is decorated with boldly conceived scenes of women in a garden enjoying music and dancing. The designs of both jars are the same, with the image of a garden party wrapping seamlessly around the sides.[1] One woman is seated in a chair, surrounded by attendants holding fans and musical instruments wrapped in brocaded bags, and the festivities appear to be for her entertainment. Folding screens, painted an orange-pink color but otherwise undecorated, separate the seated woman and her attendants from the musicians and dancer. The musicians are variously playing a drum on a stand, a pair of wooden clappers, a horizontal flute, and (just visible on the far left) a double-reed instrument with vertical pipes. The figures are large, their costumes and coiffures are elaborately detailed, and their features are delicately rendered in fine lines. Around the neck of each jar are painted rocks and floral sprays, and on the shoulders is a pattern of random polygons conventionally referred to as "cracked ice."

The combination of a strong underglaze cobalt blue with brilliant overglaze enamel colors is termed *wucai*, literally "five colors," although the palette is in fact much broader. The unfired porcelain jar was first painted with the cobalt blue parts of the design, then covered with a clear glaze and fired. In a second step, the enamel colors, which are essentially finely ground colored glass, were painted over the clear glaze to complete the design, and the jar was fired again at a lower temperature to fuse the enamels to the glazed surface. The combination of underglaze blue and brilliant *wucai* colors is an innovation of the Ming Jiajing period (1522–1622).[2] Used to render narrative pictorial designs on Transitional Period porcelains, it often imitates the composition and effect of paintings on paper or silk.

Wucai jars with images of women dancers and musicians appear to have been fashionable in the late Ming and early Qing. A single jar in the Rijksmuseum, Amsterdam, has the same design elements, although the details are somewhat different.[3] A similar large jar with a closely related image of the women musicians was sold at Sotheby's New York in 2001.[4] Like the Norton jars, both of those have rocks and flowers and the cracked ice pattern around the neck. Also painted in a style and palette similar to the Norton jars is an important *wucai* enamel-decorated jar in the Art Institute of Chicago depicting a mythological scene taking place in the palace of the Moon Goddess Chang'e.[5] The Chicago jar is especially important for an inscription dating it to the Shunzhi reign, equivalent to 1646, the second year of the Qing dynasty, which helps to locate this significant group of *wucai* enamel porcelains in the Transitional Period at the end of the Ming and beginning of the Qing.

NOT PREVIOUSLY PUBLISHED

NOTES

1 Slight differences in size, color, and handling of the painted decoration between the two jars raise the question of whether they were intended as a formal pair or represent two identical vessels made to the same design.

2 Valenstein, *Handbook*, pp. 191, 193.

3 Jörg, *Chinese Ceramics in the Collection of the Rijksmuseum*, cat. 75.

4 Sotheby's New York, *Fine Chinese Ceramics and Works of Art*, September 19, 2001, lot. 140. This jar preserves its original cover.

5 Little, *Chinese Ceramics of the Transitional Period*, cat. 42; the jar is in the Russell Tyson Collection, The Art Institute of Chicago.

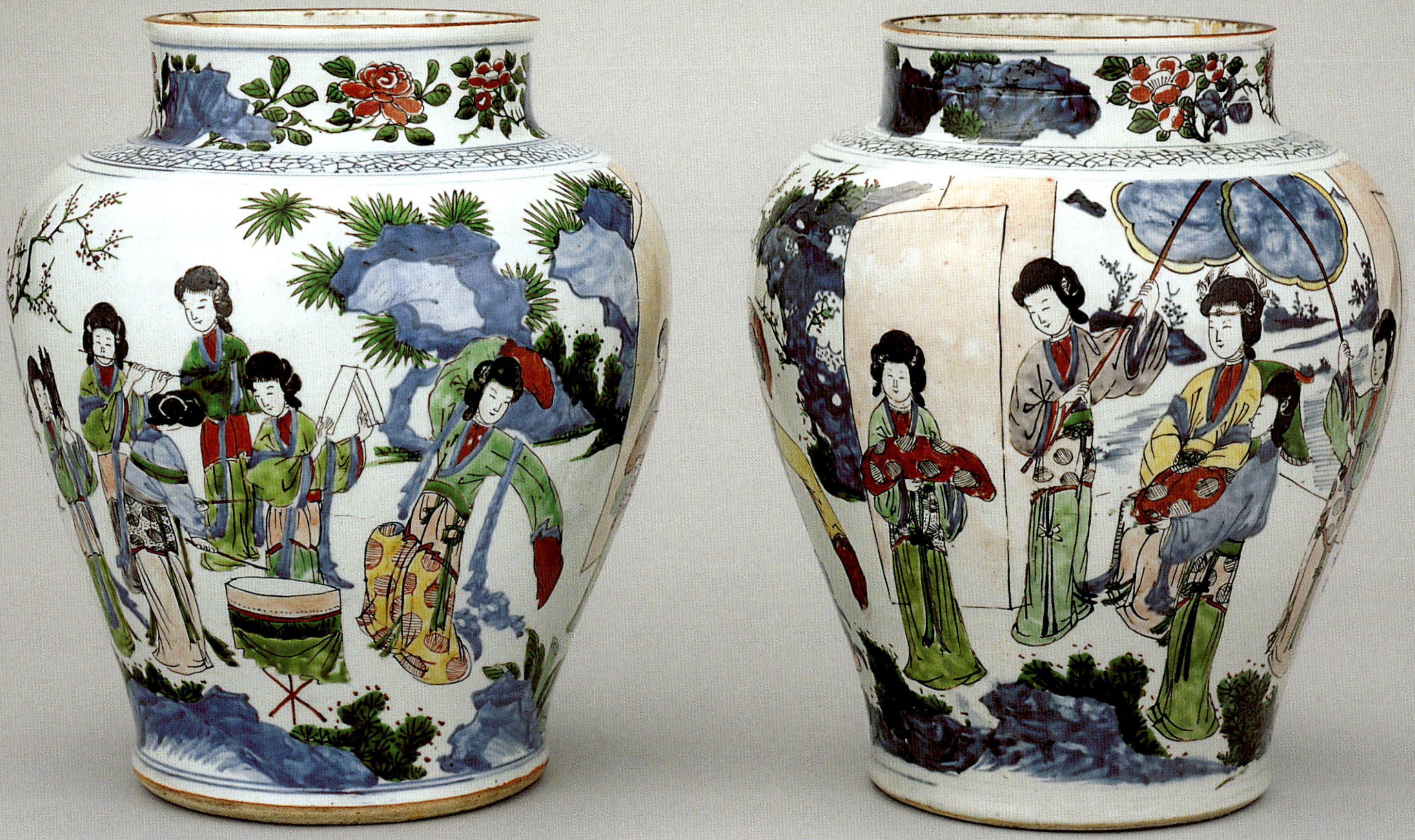

83 PLATE WITH "SEA HORSES" AND AUSPICIOUS DESIGNS

Qing dynasty, ca. 1660–70
Porcelain, colored enamel on biscuit, 2 3/16 × diam. 10 11/16 in. (5.6 × 27.1 cm)
Bequest of R.H. Norton, 53.234

The dark green background, painted over spiraling lines, and the crashing white waves around the rim of the *Plate with "sea horses" and auspicious designs* represent the ocean, over which float a remarkable array of decorative motifs. Toward the center of the plate are four emblems alternating with four horses. Starting at the upper right, these include a set of wooden clappers, the attribute of the Daoist Immortal Cao Guojiu; a pair of curving, pointed objects that represent two rhinoceros horns, emblems of wealth; two leaves with circular designs that may be palm-leaf fans, representing the Daoist Immortal Zhongli Quan; and a single green Artemisia leaf, which wards off evil influences.

The fantastically colored horses flying over the ocean are most likely *haima* or legendary "sea horses." Each has a flamelike lightning bolt indicating its miraculous or divine powers. Some writers[1] have identified such horses as the eight magic steeds of King Mu of the Zhou, who supposedly hitched his team to a chariot and visited the Daoist Queen Mother of the West.[2] A more likely identification is to be found in the early seventeenth-century encyclopedia *Sancai tuhui*.[3] In the section on real and imaginary animals, the description of the "sea horse" begins with a citation of the *Shanhaijing* (The Classic of Mountains and Seas), itself a compilation of geographic fact and fantasy that dates to the Eastern Zhou and Han dynasty.[4] The text describes a creature from the Northern Sea that is superior at galloping and appropriate for the decoration of colored robes. The drawing of the horses on the Norton *Plate*, especially the steed in the center, is very close in style to the woodblock illustration in the *Sancai tuhui*.

The image of sea horses appears on blue and white porcelains in the fourteenth century[5] as well as on a surprising range of porcelains throughout the Yuan, Ming, and early Qing dynasty. The rendering of the design that we see on the Museum's *Plate* is painted in a rich palette of enamel colors applied directly to the unglazed porcelain body or biscuit. The painting is skillful and wonderfully animated, exploiting the wide range of enamel colors to magical effect. A very similar plate in the Butler family collection[6] is unusual in having a glazed "channel" foot-ring—that is, a double foot-ring with a clear glaze between the unglazed edges of the ring. The Norton *Plate* has just such an elaborate foot (on the underside and not visible in the photo). Dense combinations of auspicious designs seem to be a preoccupation of the Qing dynasty. The early Qing *Plate with "sea horses" and auspicious emblems* is symbolic of good fortune in a general sense without having the symbols arranged as puns and rebuses in a way that characterizes later Qing designs.

PUBLISHED

Jayne, *The Chinese Collections*, no. 355

NOTES

1 See, for example, Beurdeley and Raindre, *Qing Porcelain*, cat. 111.
2 Mu's fictional "biography," the *Mu tianzi zhuan* (Biography of Mu, the Son of Heaven), probably dates to the fourth century BCE; see Nienhauser, *The Indiana Companion*, pp. 632–33.
3 Compiled by Wang Qi (*jinshi* degree, 1565) and completed in 1607, the woodblock–illustrated encyclopedia describes real and legendary subjects from the three realms—Heaven, earth, and man. See Wilkinson, *Chinese History*, p. 692, n. 13.
4 Nienhauser, *The Indiana Companion*, pp. 671–72.
5 Pope, *Fourteenth-Century Blue-and-White*, pl. 29.
6 Butler and others, *Seventeenth-Century Chinese Porcelain*, cat. 124. There is another in the Musée Guimet, Paris. See *Oriental Ceramics*, vol. 7, Musée Guimet, fig. 146.

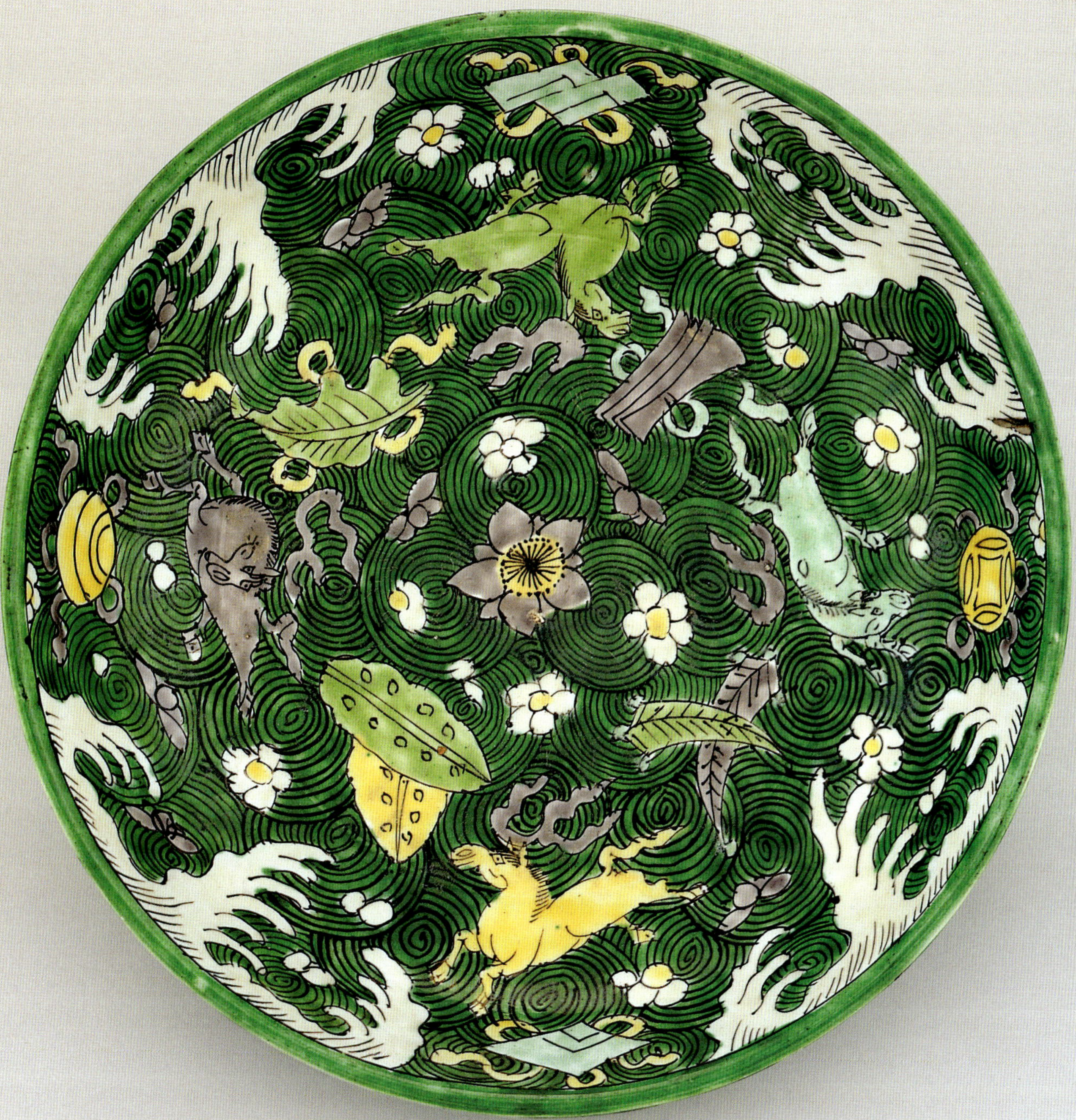

84 PAIR OF BOWLS WITH DRAGONS AND PHOENIXES

Qing dynasty, Kangxi mark and period (1662–1722)
Porcelain, overglaze enamel on biscuit, 2 3/8 × mouth diam. 4 11/16 in. (6 × 11.9 cm)
Gift of Catherine Halliday in memory of Herbert Bernenko, 2002.14a-b

The design of green dragons and phoenixes on these two bowls, part of a set of vessels, probably designates them for use by a second-rank imperial concubine of the Qing dynasty.[1] The brilliant green and yellow colors are transparent enamels applied to the biscuit, that is, directly to the fired but unglazed porcelain body. The same enameling technique is used on another plate in the Museum (cat. 83) to produce rich, deep colors. On the two *Bowls*, the design of dragons, phoenixes, and stylized clouds was first delicately incised into the surface. The enamel colors fill these fine grooves, producing the slightly darker outlines and details of the design. The carving is lively and fine, and there is a slight iridescent sheen to the green enamel. Bowls of this type were widely imitated throughout the Qing dynasty, and these qualities, along with the well-written underglaze blue six-character Kangxi mark on the inside of the foot, help identify them as late seventeenth to early eighteenth century imperial productions.

Like many Qing imperial porcelains, the bowls are a recreation of a Ming-dynasty type, and the design of green dragons against a brilliant yellow ground has many Ming prototypes. The technique of using colored enamels or low-fired lead glazes on the biscuit was also a Ming innovation, but until recent archaeological discoveries it was not entirely clear at what date such decoration begins. Certain well-known examples, such as the leys jar in the Percival David Foundation, London, have Chengde reign marks (1506–21), and the enamel-on-biscuit technique used to decorate similar porcelains is well documented through the late Ming and throughout the Qing.[2] Excavations in the Yongle era (1403–24) strata at Jingdezhen, however, have revealed the earliest Ming examples of enamel on biscuit decoration. A small pear-shaped ewer reconstructed from shards is decorated with dragons and clouds incised into the porcelain body and then covered with low-fired yellow-brown and green lead glazes.[3]

Although this particular ewer is not marked, imperial reign marks, too, are an innovation of the Yongle period. Yongle marks in modified seal script and standard script are very rare, while marks for the succeeding Xuande reign are more common.[4] Early Qing examples can have contemporary marks or remain unmarked. An interesting pair of relatively crude bowls[5] with dragons and phoenixes painted in enamel on biscuit and datable to the Shunzhi period (1644–61), the first reign of the Qing dynasty, have spurious Ming Jiajing marks (1522–66), suggesting that the Qing potters clearly remembered their Ming sources but no longer knew just how long these designs and the technique associated with them had persisted.

NOT PREVIOUSLY PUBLISHED

NOTES

1 Vainker, *Chinese Pottery and Porcelain*, p. 211, citing the 1766 *Huangchao liqi tushi*, although it has not been possible to locate the text in question. See also Jörg, *Chinese Ceramics in the Collection of the Rijksmuseum*, cat. 230, citing Liu, *Ch'ing Official and Popular Wares*, pp. 40–43: "green bowls with purple dragons for *guiren*, court ladies of the 5th rank."
2 See, for example, Medley, *The Chinese Potter*, fig. 154, pp. 207, 223.
3 Chang Foundation, *Imperial Hongwu and Yongle Porcelain*, cat. 109. The authors identify the technique as a Yongle period innovation.
4 Medley, *The Chinese Potter*, pp. 187–87, 214.
5 Little, *Chinese Ceramics of the Transitional Period*, cat. 45; the bowls are in the Asian Art Museum, San Francisco.

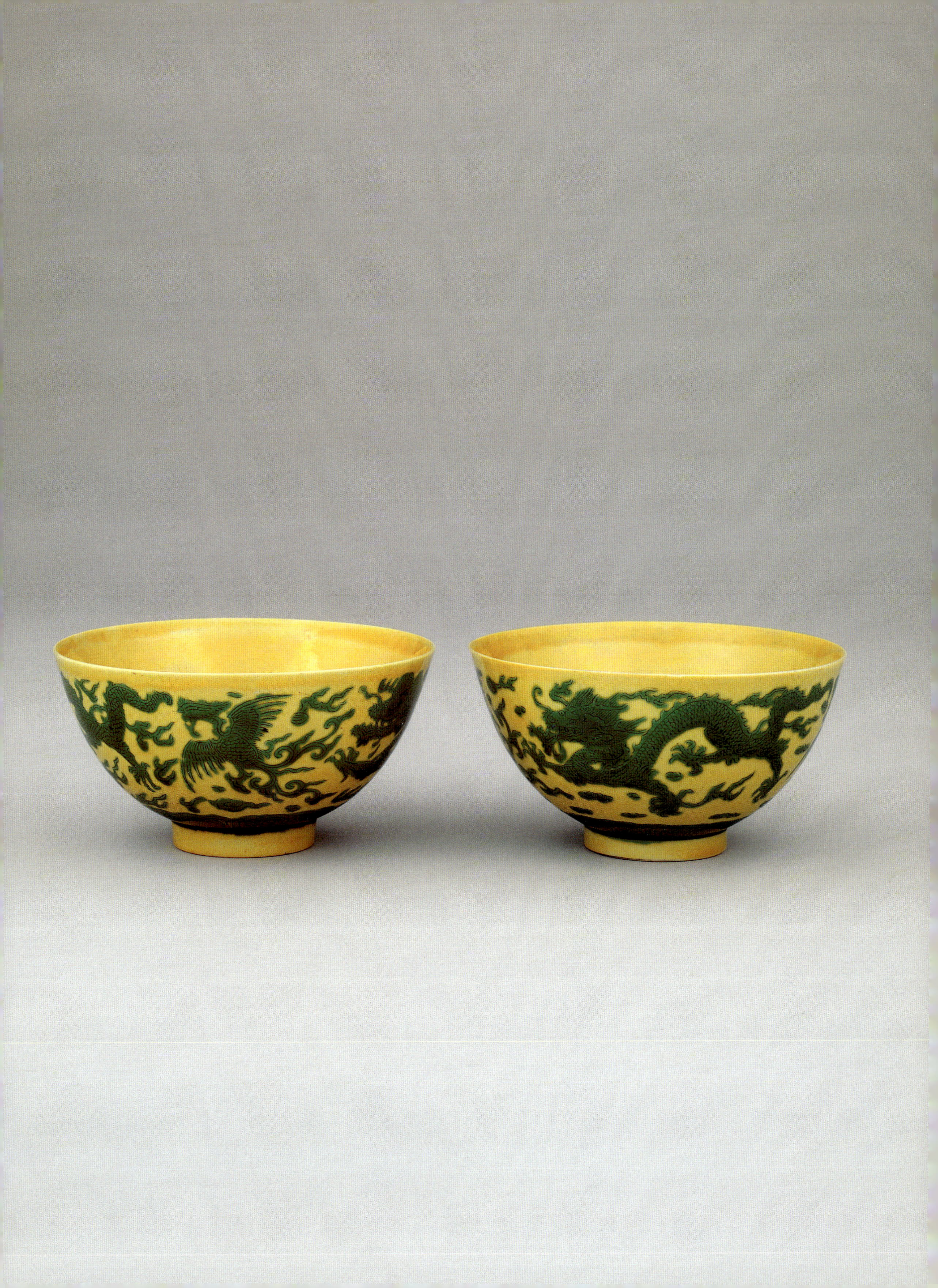

85 "CHINESE IMARI" CHARGER

Qing dynasty, Kangxi period (1662–1722), early 18th century
Porcelain, overglaze *famille verte* enamel decoration with gilding,
2 ½ × diam. 21 ⅛ in. (6.4 × 53.7 cm)
Bequest of Leonard and Sophie Davis, 2001.162

This sumptuous large platter, or *Charger*, is decorated in deep blue, red, and various green overglaze enamels with many details painted in gold. The central design depicts a spray of flowers in a vase, resting on a small stand on top of a pedestal. The platter's broad rim is decorated with six compartments that alternate highly stylized red and gold chrysanthemums on a blue ground with birds or butterflies and flowers on a white ground. The decoration of the dish is an amalgam of Chinese and Japanese designs. Designs of baskets or vases of flowers on Chinese export porcelains are well known; they appear in a wide variety of sizes, styles, and degrees of complexity, reflecting the original cost of the plate or platter.

Japanese potters began carefully to copy and adapt these designs at a time when the turmoil of the Ming–Qing transition interrupted production at Jingdezhen.[1] The most clearly Japanese design elements on this *Charger* are the highly stylized chrysanthemum flowers and the meandering line separating the six compartments on the rim. This lobed form, outlined in red and highlighted with gold, is a Japanese convention (with a complex history reaching back to Chinese designs) for representing the shape of clouds. Several of the design elements have Buddhist associations, although they are most likely used here for decorative effect. The garden railing grille has a design of swastikas, which are one emblem of the Buddha, and the finials on the posts take the form of lotus flowers and seed pods, another Buddhist motif. Even the vase itself has an everted rim decorated with lotus-petal lappets, copying perhaps elements of the design of Tibetan Buddhist altar vessels.[2]

Imari is the name of a seaport near Arita on the southern Japanese island of Kyushu. In 1604, Korean potters, brought to Japan in the aftermath of a failed invasion, began to work at Arita using local deposits of kaolin to successfully mass-produce porcelains in Japan.[3] After the mid-seventeenth and throughout the eighteenth century, Japanese imitations of Chinese overglaze enamel wares were exported to Southeast Asia and Europe, especially to Holland, which maintained the only direct commercial contacts with the Japanese.[4] So-called Ko-Imari (old Imari) wares were much sought after and imitated in Europe, and, after the Chinese re-established large-scale production at Jingdezhen in the late seventeenth century, they too made Japanese-style "Chinese Imari" overglaze enamel porcelains for the export market. The early eighteenth-century date for the Norton *Charger* is supported by an almost identical platter of slightly smaller size that was in the collection of Augustus the Strong and bears the incised Johanneum mark, documenting its presence in Dresden before 1727.[5]

NOT PREVIOUSLY PUBLISHED

NOTES

1 See, for example, Idemitsu Museum, *The Inter-Influence of Ceramic Art*, cat. 5, a blue and white charger with a vase of flowers surrounded by a wide border with eight floral panels.
2 See examples in Tsai, *Monarchy and Its Buddhist Way*, cats. 88–90.
3 Idemitsu Museum, *The Inter-Influence of Ceramic Art*, English summary, p. 3.
4 Emerson and others, *Porcelain Stories*, p. 180.
5 Ralph M. Chait Galleries, New York; see *Orientations* (December 2001), p. 1. The first Dresden inventory is dated 1721 but includes entries up to 1727; see Strober, "*La maladie de la porcelaine*," p. 10. There is another almost identical charger in the Victoria and Albert Museum from the Salting Bequest; see Victoria and Albert Museum, *Far Eastern Ceramics*, no. 204.

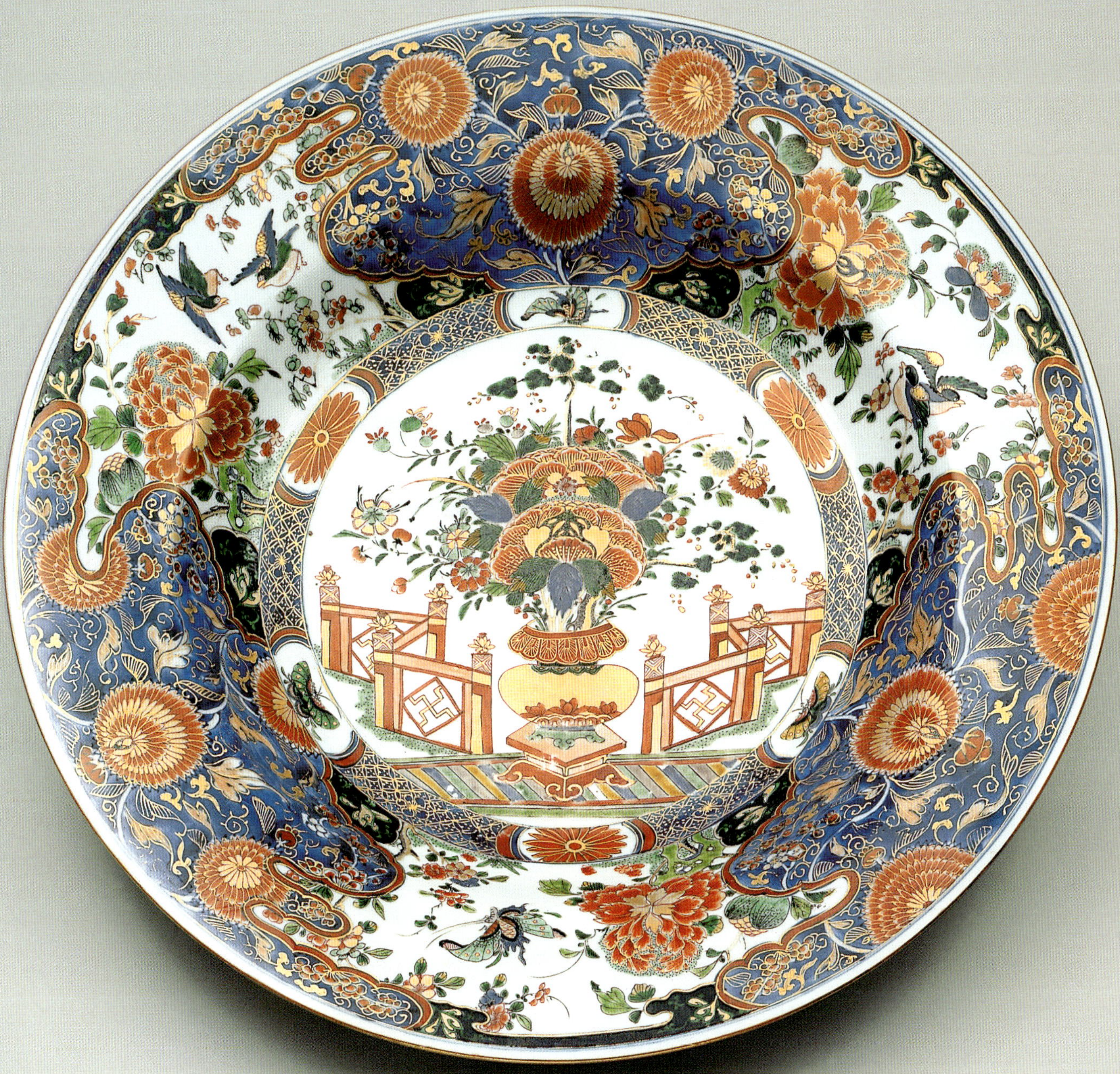

86 PAIR OF COVERED JARS WITH PHOENIXES

Qing dynasty, Kangxi period (1662–1722)
Porcelain, underglaze cobalt blue and overglaze enamel decoration with gilding, each 23 ½ × diam. 14 ½ in. (59.7 × 36.8 cm)
Bequest of Leonard and Sophie Davis, 2001.163a-b, 2001.164a-b

Painted overglaze enamel garden scenes rendered in a wonderful range of bright colors highlighted with gold decorate these two very large *Covered jars*. The sides of both jars are wrapped with single, seamless compositions of real and mythological birds, flowers of all kinds but especially peonies, and fantastic garden rocks assembled to form *jiashan*, or miniature mountains. Conventionally referred to as phoenixes, these Chinese mythological birds are *feng-huang*, the male *feng* and female *huang*, auspicious birds whose appearance heralds peace in the land.[1]

Qing porcelains with a broad palette of overglaze enamel colors that includes a wide range of greens are conventionally catalogued in the West as *famille verte* porcelains.[2] They are direct descendants of Ming dynasty *wucai*, "five-color" decoration, in overglaze enamel with underglaze cobalt blue (see cat. 82). Early Qing porcelains with painted decoration of birds and flowers seem to reach back to the Song dynasty for inspiration; the garden rocks or bits of ground firmly anchored to the bottom edge of the jar and the blank backgrounds recall Song-style paintings. It may have been the possibilities of an expanded palette that inspired early Qing potters to produce variations on elaborate bird-and-flower designs. A large overglaze enamel jar in the Metropolitan Museum of Art, dated to the late Transitional Period, about 1662 to 1683, is decorated with a pheasant on a wonderful garden rock pierced with wide holes.[3] A Kangxi period vase in the National Palace Museum, Beijing, is decorated with fantastic birds perched on truly bizarre rocks consisting of multicolored rectangles that seem suspended in space.[4] A five-piece garniture—two beaker-shaped vases and three covered jars approximately the same size as these Norton jars—in the collection of Augustus the Strong in Dresden can be dated to approximately 1700 to 1720.[5] Originally part of two different five-piece sets, all those vessels are decorated with versions of birds, flowers, and garden rocks designs, emphasizing blue rocks that are relatively close in style to rocks on earlier Transitional Period porcelains. The two Norton *Covered jars* reproduce the same design, but there are significant variations in the rendering of the design, raising intriguing questions about what constitutes a "pair" or "set" and the various decorative uses to which Europeans put Chinese porcelains.

NOT PREVIOUSLY PUBLISHED

NOTES

1 See the entry in the 1607 encyclopedia *Sancai tuhui* on "Birds," *juan* 1:1 "*feng*," reprint, p. 2,173. In some case the male is distinguished by serrated tail feathers, his mate by feathers with an undulating outline.
2 Jacquemart and Le Blant, *Histoire artistique, industrielle et commerciale de la Porcelaine*, pp. 67–68, introduced the term *famille verte* for transparent overglaze enamel decoration with green as predominant color. Chinese use the term *yingcai*, literally "hard colors," for these and other overglaze enamel wares. See Valenstein, *Handbook*, p. 227.
3 *Oriental Ceramics*, vol. 11, fig. 110.
4 Rogers and others, *China 5,000 Years*, cat. 145.
5 Kerr, "A Passionately Immoderate and Incurable Addiction," fig. 8, pp. 42–43.

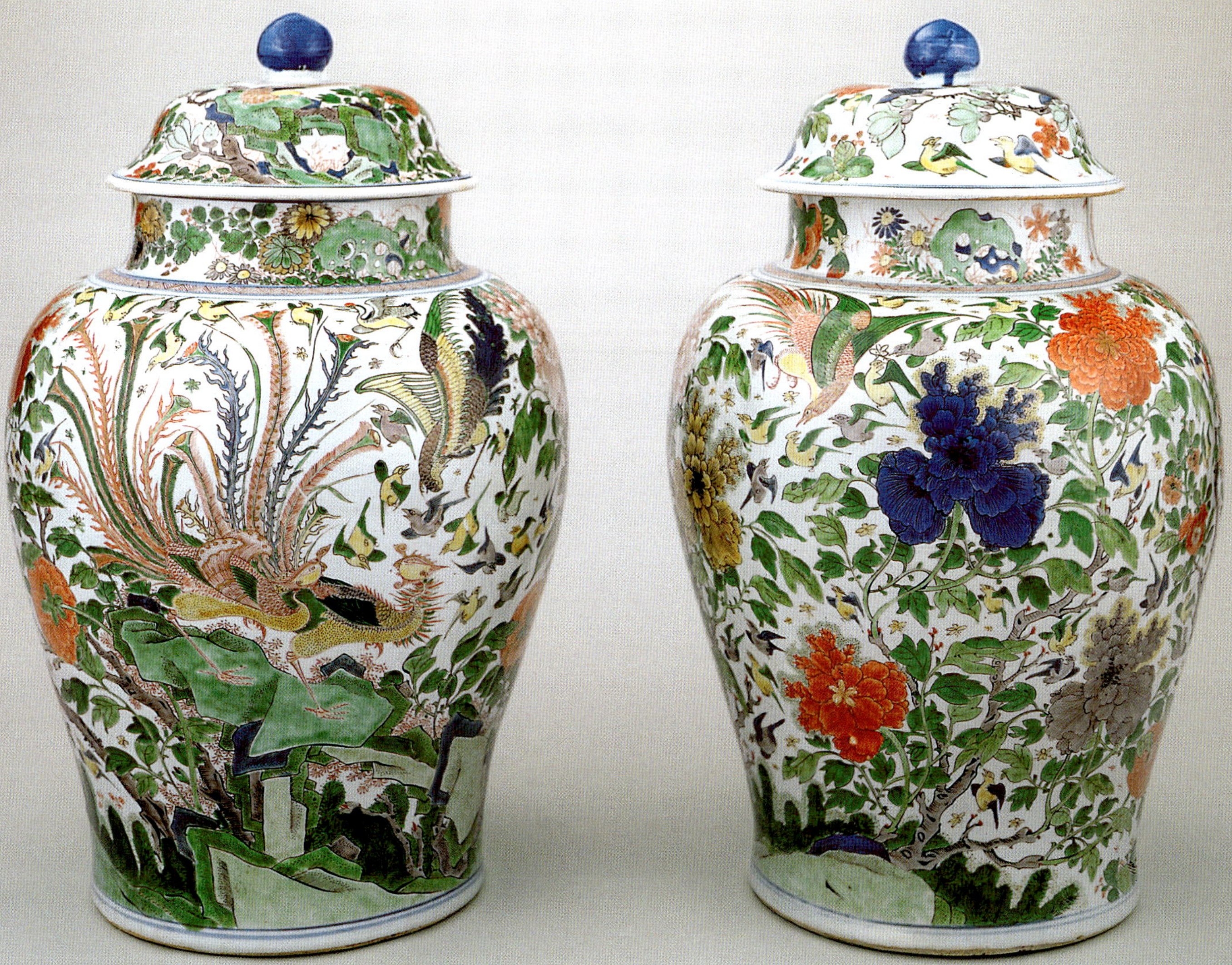

87 CHARGER WITH PHOENIXES AND EIGHT LANDSCAPES

Qing dynasty, Kangxi period (1662–1722)
Porcelain, overglaze *famille verte* enamel decoration with gilding,
3 ⅛ × diam. 22 in. (7.9 × 55.9 cm)
Bequest of Leonard and Sophie Davis, 2001.165

Like the *"Chinese Imari" charger* (cat. 85), this *Charger with phoenixes and eight landscapes* is an exuberantly decorated porcelain produced in the late seventeenth or early eighteenth century for the export market. While the designs that fill the surface are Chinese, such a very large platter is a foreign shape intended almost certainly for display and not for use. The sky in the central medallion is filled with auspicious "five-colored clouds,"[1] and there is a gold sun among the clouds on the right. Indeed, a small gold disk, sometimes representing the sun or occasionally the moon, appears in each of the eight landscapes that surround the central phoenixes. The mythological birds in a garden setting are reminiscent of the Museum's *Pair of covered jars* (cat. 86).

Many plates and platters produced for the export market were decorated with a central medallion surrounded by compartments; this *Charger* elaborates on that format by presenting landscape paintings in all compartments. Starting at the top and proceeding clockwise, these images include a man sitting in a pavilion gazing at the reflection of the moon in the water. This is followed by a scene of two figures on a nearby shore, with the sun shown setting behind blue and green mountains and pagodas. In the next compartment is a man seated in a small pavilion gazing at a lake, with flocks of birds in the distance and goldfish swimming in the water below. The following scene shows a large temple building with blue and gold roofs where two monks, identified by their shaved heads, have come to worship a seated image of the bodhisattva Guanyin. The landscape at the bottom of the plate depicts a man crossing an arched bridge under a willow tree, while another figure poles a small boat in the middle distance. Next are two figures, wearing blue, yellow, and green robes, sitting on the bank of a pond filled with lotuses. In the subsequent scene a man is riding a donkey with his servant following behind him; a stele (an inscribed tablet) stands on the far right, and a temple gate is just visible behind the large pine. The final scene shows the environs of a Buddhist temple with a multistoried pagoda in the foreground and the sun setting among distant peaks.

These eight images are like the pages of an album of paintings mounted around the dish. Taken together, they enumerate the activities of a cultivated gentleman, who would enjoy nature and visit scenic or historical places. Individual motifs recall images from classic Chinese poetry, although it is difficult to associate a particular scene with a specific poem. The remarkable amount of detail in individual scenes, the rich colors highlighted with gold, the many layers of poetic meanings in the landscape, and auspicious emblems on the rim all combine to produce a sumptuous display object that rewards careful observation.

NOT PREVIOUSLY PUBLISHED

NOTE

1 See Cammann, *China's Dragon Robes*, reprint, pp. 84–85, for five-colored clouds.

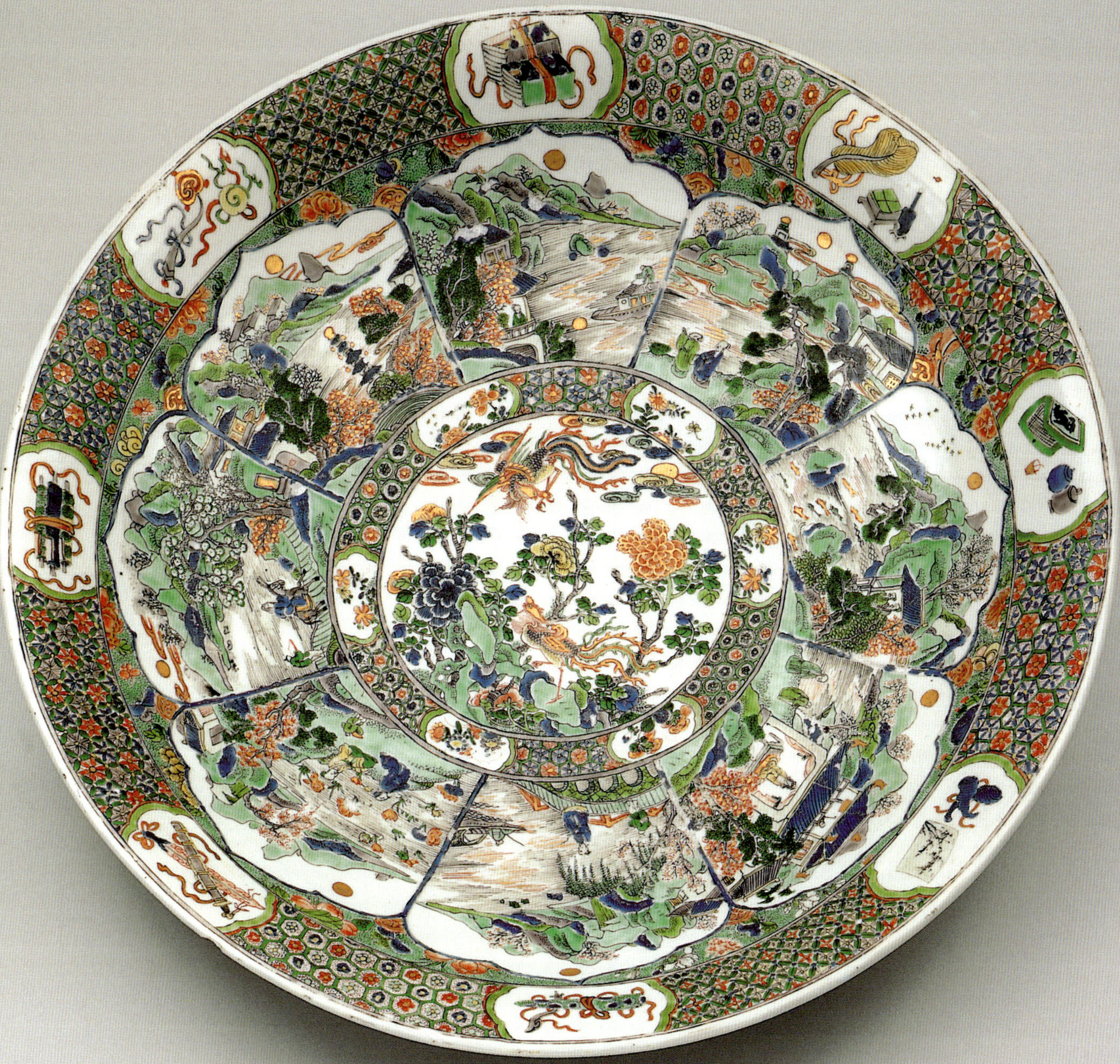

88 VASE IN THE FORM OF A SQUARE HU

Qing dynasty, Qianlong mark and period (1736–95)
Porcelain, underglaze cobalt blue and white decoration,
19 × 11 1/2 × 9 1/2 in. (48.3 × 29.2 × 24.1 cm)
Bequest of Mrs. Eugene L. Garbaty, 94.121

This Qianlong imperial *Vase in the form of a square hu* reproduces a shape well known from Shang dynasty bronzes. Like the Norton's ritual vessel *hu* (cat. 2), the Qing porcelain vase has a wide mouth, two vertical tubular handles, a broad and rounded body, and a sturdy, flaring foot. The underglaze cobalt blue decoration, however, does not reinterpret ancient forms but uses the vocabulary of Yuan and early Ming dynasty porcelain painting. A fourteenth-century design of splashing waves decorates the narrow band around the mouth, the two handles, and the foot. The designs of scrolling stems, pointed leaves, and oversize flowers filling the range between the handles and the background of the body also recreate fourteenth- and fifteenth-century porcelain decoration.

The pointed oval panel on the center of the body is a typically Qing dynasty addition to the many layers of decoration. In the form of a peach, it is filled with branches of ripe peaches, which recall the legendary peaches that grow in the orchard of the Daoist Queen Mother of the West. Those magic peaches conferred immortality on those who managed to eat them, and the peach is thus an emblem of long life. The elegant bats that fly around the peaches are part of a Qing taste for multiple auspicious emblems. The Chinese word for bat is a homophone for the word for good fortune, and since good fortune conventionally comes in five forms, five bats become a rebus for the five good fortunes. One of the bats is holding a swastika suspended on a ribbon; an emblem of the Buddha, the swastika is also a symbolic stand-in for the word for ten-thousand. Combined with the bats it invokes myriad good fortune.

While this large vessel ultimately copies an ancient bronze, the Song dynasty provides closer precedents for such porcelains. The interest in research on ancient vessels in the early twelfth century led to the revival of bronze forms in ceramics. Song examples appear in just a very few monochrome types, notably blue-green celadons, which might have recalled the patina on ancient bronzes, and *guan* wares, which have a bluish or gray-white glaze and a very distinct pattern of cracks. Two Song *guan* vases in the form of bronze *hu* from the Qing imperial collection are now in the Percival David Foundation of Chinese Art, London. One of these[1] has a rounded body with a slightly squared-off neck and a band of scrolling vines in low relief. The other,[2] rectangular in section, has plain raised bands around the mouth and between the tubular handles. Among the many Qing imitations of Song archaistic *guan* wares are a large Yongzheng-era (1722–35) vase[3] in the National Palace Museum, Taipei, and a Qianlong mark and period octagonal *hu*-shaped vase in the British Museum.[4] The Norton *Vase in the form of a square hu* takes the form of an ancient bronze, as seen through the intermediary of Song imperial porcelains, and embellishes it with designs that recall the best of early Jingdezhen blue and white porcelains.

NOT PREVIOUSLY PUBLISHED

NOTES

1 Hardy, *Illustrated Catalogue*, pl. II: no. 8. The scrolling design is almost completely obscured by the thick glaze. A Qianlong poem, referring to the vase as a *ping* (vase), not a *hu*, is engraved in the glaze on the bottom and dated in accordance with 1790.

2 Ibid., pl. I: no. 5.

3 National Palace Museum, *Qingdai danseyou ci*, cat. 81; the vase is just over 18 1/2 inches tall.

4 Jenyns, *Later Chinese Porcelain*, pl. LXIV: 2.

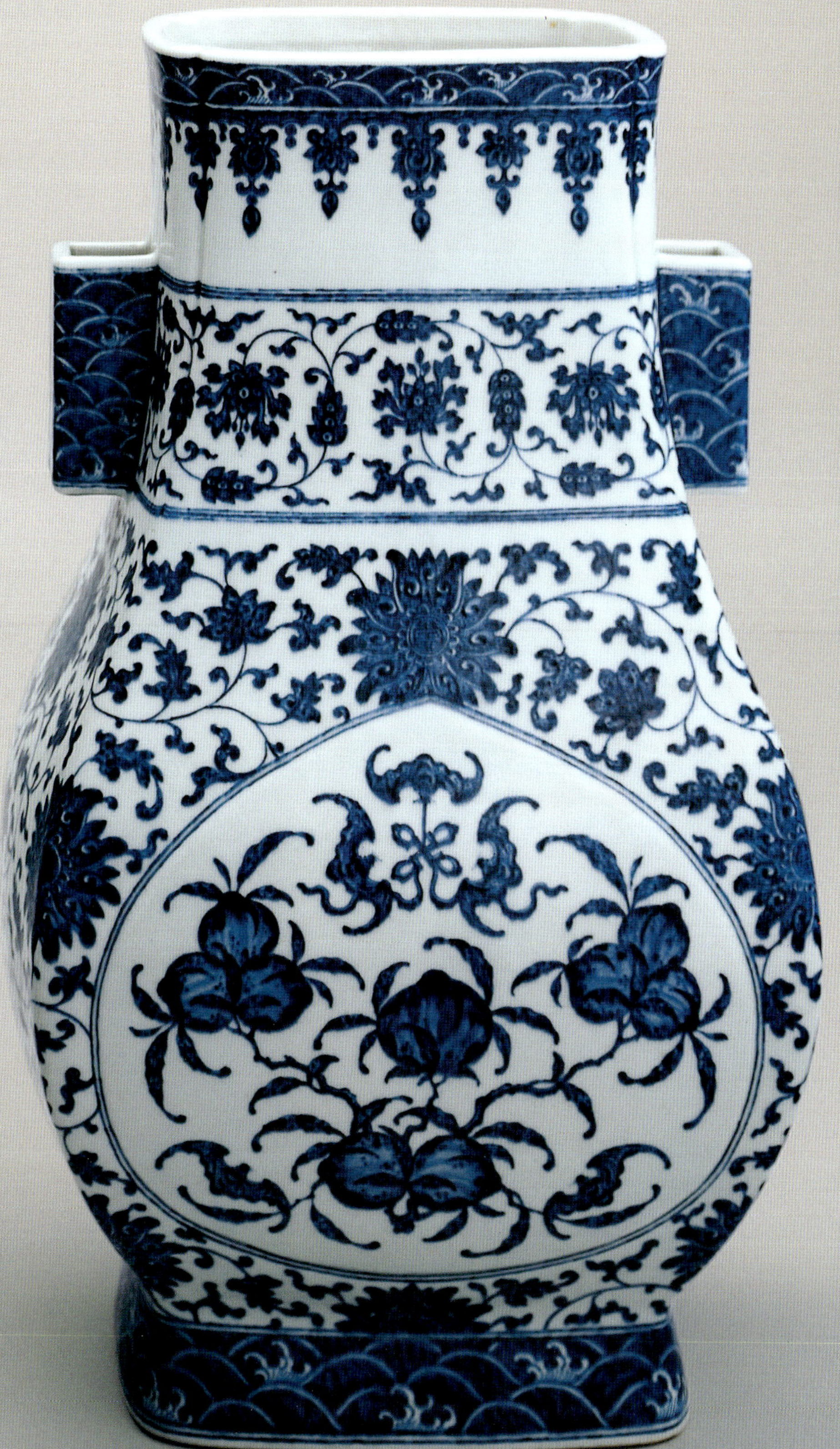

89 PUNCH BOWL WITH FOX-HUNTING SCENES

Qing dynasty, manufactured ca. 1750–70
Porcelain, overglaze enamel decoration, 6 5/16 × diam. 15 3/8 in. (16 × 39.1 cm)
Gift of Mr. and Mrs. George P. Bissell, Jr., 2002.17.1

90 "ROSE MANDARIN" PUNCH BOWL

Qing dynasty, mid-19th century
Porcelain, overglaze enamel decoration, 5 7/8 × diam. 14 3/4 in. (14.9 × 37.5 cm)
Gift of Mr. and Mrs. Thor H. Ramsing, 2000.144

Porcelains manufactured for European and American markets form an important part of Chinese export production of the seventeenth to nineteenth century. As they had been for centuries, Chinese potters proved themselves admirably adaptable to new and changing markets. Punch bowls were ordered almost exclusively for sale and use in England and North America. This *Punch bowl with fox-hunting scenes* (top) is one of a pair that reproduces four scenes of fox hunting, with two scenes on each bowl separated by floral designs surrounded by rococo-style frames. The scene partly visible here is taken from the painting *Beating and Trailing for a Hare* by James Seymour (1702–1752), one of four paintings reproduced as mezzotints by Thomas Burford (ca. 1710–1774) in 1753 and reprinted in 1787.[1] The clarity of the design, which remains quite close to its printed model, and the "spear-point" border on the interior rim of the bowl (a Chinese design adapted for European export porcelains) indicate that this *Punch bowl* was decorated just after the middle of the eighteenth century.

By the second half of the eighteenth century the range of transparent overglaze enamel colors in combinations emphasizing greens or opaque pinks and reds were well known to customers for Chinese export porcelains. These palettes would be dubbed *famille verte* and *famille rose* in Jacquemart and Le Blant's 1862 *Histoire artistique, industrielle et commerciale de la Porcelaine.*[2] Toward the end of the eighteenth and throughout the nineteenth century, Western taste favored increasingly florid overglaze enamel colors and combinations of "Chinese" designs. In general, figures on Chinese porcelains were dubbed "mandarins," and a relatively distinctive combination of elaborate floral designs surrounding figure scenes earned the name "Rose Mandarin."[3] The Norton *"Rose Mandarin" punch bowl* is a good example of the type. Such Rose Mandarin (sometimes called Rose Medallion) designs also proved popular in Muslim markets, and there is a significant body of pieces painted with similar designs as wares for the West but inscribed in Arabic and Persian for customers in Qajar Iran.[4] Chinese motifs and European designs form a decorative amalgam that covers every surface of the Norton *"Rose Mandarin" punch bowl* and contrasts with the more open and reserved treatment of the eighteenth-century fox-hunting bowl, clearly illustrating the shifting tastes of European and American customers for Chinese porcelain.

NOT PREVIOUSLY PUBLISHED

NOTES

1 Phillips, *China-Trade Porcelain*, pl. 133 and pl. 59; see also Krahl and Harrison-Hall, *Ancient Chinese Trade Ceramics*, cat. 46, who give a different identification of the artists, citing Howard and Ayers, *China for the West*, vol. 1, p. 280:b, and Hervouët and Bruneau, *La porcelaine des compagnies des Indes*, nos. 3.25:a,b. See also Hyde, *Oriental Lowestoft*, pl. XVII: figs. 69–71.

2 The mostly transparent enamels of *famille verte* are described on pp. 67–68, and the opaque colors, including a distinctive pink, are described on pp. 72 ff.

3 See Mudge, *Chinese Export Porcelain*, p. 167. I believe the "rose" refers to the elaborate flowers in the border and medallion designs on these wares and not to the *famille rose* palette, a term first published only in 1862; see n. 2 above.

4 See Howard and Ayers, *China for the West*, vol. 2, nos. 495–97.

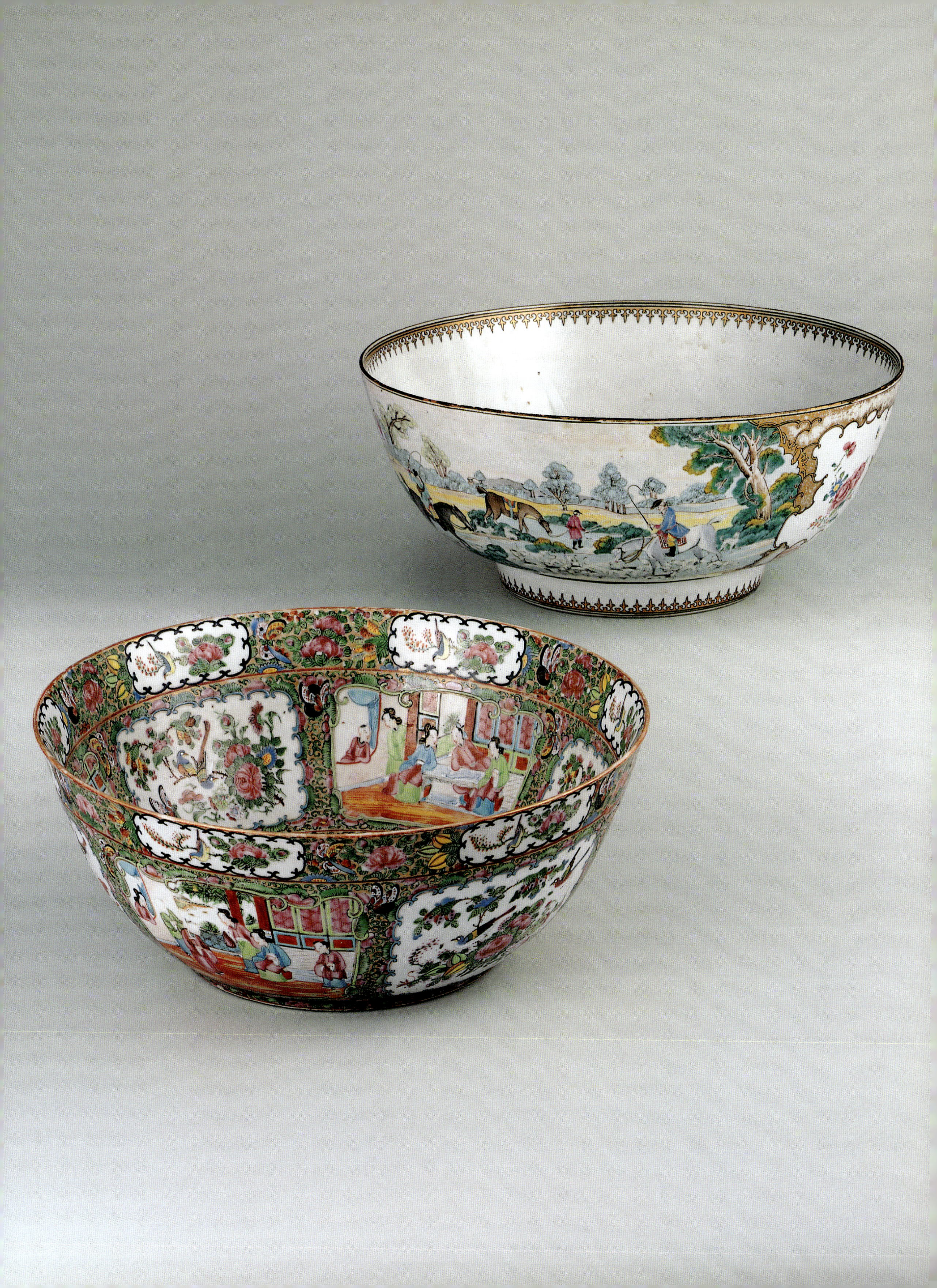

91 INDIVIDUAL CHIMESTONE (*TEQING*)

Qing dynasty, Qianlong period, dated 1761
Green jade and gold lacquer, 17 ¼ × 12 × 1 ⅛ in. (43.8 × 30.5 × 2.9 cm)
Gift of R.H. Norton, 42.20

92 INDIVIDUAL CHIMESTONE (*TEQING*)

Qing dynasty, Qianlong period, dated 1761
Green jade and gold lacquer, 26 ¾ × 15 ¼ × 1 ⅛ in. (67.9 × 38.7 × 2.9 cm)
Gift of R.H. Norton, 42.21

These two individual chimestones (*teqing*) are number eight (left) and number twelve (right), the latter being the smallest from a set of twelve, graduated in size, completed in 1761.[1] Cut from dark green Central Asian jade, they are decorated on both sides. The sides we see here are inscribed in archaistic seal script characters with the number and musical note of the stone (the line of six characters reading right to left along the top of the inscription) and the date (in seven columns of slightly smaller characters), which details the year, month, and the very day their carving was finally, and officially, complete. While the characters are engraved in the stone and filled with gold pigment, the design of dragons pursuing a flaming jewel is painted on the surface in slightly raised lines of gold lacquer.

The chance discovery in 1759 of a partial set of Zhou dynasty bronze bells inspired the Qianlong emperor to commission sets of bells for court ritual music. Following Confucian traditions regarding ritual music, corresponding sets of jade chimestones were also ordered for use in court ceremonies within the Forbidden City and in Qing imperial temples. At least four sets of individual chimestones, each stone corresponding to a month of the lunar calendar and played at the appropriate time of the year, were made in 1761. Two complete sets of twelve remain in China,[2] and the Norton chimestones are from another, dispersed set. Although Horace Jayne asserted that they were made for presentation to the Temple of Confucius in Beijing,[3] no inscriptions on extant stones contain references to particular temples or palaces, and we do not know where these two were used.

Chimestones, however, are among the most ancient Chinese musical instruments, and one of the best known is a large Shang dynasty hardstone chime, engraved with a design of a tiger and dating to about 1200 BCE, that was excavated in 1950 at Anyang, the site of the last Shang capital.[4] The inverted V-shape of chimestones was probably the standard form of this instrument by the Zhou dynasty, when sets of sixteen stones (*bianqing*), generally smaller than *teqing* and suspended together on one rack, became standard.[5] There was ample precedent in the Confucian Classics for the use of chimestones in ritual music, and Qianlong imperial texts make constant references to these sacred texts. The proper performance of ritual music, like the correct performance of any ritual, helped to legitimize the rule of the Manchu Qing emperors, and the spectacular size—and number—of individual jade chimestones is just one reflection of this crucial aspect of Qing imperial rule.

PUBLISHED

91: Nott, *Chinese Jades*, no. 21; Jayne, *The Chinese Collections*, nos. 226–27
92: Nott, *Chinese Jades*, no. 22; Jayne, *The Chinese Collections*, nos. 226–27

NOTES

1 The chimestones are discussed at length in the essay "Qianlong Imperial Jades in the Norton Museum of Art" in this catalogue.
2 One is in the Forbidden City and the other in the Qing imperial palace at Shenyang, the former Manchu Qing capital north of the Great Wall.
3 Jayne, *The Chinese Collections*, nos. 226–27.
4 Rogers and others, *China 5,000 Years*, cat. 9.
5 Bartholomew and Clark, "The Walters Art Gallery," p. 133. This article is a seminal study of jade chimestones. For archaeologically excavated sets of bells and chimestones, see So, ed., *Music in the Age of Confucius*, focusing on the tomb of Marquis Yi of Zeng (d. 433 BCE).

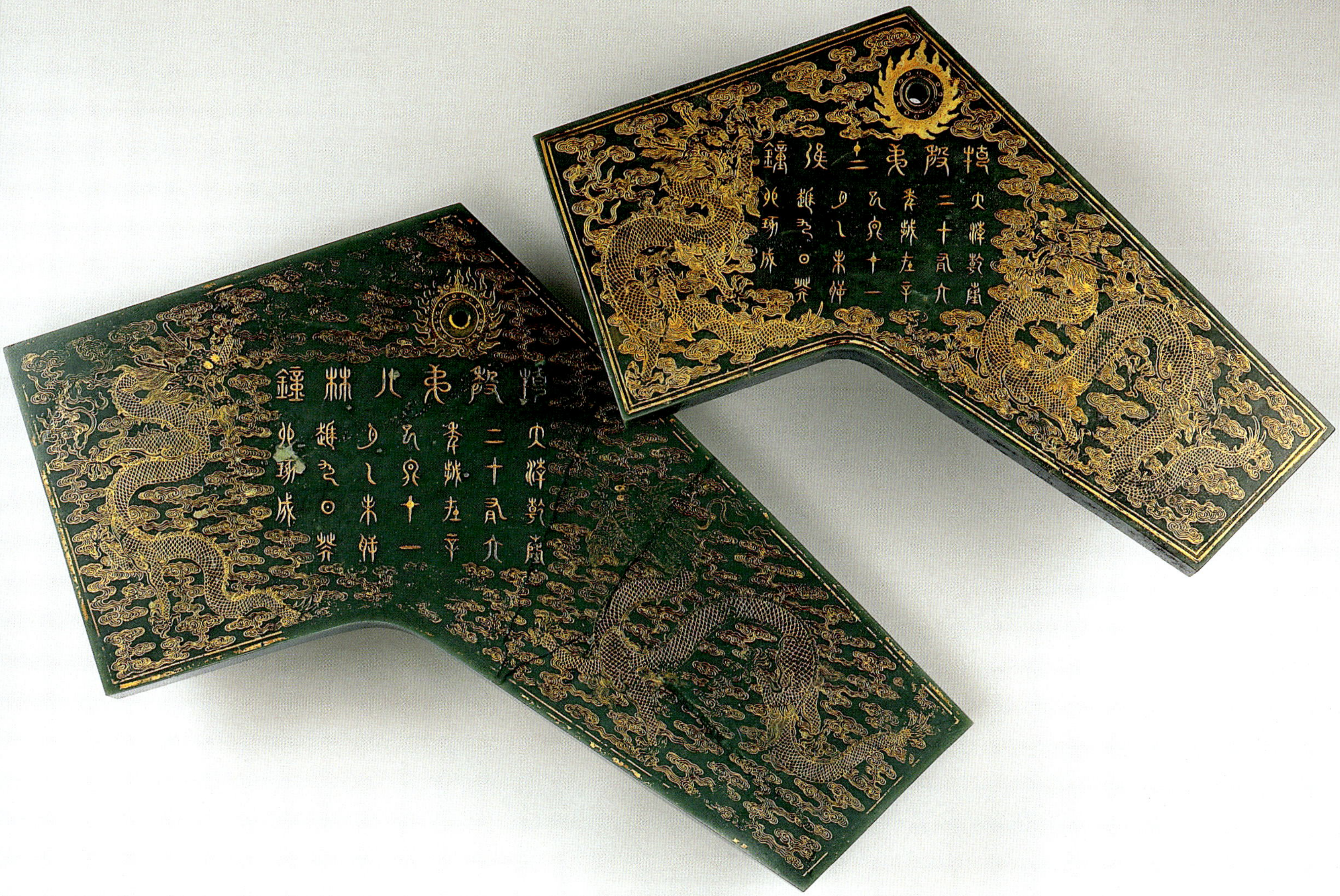

93 VASE IN THE FORM OF A HU

Qing dynasty, Qianlong period, dated 1778
Green jade, traces of gold, 17 ¼ × 9 ⅞ × 6 ⅜ in. (43.8 × 25.1 × 16.2 cm)
Gift of R.H. Norton, 42.77

The long inscription between the bands on the front of this massive jade *Vase in the form of a hu* gives the date, 1778, and tells the story of one of the most notorious cases of official corruption in eighteenth-century China.[1] Qing conquests of the territories of Central Asia brought the vast areas of Xinjiang, literally the "new frontier," under Chinese domination and established the western borders of modern China. The Kunlun Mountains and the Chinese side of the Pamirs were the location of deposits of nephrite — true jade — the majority of which officially belonged to the Imperial Household Department. The Chinese conscripted local Muslims to gather jade boulders from the rivers on either side of the city of Khotan and to mine jade from deposits in the Mirtagh Mountains. Among other official and ritual uses for jade, it was the goal of the emperor to acquire blocks big enough to carve sets of individual chimestones (*teqing*) for use in the performance of court and ritual music (see cats. 91, 92).

Although local officials were allowed to keep small amounts of jade for sale, the bulk was to be shipped to the imperial jade-carving workshops in Beijing. Official corruption, however, was a fact of life in the administration of the empire, and emperors had to balance tolerance of small-scale money-making schemes with large-scale corruption that threatened their own sources of income and the stability of the state. Sent in 1776 to rule an area centered on the city of Yarkand, the Detached Grand Minister Gao Pu was officially a bondservant, technically a slave of the imperial clan, but in reality a powerful official who owed his allegiance directly to the Qianlong emperor. Gao Pu quickly became involved in large-scale jade mining, at one point conscripting over 3,000 of the Muslim inhabitants of the region to work without pay. He and local merchants devised complex schemes to ship the jade to Suzhou, the southern Chinese city where the best jade-carving workshops were located. The profits from diverting the precious stone to the burgeoning private market were to be shared among a group of conspirators, and bribery helped to corrupt officials along the shipping routes. The scheme, unparalleled up to that time for its scale,[2] was soon exposed and Gao Pu was executed in 1788— the date inscribed on the Norton vessel. There is one other inscription on the hu, the four-character phrase *Qianlong fang gu*, on the bottom. Meaning "imitating antiquity in the Qianlong reign," it classifies the archaistic form of the vessel, which imitates an ancient bronze (see cat. 2). Deliberately simple — almost crude — in its carving, the Norton *Vase in the form of a hu* provides a large surface on which the emperor could make an emphatic statement of his power and advertise the just punishment of corrupt officials.

PUBLISHED

Nott, *Chinese Jades*, no. 78; Jayne, *The Chinese Collections*, no. 247

NOTES

1 The jade *hu* is discussed at length in the essay "Qianlong Imperial Jades in the Norton Museum of Art" in this catalogue.

2 The fines levied against the main group of conspirators totaled 270,000 taels or Chinese ounces of silver. In addition, the emperor recovered literally tons of smuggled jade and substantial amounts of confiscated property from many of those punished.

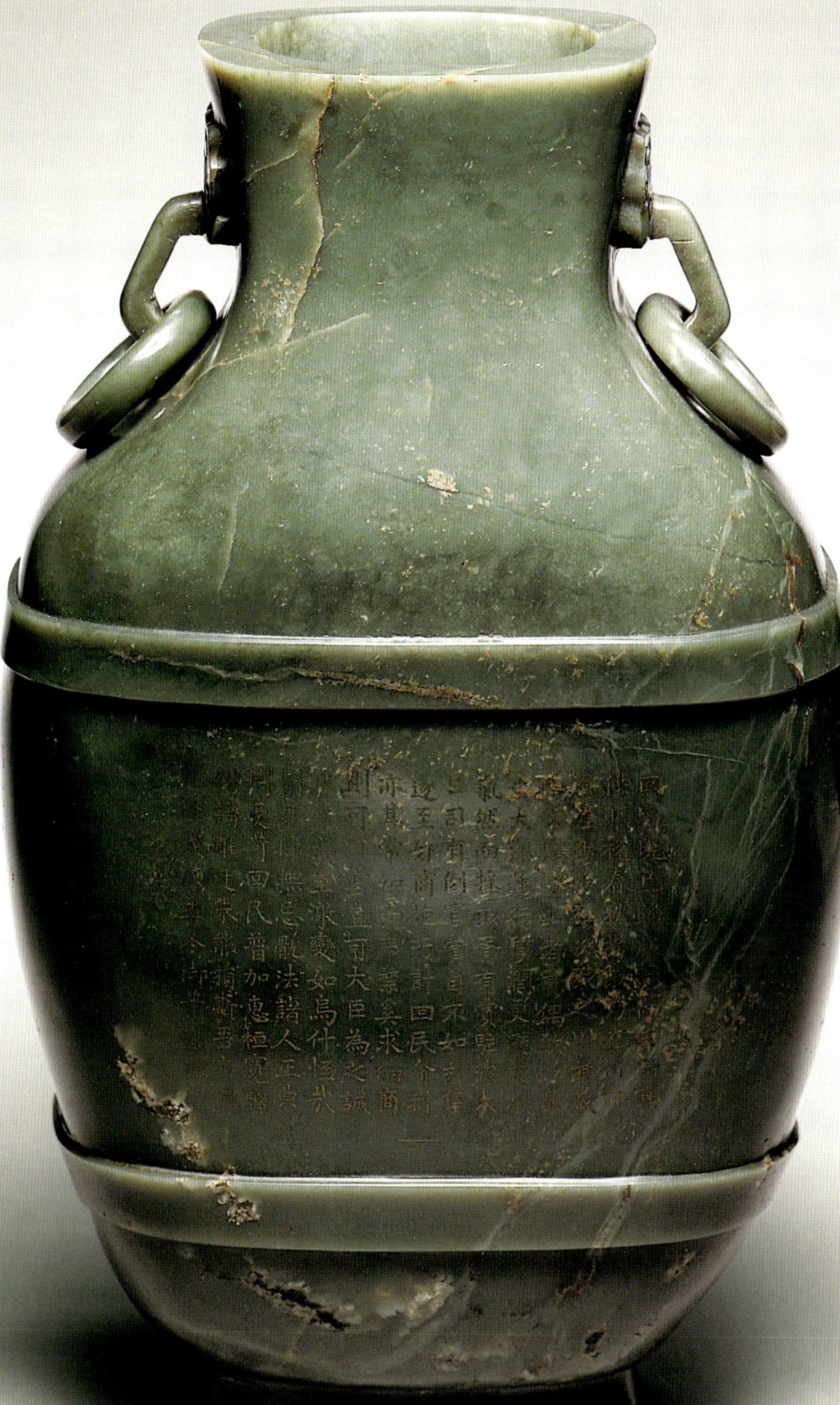

94 BOWL WITH SEVEN BUDDHAS

Qing dynasty, Qianlong period, dated 1777
Green jade, traces of gold, 5 7/8 × diam. 9 1/2 in. (14.9 × 24.1 cm)
Gift of R.H. Norton, 42.66

In 1777, tribute presented to the imperial court from the sixth Panchen Lama (one of the incarnations or "living Buddhas" who, along with the Dalai Lama, were the leaders of the Yellow sect of Tibetan Buddhism) included a Tibetan scroll depicting seven Buddhas.[1] According to the lengthy Qianlong imperial text (not visible in the photograph) engraved on the rounded bottom of the *Bowl with seven Buddhas*, it was one official—the Grand Lama of Beijing, Rolpay Dorje—who correctly identified the Buddhas and their lineages from Tibetan and Chinese sutras (the sacred texts of Buddhism). Rolpay Dorje was the current incarnation of a lineage of Mongol lamas resident in Beijing and an important advisor to the Qianlong emperor. Tibetan Buddhism had long been the religion of the Manchu Qing imperial clan, and a substantial body of Tibetan Buddhist architecture and religious objects remains in the Forbidden City in Beijing,[2] the imperial summer villa at Rehe (Jehol), and the palace at Shenyang, both north of the Great Wall.

The seven Buddhas include Shakyamuni, the historical Buddha, and the six Buddhas—manifestations of the same Buddha nature—who preceded Shakyamuni in past ages. The ultimate identity of all seven Buddhas is probably reflected in the use of an identical image to represent each figure. The seven texts engraved and filled with gold pigment between the images are attributed to the individual Buddhas.[3] The long text on the bottom of the bowl records that the emperor ordered the construction of a stupa, a Tibetan-style reliquary shrine, to contain the scroll of seven Buddhas. Although the stupa has not been identified, or possibly no longer exists, it was not necessarily a free-standing building but more likely a smaller shrine in the form of a stupa, perhaps even a gilt-bronze container for the scroll.[4] In 1779, the sixth Panchen Lama, who had earlier sent the original scroll in tribute, expressed his desire to be present at the celebrations of the Qianlong emperor's seventieth birthday. An official visit by a Panchen Lama was almost unprecedented, and the emperor made elaborate preparations, including the construction of a Tibetan-style monastery and temple for the Panchen Lama at Rehe.[5] The Panchen Lama was also received by the emperor in Beijing where, in 1780, he died suddenly of smallpox. This tragic and highly inauspicious death prompted the Qianlong emperor to construct a golden stupa to contain the Lama's embalmed body on the long road back to Tibet and to build a white stone stupa to hold the gifts and relics he had brought with him on his ill-fated journey.

PUBLISHED

Nott, *Chinese Jades*, no. 67; Jayne, *The Chinese Collections*, no. 217

NOTES

1 The bowl is discussed at length in the essay "Qianlong Imperial Jades in the Norton Museum of Art" in this catalogue.
2 On Tibetan Buddhist relics in Beijing, see Palace Museum, *Qinggong Zangzhuan Fojiao wenwu*.
3 Although the Buddhas are not identified here, a carved lacquer bowl in the National Palace Museum, Taipei, has the identical texts carved between seven Buddha images, and the names of each are inscribed above the images. See Tsai, *Monarchy and Its Buddhist Way*, no. 85, reproduced as fig. 3 on page 58 of this catalogue.
4 I am grateful to Prof. Susan Naquin who discussed this possibility in a personal communication, October 2002.
5 On the Panchen Lama's visit, see Bartholomew, "*Thangkas*," pp. 174–78.

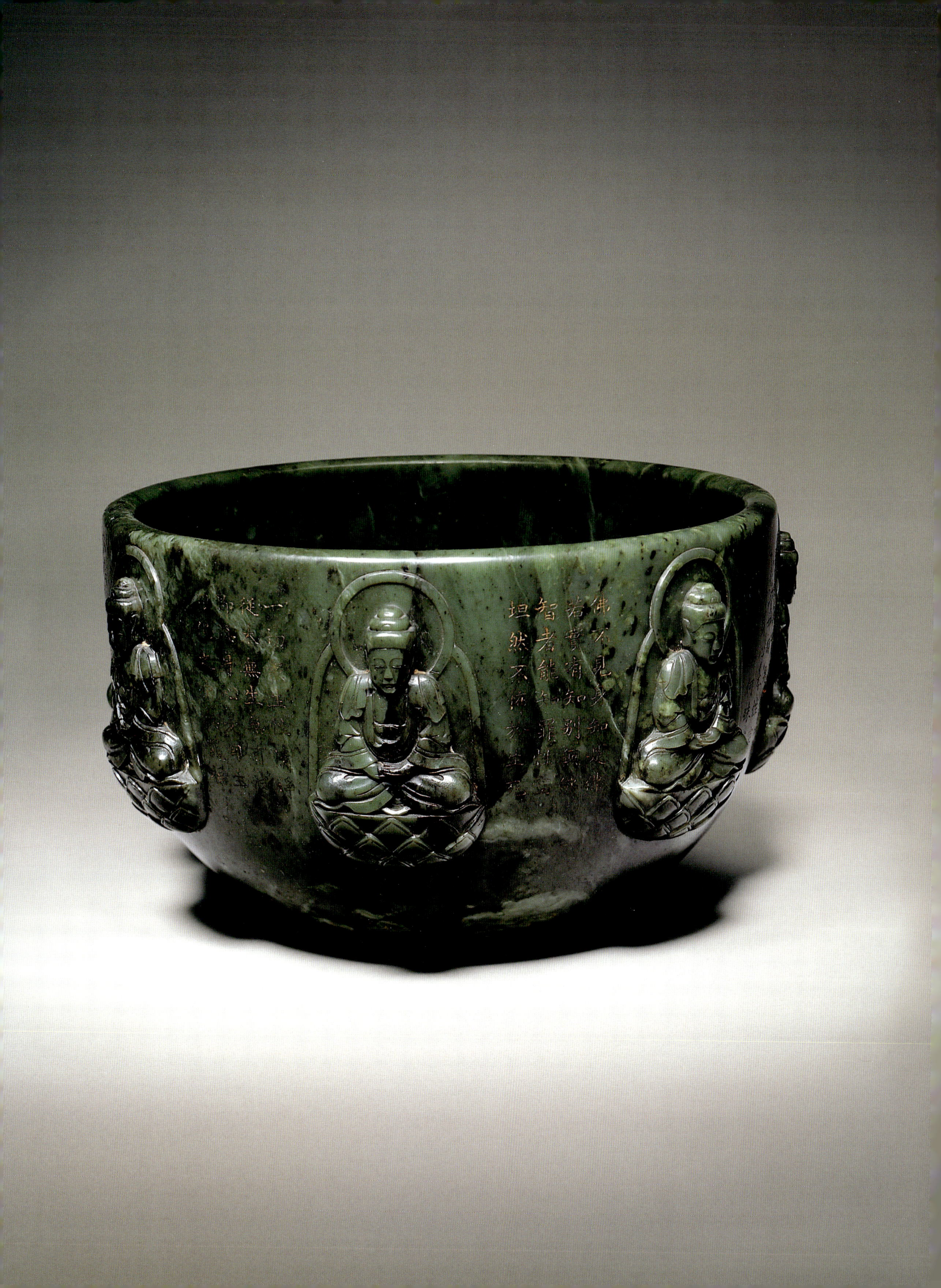

95 FIGURE OF MULAN ON HORSEBACK

Qing dynasty, 18th century
White jade, 8 1/2 × 4 1/2 × 2 in. (21.6 × 11.4 × 5.1 cm)
Gift of R.H. Norton, 42.9

The story of Mulan is first recorded in an anonymous ballad of the fifth or sixth century; the tale is set in the Northern Wei dynasty, a time when northern China was ruled by emperors of the Tuoba clan of the Xianbei. The emperors conscripted men to fight their wars, but the young girl Mulan purchased a horse and took up weapons to fight in her aged father's place. Dressed as a man and distinguishing herself in battle, she remained unrecognized by her fellow soldiers. Returning to her family after ten years' absence, she doffed her armor and took up again her role as a dutiful daughter.[1] The story of Mulan was the inspiration for at least one sixteenth-century *zaju* drama, a theatrical form mixing music, poetry, drama, and action that had developed into an important literati art form by the Ming dynasty. Xu Wei's (1521–1593) drama *Zi Mulan ti fu congjun* (The Heroine Mulan Joins the Army for Her Father) is one of a group of four plays of which two in particular focus on the courage, determination, and superiority of their female characters.[2]

The figure of Mulan is also represented in woodblock prints, which appeared in increasing numbers in the late Ming and early Qing as illustrations to published plays and popular fiction or as compendia of images. A two-page image of Mulan appears in a collection called *Lienü zhuan* (Biographies of exemplary women), first published in the Ming Wanli era (1573–1619) with designs attributed to the well-known artist Qiu Ying (act. early 16th century), and later recut and reprinted in the Qing Qianlong era.[3] She is shown wearing a man's helmet and robes and carrying a sword, while soldiers wait with a horse that is remarkably similar to the mount we see in the Museum's jade carving. Both these animals are square-headed ponies richly caparisoned with large hanging tassels.

While Mulan is conventionally shown wearing a helmet with a plume on top, in the Norton figure she has a long veil over her hair and a large peony flower on top of her head. While she still has her horse and sword, she is depicted as a mature woman dressed in long, flowing robes, not in the costume of a soldier. The robes recall the female manifestations of the bodhisattva Guanyin that were favored in later Chinese popular Buddhism. Guanyin's role as a protector of people in danger seems here to be mingled with Mulan's identity as a virtuous woman who spared her father (and a younger brother, in some versions of the tale) the dangers of war, and this hybrid jade image of *Mulan on horseback* borrows many traits from Guanyin to depict the legendary heroine.

PUBLISHED

Nott, *Chinese Jades*, no. 10; Jayne, *The Chinese Collections*, no. 229

NOTES

1 See Frankel, *The Flowering Plum*, pp. 68–72, for the text, translation, and succinct commentary on the poem.
2 Nienhauser, *The Indiana Companion*, pp. 436–37.
3 Zhou Wu, *Zhongguo banhuashi tulu*, p. 117, reproducing facing pages, *juan* 9:33b–34a.

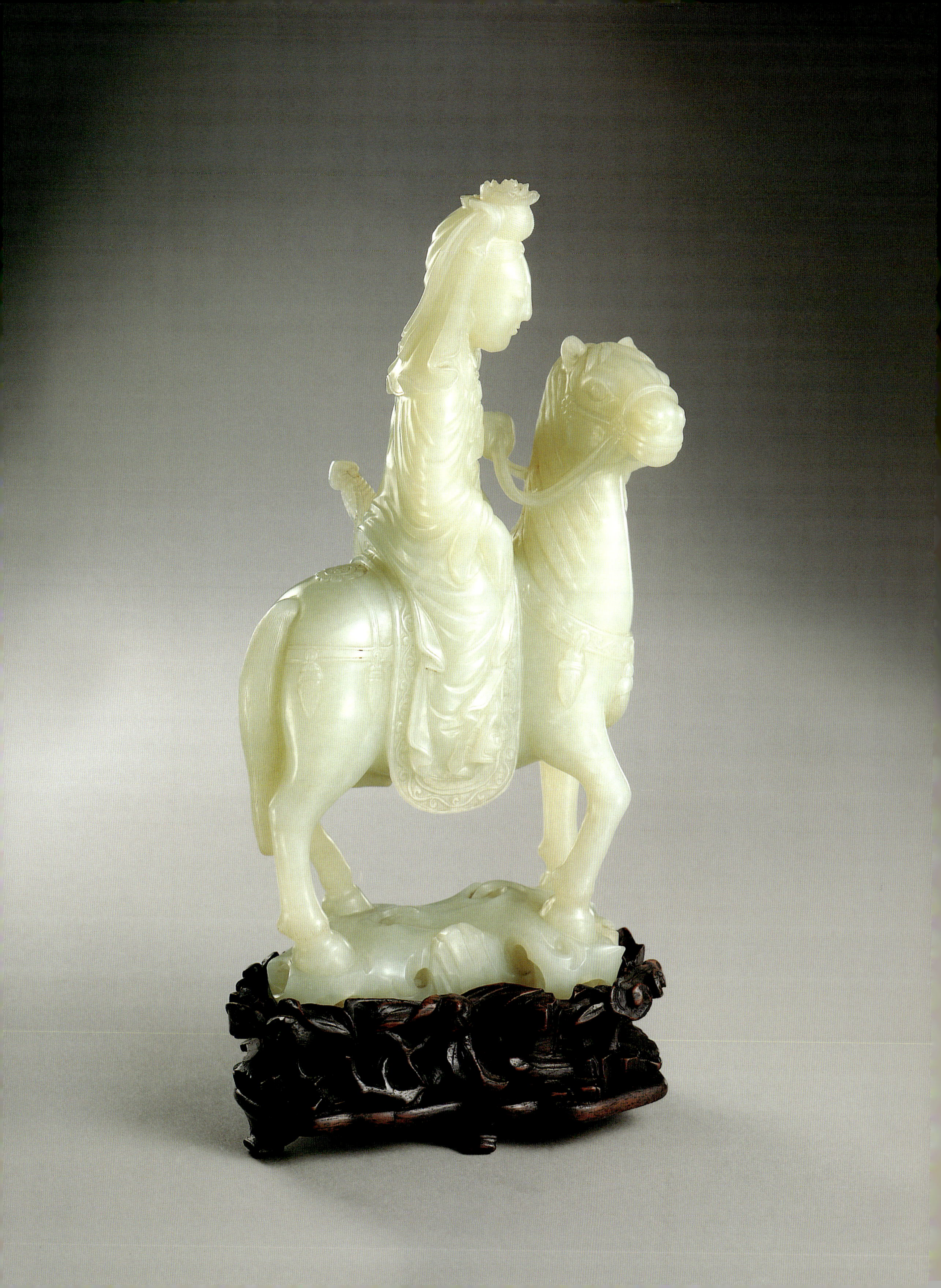

96 GREEN JADE MOUNTAIN

Qing dynasty, Qianlong period (1736–95)
Green jade, 6 5/8 × 9 1/2 × 4 in. (16.8 × 24.1 × 10.2 cm)
Gift of R.H. Norton, 42.16

97 WHITE JADE MOUNTAIN

Qing dynasty, Qianlong period (1736–95)
White jade, 7 × 10 3/8 × 3 1/2 in. (17.8 × 26.4 × 8.9 cm)
Gift of R.H. Norton, 42.15

These two "mountains" are miniature landscapes carved on jade rocks. The most highly valued jade from Chinese Central Asia came from the rivers that flowed down from the Kunlun Mountains near the city of Khotan. Members of the local Muslim population were conscripted by the Chinese to comb the riverbeds for jade pebbles and rocks. Landscapes carved on pieces of jade often preserved some of the natural shape of the stone, especially if it suggested a mountain form. The carving, too, preserved traces of the weathered skin, which had a different texture or color from the jade interior. The jade carvers left some of the brown stain from the surface on the *White jade mountain* on the right to suggest, perhaps, a trace of color in the landscape.

The subjects depicted on these two jades are processions through mountain landscapes, in which many of the figures bear auspicious emblems. The route of the *White jade mountain* begins on the back side of the stone; horsemen on the visible side are emerging from the mouth of a cave at the left-hand edge. Each figure carries weapons, such as bows and arrows, or various objects. The fourth figure from the left, about in the center of the composition, is holding a large vase from which emerges a V-shaped chimestone (see cats. 91, 92) and three halberd blades, details which are barely visible in the photograph. This odd combination forms a rebus that signifies a wish to rise easily to the highest official ranks. The procession continues to the top center of the boulder where two tiny horsemen gallop toward distant palace or temple buildings on a high terrace. The giant grotto that contains these figures suggests that this is a magical paradise or realm of Daoist Immortals, which were reached by passage through a cave.[1]

Having passed through a cave, the procession on the *Green jade mountain* (left) follows a road that winds downward from the upper left. The most clearly readable auspicious emblem here is the elephant with a large vase on its back at the bottom center. This particular motif occurs frequently in Qing dynasty decorative arts; modeled in a wide variety of precious materials, pairs of elephants supporting large vases sometimes flanked imperial thrones, and the combination forms another rebus. The phrase *tai ping you xiang* describes literally what we see, that "with the large vase there is an elephant." Written with different characters, however, these words announce that "[in an era of] great peace, there are signs." The "signs" are any of a number of phenomena—the reported appearance of legendary animals, stalks of grain with double heads, or brilliantly colored clouds—that indicate Heaven's blessing on the current dynasty. Although we need not give too much emphasis to the auspicious rebuses on these two jade mountains, the use of such puns and emblems as the basis of decorative schemes becomes common in the Qing and more frequent as the dynasty progresses.

PUBLISHED

96: Nott, *Chinese Jades*, no. 17; Jayne, *The Chinese Collections*, no. 202
97: Nott, *Chinese Jades*, no. 16; Jayne, *The Chinese Collections*, no. 203

NOTE

1 For an extended discussion of this theme, see Munakata, *Sacred Mountains*, esp. section III, "Mountains and Daoistic Images of the Immortals' Realm," pp. 111–72.

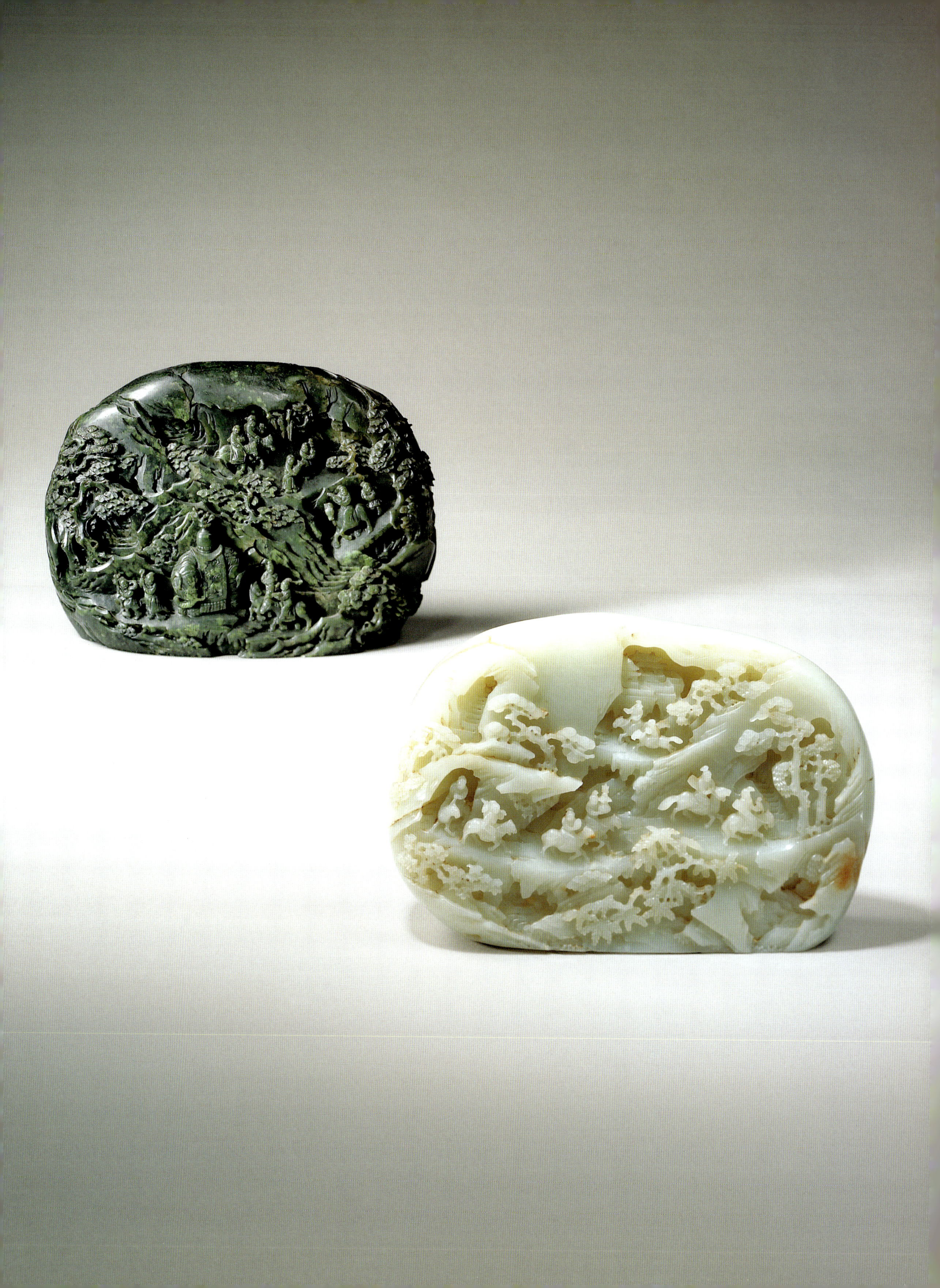

98 MOUNTAIN WITH IMMORTALS

Qing dynasty, 18th–19th century
Amber, 12 ½ × 19 ¼ × 7 ½ in. (31.8 × 48.9 × 19.1 cm)
Gift of R.H. Norton, 42.17

This carving of a *Mountain with Immortals* preserves the shape of an extraordinarily large piece of amber. Amber is not the fossilized remains of pine tree resins but the actual ancient resins from a wide variety of conifers and broad-leaved trees. A combination of conditions was necessary to concentrate, bury, and preserve tree resins, and deposits of amber, though widely scattered across the world, are rare.[1] The source for the Norton amber *Mountain* is most likely northern Myanmar (Burma) where deposits were found in the Hukawng valley. Amber from this region was exported to China, perhaps beginning in very early times, as was Burmese jadeite in the eighteenth century (see cat. 104).[2] As on the green and white carved jade *Mountains* (cats. 96, 97), the landscape on the *Mountain with Immortals* represents mountains that have magical associations. The group of palace buildings nestled in a mountain valley at the top of the carving includes a gate as well as an open pavilion, suggesting passage from a realm beyond the present scene. The steps of the narrow pathway wind down the right-hand edge of the carving, and two figures accompanied by a servant are walking along a terraced mountain road. The two are depicted as aged scholars with long beards and wearing flowing robes; one leans on a walking stick. Although these attributes are seen in images of Laozi, the founder of historical Daoism, they have also been used to represent both specific Daoist Immortals and figures like the present ones, who cannot be identified with any particular legendary or historical individuals. The bottom of the piece of amber is carved with a dragon among clouds, further supporting the interpretation of this as a magical landscape.

PUBLISHED

Nott, *Chinese Jades*, no. 18; Jayne, *The Chinese Collections*, no. 253

NOTES

1 Grimaldi, *Amber*, pp. 12–13, map p. 20.
2 Ibid., pp. 41–42. Page 41 shows a piece of Burmese amber, 19 ½ inches long, discovered in 1860 and later presented to the Natural History Museum, London, which has a deep red-brown color and a pattern of fractures very similar to the Norton carving. See pp. 194, 199, 202 for a discussion of the history of amber in China, citing Berthold Laufer, "Historical Jottings on Amber in Asia," *Journal of the American Anthropological Association* 1 (1907), p. 3.

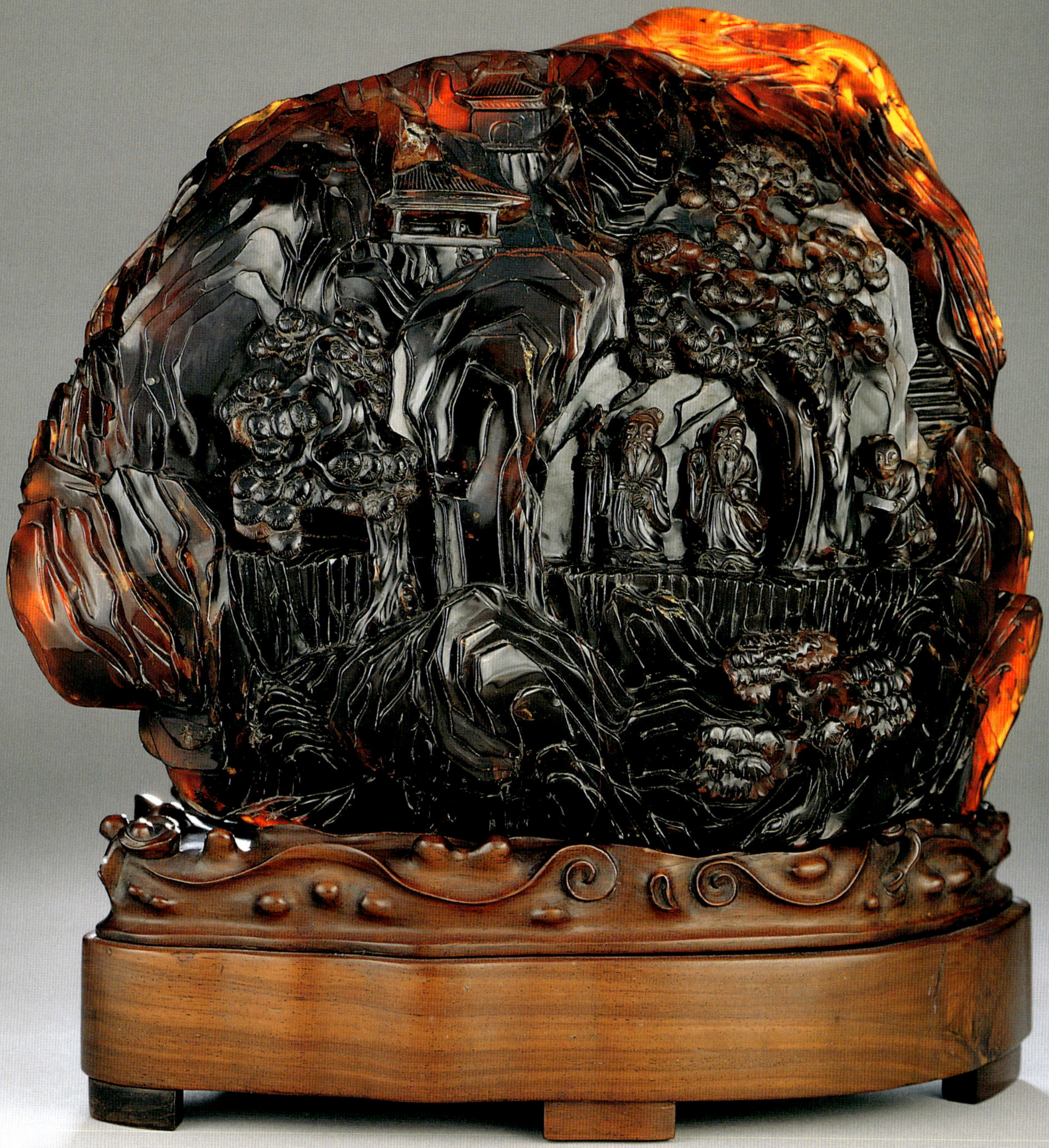

99 RECUMBENT WATER BUFFALO

Qing dynasty, mid- to late 18th century
Dark green jade, 4 5/8 × 11 3/8 × 6 3/8 in. (11.7 × 28.9 × 16.2 cm)
Gift of R.H. Norton, 42.19

The Norton *Recumbent water buffalo* is one of a surprisingly large group of similar jade animals that raise many unsolved questions of style, provenance, and date. In general they have the same attributes we see here, which are based on observation of these common domestic animals. They lie placidly with their legs folded under or alongside them, the body curves, and the head is turned as if looking up at the viewer. Broad horns sweep back from the flat head, and curled tails typically rest on the animal's haunches. In most examples the bottom of the jade is also carefully modeled. What distinguishes one from the other is the great variety of size, the various colors of the jades, and the relative naturalism of the carving.

One of the largest of these buffaloes, one whose history is probably the source of some of the confusion about the group, was in the bequest of O.C. Raphael to the Fitzwilliam Museum, Cambridge. Approximately sixteen inches long and carved of mottled green jade, it was exhibited at the Burlington Fine Arts Club, London, in 1915.[1] The catalogue stated that the buffalo, a horse, and a "dragon-horse" stood until 1900 in the Forbidden City, with the implication that they were looted in the aftermath of the Boxer Rebellion. An unidentified "manuscript catalogue that existed in the Palace" listed these as Han dynasty carvings, although the Burlington catalogue tentatively dates the massive buffalo to the sixth century.[2] This buffalo and an accompanying horse had supposedly been brought to the Forbidden City by the Ming Yongle emperor (r. 1403–24). A version of this chain of events is repeated by Una Pope-Hennessey as early as 1923.[3]

It is perhaps echoes of the story of the Yongle-era buffalo that have led to some of the larger of these jade animals being dated to the Ming, but in truth there are very few securely dated examples from any period. A tiny jade recumbent buffalo from the ca. 1200 BCE tomb of Fu Hao demonstrates that the pose, with the head turned back, is a natural one for representation.[4] Na Zhiliang notes that carvings of the Tang through the Ming (a period of almost 1,000 years) share many of the same general characteristics.[5] The dating of the Norton *Buffalo* to the eighteenth century is based in part on the quality of the stone. The jade is dramatically mottled with different colored inclusions, ranging from black to cool gray and even deeply translucent areas. This type of dark green jade is associated with jade from Central Asia, which came under Chinese domination in the mid-eighteenth century and provided large pieces of jade for just this type of carving.[6] The soft, almost muted polish of the surface, which avoids any glossiness and seems to allow the inner quality of the jade to shine through, is typical of jades dated by inscription, often only a reign mark, to the reign of the Qianlong emperor (1736–95).

PUBLISHED

Nott, *Chinese Jades*, no. 19; Hartman, *Chinese Jade of Five Centuries*, p. 56, pl. 9; Jayne, *The Chinese Collections*, no. 238

NOTES

1 *Catalogue of a Collection of Objects of Chinese Art*, p. 35, pl. XXII.
2 Ibid., pp. 28–29.
3 Pope-Hennessey, *Early Chinese Jades*, p. 107. See also Gray and others, *Chinese Jade Throughout the Ages*, p. 118.
4 *Yinxu Fu Hao mu*, pl. 136.2.
5 *Yuqi tongshi*, vol. 1, p. 158, fig. 62B.
6 See the discussion of jade mining in the essay "Qianlong Imperial Jades in the Norton Museum of Art" in this catalogue, pp. 64–65.

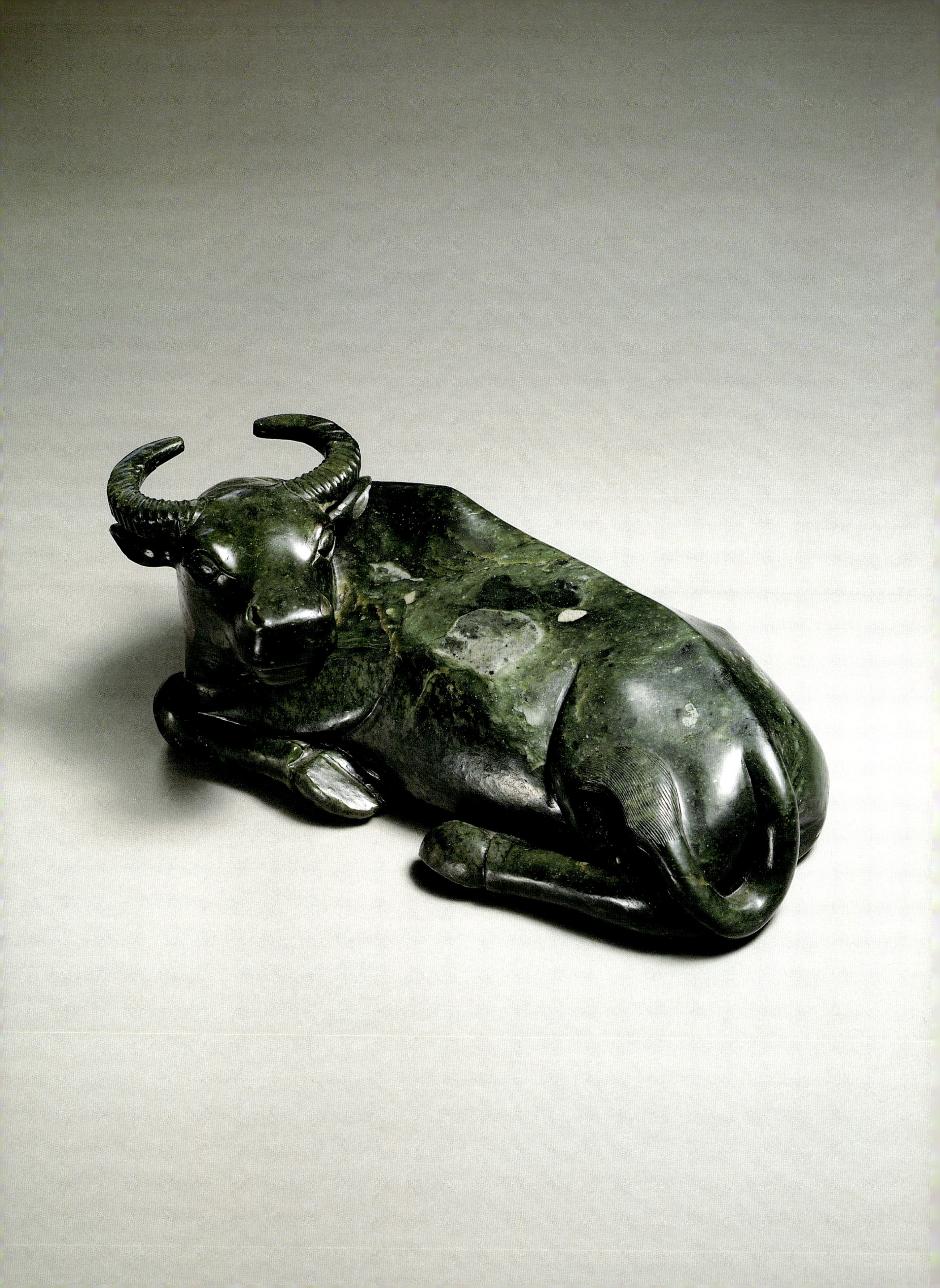

100 INCENSE BURNER IN THE FORM OF A SQUARE DING

Qing dynasty, 18th–19th century
Lapis lazuli, 7 ¾ × 5 ⅝ × 3 in. (19.7 × 14.3 × 7.6 cm)
Gift of R.H. Norton, 42.98a-b

101 INCENSE BURNER

Qing dynasty, 18th–19th century
Malachite, 7 ⅛ × 7 ¼ × 5 ½ in. (18.1 × 18.4 × 14 cm)
Gift of R.H. Norton, 42.97a-b

Carved from semiprecious stones, these two covered vessels take the form of archaistic *ding*, or ritual food containers on legs (see cats. 5, 6). Although *ding* are usually tripods, square *fang ding*, with four legs, appeared about 1200 BCE, and are also a well-known ritual bronze shape.[1] Superficially similar to functioning incense burners, their solid covers and valuable materials probably prevented their actual use as anything but decorative objects. Both take ancient designs and interpret them freely in their decoration.[2]

The deep blue, lapis lazuli vessel (left) is thick and elaborately carved. Squared spirals form the four legs, which resemble those of heavy pieces of furniture. Symmetrically placed mythological birds are the central decorative motif on the body, and the square flanges of Shang and Zhou bronzes are here treated as sharp, flamelike projections. The rim of the vessel has two thick handles that are relatively close to ancient bronze prototypes, but the mythological lion and cub on the cover are a much later addition to the Chinese decorative repertoire, most likely associated with Buddhism. This vessel retains what is probably its original wood base, which is decorated with interlaced cords, circular *bi* disks (see cat. 41), and bats with outspread wings. Bats, *fu* in Chinese, are a pun on the identically pronounced character meaning "good fortune," and function as much as a decorative element as an auspicious talisman.

The malachite vessel (right) posed a special challenge to the artisans who made it. The very uneven structure of the stone, which is riddled with small voids and fissures, caused them to adjust details of the design and fill the voids with colored material that mimics the surrounding stone. The decoration on the body of the vessel, which is also very thick and heavy, is a masklike face borrowed from the typical decoration of Shang and Zhou bronzes. The legs are high-relief animal-heads with feet projecting below them. Two fantastic animal-heads with tongues that extend as a scrolling floral ornament form the broad handles, and a coiling dragon, now damaged, surmounts the solid cover.

PUBLISHED

100: Nott, *Chinese Jades*, no. 99
101: Nott, *Chinese Jades*, no. 98

NOTES

1 Colin Mackenzie's essay in this catalogue notes the appearance of innovative square bronzes in tombs at Anyang. See pp. 45–46.
2 On later reinterpretations of the *ding* form, see Rawson, "The Ancestry of Chinese Bronze Vessels," pp. 51–73.

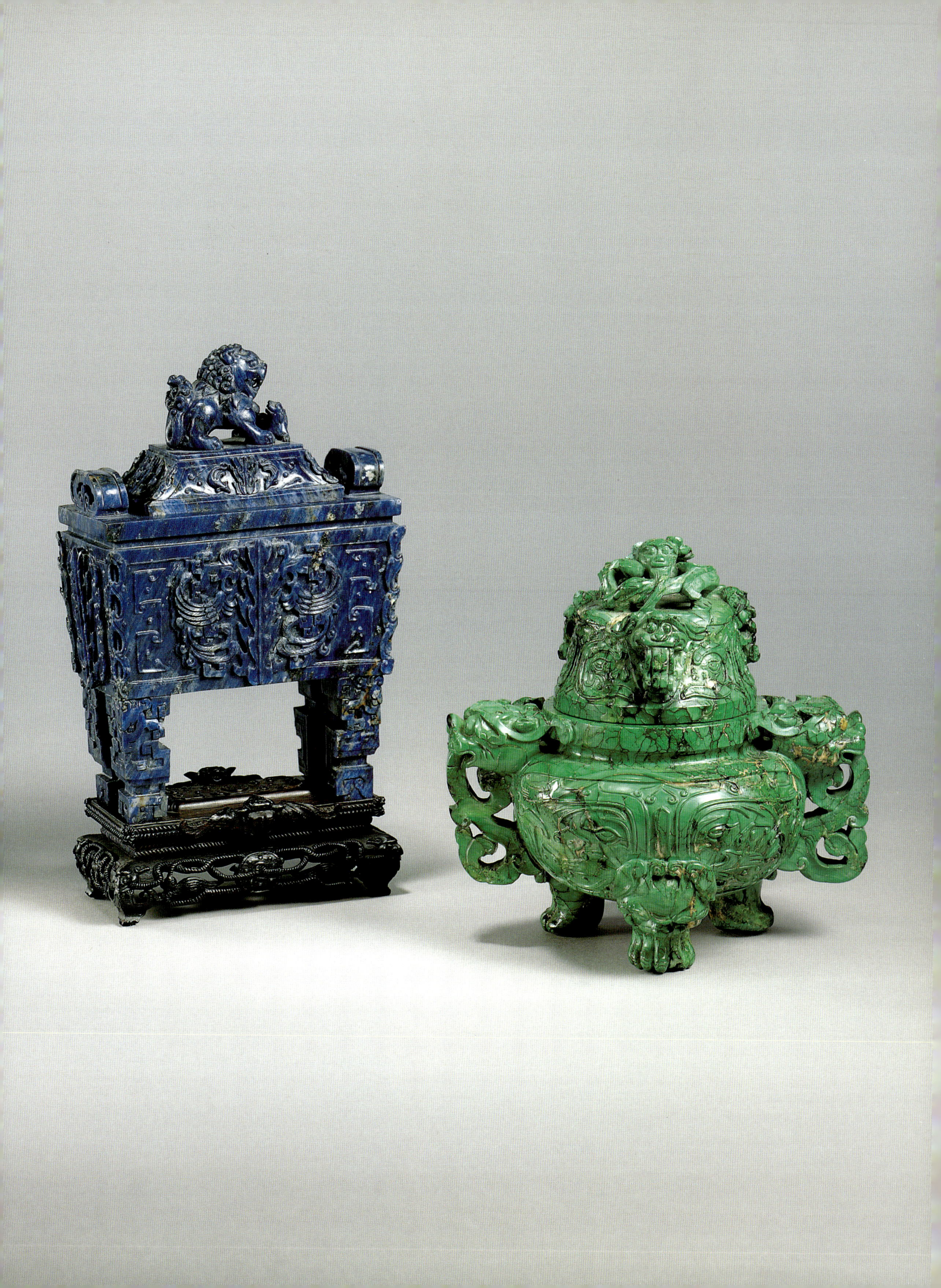

102 **COVERED INCENSE BURNER IN THE FORM OF A DING**

Qing dynasty, 18th century
Rock (quartz) crystal, 8 7/8 × 7 3/4 × diam. 5 5/8 in. (22.5 × 19.7 × 14.3 cm)
Gift of R.H. Norton, 42.105

103 **VESSEL IN THE FORM OF A GUANG**

Qing dynasty, 18th century
Rock (quartz) crystal, 6 3/8 × 10 1/2 × 5 1/2 in. (16.2 × 26.7 × 14 cm)
Gift of R.H. Norton, 42.106

Like the lapis lazuli and malachite *Incense burners* (see cats. 100, 101), the *Covered incense burner in the form of a ding* and the *Vessel in the form of a guang* are archaistic recreations of ancient ritual bronzes. Both are rather free interpretations of the past, translating the original shape into a new medium and giving it new uses while invoking ancient associations. The tripod incense burner (left) is carved from two pieces of transparent rock crystal, one for the tall cover and one for the body. Animal heads and thick paws form the legs of the vessel, and the handles on the body (and three smaller decorative handles on the cover) take the form of animal masks supporting freely moving rings, a feature that first appears on late Shang and early Western Zhou bronzes. The cover is pierced under the dragon on the very top, and the vessel could, in theory, function as an incense burner, but the valuable material probably prevented it from being anything other than an object for opulent display. The vessel in the form of a *guang* (right) also replicates an important bronze form (see cat. 1) but without the cover of the Shang original. The loop handle under the spout makes this vessel completely impractical. The division of the sides into horizontal ranges echoes Shang style, although the beauty of the material, rather than any elaborate surface carving, is the main decoration. The squared-off vertical flanges characteristic of Shang and Zhou bronzes are here interpreted as rows of stylized insects.

Shortly after the opening of his Gallery in West Palm Beach, Ralph Norton acquired just over 100 carved jades and hardstones from the dealer Stanley Charles Nott. Norton himself designed top-lighted cases for this large group, which served to display the Chinese collection as it expanded in later years. Horace Jayne's 1972 catalogue notes that "Mr. Norton's interest in the exotic carvings first acquired was not profound. He looked upon their addition, however, as a worthy means to complement his already important holdings in fields of Western painting and sculpture, and serve to direct attention of visitors to the art of the Far East."[1] Although the original group of eighteenth- and nineteenth-century jades and hardstones was reduced by the sale or trade of lesser quality objects for other Chinese acquisitions, the majority, including these quartz-crystal vessels, remained in the Museum, where they continue to display much of their initial appeal.

PUBLISHED

102: Nott, *Chinese Jades*, no. 251; Jayne, *The Chinese Collections*, no. 106
103: Nott, *Chinese Jades*, no. 252; Jayne, *The Chinese Collections*, no. 107

NOTE

1 *The Chinese Collections*, part 4, n.p.

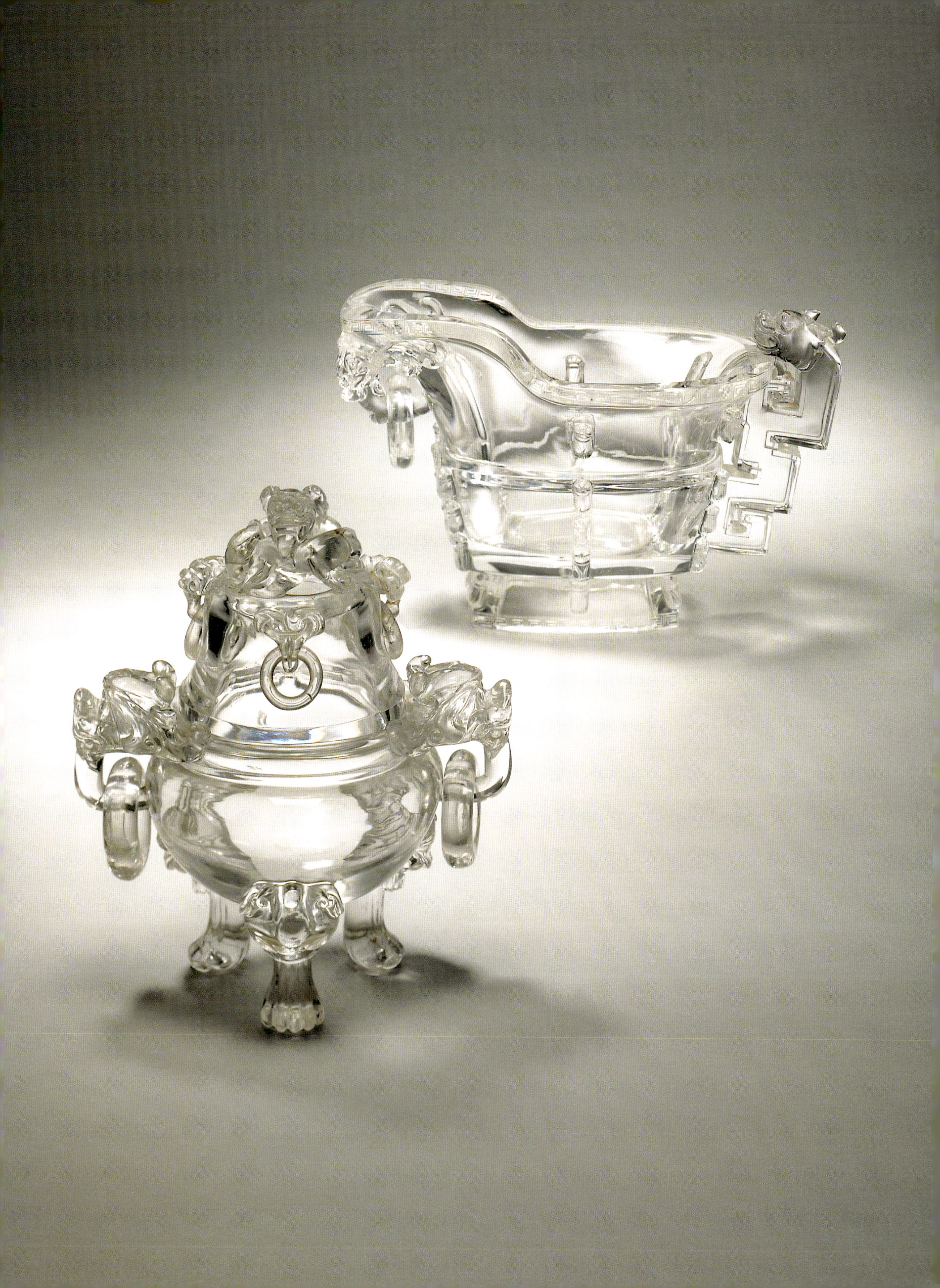

104 PAIR OF JADEITE BRACELETS

Qing dynasty, late 18th–early 19th century
Jadeite, each $\frac{5}{16}$ × diam. 3 $\frac{1}{8}$ in. (.8 × 7.9 cm)
Gift of Mrs. Bartlett Richards, 65.14, 66.1

Jadeite is a mineral distinct from nephrite, or true jade, although the Chinese word *yu* is used to name both these and many precious stones.[1] The major source for jadeite is the region near Tawmaw in northern Myanmar (Burma), but supplies of the mineral did not reach China in any significant quantities until after the late eighteenth century, when Chinese attempts to conquer the region came to an end and trade began on a significant scale. (See also cat. 98, for amber from Myanmar.) The fine carving of this rare matching *Pair of Jadeite Bracelets* highlights the color and transparency of the jadeite. Some areas of the stone are deep transparent green while others are a lighter, translucent, green. Dragons flying through clouds decorate the bracelets, and the jadeite carvers have adjusted the designs so that the heads of the dragons are cut from the deepest green areas (two of four heads appear toward the top of the photograph). Parts of the dragons' scaly backs appear among the swirling clouds. In a few places tiny holes pierce the bracelets, especially through the dragons' mouths. Most jadeite bangles are plain circlets that depend on the quality of the stone and the polish for their appeal, making elaborately carved examples like the Norton *Bracelets* highly unusual.

PUBLISHED

Jayne, *The Chinese Collections*, no. 249

NOTE

1 Jadeite is sometimes referred to as *feicui yu*, meaning "kingfisher feather-blue jade."

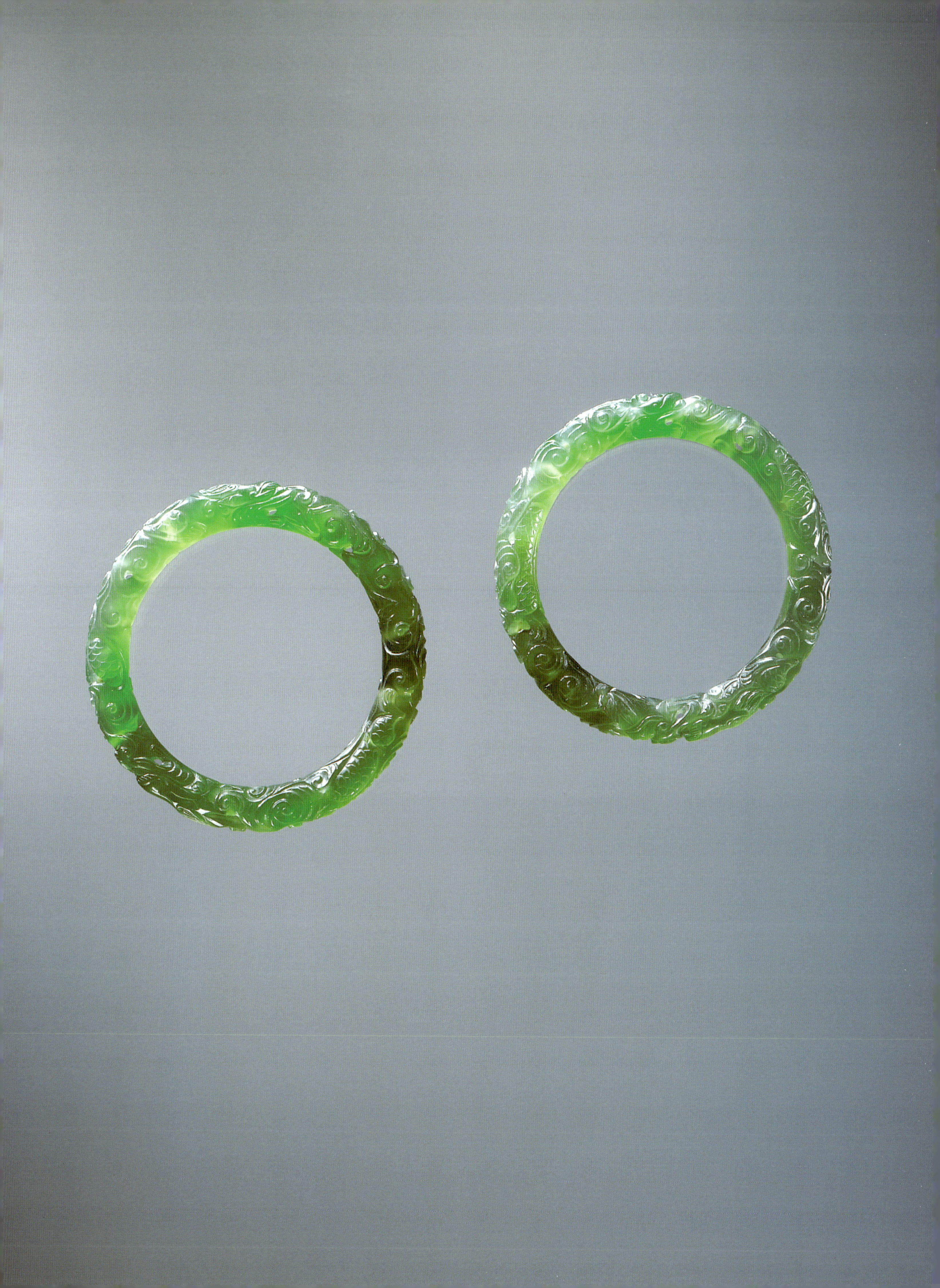

105 VESSEL IN THE FORM OF A RHYTON

Qing dynasty, 18th century
Yellow jade, 6 1/2 × 3 5/8 × 1 7/8 in (16.5 × 9.2 × 4.8 cm)
Gift of R.H. Norton, 42.24

A rhyton is a drinking vessel made originally from an ox or buffalo horn but imitated in many different media.[1] The Hellenistic vessel type was widely dispersed across Eurasia, and an early and well-documented example carved in jade was discovered in the tomb of the King of Nanyue, who died around the year 122 BCE.[2] It takes the form of a narrow horn with stylized decoration around the top derived from animal or cloud forms and a point tapering to a spiraling projection that wraps back around the base of the horn. Some later Chinese versions of the rhyton form are titled *bei*, or "cup," while others are called *guang*, the same character as the Shang wine-pouring vessel (cat. 1).[3] Examples dated by scholars as early as the Song dynasty and many examples of Ming and Qing workmanship have a dragon's or monster's head biting the bottom of the horn, as we see in this Norton example. Chinese vessels with animal-heads at the bottom are probably the reflection of Tang imports from Sassanian Persia that were imitated in seventh-century China.[4]

Though the smaller animals on the outside of Norton vessel are sometimes identified as *chilong*, a kind of dragon, they are rather feline creatures that replicate the animals on Han jade carvings, such as the *Sword guard* in the Norton collection (cat. 46).[5] The convention of showing such creatures biting the rim of a cup or other vessel appears at least as early as the Song dynasty,[6] and there is a small group of jade cups with creatures biting the rim or top of the handle, the earliest of which dates to the fifteenth century.[7] The Norton vessel has a distinctly yellow tone when compared to the greenish or even blue tints of so-called white jade. Probably reflecting a contemporary supply of deep yellow-colored jade, a number of small carvings, often with brown inclusions, were made in the early Ming, in the fourteenth and fifteenth centuries.[8] The Norton rhyton, however, is most likely a Qing dynasty vessel. The carving is relatively sculptural, and the small felines are particularly animated. One senses that the jade carver did not attempt to recreate an awkward, archaistic vessel, but rather used a fine piece of yellow-toned translucent jade to its best advantage.

PUBLISHED

Nott, *Chinese Jades*, no. 25; Hartman, *Chinese Jade of Five Centuries*, pl. 26; Jayne, *The Chinese Collections*, no. 231

NOTES

1 See Boardman, *The Diffusion of Classical Art*, fig. 4.20, for a Graeco-Persian silver rhyton in the Toledo Museum of Art (1988.23).
2 *Xi Han Nanyue wang mu*, vol. 2, color pl. XV, pl. 118:1. The tomb is located in the modern city of Guangzhou (Canton) on China's southeastern coast.
3 See, for example, Chang, *Gongting zhi ya*, cat. 34, for a Western Han jade with a Qianlong imperial inscription on the interior celebrating it as a "Khotan green jade dragon-tail *guang*."
4 Watt, *Chinese Jades from Han to Ch'ing*, cat. 29.
5 The Western Han jade rhyton, formerly in the Qing imperial collection, cited in Chang (see n. 3), has a dragon coiled around the body of the vessel.
6 See *Oriental Ceramics*, vol. 8, cat. 183, for an *yinqing* cup, dated Southern Song or Yuan dynasty, 13th century.
7 These testify to the export of Chinese exotic forms to West Asia and Europe: one is inscribed with the name of Ulug Beg, who ruled in Samarkand (1447–49) (see Hansford, *Chinese Carved Jades*, no. 79); another was the gift of Shah Abbas to the Ardebil Shrine in 1611 (ibid., no. 80B; and see cat. 76, n. 5, above); a third belonged to Cardinal Mazarin (d. 1661) and later Louis XIV (see Pirazzoli-t'Serstevens, "Un jade chinois des collections de Louis XIV").
8 Watt, *Chinese Jades from Han to Ch'ing*, p. 29.

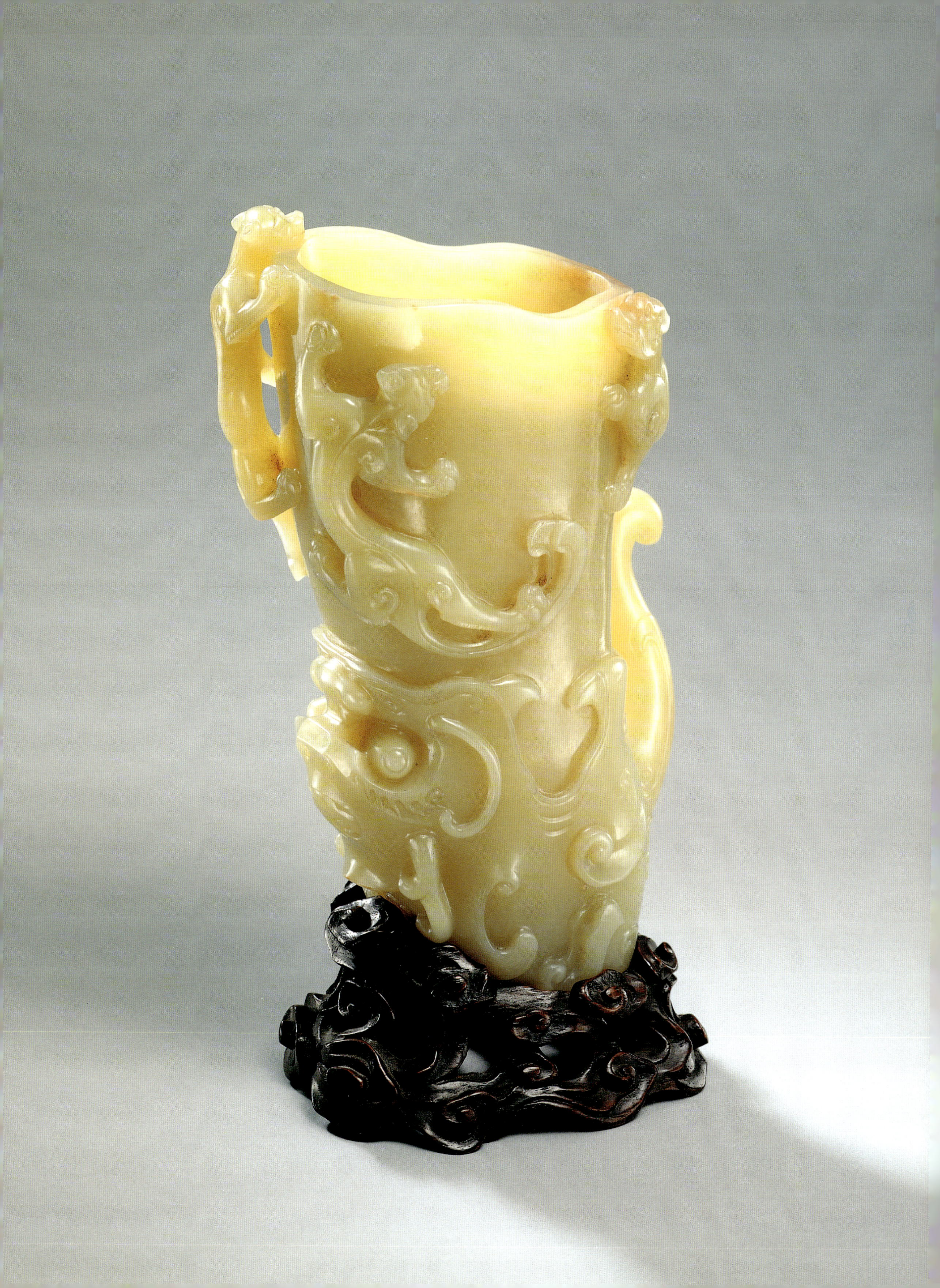

106 PILGRIM BOTTLE

Qing dynasty, 18th century
Green jade, 13 × 7⅞ × 2⅛ in. (33 × 20 × 5.4 cm)
Gift of R.H. Norton, 42.31a-b

107 PILGRIM BOTTLE

Qing dynasty, 18th century
White jade, 9¾ × 2⅛ × 5⅞ in. (24.8 × 5.4 × 14.9 cm)
Gift of R.H. Norton, 42.33a-b

These jade vessels derive their shape, however distantly, from water flasks, and their circular bodies with flat sides provide ample surfaces for decorative carving. The cover and neck of the larger, dark green *Pilgrim bottle* (left) are decorated with stylized palmette designs that first appear on blue and white porcelains of the fourteenth and fifteenth centuries.[1] The handles are in the form of *ruyi* scepters, a ceremonial object originally held by Buddhist figures and later adopted as a scholar's auspicious emblem. *Ruyi* means "as you wish," with the implication that one's desires will be granted, and the lobed head of the *ruyi*, here projecting from the neck of the vessel, is shaped like the magical *lingzhi* fungus that imparts immortality. The gently swelling sides of the bottle are decorated with scrolling floral ornament and the Eight Emblems of the Buddha. There are four emblems on each side, alternating with large flowers. Reading clockwise from the top, they are the canopy, endless knot, conch-shell trumpet, and the Wheel of the Law. The *ruyi* and the Eight Emblems are a general wish for good fortune and not specifically religious in meaning. A similar though more ornate green jade bottle in the Lady Lever Art Gallery, Port Sunlight, has the Eight Emblems arrayed around an eight-pointed floral ornament and retains its original gilt-bronze stand.[2]

The handles on the smaller, white jade *Pilgrim bottle* (right) take the form of elephants' heads supporting free-moving rings. Ring handles appear on ancient bronzes, although the animal-head is usually an ox with spreading horns or a mythological creature. The decoration on the two sides of the bottle imitates paintings on circular fans or album leaves. On the side on view are plum blossoms, which are particularly appropriate to the white color of the jade. Plum blossoms, or flowering prunus, are a complex symbol with a long history in Chinese literature, painting, and decorative arts. Blooming in isolated places, they are an emblem of the scholar-recluse. As the first flowers to appear in the new year, often blooming while there is snow on the ground, they are an emblem of renewal. The delicate blossoms, which only last a brief time, are a metaphor for the transience of life.[3] The jade carvers here have incorporated in the composition the natural vein of thin rust brown coloration that runs along the branch growing up over the edge of the bottle on the upper left. Thus what might have been considered a flaw becomes part of the design, a technique surprisingly common in decorative jades such as these.

PUBLISHED

106: Nott, *Chinese Jades*, no. 33
107: Nott, *Chinese Jades*, no. 34; Jayne, *The Chinese Collections*, no. 211

NOTES

1 The design seems to conflate early designs of leaves that have round lobes and sharp points with cloud-shaped panels that commonly decorate the shoulders or necks of porcelain vessels.
2 Gray and others, *Chinese Jade Throughout the Ages*, no. 418. By reputation this object is from the Yuanming Yuan, the Qing imperial summer palace looted by British and French forces in 1860.
3 On the many meanings of plum blossoms, see especially Bickford and others, *Bones of Jade*, pp. 17–43.

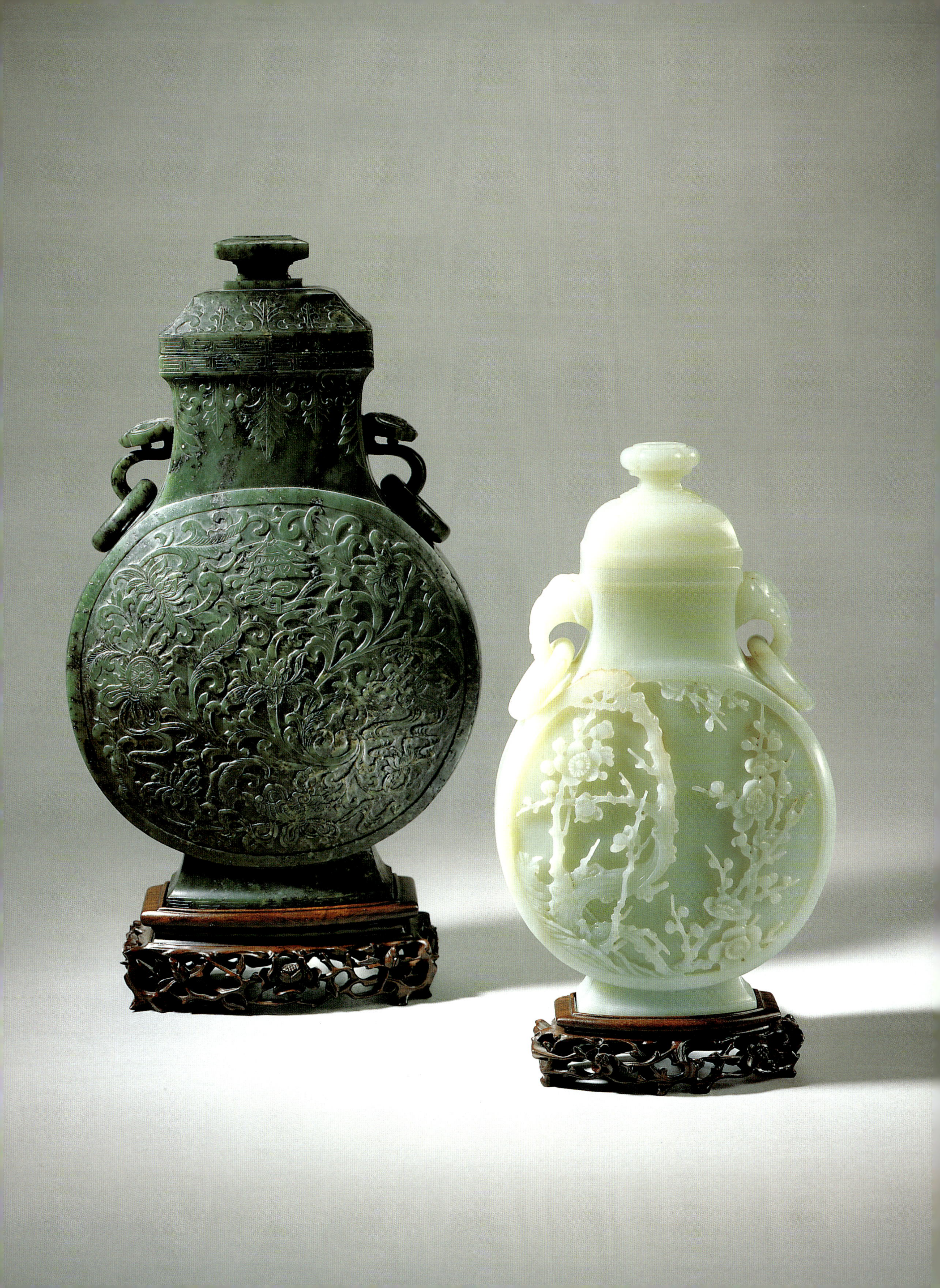

108 **BOWL IN MUGHAL STYLE**

Qing dynasty, late 18th century
Jade, 2 5/8 × diam. 4 5/8 in. (6.7 × 11.7 cm)
Gift of R.H. Norton, 42.75

"Mughal" style with respect to Chinese jades generally refers to objects from the late eighteenth century that imitate a range of carved jades that came to China from the Mughal territories of northern India as well as from the Ottoman empire (with its capital at modern Istanbul) and perhaps workshops in Muslim regions of Chinese Central Asia.[1] Inscriptions by the Qianlong emperor on foreign jades in the imperial collection refer to Mughal India as *Hendusitan*, the transcription of Hindustan, and a wide variety of jades from various sources were catalogued in the imperial collection as Hindustan or Mughal jades. Chinese jades inspired by these models combine exotic designs with Chinese forms and motifs. The fine fluting and abstract floral motifs seen on jades from Mughal India are reflected in Chinese pieces that use stylized chrysanthemum flowers as the main decorative motif. Chrysanthemum flowers are carved on the bottom, inside and out, of the Norton *Bowl in Mughal style*, and the fluting of the foot and the sides of the bowl repeats this motif. The shape of the bowl is typically Chinese; it may once have had a cover and certainly had a decorative display stand.[2]

The designs in the broad band around the rim have a long tradition in China, although they too may ultimately be foreign in origin. The band includes the Eight Emblems of the Buddha, and the most clearly visible are the furled umbrella, lotus flower, and vase on the interior wall and the Wheel of the Law in the center of the exterior. The design of stylized palmettes that hangs down from the rim and separates the Eight Emblems has been distorted, perhaps to give it a more "Mughal" feel, but it appears on Chinese blue and white porcelains of the late fourteenth to early fifteenth century. The same designs—Eight Emblems and palmettes—appear in a different configuration on the Norton green jade *Pilgrim bottle* (cat. 106). Finally, perhaps to replicate the translucency of white Mughal jades, Chinese artisans carved the walls of jades such as this bowl to extraordinary thinness, sometimes less than one millimeter. The design motifs here are carved in very low relief and match each other on the inside and the outside. These convex designs act like miniature lenses, concentrating the light that passes through the almost transparent jade and highlighting the extraordinarily delicate carving.

PUBLISHED

Nott, *Chinese Jades*, no. 76; Jayne, *The Chinese Collections*, no. 221

NOTES

1 The National Palace Museum exhibition catalogue *Gugong suozang hendusitan yuqi tezhan tulu* is still the most important publication on this phase of Chinese jade carving and the source for much of the present discussion.

2 See ibid., pl. 75, for a pair of similarly shaped bowls with their covers.

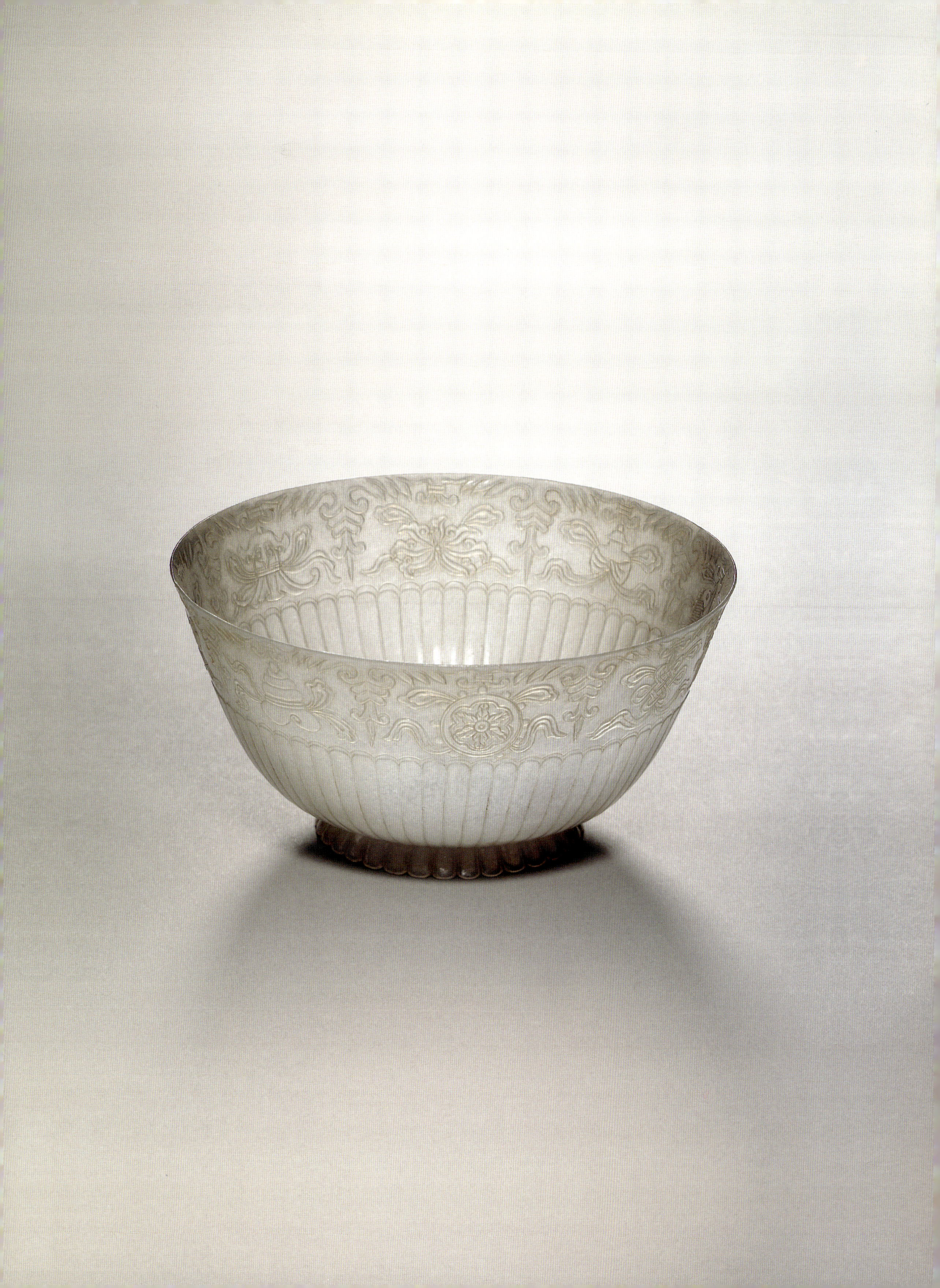

109 PAIR OF LACQUERED CABINETS WITH CUPBOARDS

Late Ming–early Qing dynasty, probably mid- to late 17th century
Wood, painted lacquer with gold, each cabinet 79 1/4 × 52 5/8 × 24 3/8 in. (201.3 × 133.7 × 69.1 cm), each cupboard 32 3/4 × 52 5/8 × 24 3/8 in. (83.2 × 133.7 × 69.1 cm)
Bequest of Leonard and Sophie Davis, 2001.173a-b, 2001.174a-b

Modern taste favors Chinese hardwood furniture, where the color of the hardwood and elegant lines create the aesthetic appeal, in the Ming and Qing dynasties sumptuous lacquer-decorated pieces were the most luxurious furniture for upper-class mansions and imperial palaces.[1] Although large amounts of lacquer furniture must have been manufactured, relatively few examples have survived. The Norton *Pair of lacquered cabinets with cupboards* is remarkable for the quality of its decoration and the preservation of a complete suite of four pieces — two cabinets and two matching cupboards — in extraordinarily fine condition.

Combining several lacquer-painting techniques, the decoration covers every surface except the backs and bottoms. The edges are decorated with scrolling flowers and dragons pursuing roundels containing stylized characters reading *shou*, or "long life." The sides and doors of the upper cupboards are covered with round bird-and-flower paintings. The cabinet doors are painted (from top to bottom) with palace and landscape views, figure compositions, and panels of birds and flowers. All of the open areas of the decoration on the front of the cupboards and cabinets are filled with precise geometric designs (the backgrounds on the sides are plain), consisting almost exclusively of miniature interlocking swastikas or diaper patterns including swastikas.[2] Most of the lacquer decoration on the cabinets is rendered in the painstaking technique of *tianqi*, or "filled-in" lacquer.[3] The details of the design are cut into a solid background and filled in with contrasting colored lacquer; the whole is then carefully polished, leaving a smoothly decorated surface. Many of the details are outlined in gold, in a technique called *qiangjin*, where a fine line is engraved in the surface and filled with gold leaf.[4] In such details as the faces and hands, the artists have inlaid areas of cream-colored lacquer and most likely rendered the details with tung-oil based paints, achieving a level of painterly modeling not possible with pigment in lacquer.

Because there are few surviving examples of painted lacquer furniture, dating this Norton suite is difficult. In the second half of the sixteenth century, there was a growing taste for elaborate polychrome decoration in many media, including lacquers. The late sixteenth and early seventeenth century saw the culmination of a tradition that, after the end of the Ming Wanli reign in 1619, gradually became more restrained in style while lasting into the Qing dynasty.[5] Some smaller lacquered objects have designs perhaps comparable to those seen here. A square stand in Edinburgh dated to 1623, for example, combines *tianqi* and *qiangjin* techniques as well as dense swastika patterns.[6] The cloisonné enamel hardware on the Norton furniture — a complete set of twenty pieces — may provide further clues to dating. It is embellished with designs of lotus flowers and scrolling vines set against a bright blue background; the details of the flowers are comparable to the designs on cloisonné enamel vessels datable to the first half of the seventeenth century.[7] Thus the modest evidence we can muster points to a date in the mid- to late

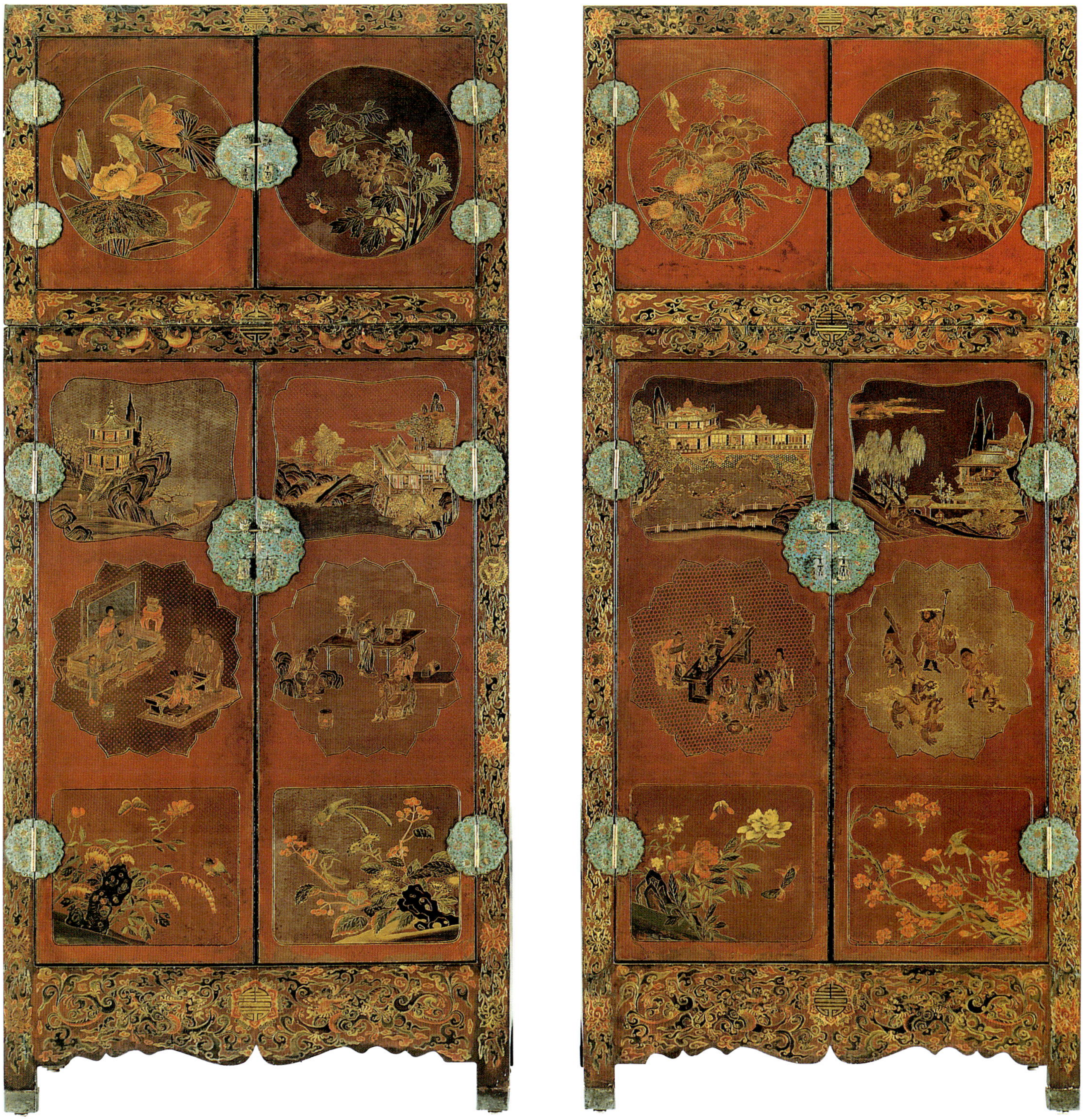

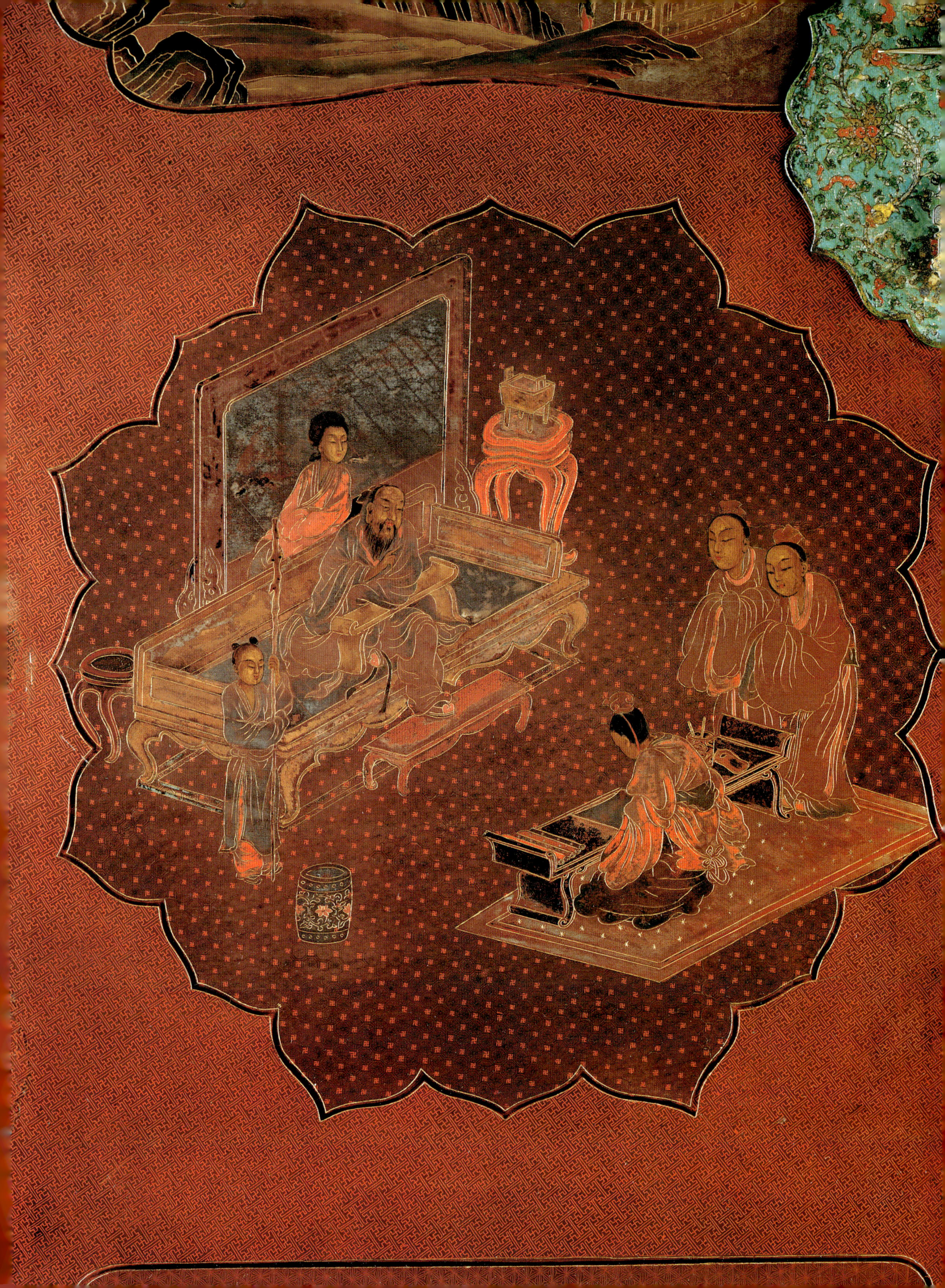

seventeenth century for this sumptuous suite of lacquer furniture.

It is in the figure compositions that the skill of the lacquer painters shows most clearly. In the detail seen here (opposite), the artists illustrate a famous scene from ancient history. The First Emperor of Qin (r. 246–210 BCE) ruthlessly executed scholars and burned numerous texts in a ruthless attempt to suppress Confucianism. At the beginning of the succeeding Western Han dynasty, the new emperor sent emissaries to the aged scholar Fu Sheng, who had memorized the *Shujing* (The Book of Documents) from the Confucian Classics.[8] We see Fu Sheng seated on a couch, leaning on an armrest and dictating the text and commentary to the imperial emissary, who sits at a low desk on a mat. Fu Sheng's granddaughter is leaning over his shoulder, helping to make clear his archaic, provincial Chinese. The composition is probably adapted from an unidentified painting or woodblock illustration, as the other figure compositions on the cabinets seem to be.

PUBLISHED

Medley, "Lacquered Furniture," pp. 72–73, pls. 2a,b.

NOTES

1 See Clunas, "Furnishing the Self in Early Modern China," esp. pp. 23–24.

2 The swastika, pronounced *wan*, is an emblem of the Buddha as well as a rebus for the word "ten thousand," thus a good-luck charm invoking the Buddha's blessing for long life.

3 See Garner, *Chinese Lacquer*, pp. 179–94. See also Wang, ed., *Xiushi lu jieshuo*, no. 100, pp. 95–99, for the description and Wang's extensive commentary on the technique. Probably the earliest example comes from a mid- to late-Southern Song (13th century) tomb in Jiangsu; see Kuwayama, "Recently Discovered Sung Lacquers," pp. 44–45.

4 Wang, ed., *Xiushi lu jieshuo*, no. 131, pp. 136–40.

5 See Watt, *The Sumptuous Basket*, pp. 22–24.

6 Hu and Wilkinson, *Chinese Lacquer*, no. 39. See also Shangraw, "Chinese Lacquers in the Asian Art Museum," pp. 39–40, for a lacquer box with basketry sides, datable to the early 17th century, with filled-in decoration carefully outlined in gold. And for a piece with a Qianlong mark, see British Museum, *Chinese and Associated Lacquer*, no. 172, pl. 75b, an octagonal, filled-in lacquer tray that has a miniature swastika diaper pattern background.

7 See Brinker and Lutz, *Chinese Cloisonné: The Pierre Uldry Collection*, esp. cats. 124–27. The details include mirror-image double petals in the center and ogee-shaped petals marking the axis of the highly stylized flowers. Medley, "Lacquered Furniture," pp. 72–73, states that the cloisonné can be firmly dated to the middle of the 16th century, giving that date to the lacquer decoration as well, but in light of recently published examples her dating seems too early.

8 I am grateful to Stephen Little for identifying this scene. Cahill (*Parting at the Shore*, p. 156) says Fu Sheng had hidden the text in the wall of his house and spent the end of his life expounding the text to the imperial emissary.

110 COROMANDEL SCREEN

Qing dynasty, Qianlong reign, dated 1793
Carved lacquer on wood, each panel 106 in. × 17 in. (269.2 × 43.2 cm); fully extended, approximately 204 inches wide (518.2 cm)
Bequest of Leonard and Sophie Davis, 2001.177

This imposing *Screen* is made of twelve wood panels, each almost nine feet tall and decorated on both front and back with a distinctive carved and colored lacquer technique referred to in the West as "Coromandel lacquer." The term is a misnomer, implying a connection with the Coromandel coast of southeastern India, which, curiously, only came into use in the early twentieth century.[1] Before then such Chinese screens were referred to in English as "Bantam work," after the Dutch East India Company trading station on Java, where lacquer for export was collected for shipment to Europe.[2] Large numbers of Coromandel screens were exported to Europe in the late seventeenth and eighteenth century, where they had a profound effect on the fashion for *chinoiserie*, the taste for goods in imaginative Chinese styles.

The "Coromandel" lacquer decoration technique is called *kuancai* in Chinese, a term best rendered as "intaglio-carved and colored" lacquer to distinguish it among a great number of carved lacquer techniques. The late sixteenth- to early seventeenth-century *Xiushi lu*, the Treatise on Lacquer Decoration, gives a succinct description: "One carves the design in intaglio, like woodblocks for printing, and then fills it in with different colors, whence the name."[3] Huang Cheng, the original compiler of the *Xiushi lu,* was from Huizhou, Anhui province, and a lacquer craftsman himself, as was Yang Ming, whose commentary on the text clarifies much of what Huang recorded. Since the term *kuancai* first appears in the *Xiushi lu*, it is possible that the technique originated in the Huizhou region, long an important center of lacquer production, in the sixteenth century.[4] For *kuancai* or Coromandel lacquer, a relatively thick layer made of an adhesive, probably containing an amount of lacquer, and a filler was built up on the wood panel.[5] The surface was finished with layers of shiny black, dark brown, or red lacquer. All the details of the design were then cut through the lacquer surface into the layer below, leaving the background raised. The exposed filler, which is almost always a dull gray, was given a coat of whiting and then brightly colored, using either lacquer or tung oil–based paints, gold or silver, or combinations of all these.

The decoration of Coromandel screens conventionally reflects certain subjects, and the Norton screen depicts a typically elaborate scene in a palace garden. It is framed by a wide border with dragons among clouds and fantastic, mythological birds. Coromandel screens were commissioned as gifts, and several, like this one, have long inscriptions on the back. The inscription on the Norton screen is an imperial proclamation granting honorary rank to a high official, and it includes a date in the Qianlong reign equivalent to 1793. Most Coromandel screens with dated inscriptions were produced in the seventeenth century, with a smaller number manufactured early in the eighteenth century; the Norton *Coromandel screen* is unusual in having a relatively late date.[6]

NOT PREVIOUSLY PUBLISHED

NOTES

1 Garner, *Chinese Lacquer*, p. 260.
2 Jourdain and Jenyns, *Chinese Export Art*, p. 21.
3 The translation of the passage is mine, following the text printed in Wang, ed., *Xiushi lu jieshuo*, no. 129, pp. 135–36.
4 Chou, *Qing Kangxi*, p. 24.
5 The formulas are not clearly understood. See Wang, ed., *Xiushi lu jieshuo*, p. 135.
6 See "Coromandel Screen," in National Gallery of Art, *Decorative Arts*, Part II, esp. p. 277.

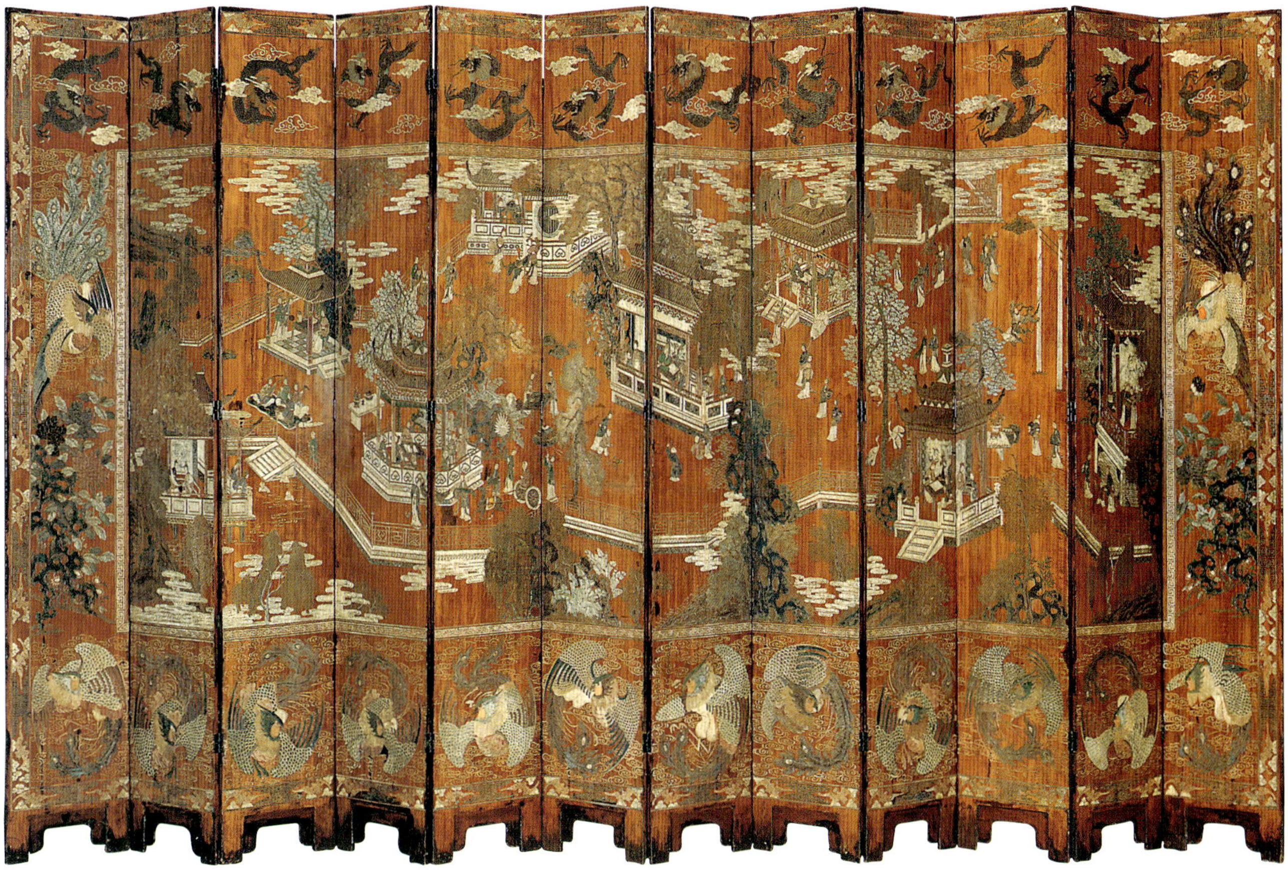

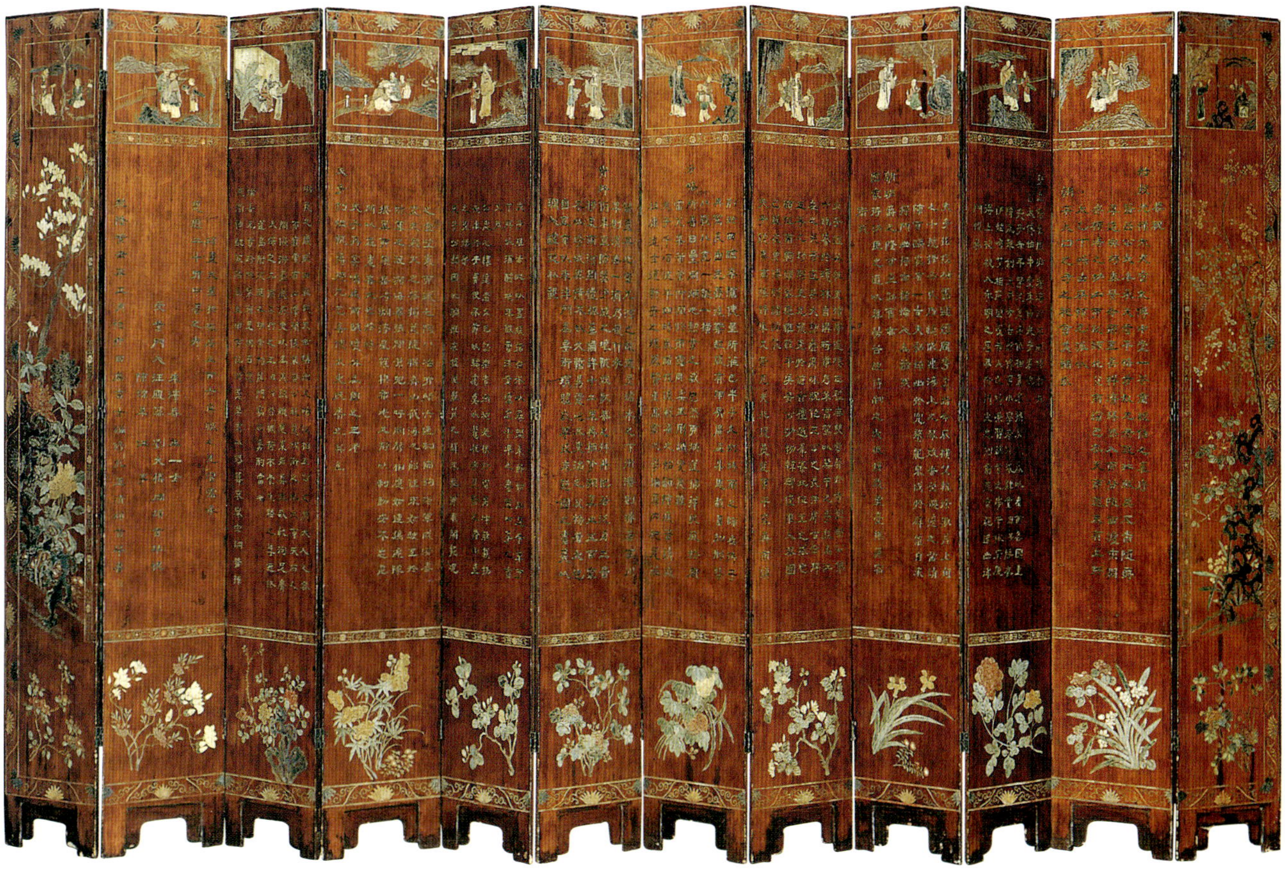

BIBLIOGRAPHY

Anyang Yinxu Guojiazhuang Shang dai muzang: 1982 nian–1992 nian kaogu fajue baogao (*Guojiazhuang Cemetery of the Shang Period within the Yin Ruins, Anyang: Excavations in 1982–1992*). Beijing: Zhongguo Dabaike quanshu chubanshe, 1998.

Archaeology Institute of Liaoning and the Museum of Chaoyang City, comps. "Chaoyang Shi'ertai xiang zhuanchang 88M1 fajue jianbao (Excavation of a Tomb (coded 88M1) in a Brickyard at Shi'ertai Township, Chaoyang)." *Wenwu* 1997.11, pp. 19–32.

Art of the Houma Foundry. Compiled by the Institute of Archaeology of Shanxi Province and others. Princeton: Princeton University Press: 1996.

Avril, Ellen B. *Chinese Art in the Cincinnati Art Museum*. Cincinnati: Cincinnati Art Museum, 1997.

Bagley, Robert W. "An Early Bronze Age Tomb in Jiangxi Province." *Orientations* (July 1993), pp. 20–36.

———. "Shang Archaeology." In Loewe and Shaughnessy, *The Cambridge History of Ancient China*, pp. 124–231.

———. "Shang Ritual Bronzes: Casting Technique and Vessel Design." *Archives of Asian Art* 43 (1990), pp. 6–20.

———. *Shang Ritual Bronzes in the Arthur M. Sackler Collections*. Washington, D.C.: Arthur M. Sackler Foundation, and Cambridge, Mass.: Harvard University, Arthur M. Sackler Museum, 1987.

———, ed. *Ancient Sichuan: Treasures from a Lost Civilization*. Seattle and Princeton: Seattle Art Museum and Princeton University Press, 2001.

Baoji Yu guo mudi (*Yu State Cemeteries in Baoji*). Compiled by Lu Liancheng, Hu Zhisheng, and the Baoji Municipal Museum. In Chinese with English abstract. 2 vols. Beijing: Wenwu chubanshe, 1988.

Barnard, Noel. *Bronze Casting and Bronze Alloys in Ancient China*. Canberra: Australian National University, 1961.

Barnhart, Richard M., and others. *The Jade Studio: Masterpieces of Ming and Qing Painting and Calligraphy from the Wong Nan-p'ing Collection*. New Haven: Yale University Art Gallery, 1994.

Bartholomew, Terese Tse. "*Thangkas* for the Qianlong Emperor's Seventieth Birthday." In Marsha Weidner, ed., *Cultural Intersections in Later Chinese Buddhism*, pp. 170–88.

———, and Mitchell Clark. "The Walters Art Gallery 1764 Jade *Qing* Lithophone and Related Pieces." *The Journal of the Walters Art Gallery* 49–50 (1991–92), pp. 131–40.

Berliner, Nancy, and others. *Beyond the Screen: Chinese Furniture of the 16th and 17th Centuries*. Boston: Museum of Fine Arts, 1996.

Beurdeley, Michèle, and Guy Raindre. Translated by Charlotte Chesnay. *Qing Porcelain: Famille Verte, Famille Rose, 1644–1912*. New York: Rizzoli, 1987.

Bickford, Maggie, and others. *Bones of Jade, Soul of Ice: The Flowering Plum in Chinese Art*. New Haven: Yale University Art Gallery, 1985.

Bishop, Heber Reginald. *Investigations and Studies in Jade*. 2 vols. New York (privately printed), 1906.

Boardman, John. *The Diffusion of Classical Art in Antiquity*. Princeton: Princeton University Press, 1994.

Brinker, Helmut, and Albert Lutz. *Chinese Cloisonné: The Pierre Uldry Collection*. Translated by Susanna Swoboda. Exh. cat., New York, The Asia Society Galleries, 1989.

British Museum. *Chinese and Associated Lacquer from the Garner Collection*. Exh. cat., London, 1973.

Bulletin of the Museum of Far Eastern Antiquities. "The Exhibition of Early Chinese Bronzes." *Bulletin of the Museum of Far Eastern Antiquities* 6 (1934), pp. 81–132.

Burlington Fine Arts Club. *Catalogue of a Collection of Objects of Chinese Art*. London (privately printed for the Burlington Fine Arts Club), 1915.

Butler, Sir Michael, Margaret Medley, and Stephen Little. *Seventeenth-Century Chinese Porcelain from the Butler Family Collection*. Alexandria, Va.: Art Services International, 1990.

Cahill, James. *The Compelling Image: Nature and Style in Seventeenth-Century Chinese Painting*. Cambridge, Mass.: Harvard University Press, 1982.

———. *The Distant Mountains: Chinese Painting of the Late Ming Dynasty, 1570–1644*. New York and Tokyo: Weatherhill, 1982.

———. *Paintings of the Zhi Garden by Zhang Hong: Revisiting a Seventeenth-Century Chinese Garden*. Los Angeles: Los Angeles County Museum of Art, 1996.

———. *Parting at the Shore: Painting of the Early and Middle Ming Dynasty, 1368–1580*. New York and Tokyo: Weatherhill, 1978.

Cammann, Schuyler v.R. *China's Dragon Robes*. New York: The Ronald Press, 1952. Reprint with corrections, Chicago: Art Media Resources, Ltd., n.d.

Catalogue of the International Exhibtion of Chinese Art, 1935–36. London: Royal Academy of Arts, 1935.

Ch'en, Kenneth. *Buddhism in China: A Historical Survey*. Princeton: Princeton University Press, 1964.

Chang Foundation. *Imperial Hongwu and Yongle Porcelain Excavated at Jingdezhen*. Exh. cat. (in Chinese and English), Taipei, 1996.

Chang Li-tuan. *Gongting zhi ya* (*The Refined Taste of the Emperor: Special Exhibition of Archaic and Pictorial Jades of the Ch'ing Court*). In Chinese and English. Taipei: National Palace Museum, 1997.

Chang, K.C. "Yangshao Culture (5000–3000 BC)." In Loewe and Shaughnessy, *The Cambridge History of Ancient China*, pp. 49–52.

Chang, Kwang-chih (K.C. Chang). *Shang Civilization*. New Haven and London: Yale University Press, 1980.

Changsha Mawangdui yihao Han mu (Han tomb no. 1 at Mawangdui, Changsha). 2 vols. Beijing: Wenwu chubanshe, 1973.

Chase, W. Thomas, and others. *Ancient Chinese Bronze Art: Casting the Precious Sacral Vessel*. New York: China Institute in America, 1991.

Chavannes, Édouard. *Mission archaéologique dans la Chine septentrionale*. 4 vols. Paris: E. Leroux, 1909–15.

Childs-Johnson, Elizabeth. "The *Jue*-Vessel and Its Ritual Use in the Ancestor Cult of Shang China." *Artibus Asiae* 48, nos. 3–4 (1987), pp. 171–96.

Chou, Ju-hsi. *Circles of Reflection: The Carter Collection of Chinese Bronze Mirrors*. Cleveland: The Cleveland Museum of Art, 2000.

Chou, Kung-hsin. *Qing Kangxi qianqi kuancai "Han gong chunxiao" qi pingfeng yu Zhongguo qigongyi zhi Xi quan* (A Kangxi Coromandel lacquer "Spring in the Han palace" screen and the transmission of Chinese lacquer art to the West). Taipei: National Palace Museum, 1991.

Chou, Kung-shin [*sic*, for hsin]. "French Jesuits and Chinese Lacquer in the Late 17th Century." *Oriental Art* 44, no. 4 (Winter 1999), pp. 33–37.

Clapp, Anne De Coursey. *The Painting of T'ang Yin*. Chicago and London: University of Chicago Press, 1991.

Clark, Walter Eugene, ed. *Two Lamaistic Pantheons*. Cambridge, Mass.: Harvard University Press, 1937.

Clunas, Craig. "Furnishing the Self in Early Modern China." In Berliner and others, *Beyond the Screen*, pp. 21–35.

Contag, Victoria, and Wang Chi-ch'ien. *Seals of Chinese Painters and Collectors of the Ming and Ch'ing Periods*. Rev. ed. with supplement. Hong Kong: Hong Kong University Press, 1966.

Cooke, Bill, and others. *Imperial China: The Art of the Horse in Chinese History*. Exh. cat., Lexington, Kentucky Horse Park and International Museum of the Horse, 2000.

Curtis, Julia. *Chinese Porcelains of the Seventeenth Century: Landscapes, Scholars' Motifs and Narratives*. New York: China Institute Gallery, 1995.

Deng Cong, ed. *Nan Zhongguo ji linjin diqu gu wenhua yanjiu* (*Ancient Cultures of South China and Neighbouring Regions*). Hong Kong: Centre for Chinese Archaeology and Art, ICS, and The Chinese University of Hong Kong, 1994.

Dickinson, Gary, and Linda Wrigglesworth. *Imperial Wardrobe*. London: Bamboo Publishing Ltd., 1990.

Dien, Albert E. "A Study of Early Chinese Armor." *Artibus Asiae* 43, nos. 1–2 (1981–82), pp. 5–66.

E'ertai, Zhang Tingyu, and others, comp. *Guochao gongshi* (History of the palace in the present [Qing] dynasty). Completed 1769. Reprint, 2 vols. Beijing: Beijing guji chubanshe, 1987.

Eberhard, Wolfram. *A Dictionary of Chinese Symbols: Hidden Symbols in Chinese Life and Thought*. London: Routledge and Keegan Paul, 1986.

Emerson, Julie, Jennifer Chen, and Mimi Gardner Gates. *Porcelain Stories: From China to Europe*. Seattle: University of Washington Press, 2000.

Farquhar, David. "Emperor as Bodhisattva in the Governance of the Ch'ing Empire." *Harvard Journal of Asiatic Studies* 38 (1978), pp. 5–34.

Fong, Wen C. *Between Two Cultures: Late-Nineteenth- and Twentieth-Century Chinese Paintings from the Robert H. Ellsworth Collection in The Metropolitan Museum*. New York: The Metropolitan Museum of Art, 2001.

———, ed. *The Great Bronze Age of China: An Exhibition from the People's Republic of China*. New York: The Metropolitan Museum of Art, 1980.

———, and James C.Y. Watt. *Possessing the Past: Treasures from the National Palace Museum, Taipei*. New York: The Metropolitan Museum of Art, 1996.

Frankel, Hans H. *The Flowering Plum and the Palace Lady: Interpretations of Chinese Poetry*. New Haven and London: Yale University Press, 1976.

Gaocheng Taixi Shang dai yizhi (*A Shang Site at Taixi, Gaocheng*). Beijing: Wenwu chubanshe, 1985.

Garner, Sir Harry. *Chinese Lacquer*. London: Faber and Faber, 1979.

Getty, Alice. *The Gods of Northern Buddhism: Their History and Iconography*. Oxford: Clarendon Press, 1914. 2d ed., 1928. Reprint, New York: Dover Books, 1988.

Gompertz, Godfrey St. George Montague. *Chinese Celadon Wares*. London: Faber and Faber, 1958.

Gray, Basil, Jessica Rawson, John Ayers, and others. *Chinese Jade Throughout the Ages*. London: Victoria and Albert Museum, 1975.

Grimaldi, David A. *Amber: Window to the Past*. New York: Harry N. Abrams, 1996.

Gujin tushu jicheng. Full title: *Qinding gujin tushu jicheng* (Imperially sponsored synthesis of books and illustrations of ancient and modern times). Compiled by Chen Menglei and others, 10,000 *juan*, 1726. Reprint, 808 vols. Shanghai: Zhonghua shuju, 1934.

Guo Baojun. *Shang Zhou tongqi qun zonghe yanjiu* (*A Comprehensive Study of the Shang and Zhou Bronze Vessel Group*). Beijing: Wenwu chubanshe, 1981.

Hansford, S. Howard. *Chinese Carved Jades*. London: Faber and Faber, 1968.

Hardy, S. Yorke. *Illustrated Catalogue of Tung, Ju, Kuan, Chün, Kuang-tung and Glazed I-hsing Wares in the Percival David Foundation of Chinese Art*. London: Percival David Foundation of Chinese Art, 1953.

Harrist, Robert E., Jr. *Power and Virtue: The Horse in Chinese Art*. New York: China Institute Gallery, 1997.

Hartman, Joan M. *Chinese Jade of Five Centuries*. Rutland, Vt., and Tokyo: Charles E. Tuttle, 1969.

Hasebe, Gakuji, chief ed. *Chūgoku no tōji* (Ceramics of China). 12 vols. Tokyo: Heibonsha, 1995–99.

Hayashi, Minao. *Chūgoku kogyokuki sōsetsu* (*Surveys on Ancient Chinese Jades*). Tokyo: Yoshikawa Kobunkan, 1999.

Hebei sheng chutu wenwu xuanji (Selection of cultural relics unearthed in Hebei province). Hebei sheng bowuguan, wenwu guanlichu, eds. Beijing: Wenwu chubanshe, 1980.

Hervouët, François and Nicole, and Yves Bruneau. *La porcelaine des compagnies des Indes, à décor occidental*. Paris: Flammarion, 1986.

Hevia, James. "Looting Beijing: 1860, 1900." In Liu, *Tokens of Exchange*, pp. 192–213.

Ho, Chuimei, ed. *New Light on Chinese Yue and Longquan Wares*. Hong Kong: University of Hong Kong, 1994.

Ho, Wai-kam, and Judith G. Smith, eds. *The Century of Tung Ch'i-ch'ang: 1555–1636*. 2 vols. Seattle and London: University of Washington Press, 1992.

Hobson, R.L. *The Wares of the Ming Dynasty*. New York: Charles Scribner's Sons, 1923.

———, and A.L. Heatherington. *The Art of the Chinese Potter from the Han Dynasty to the End of the Ming*. London: Benn Ltd., 1923. Reprint: *The Art of the Chinese Potter: An Illustrated Survey*. New York: Dover Publications, 1982.

Houma zhutong yizhi (*Bronze Foundry Sites at Houma*). Compiled by the Institute of Archaeology of Shanxi Province. 2 vols. In Chinese with English abstracts. Beijing: Wenwu chubanshe, 1993.

Howard, David S., and John Ayers. *China for the West: Chinese Porcelain and Other Decorative Arts for Export Illustrated from the Mottahedeh Collection*. 2 vols. New York: Sotheby Parke Bernet, 1978.

Hsu, Cho-yun, and Katheryn M. Linduff. *Western Chou Civilization*. New Haven and London: Yale University Press, 1988.

Hu, Shih-chang, and Jane Wilkinson. *Chinese Lacquer*. Edinburgh: National Museums of Scotland, 1998.

Hua Jueming. *Zhongguo gudai jinshu jishu — tong he tie zaojiu de wenming* (Metallurgy in ancient China—a civilization of bronze and iron achievements). Zhengzhou: Daxiang chubanshe, 1999.

Huangchao liqi tushi (Illustrated court regalia of the present [Qing] dynasty). Compiled by Prince Yinlu and others. Completed 1759, revised 1766. See *Siku quanshu*, vol. 656.

Hucker, Charles O. *A Dictionary of Official Titles in Imperial China*. Stanford: Stanford University Press, 1985.

Hummel, Arthur W., ed. *Eminent Chinese of the Ch'ing Period (1644–1912)*. 2 vols. Washington, D.C.: The Library of Congress, 1943.

Hurvitz, Leon, trans. *Scripture of the Lotus Blossom of the Fine Dharma (The Lotus Sutra)*. New York: Columbia University Press, 1976.

Hyde, J.A. Lloyd. *Oriental Lowestoft, Chinese Export Porcelain, Porcelaine de la Cie des Indes*. 3d ed. Newport, Monmouthshire: The Ceramic Book Company, 1964.

Idemitsu Museum of Arts. *The Inter-Influence of Ceramic Art in East and West*. Exh. cat., Tokyo, 1990.

Imperial Tombs of China. Orlando Museum of Art, Wonders/Memphis International Cultural Series, and the State Bureau of Cultural Relics of the People's Republic of China. Memphis: Wonders, 1995.

Jacquemart, Albert, and Edmond Le Blant. *Histoire artistique, industrielle et commerciale de la Porcelaine*. Paris: J. Techener, 1862.

Jayne, Horace H.F. *A Handbook of the Chinese Collections in the Norton Gallery and School of Art*. West Palm Beach, Fl.: Palm Beach Art Institute, Inc., 1972.

Jenyns, Soame. *Later Chinese Porcelain: The Ch'ing Dynasty (1644–1911)*. London: Faber and Faber, 1951. 4th ed., 1971.

Jörg, Christiaan J.A., in collaboration with Jan van Campen. *Chinese Ceramics in the Collection of the Rijksmuseum, Amsterdam: The Ming and Qing Dynasties*. London, Philip Wilson, 1997.

Jourdain, Margaret, and R. Soame Jenyns. *Chinese Export Art in the Eighteenth Century*. Country Life, Ltd., 1950. Reprint, Feltham, Middlesex: Spring Books, 1967.

Juliano, Annette L. *Teng-hsien: An Important Six Dynasties Tomb*. Ascona, Switzerland: Artibus Asiae Publishers, 1980.

———, and Judith A. Lerner. *Monks and Merchants: Silk Road Treasures from Northwest China, Gansu and Ningxia, 4th–7th Century*. New York: Harry N. Abrams, 2001.

Kaikodo Journal, "A Natural Selection." Compiled by Howard Rogers, Arnold Chang, Mary Ann Rogers, and others. Vol. 19 (Spring 2001).

Karetzky, Patricia Eichenbaum. *Court Art of the Tang*. Lanham, New York: University Press of America, 1996.

Karlgren, Bernhard. *A Catalogue of the Chinese Bronzes in the Alfred E. Pillsbury Collection*. Minneapolis: University of Minnesota Press, 1952.

———. "Marginalia on Some Bronze Albums." *Bulletin of the Museum of Far Eastern Antiquities* (Stockholm), no. 31 (1959), pp. 289–331.

Kaufman, Walter. *Musical References in the Chinese Classics*. Detroit: Information Coordinators, 1976.

Keightley, David N. "The Shang: China's First Historical Dynasty." In Loewe and Shaughnessy, *The Cambridge History of Ancient China*, pp. 232–91.

———. *Sources of Shang History: The Oracle-Bone Inscriptions of Bronze Age China*. Berkeley: University of California Press, 1978.

Kerr, Rose. "'A Passionately Immoderate and Incurable Addiction to Buying Porcelain': The Collection of Augustus the Strong at Dresden." *Orientations* (November 2001), pp. 39–44.

Kingery, W. David, and Pamela B. Vandiver. *Ceramic Masterpieces: Art, Structure, and Technology*. New York: The Free Press, 1986.

Krahl, Regina, and Jessica Harrison-Hall. *Ancient Chinese Trade Ceramics from the British Museum, London*. Exh. cat. (in Chinese and English), Taipei, National Palace Museum, 1994.

Kuwayama, George. "Recently Discovered Sung Lacquers." In Watson, *Lacquerwork in Asia and Beyond*, pp. 40–69.

———, ed. *Ancient Mortuary Traditions of China: Papers on Chinese Ceramic Funerary Sculpture*. Los Angeles: Los Angeles County Museum of Art, 1991.

———, ed. *New Perspectives on the Art of Ceramics in China*. Los Angeles: Los Angeles County Museum of Art, 1992.

Lam, Peter Y.K., ed. *Nanyue Wang mu yuqi* (Jades from the tomb of the King of Nanyue). Hong Kong: The Chinese University of Hong Kong, 1991.

Lang Xiuhua. "Biyu teqing" (A *teqing* of green jade). In *Gugong bowuyuan cangbaolu* (Record of treasures in the Palace Museum), p. 250. Hong Kong: Joint Publishing Co., 1985.

Laufer, Berthold. *Chinese Pottery of the Han Dynasty*. Leiden: E.J. Brill Ltd., 1909. Reprint, Tianjin, 1940.

———. *Jade: A Study in Chinese Archaeology and Religion*. Chicago: Chicago Field Museum of Natural History, 1912. Reprint, New York: Dover Publications, 1974.

Lawton, Thomas, and others. *Asian Art in the Arthur M. Sackler Gallery: The Inaugural Gift*. Washington, D.C.: Smithsonian Institution, 1987.

Ledderose, Lothar. *Ten Thousand Things: Module and Mass Production in Chinese Art*. Princeton: Princeton University Press, 2000.

Lefebvre d'Argencé, René-Yvon. *Chinese Jades in the Avery Brundage Collection*. 2d rev. ed. San Francisco: Asian Art Museum of San Francisco, 1977.

———, and others. *Chinese, Korean, and Japanese Sculpture: The Avery Brundage Collection*. San Francisco: Asian Art Museum of San Francisco, and Tokyo: Kodansha International, 1974.

Legge, James, trans. *The Li Ki* [the *Liji*, or *Book of Rites*]. Vols. XVII–XVIII in *The Sacred Books of the East*, edited by F. Max Müller. Oxford: Clarendon Press, 1885. Reprint, 2 vols. New York: University Books, 1967.

———, trans. *The She King* [the *Shijing*, or *Book of Songs*]. Oxford: Oxford University Press, 1893–95.

———, trans. *The Shoo King* [the *Shujing*, or *Book of Documents*]. Oxford: Oxford University Press, 1893–95.

———, trans. *The Works of Mencius*. Oxford: Oxford University Press, 1893–95.

Leidy, Denise P., Wai-fong Anita Siu, and James C.Y. Watt. *Chinese Decorative Arts*. New York: The Metropolitan Museum of Art, 1997.

Li Chi (Li Ji). *Anyang*. Seattle: University of Washington Press, 1977.

Li Ji and Wan Jiabao. *Yinxu chutu qingtong ding xing qi zhi yanjiu* (*Studies of the Bronze Ting-Cauldron Excavated from Hsiao T'un and Hou Chia Chuang, Its Casting Process and Decorative Patterns*). Archaeologica Sinica, New Series, no. 4. Nangang: Institute of History and Philology, Academica Sinica, 1970.

———. *Yinxu chutu qingtong gu xing qi zhi yanjiu* (*Studies of the Bronze Gu-Beaker Excavated from Hsiao T'un and Hou Chia Chuang, Its Casting Process and Decorative Patterns*). Archaeologica Sinica, New Series, no. 1. Nangang: Institute of History and Philology, Academica Sinica,1964.

———. *Yinxu chutu qingtong jia xing qi zhi yanjiu* (*Studies of the Bronze Chia-Vessel Excavated from Hsiao T'un and Hou Chia Chuang, Its Casting Process and Decorative Patterns*). Archaeologica Sinica, New Series, no. 3. Nangang: Institute of History and Philology, Academica Sinica, 1968.

———. *Yinxu chutu wushisan jian qingtong rongqi zhi yanjiu* (*Studies of Fifty-Three Ritual Bronzes Excavated from Hsiao T'un and Hou Chia Chuang, Their Casting Process and Decorative Patterns*). Archaeologica Sinica, New Series, no. 5. Nangang: Institute of History and Philology, Academica Sinica, 1972.

Li Xueqin. *Eastern Zhou and Qin Civilizations*. Translated by K.C. Chang. New Haven: Yale University Press, 1985.

———. "Liangzhu Culture and the Shang Dynasty *Taotie* Motif." In Whitfield, *The Problem of Meaning in Early Chinese Ritual Bronzes*, pp. 56–66.

Li, Jian. *Changsha Ceramics, Featuring Gifts from Dr. and Mrs. Wally Zollman and Keith Uhl Clary*. Indianapolis: Indianapolis Museum of Art, 1993.

Liang Siyong and Gao Quxun. *Houjiazhuang: Henan Anyang Houjiazhuang Yin dai mudi* (Houjiazhuang: The Yin cemetery at Houjiazhuang, Anyang, Henan). Vol. 2, Tomb HPKM 1001. Taipei: Institute of History and Philology, Academica Sinica, 1962.

Liangzhu wenhua yuqi (Jades from the Liangzhu culture). Compiled by the Zhejiang sheng bowuguan, Shanghai shi wenwu guanli weiyuanhui, Nanjing bowuyuan. Hong Kong: Wenwu chubanshe, in association with Liangmu chubanshe, 1989.

Lingjiatan yuqi (*Jade Unearthed from Lingjiatan*). Compiled by Anhui Sheng wenwu kaogu yanjiusuo. Beijing: Wenwu chubanshe, 2000.

Little, Stephen. *Chinese Ceramics of the Transitional Period: 1620–1683*. Exh. cat., New York, China Institute in America, 1983.

Liu Liang-yu (Liu Liangyou). *Ch'ing Official and Popular Wares*. Taipei: Aries Gemini Publications, 1991.

Liu, Lydia H. *Tokens of Exchange: The Problem of Translation in Global Circulations*. Durham, N.C., and London: Duke University Press, 1999.

Loehr, Max. *Ancient Chinese Jades from the Grenville L. Winthrop Collection in the Fogg Art Museum, Harvard University*. Cambridge: Fogg Art Museum, Harvard University, 1975.

———. "The Bronze Styles of the Anyang Period (1300–1028 BC)." *Archives of the Chinese Art Society of America* 7 (1953), pp. 42–53.

———. *Ritual Vessels of Bronze Age China*. New York: The Asia Society, 1968.

Loewe, Michael, and Edward L. Shaughnessy. *The Cambridge History of Ancient China: From the Origins of Civilization to 221 B.C.* Cambridge: Cambridge University Press, 1999.

Longmen shiku (The cave-temples of Longmen). Compiled by Longmen wenwu baoguansuo. Beijing: Wenwu chubanshe, 1980.

Loo, C.T. *Archaic Chinese Jades: Special Exhibition*. Introduction by Horace H.F. Jayne. Philadelphia: The University Museum, 1940.

———. *An Exhibition of Chinese Archaic Jades*. Preface by C.T. Loo; introduction and catalogue by Lindsay Hughes Cooper. West Palm Beach, Fl.: The Norton Gallery of Art, 1950.

———. *Exhibition of Chinese Arts: Special Sale: November 1, 1941 to April 30, 1942*. Exh. cat., New York, C.T. Loo and Co., 1941.

———, and Paul Pelliot. *Jades Archaïques de la Chine appartenant à C.T. Loo et Cie*. Paris and Brussels: Librarie Nationale d'Art et d'Histoire, G. van Oest, 1925.

Lopez, Donald S., Jr., ed. *Religions of China in Practice.* Princeton: Princeton University Press, 1996.

Los Angeles County Museum of Art. *The Quest for Eternity: Chinese Ceramic Sculptures from the People's Republic of China.* Exh. cat., Los Angeles, 1987.

Lovell, Hin-cheung, ed. *Transitional Wares and Their Forerunners.* Hong Kong: OCS, 1981.

Lowe Art Museum. *Ancient Chinese Painting.* Exh. cat., Miami, Dec. 1973–Jan. 1974.

Lu Liancheng. *Qingtong wenhua de baoku: Yinxu fajue ji* (A treasury of bronze culture: notes on the excavation of Yinxu). Chengdu: Sichuan jiaoyu chubanshe, 1996.

Lubar, Steven, and W. David Kingery, eds. *History from Things: Essays on Material Culture.* Washington, D.C., and London: Smithsonian Institution Press, 1993.

Lülü zhengyi. Full title: *Yuzhi lülü zhengyi,* 5 *juan.* Compiled by He Guozong and others, 1723. Reprint, Shanghai: Shangwu yinshuguan, 1936. See *Siku quanshu,* vol. 215.

Lülü zhengyi houbian. Full title: *Yuzhi lülü zhengyi houbian,* 128 *juan.* Compiled by Prince Yinlu and others, 1746; 8 *juan* supplement, 1789. See *Siku quanshu,* vols. 215–17.

Luyi Taiqinggong Chang Zi Kou mu (*Taiqinggong Changzikou Tomb in Luyi*) [*sic*]. Compiled by Henan Sheng Wenwu Kaogusuo. Zhengzhou: Zhongzhou Guji chubanshe, 2000.

Mancheng Han mo fachu baogao (*Excavation of the Han Tombs at Man-ch'eng*). Compiled by Zhongguo shehui kexueyuan kaogu yanjiusuo, Hebei sheng wenwu guanlichu. 2 vols. Beijing: Wenwu chubanshe, 1980.

Matsubara, Saburo. *Chinese Buddhist Sculpture: A Study Based on Bronze and Stone Statues Other than Works from Cave Temples.* In Japanese. 2 vols. Tokyo: Yoshikawa Kobunkan, 1966.

Medley, Margaret. *The Chinese Potter: A Practical History of Chinese Ceramics.* Oxford: Phaidon Press, 1976 (1982).

———. *Illustrated Catalogue of Celadon Wares.* London: Percival David Foundation of Chinese Art, 1977.

———. *Illustrated Catalogue of Porcelains Decorated in Underglaze Blue and Copper Red in the Percival David Foundation of Chinese Art.* London: Percival David Foundation of Chinese Art, 1963.

———. "Lacquered Furniture." In Watson, ed., *Lacquerwork in Asia and Beyond,* pp. 70–84.

Millward, James A. *Beyond the Pass: Economy, Ethnicity, and Empire in Qing Central Asia, 1759–1864.* Stanford: Stanford University Press, 1998.

Mino, Yutaka, and James Robinson. *Beauty and Tranquility: The Eli Lilly Collection of Chinese Art.* Indianapolis: Indianapolis Museum of Art, 1983.

Mino, Yutaka, and Katherine R. Tsiang. *Ice and Green Clouds: Traditions of Chinese Celadon.* Bloomington: Indiana University Press, 1986.

Misugi, T. *Chinese Porcelain Collections in the Near East: Topkapi and Ardebil.* 3 vols. Hong Kong: Hong Kong University Press, 1981.

Mizuno, Seiichi. *Bronzes and Jades of Ancient China.* Tokyo: Nihon Keizai, 1959.

Mou Yongkang, Wang Mingda, Huang Xuanpei, Sun Weichang, Zou Houben, Wang Junguo. *Liangzhu wenhua yuqi* (Jades of the Liangzhu culture). Beijing and Hong Kong: Wenwu chubanshe and Woods Publishing, 1989.

Mudge, Jean McClure. *Chinese Export Porcelain for the American Trade, 1785–1835.* 2d. rev. ed. Newark: University of Delaware Press, and London and Toronto: Associated University Presses, 1981.

Mullikin, Mary Augusta, and Anna M. Hotchkis. *Buddhist Sculptures at the Yun Kang Caves.* Peiping (Beijing): Henri Vetch, 1935.

Munakata, Kiyohiko. *Sacred Mountains in Chinese Art.* Exh. cat., Urbana-Champaign, Krannert Art Museum at the University of Illinois, 1991.

Munsterberg, Hugo. *Art of the Far East.* New York: Harry N. Abrams, 1968.

Museum Rietberg. *Chinesische Skulpturen der Sammlung Eduard von der Heydt; beschreibender Katalog von Osvald Sirén.* Zurich, 1959.

Na Zhiliang (Na Chih-liang). *Yuqi tongshi* (Comprehensive explanation of jades). 2 vols. Hong Kong: Kaifa Ltd., 1964.
Naquin, Susan. *Peking Temples and City Life, 1400–1900*. Berkeley: University of California Press, 2000.
National Gallery of Art. *Decorative Arts, Part II: Far Eastern Ceramics and Paintings; Persian and Indian Rugs and Carpets*. Washington, D.C., 1988.
National History Museum. *Fo diao zhi mei: Song Yuan mudiao Fo xiang jingpinzhan* (*The Splendour of Buddhist Statuaries* [sic]: *Chinese Buddhist Wooden Sculpture from Sung and Yuan Dynasties*). In Chinese with English captions. Taipei, 1997.
National Palace Museum. *Gugong suo zang Hendusitan yuqi tezhan tulu* (*Catalogue of a Special Exhibition of Hindustan Jade in the National Palace Museum*). Taipei, 1983.
———. *Haiwai yizhen: Fo xiang* (*xu*) (Treasures in overseas collections: Buddhist sculpture). Taipei, 1990.
———. *Masterpieces of Chinese Porcelain in the National Palace Museum*. Taipei, 1969.
———. *Qingdai danseyou ci tezhan mulu* (*Catalogue of a Special Exhibition of Ch'ing-Dynasty Monochrome Porcelains in the National Palace Museum*). In Chinese and English. Taipei, 1981. 4th ed., 1983.
Nienhauser, William H., Jr., ed. *The Indiana Companion to Traditional Chinese Literature*. Bloomington: Indiana University Press, 1986.
Nott, Stanley Charles. *Chinese Jades in the Stanley Charles Nott Collection*. West Palm Beach, Fl.: Norton Gallery and School of Art, 1942.
Oriental Ceramics: The World's Great Collections, vol. 3: The Museum Pusat, Jakarta. Compiled by Abu Ridho. Tokyo, New York, and San Francisco: Kodansha International, 1977 and 1982.
———, vol. 4: The Iran Bastan Museum, Teheran. Compiled by Firouz Bagherzadeh and others. Tokyo, New York, and San Francisco: Kodansha International, 1979 and 1981.
———, vol. 5: The British Museum, London. Compiled by Douglas Barnett and others. Tokyo, New York, and San Francisco: Kodansha International, 1974 and 1981.
———, vol. 6: The Percival David Foundation of Chinese Art, London. Compiled by Margaret Medley. Tokyo, New York, and San Francisco: Kodansha International, 1975 and 1982.
———, vol. 7: Musée Guimet, Paris. Compiled by Madeleine Paul-David and others. Tokyo, New York, and San Francisco: Kodansha International, 1975 and 1981.
———, vol. 8: Museum of Far Eastern Antiquities, Stockholm. Compiled by Bo Gyllensvärd. Tokyo, New York, and San Francisco: Kodansha International, 1976 and 1982.
———, vol. 9: The Freer Gallery of Art, Washington, D.C. Compiled by John A. Pope and others. Tokyo, New York, and San Francisco: Kodansha International, 1975 and 1981.
———, vol. 10: The Museum of Fine Arts, Boston. Compiled by Jan Fontein and Wu Tung. Tokyo, New York, and San Francisco: Kodansha International, 1980.
———, vol. 11: The Metropolitan Museum of Art, New York. Compiled by Suzanne G. Valenstein and others. Tokyo, New York, and San Francisco: Kodansha International, 1977 and 1982.
Palace Museum. *Qinggong Zangchuan Fojiao wenwu* (*Cultural Relics of Tibetan Buddhism Collected in the Qing Palace*). In Chinese and English. Beijing: Forbidden City Press, 1992.
Palmer, Arlene. *A Winterthur Guide to Chinese Export Porcelain*. New York: Crown, 1976.
Paludan, Ann. *The Chinese Spirit Road: The Classical Tradition of Stone Tomb Statuary*. New Haven: Yale University Press, 1991.
Parke-Bernet Galleries. *The Richard Bryant Hobart Collection of Oriental Ceramics: Part One*. Auction cat., New York, May 23, 1969.
Pearlstein, Elinor. "Ancient Chinese Jades: The Sonnenschein Legacy." *Arts of China*, vol. 29, no. 3 (May–June, 1999), pp. 98–110.
Peng Shifan, ed., *Song Yuan jinian qingbai ci* (*Dated Qingbai Wares of the Song and Yuan Dynasties*). Hong Kong: Ching Leng Foundation, 1998.
———, Zhan Kaisun, and Liu Lin. *Jiangxi Xin'gan chutu qingtong yishu* (Bronze unearthed at Xin'gan in Jiangxi). Hong Kong: Woods Publishing, 1994.
Phillips, John Goldsmith. *China-Trade Porcelain: An Account of Its Historical Background, Manufacture, and Decoration and a Study of the Helena Woolworth McCann Collection*. London: Phaidon Press, n.d. [1956?].

Pierson, Stacey, ed. *Collecting Chinese Art: Interpretation and Display*. London: Percival David Foundation of Chinese Art, 2000.

Pirazzoli-t'Serstevens, Michèle. "Un jade chinois des collections de Louis XIV au Musée Guimet." *Arts Asiatiques* 25 (1972), pp. 199–204.

Poor, Robert J. "Notes on the Sung Dynasty Archaeological Catalogs." *Archives of Asian Art* 19 (1965), pp. 33–44.

Pope, John Alexander. *Fourteenth-Century Blue-and-White: A Group of Chinese Porcelains in the Topkapu Sarayi Müzesi, Istanbul*. Rev. ed. Washington, D.C.: Freer Gallery of Art, 1970.

Pope-Hennessy, Una. *Early Chinese Jades*. London: Ernest Benn, Ltd., 1923.

Priestley & Ferraro Chinese Art. *Chinese Art 1998: A Selection for Asian Art in London, November 1998*. Sale cat., London, 1998.

———. *Out of Wind and Dust: Reflections of War and Peace in Chinese Art*. Sale cat., London, 1999.

Qufu Lu guo gucheng (Ancient capital of the state of Lu at Qufu). Compiled by Shandongsheng wenwu kaogu yanjiusuo, Shandongsheng bowuguan, Jining diqu wenwuzu, Qufuxian wenguanhui. Ji'nan: Ji Lu shuhui, 1982.

Raswki, Evelyn S. "The Creation of an Emperor in Eighteenth-Century China." In Yung and others, eds., *Harmony and Counterpoint*, pp. 150–74.

Rawson, Jessica. "The Ancestry of Chinese Bronze Vessels." In Lubar and Kingery, *History from Things*, pp. 51–73.

———. *Chinese Bronzes: Art and Ritual*. London: British Museum Publications, 1987.

———. "Western Zhou Archaeology." In Loewe and Shaughnessy, *The Cambridge History of Ancient China*, pp. 352–449.

———. *Western Zhou Ritual Bronzes from the Arthur M. Sackler Collections*. Vol. 2 of *Ancient Chinese Bronzes from the Arthur M. Sackler Collections*. Washington, D.C. and Cambridge, Mass.: The Arthur M. Sackler Foundation and the Arthur M. Sackler Museum, Harvard University, 1990.

———, and Carol Michaelson. *Chinese Jade from the Neolithic to the Qing*. London: British Museum Press, 1995.

Riddell, Sheila. *Dated Chinese Antiquities: 600–1650*. London: Faber and Faber, 1979.

Rixia jiuwen kao (Study of "Ancient accounts heard in the precincts of the Throne"). Compiled by Yu Minzhong and others, 1774, printed 1785–88. Reprint, 8 vols. Beijing: Guji chubanshe, 1983.

Rogers, Howard, and others, eds. *China 5,000 Years: Innovation and Transformation in the Arts*. New York: Guggenheim Museum, 1998.

Royal Ontario Museum. *Chinese Art in the Royal Ontario Museum*. Toronto: Royal Ontario Museum, 1972.

———. *Homage to Heaven, Homage to Earth: Chinese Treasures in the Royal Ontario Museum*. Toronto: University of Toronto Press, 1992.

———. *Royal Ontario Museum, The T.T. Tsui Galleries of Chinese Art*. Toronto: Royal Ontario Museum, 1996.

Salmony, Alfred. *Carved Jade of Ancient China*. Berkeley: Gulick Press, 1938.

———. *Chinese Jade through the Wei Dynasty*. New York: Ronald Press Co., 1963.

———. *Far Eastern Jades: Charles M. Pratt Collection*. Poughkeepsie: Vassar College Art Gallery, 1941.

Sancai tuhui (Illustrated compendium of the three realms). Compiled by Wang Qi Wang Qi (*jinshi* degree, 1565). Woodblock edition in 106 *juan*. Prefaces dated 1607, 1609. Reprint, 6 vols. Taipei: Chengwen Publishing, 1970.

Schafer, Edward H. *The Vermillion Bird: T'ang Images of the South*. Berkeley: University of California Press, 1967.

Scott, Rosemary E. *Elegant Form and Harmonious Decoration: Four Dynasties of Jingdezhen Porcelain*. Exh. cat., London, Percival David Foundation of Chinese Art, 1992.

———, ed. *The Porcelains of Jingdezhen*. London: Percival David Foundation of Chinese Art, 1992.

Shanghai Museum. *Zhongguo shuhuajia yinjian kuanshi* (Identification of seals and signatures of Chinese painters and calligraphers). 2 vols. Beijing: Wenwu chubanshe, 1987.

Shangraw, Clarence. "Chinese Lacquers in the Asian Art Museum." *Orientations* (April 1986), pp. 22–41.

———. *Origins of Chinese Ceramics.* New York: China Institute in America, 1978.

Shaughnessy, Edward L. "Western Zhou History." In Loewe and Shaughnessy, *The Cambridge History of Ancient China,* pp. 292–351.

Shi Zhangru. *Xiaotun,* vol. 1: *Yizhi de faxian yu fajue, bing bian: Yinxu muzang zhi san, Nanzu muzang fu beizu mu buyi.* (*The Yin-Shang Site at Anyang, Honan,* vol. 1: *The Site, Its Discovery and Excavations,* fasc. 3: *Burials of the South Section with Supplement to the Burials of the North Section*). Archaeologica Sinica, no. 2. Taipei: Academica Sinica, Institute of History and Philology, 1973.

Siku quanshu. Full title: *Wenyuan ge siku quanshu.* Completed 1782. Facsimile reprint, 1,500 vols. Taipei: Taiwan Commercial Press, 1983–86.

Sirén, Osvald. *Chinese Painting: Leading Masters and Principles.* 7 vols. London: Lund, Humphries, 1956, 1958. Reprint, New York: Hacker Art Books, 1973.

———. *Chinese Sculpture from the Fifth to the Fourteenth Centuries.* 4 vols. New York: Scribner's, 1925.

So, Jenny F. "Jade and Stone at Sanxingdui." In Bagley, ed. *Ancient Sichuan,* pp. 153–75.

———. "Revisiting Antiquity in Late Bronze Age China." Ip Yee Memorial Lecture delivered at the Oriental Ceramic Society of Hong Kong, November 6, 2001. Forthcoming.

———, ed. *Music in the Age of Confucius.* Exh. cat., Washington, D.C., Freer Gallery of Art and Arthur M. Sackler Gallery, Smithsonian Institution, 2000.

———, and Emma C. Bunker. *Traders and Raiders on China's Northern Frontier.* Seattle: University of Washington Press, 1995.

Soper, Alexander. "Addendum: The 'Jen Shou' Mirrors." *Artibus Asiae* 29, no. 1 (1967), pp. 55–66.

Spence, Jonathan D. *Ts'ao Yin and the K'ang-hsi Emperor: Bondservant and Master.* New Haven: Yale University Press, 1988.

Steinhardt, Nancy Shatzman. *Chinese Imperial City Planning.* Honolulu: University of Hawaii Press, 1990.

Strober, Eva. "*La maladie de la porcelaine*": *Ostasiatisches Porzellan aus der Sammlung Augusts des Starken* (*East Asian Porcelain from the Collection of Augustus the Strong*). Leipzig: Edition Leipzig, 2001.

Sun, Zhixin. "The Liangzhu Culture." In Yang, ed., *The Golden Age of Chinese Archaeology,* pp. 117–20.

Tan Derui. "Zhongguo qingtong shidai tao fan zhuzao jishu yanjiu (A study of the techniques of bronze casting with clay molds in Bronze Age China)." *Kaogu xuebao* 1999.2, pp. 211–50.

Tan Danqiong, comp. *Zhongguo taoci* (Chinese pottery and porcelain). In Chinese and English. 5 vols. Taipei: Guangfu shuju, 1980.

Tang Chung, ed. *Dongya yuqi* (*East Asian Jade: Symbol of Excellence*). 3 vols. Hong Kong: The Chinese University of Hong Kong, Centre for Chinese Art and Archaeology, 1998.

Tch'ou Tö-yi (Chu Deyi), and Paul Pelliot. *Bronzes antiques de la Chine appartenant à C.T. Loo et Cie.* Paris and Brussels: G. van Oest, 1924.

Teng Shu-p'ing (Deng Shuping). *Guoli Gugong Bowuyuan cang xinshiqi shidai yuqi tulu* (*Neolithic Jades in the Collection of the National Palace Museum*). Taipei: National Palace Museum, 1992.

Thompson, Nancy. "The Evolution of the T'ang Lion and Grapevine Mirror." *Artibus Asiae* 29, no. 1 (1967), pp. 25–40.

Thorp, Robert L., and Virginia Bower. *Spirit and Ritual: The Morse Collection of Ancient Chinese Art.* New York: The Metropolitan Museum of Art, 1982.

Tian Likun and Zhang Kefeng. "Qian Yan de jiaqi juzhuang" (A complete set of armor from the Former Yan). *Wenwu* 1997:11, pp. 72–75.

Tokiwa Daijō and Sekino Tadashi. *Shina Bukkyō shiseki* (*Buddhist Monuments in China*). 5 vols. Tokyo: Bukkyō-shiseki kenkyu-kwai, 1926–38.

Tonglüshan gu kuangye yizhi (*Ancient Mining and Smelting Site at Tonglüshan*). Compiled by Huangshi Bowuguan. Beijing: Wenwu chubanshe, 1999.

Torbert, Preston M. *The Ch'ing Imperial Household Department: A Study of Its Organization and Principal Functions, 1662–1796*. Cambridge, Mass.: Council on East Asian Studies, Harvard University, 1977.

Trubner, Henry. *Arts of the Han Dynasty*. New York: The Asia Society, 1961.

Tsai, Mei-fen. *Monarchy and Its Buddhist Way*. Taipei: National Palace Museum, 1999.

Umehara, Sueji. *Inkyo* (*Yin Hsü, Ancient Capital of the Shang Dynasty at An-Yang*). Tokyo: Asahi Shimbunsha, 1964.

———, comp. *Shina kodō seikwa* (*Selected Relics of Ancient Chinese Bronzes from Collections in Europe and America*). In Japanese with English captions and summaries. 7 vols. Osaka: Yamanaka and Co., 1933–35.

Unafraid of the Autumn Wind: Retrospective Exhibition of Paintings by Zhu Qizhan. Exh. cat., New York, China 2000 Fine Art, 1999.

Vainker, S.J. *Chinese Pottery and Porcelain: From Prehistory to the Present*. New York: George Braziller, Inc., 1991.

Valenstein, Suzanne G. *A Handbook of Chinese Ceramics*. New York: The Metropolitan Museum of Art, 1975. Revised, 1989.

Van Alphen, Jan, ed. *The Buddha in the Dragon Gate: Buddhist Sculpture of the 5th–9th Centuries from Longmen, China*. Exh. cat., Antwerp, Etnografisch Museum, 2001.

Victoria and Albert Museum. *Far Eastern Ceramics in the Victoria and Albert Museum*. London: Sotheby Parke Bernet, 1980. Originally published as *Oriental Ceramics: The World's Great Collections*, vol. 6: The Victoria and Albert Museum. Tokyo: Kodansha International, 1975.

Wan Yi. "Qingdai gongting yinyue" (Qing court music). *Gugong bowuyuan yuankan* 16 (1982:2), pp. 8–18.

———, Wan Shuqing, and Lu Yanzheng, comps. *Qingdai gongting shenghuo* (Daily life in the Forbidden City). Hong Kong: Commercial Press, 1985.

Wang Jiapeng. "Liushi Banchan de yifeng zoushu" (The memorial of the Sixth Panchen [Lama]). *Zijincheng* 44 (1988:1), pp. 17–21.

Wang Qingzheng, and George Fan, eds. *Juanceng ciqi jingpinxuan* (*Selected Ceramics from the Collection of Mr. and Mrs. J.M. Hu*). In Chinese and English. Shanghai: Shanghai Museum, 1989.

Wang Shixiang, ed. *Xiushi lu jieshuo* (Annotated explanation of the treatise on lacquer decoration). Beijing: Wenwu chubanshe, 1983.

Watson, Burton, trans. *Chuang Tzu: Basic Writings*. New York: Columbia University Press, 1964.

Watson, William. *Chinese Jade Books in the Chester Beatty Library*. Dublin: Hodges Figgis and Co. Ltd., 1963.

———. *Cultural Frontiers in Ancient East Asia*. Edinburgh: Edinburgh University Press, 1971.

———. *Pre-Tang Ceramics of China: Chinese Pottery from 4000 BC to 600 AD*. London: Faber and Faber, 1991.

———, ed. *Lacquerwork in Asia and Beyond*. London: Percival David Foundation of Chinese Art, 1982.

Watt, James C.Y. "Antiquarianism and Naturalism." In Fong and Watt, *Possessing the Past*, pp. 219–55.

———. *Chinese Jades from Han to Ch'ing*. Exh. cat., New York, The Asia Society, 1980.

———. *The Sumptuous Basket: Chinese Lacquer with Basketry Panels*. New York: China Institute in America, 1985.

———, and Michael Knight. *Chinese Jades from the Collection of the Seattle Art Museum*. Seattle: Seattle Art Museum, 1989.

———, and Anne E. Wardwell. *When Silk Was Gold: Central Asian and Chinese Textiles*. New York: The Metropolitan Museum of Art, 1997.

Weidner, Marsha. *Cultural Intersections in Later Chinese Buddhism*. Honolulu, University of Hawaii Press, 2001.

———, ed. *Latter Days of the Law: Images of Chinese Buddhism, 850–1850*. Honolulu: University of Hawaii Press, 1994.

Wen Guang and Jing Zhichun. "Chinese Neolithic Jade: A Preliminary Geoarchaeological Study." *Geoarchaeology: An International Journal*, vol. 7, no. 3 (1992), pp. 251–75.

Whitfield, Roderick, ed. *The Problem of Meaning in Early Chinese Ritual Bronzes.* London: Percival David Foundation of Chinese Art, 1992.

Wilkinson, Endymion. *Chinese History: A Manual.* Cambridge, Mass.: Harvard University Asia Center for the Harvard-Yenching Institute, 2000.

Willetts, William. *Foundations of Chinese Art: From Neolithic Pottery to Modern Architecture.* London: Thames and Hudson, 1965.

Wood, Nigel. *Chinese Glazes: Their Origins, Chemistry and Recreation.* London: A&C Black, and Philadelphia: University of Pennsylvania Press, 1999.

Wright, Arthur F. *Buddhism in Chinese History.* Stanford: Stanford University Press, 1959. Revised, 1971 (1996).

Xi Han bohua (*Western Han Silk Paintings*). Beijing: Wenwu chubanshe, 1972.

Xi Han Nanyue wang mu (*Nanyue King's Tomb of the Western Han*). Compiled by the Guangzhoushi wenwu guanli weiyuanhui, Zhongguo shehui kexue kaogu yanjiusuo, and Guangdongsheng bowuguan. 2 vols. Beijing: Wenwu chubanshe, 1991.

Xichuan Xiasi Chunqiu Chu mu (Chu tombs of the Spring and Autumn period at Xiasi). Compiled by the Institute of Archaeology (Henan Province), Danjiang Reservoir Archaeological Team, and Xichuan County Museum. Beijing: Wenwu chubanshe, 1991.

Xin'gan Shang dai da mu (The large Shang dynasty tomb at Xin'gan). Compiled by Jiangxi sheng bowuguan, Jiangxi sheng wenwu kaogu yanjiusuo, Xin'ganxian bowuguan. Beijing: Wenwu chubanshe, 1997.

Xinyang Chu mu (*Chu Tombs at Xinyang*). Beijing: Wenwu chubanshe, 1986.

Xu, Jay. "Bronze at Sanxingdui." In Bagley, ed. *Ancient Sichuan*, pp. 59–70.

Yang Boda. *Chinese Archaic Jades from the Kwan Collection.* In Chinese and English. Hong Kong: Chinese University of Hong Kong, The Art Gallery, 1994.

———. "Gansu Qijia yu wenhua chutan" (A preliminary investigation of the jades of the Qijia culture in Gansu province). *Longyou wenhua* 1997.1, pp. 10–18.

Yang Xin and others. *Three Thousand Years of Chinese Painting.* New Haven: Yale University Press, and Beijing: Foreign Languages Press, 1997.

Yang Xizhang and Yang Baocheng. "Yin dai qingtong liqi de fenqi yu zuhe" (Periodization and study of Shang dynasty ritual bronze vessels). In *Yinxu qingtongqi*, pp. 79–102.

Yang, Xiaoneng, ed. *The Golden Age of Chinese Archaeology: Celebrated Discoveries from the People's Republic of China.* Exh. cat., Washington, D.C., National Gallery of Art, 1999.

Yanshi Erlitou: 1959 nian–1978 nian kaogu fajue baogao (*The Erlitou Site in Yanshi: Excavations in 1959–78*). Beijing: Zhongguo da baikequanshu chubanshe, 1999.

Yeung Kin Fong (Yang Jianfang). *Zhongguo guyu yanjiu lunwenji* (Research papers on ancient Chinese jades). 2 vols. Taipei: Zhongzhi Art Press, 2001.

Yinxu de faxian yu yanjiu (*Archaeologogy, Excavation and Researches in the Yin Ruins*). Beijing: Kexue chubanshe, 2001.

Yinxu fajue baogao: 1958–1961 (*Excavation of Yinxu: 1958–1961*). Beijing: Wenwu chubanshe, 1987.

Yinxu Fu Hao mu (*Tomb of Lady Hao at Yinxu in Anyang*). Beijing: Wenwu chubanshe, 1980.

Yinxu qingtongqi (*Bronze Vessels from Yin Xu*). In Chinese, with English synopsis. Beijing: Wenwu chubanshe, 1985.

Yinxu yuqi (Jades from Yinxu). Beijing: Wenwu chubanshe, 1981.

Yu Anlan, ed. *Huashi congshu* (Collectanea of the history of painting). 5 vols. Shanghai: Renmin meishu chubanshe, 1963 and 1982.

Yu Jianhua, comp. *Zhongguo meishujia renming cidian* (Dictionary of Chinese painters and calligraphers). Shanghai: Renmin meishu chubanshe, 1981.

Yü, Chün-fang. "Feminine Images of Kuan-yin in Post-T'ang China." *Journal of Chinese Religions* 18 (1990), pp. 61–89.

———. "A Sutra Promoting the White-robed Guanyin as Giver of Sons." In Lopez, ed., *Religions of China in Practice*, pp. 97–105.

Yung, Bell, Evelyn S. Rawski, and Rubie S. Watson, eds. *Harmony and Counterpoint: Ritual Music in a Chinese Context*. Stanford: Stanford University Press, 1996.

Yungang shiku (The Yunkang caves). Compiled by the Committee in Charge of Cultural Relics and the Institute for the Preservation of the Yunkang Caves of Shansi Province. In Chinese with English supplement. Beijing: Beijing: Wenwu chubanshe, 1977.

Yuzhi shi siji. Full title: *Qing Gaozong yuzhi shi siji*. (Fourth compilation of imperial poetry). 100 *juan*, printed 1783. Reprint, vols. 7–8 in *Qing Gaozong yuzhi shi wen quanji* (Complete collected poems and writings of Qing Gaozong [the Qianlong emperor]). Taipei: National Palace Museum, 1976.

Yuzhi wen chuji. Full title: *Qing Gaozong yuzhi wen chuji* (First compilation of writings of Qing Gaozong [the Qianlong emperor]). 30 *juan*, printed 1763. Reprint, vol. 10 in *Qing Gaozong yuzhi shi wen quanji*. Taipei: National Palace Museum, 1976.

Yuzhi wen erji. Full title: *Qing Gaozong yuzhi wen erji* (Second compilation of writings of Qing Gaozong [the Qianlong emperor]). 44 *juan*. Preface dated 1786. See *Siku quanshu*, vol. 1301, pp. 271–562.

Zeng Hou Yi mu (Tomb of Marquis Yi of Zeng, Hubei Provincial Museum). Compiled by Institute of Archaeology, Chinese Academy of Social Sciences. 2 vols. Beijing: Wenwu chubanshe, 1989.

Zhengzhou Shang cheng (*The Site of Shang Dynasty City in Zhengzhou: A Report on the 1953–1985 Excavations*). 3 vols. Beijing: Wenwu chubanshe, 2001.

Zhongguo gu qingtongqi xuan (*A Selection of Ancient Chinese Bronzes*). Beijing: Wenwu chubanshe, 1976.

Zhongguo Han Yangling caiyong (*The Coloured Figurines in Yang Ling Mausoleum of Han in China*). Compiled by Shaanxi Provincial Archaeological Institute. Xi'an: Shaanxi Travel and Tourism Press, 1992.

Zhongguo meishu quanji, diaosu bian 3: *Wei Jin Nan-Bei chao diaosu* (Complete arts of China, sculpture, vol. 3: Wei, Jin, and Northern and Southern dynasties). Liu Shuzhong, chief ed. Beijing: Xinhua shudian, 1988.

Zhongguo meishu quanji, diaosu bian 4: *Sui Tang diaosu* (Complete arts of China, sculpture, vol. 4: Sui and Tang dynasties). Compiled by Shi Yan and Ren Rong. Beijing: Xinhua shudian, 1988.

Zhongguo meishu quanji, diaosu bian 6: *Yuan Ming Qing diaosu* (Complete arts of China, sculpture, vol. 6: Yuan, Ming, and Qing dynasties). Yang, Boda, chief ed. Beijing: Renmin meishu chubanshe, 1988.

Zhongguo yuqi quanji 3: *Chunqiu, Zhanguo* (Complete jades of China, vol. 3: Spring and Autumn and Warring States periods). Jia E, chief ed. Shijiazhuang: Hebei meishu chubanshe, 1993.

Zhou Wu, ed. *Zhongguo banhua shi tulu* (Illustrated history of Chinese woodcuts). 2 vols. Shanghai: Renmin meishu chubanshe, 1988.

Zhu Fenghan. *Gudai Zhongguo qingtongqi* (Ancient Chinese bronzes). Tianjin: Nankai Daxue chubanshe, 1995.

Zwalf, W., ed. *Buddhism: Art and Faith*. London: British Museum Publications Ltd., 1985.

CHINESE CHARACTER GLOSSARY

An Lushan (703–757) 安祿山
baoyi 包衣
bianqing 編磬
Bide 比德
Bishu Shanzhuang 避暑山庄
bozhong 鎛鐘
Cao Guojiu 曹國舅
ce 冊
Chang Zi Kou 長子口
Chen Hongshou (1598–1652) 陳洪綬
Chen Yang (act. late 11th century) 陳暘
Chongxiu Xuanhe bogutu 重修宣和博古圖
Chuoketuo (d. 1789) 綽克托
Cizhou ware 磁州窰
cong 琮
Cui Yingying 崔鶯鶯
da chen 大臣
Da Ming Wanli nian zhi 大明萬曆年製
Da Qing huidian shili 大清會典事例
Da Qing Qianlong nian zhi 大清乾隆年製
Da Qing Qianlong xinsi nian jingzao 大清乾隆辛巳年敬造
Dehua porcelain 德化窰
ding 鼎
Dong Bangda (1699–1764) 董邦達
Dong Gao (1740–1818) 董誥
Dong Qichang (1555–1636) 董其昌
Dong Yuan (d. 962) 董源
Duan Yucai (1735–1815) 段玉裁
Emperor Yao 堯
Empress Dou (d. 135 BCE) 竇太后
Erchi jushi 二癡居士
fang ding 方鼎
fang gu 方觚
fang jia 方斝
fang yi 方彝
fang zun 方尊
fenghuang 鳳凰
Fu Ding 父丁
Fu Hao (ca. 1200 BCE) 婦好
Fuchang 阜長
Gao Bin (1683–1775) 高斌
Gao Heng (d. 1768) 高恆
Gao Pu (d. 1778) 高樸
ge 戈
Gongyang zhuan 公羊傳
gu 觚
Gu Yun (1835–1896) 顧澐
guan wares 官窰
guang 觥
Guanshiyin 觀世音
Guanyin 觀音
gui 簋
Guo state 虢國
Guochao gongshi 國朝宮史
Guochao huazheng lu 國朝畫徵錄
Guoshi 國師
gutiao (striking end) 鼓條
gutiao (thigh end) 股條
Guyang Cave 古陽洞
Guyu tukao 古玉圖考
haima 海馬
Han Jingdi (r. 156–142 BCE) 漢景帝
Han Wendi (r. 179–157 BCE) 漢文帝
he 盉
He Guozong (d. 1766) 何國宗
He Tan Jia 河壇甲
hu 壺
Huangchao liqi tushi 皇朝禮器圖式
huangzhong 黄鐘
Huiyu xing 回玉行
ji (*jie*) 偈
jia 斝
Jiajing period (1522–66) 嘉靖
jiao 角
jiashan 假山

jing 經
Jiu qu (Nine Bends river) 九曲
ju bi 駐彼
jue 爵
Juluxian 鉅鹿縣
Juran (act. ca. 960–95) 巨然
Langrun 朗潤
lei 罍
leiwen 雷紋
li 鬲
li ding 鬲鼎
Li Ji 禮記
Li Tang (ca. 1050–after 1130) 李唐
Liang Guozhi (1723–1787) 梁國治
liangdang 兩當 or 裲襠
Lianghuai 兩淮
lingbi stone 靈璧石
lingzhi 靈芝
Lülü zhengyi 律呂正義
Lülü zhengyi houbian 律呂正義後編
Majiayao 馬家窯
Mi'ertaishan 密爾岱山
mingqi 冥器
Mingtang 明堂
Mu tianzi zhuan 穆天子傳
Murong Xianbei 慕容鮮卑
Nanyue Wang 南越王
Neidi 內地
Ni Zan (1301–1374) 倪瓚
Nu'erhachi (Nurhaci, 1559–1626) 努爾哈赤
pan 盤
Pan Geng 盤庚
Panchen Lama E'erdeni 班神額爾得呢喇嘛
ping 瓶
pou 瓿
Prince Yinlu (Yunlu, 1695–1767) 胤祿 (允祿)
qi (ax head) 戚
qi (essence) 氣
Qi fo ta beiji 七佛塔碑記
Qianji Si 潛溪寺
Qianlong fanggu 乾隆倣古
Qianlong nian zhi 乾隆年製
qilin 麒麟
Qinding Da Qing huidian tu 欽定大清會典圖
qing 磬
Qing Gaozong yuzhi shi 清高宗御製詩
Qing Gaozong yuzhi wen 清高宗御製文
Qing Shilu 清實錄
Qingchao wenxian tongkao 清朝文獻通考
ren 仁
Ren Bonian (Ren Yi, 1840–1896) 任伯年 (任頤)
Ren Xiong (1820–1857) 任熊
Ren Xun (1835–1893) 任熏
sancai 三彩
Sancai tuhui 三才圖會
Setiba'erdi 色提巴爾第
Shanhaijing 山海經
Shao 韶
shendao 神道
shi zhuo cheng da yu weng 師琢成大玉甕
Shijing 詩經
Shiku Si 石窟寺
Shiliao xunkan 史料旬刊
shizi 獅子
Shujing 書經
Shuowen jiezi zhu 說文解字注
Si Mu Wu *fang ding* 司母戊方鼎
Si Mu Xin *fang ding* 司母辛方鼎
Song Taizong (r. 976–97) 宋太宗
Songzi Guanyin 送子觀音
tai ping you xiang 太瓶有象 and 太平有像
Tang Gaozong (r. 649–83) 唐高宗
Tang Yin (1470–1524) 唐寅
taotie 饕餮
teqing 特磬
Teqing ming 特磬銘
Tianqi period (1621–27) 天啓
Tianshen Tan 天神壇
Wang Hui (1632–1717) 王翬
Wang Jiu (ca. 1715–ca. 1788) 王玖
Wang Jiu zhi yin 王玖之印
Wang Meng (1308–1385) 王蒙
wen hu 溫壺
Wen Zhengming (1470–1559) 文徵明
wenjiuzun 溫酒尊
Wu (Suzhou) 吳
Wu Changshuo (or Changshi, 1844–1927) 吳昌碩
Wu Dacheng (1835–1902) 吳大澂
Wu Ding 武丁
Wu Li (1632–1718) 吳歷
Wu Zetian (r. 690–705) 武則天
wucai 五彩
Wuliangshou Fo 無量壽佛
Wumen 吳門
Wushi 烏什
Wuying dian 武英殿
xi 觿
Xi Huangsi 西黃寺
Xiangshan 香山
Xiangyu (233–202 BCE) 項羽
xing 興
Xiyu wenjian lu 西域聞見錄
Xu Shen (act. ca. 100 CE) 許慎
Xu You 續幽
Xukongzang 虛空藏
Xumifushou Temple 須彌福壽之廟
yan 甗
Yan Liben (ca. 600–673) 閻立本
Yan Lide (d. 656) 閻立德
yang 陽
Yijing 易經
yin 蔭 or 廕
yingqing 影青
Yinxu 殷墟
Yonggui (d. 1783) 永貴
you 卣
yu 玉
yudao 御道
yue 鉞 (戉)
Yue ware 鉞窯
Yueshu 樂書
Yun Shouping (1633–1690) 惲壽平
Zhang Hong (1577–ca. 1652) 張宏
Zhang Luan (d. 1778) 張鑾
Zhang Sheng 張生
Zhang Zhao (1691–1745) 張照
Zhangjia hutuketu 章嘉呼圖克圖
zhi 觶
Zhi 址
Zhixin 志新
Zhonghe shaoyue 中和韶樂
Zhongli Quan 鍾離權
Zhongshan 中山國
Zhou Chen (ca. 1450–after 1535) 周臣
Zhou Li 周禮
Zhu Qizhan (1892–1996) 朱屺瞻
zhucha Ye'erjiang dachen 駐劄葉爾羌大臣
zun 尊

INDEX

References to illustrations are in **boldface**.

CREDITS

All color photographs in this book are © Bruce M. White, except catalogue plates 72–75, which are by C.J. Walker.

Black-and-white illustrations in the essays are from the sources listed at the right.

JENNY F. SO

1 After Mou and others, *Liangzhu wenhua yuqi*, pl. 4
2 After Mou and others, *Liangzhu wenhua yuqi*, no. 132
3 After Bagley, ed., *Ancient Sichuan*, no. 51
4 After Bagley, ed., *Ancient Sichuan*, p. 162, fig. 53.1
5 Photograph © Bruce M. White
6 Photograph courtesy Jenny F. So
7 After *Wenwu* 1986.8, pl. 2:1
8 After *Lingjiatan yuqi*, no. 1
9 After Mou and others, *Liangzhu wenhua yuqi*, no. 203
10 After Tang, ed., *Dongya yuqi*, vol. 2, p. 59, fig. 42.6
11 After Tang, ed., *Dongya yuqi*, vol. 2, p. 51, fig. 42.3
12 After *Xinyang Chu mu*, p. 115, fig. 79
13 After Lam, ed., *Nanyue Wang mu yuqi*, pl. 52
14 After *Xi Han bohua*, pl. 6
15 After *Yinxu Fu Hao mu*, pp. 194–95, fig. 97

COLIN MACKENZIE

1 After *Yinxu de faxian yu yanjiu*, p. 85, fig. 42, and p. 263, fig. 135
2 After images from Shi Zhangru, *Xiaotun*, vol. 1: *Yizhi de faxian yu fajue*: fasc. 3, Yinxu tombs part 3: *Nanzu muzang fu beizu mu buyi*
3 After images from *Gu qiwu yanjiu zhuankan*, Li Ji and Wan Jiabao, editors, no. 3: *Yinxu chutu qingtong jia xing qi zhi yanjiu*; no. 4: *Yinxu chutu qingtong ding xing qi zhi yanjiu*; no. 5: *Yinxu chutu wushisan jian qingtongqi zhi yanjiu*; and Zhu Fenghan, *Gudai Zhongguo qingtongqi*, p. 707, fig. 10:28
4 After *Yinxu qingtongqi*, figs. 2–3
5 After *Yinxu qingtongqi*, figs. 21:4; 28:4,6; 17; 22:1,2; 27:1
6 Norton Museum of Art photo
7 After *Yinxu qingtong qi*, fig. 15:2
8 Photograph © Bruce M. White
9 After *Yinxu de faxian yu yanjiu*, p. 284, fig. 153:3
10 After "1980 nian Henan Anyang Dasikongcun M539 fajue jianbao," *Kaogu* 1992.6, pp. 509–17, figs. 3–6
11 After "Yinxu Qijiazhuang dong 269 hao mu," *Kaogu xuebao* 1991.3, pp. 325–52, figs. 5, 7, 9, 10, 12
12 After *Anyang Yinxu Guojiazhuang Shang dai muzang*, pp. 70–126
13 After *Yinxu qingtongqi*, figs. 86:1, 87:5
14 After *Luyi Taiqinggong Chang Zi Kou mu*, p. 7, fig. 4, and p. 11, fig. 6
15 After images from *Luyi Taiqinggong Chang Zi Kou mu*

JOHN R. FINLAY

1 Photograph: Peter Harholdt
2 After Bishop, *Investigations and Studies*, vol. 2, facing p. 202; Avery Architectural and Fine Arts Library, Columbia University in the City of New York
3 After Tsai, *Monarchy and Its Buddhist Way*, cat. 85
4 Photo © Bruce M. White
5 Courtesy of the C.V. Starr East Asian Library, Columbia University in the City of New York
6 After Bishop, *Investigations and Studies*, vol. 1, facing p. 24; Avery Architectural and Fine Arts Library, Columbia University in the City of New York
7 After Chang, *Gongting zhi ya*, cat. 51